THE AKUNIN PROJECT

The Mysteries and Histories of Russia's Bestselling Author

The Akunin Project is the first book to study the fiction and popular history of Grigorii Chkhartishvili, one of the most successful writers in post-Soviet Russia. In the first two decades of the twenty-first century, Chkhartishvili published over sixty books under the pen names Anatolii Brusnikin, Anna Borisova, Akunin-Chkhartishvili, and, most commonly, Boris Akunin. His series featuring the tsarist secret policeman Erast Fandorin has sold over 15 million books in Russia alone, making Akunin one of the bestselling authors of the post-Soviet era. Combining intertextuality, allusions, pastiche, and other markers of postmodern playfulness, many of Akunin's works have been translated into English and have also been adapted for film and television. Akunin's public profile has been further enhanced by his active involvement in mass political protests against Vladimir Putin.

Despite Akunin's international reputation as a celebrated writer, there is very little critical work on his literary output and his mysterious persona. Bringing together scholars of literature, history, and culture, *The Akunin Project* fills this gap by exploring the author's bestselling adventure novels and recent histories of the Russian state. The book includes translations of five short works previously unavailable in English as well as an interview with the author.

ELENA V. BARABAN is an associate professor of Russian in the Department of German and Slavic Studies at the University of Manitoba.

STEPHEN M. NORRIS is the Walter E. Havighurst professor of Russian History and the Director of the Havighurst Center for Russian and Post-Soviet Studies at Miami University in Ohio.

The Akunin Project

The Mysteries and Histories of Russia's Bestselling Author

Edited by ELENA V. BARABAN and
STEPHEN M. NORRIS

UNIVERSITY OF TORONTO PRESS
Toronto Buffalo London

© University of Toronto Press 2021
Toronto Buffalo London
utorontopress.com
Printed in the U.S.A.

ISBN 978-1-4875-0826-5 (cloth)   ISBN 978-1-4875-3789-0 (EPUB)
ISBN 978-1-4875-2576-7 (paper)   ISBN 978-1-4875-3788-3 (PDF)

Library and Archives Canada Cataloguing in Publication

Title: The Akunin project : the mysteries and histories of Russia's bestselling
    author / edited by Elena V. Baraban and Stephen M. Norris.
Names: Baraban, Elena V. (Elena Viktorovna), 1969– editor. |
    Norris, Stephen M., editor.
Description: Includes bibliographical references and index.
Identifiers: Canadiana (print) 20200286390 | Canadiana (ebook) 2020028648X |
    ISBN 9781487508265 (cloth) | ISBN 9781487525767 (paper) |
    ISBN 9781487537890 (EPUB) | ISBN 9781487537883 (PDF)
Subjects: LCSH: Akunin, B. (Boris) – Criticism and interpretation.
Classification: LCC PG3478.K78 Z49 2021 | DDC 891.73/5–dc23

University of Toronto Press acknowledges the financial assistance to its
publishing program of the Canada Council for the Arts and the Ontario Arts
Council, an agency of the Government of Ontario.

Canada Council   Conseil des Arts
for the Arts   du Canada

ONTARIO ARTS COUNCIL
CONSEIL DES ARTS DE L'ONTARIO
an Ontario government agency
un organisme du gouvernement de l'Ontario

Funded by the   Financé par le
Government   gouvernement
of Canada   du Canada

Canada

Contents

Part Three: Buried Secrets and Historical Spies in Akunin's Works

Part Four: Rewriting the History of Russia

Part Five: New Pseudonyms and Projects: Anatolii Brusnikin and Akunin-Chkhartishvili

Part Six: Boris Akunin as a Literary and Commercial Project

Acknowledgments

Many people have contributed to the success of this volume. We thank our respective institutions, Miami University and the Department of German and Slavic Studies at the University of Manitoba, for contributing part of the publishing subvention funds for this project.

We are also grateful to anonymous reviewers of this collected volume who gave inspiring and constructive feedback on the manuscript. At the University of Toronto Press, our heartfelt appreciation goes to Stephen Shapiro for his encouragement, commitment to the project, and helpful suggestions that made the publication a smooth process.

Our special thanks go to Ben Sutcliffe of Miami University (Ohio) for reviving our interest in Akunin. We are also grateful to Boris Akunin for his prompt responses to our queries and his support of the project. We extend our thanks to all contributors to the volume for their work and responsiveness to our editorial suggestions.

Note on Transliteration

The transliterations in this volume follow the Library of Congress (LoC) guidelines, except in cases where an accepted English spelling of a name already exists (e.g., Tolstoy instead of Tolstoi, Dostoevsky instead of Dostoevskii).

THE AKUNIN PROJECT

The Mysteries and Histories of Russia's
Bestselling Author

1 The Akunin Project: Introduction

ELENA V. BARABAN and STEPHEN M. NORRIS

STEPHEN M. NORRIS: *I first met Grigorii Chkhartishvili, better known by his pseudonym Boris Akunin, in July 2008. We talked at a coffee house near Chistye prudy. Chkhartishvili agreed to be interviewed for a book I was writing on recent Russian blockbuster movies: he had authored the script for the film based on his best-selling novel,* Turkish Gambit. *Our conversation veered towards other topics, including his then-new series,* Brotherhood of Death, *which he termed as a "cinema-novel." It was then, as he discussed these books, that I realized just how carefully planned Akunin's entire output was. It was there, in Moscow in 2008, where I first realized it was a project: in fact, the notes I took of my meeting have "Akunin project" written in the margins.*

When I asked Chkhartishvili/Akunin about his "cinema-novels," he answered first by stating he was deeply interested in the "new market strategy" of promotion and combining it with "other aspects of marketing," what we would call cross-media marketing. Chkhartishvili's initial plan for "Boris Akunin" was to launch simultaneously a series of ten novels, ten movies, and ten television serials that would all overlap and reinforce each other. Each product would reflect the specifics of its media form, each could be marketed through the others (the films would have ads for the novels and TV shows, for example), and each would focus on a similar narrative, but the outcomes would change from book to show to film. Chkhartishvili wrote ten scripts for the films in the mid-1990s and received a contract to film them, but the project broke down for financial reasons. Instead, he told me in 2008, he decided to start a detective series where he wrote each entry using a different nineteenth- or early twentieth-century genre: this was the birth of his Fandorin series.

Akunin returned to the scripts in 2007, altered them slightly, and published them as the Brotherhood of Death *"cinema-novels." Yet that meeting in Moscow pointed out a singular fact about the remarkable career of the writer best known as Boris Akunin: namely, just how much we should understand it as a project, complete with a clear marketing strategy, and a genre-bending effort to rethink the very nature of Russian literature.*

ELENA V. BARABAN: *I became interested in Boris Akunin's page-turners about Erast Fandorin when they first appeared in 1998. Working then on my PhD thesis on post-Soviet detective fiction, I was happy to include a chapter on Akunin, whose work was so much better than most crime fiction that flooded the Russian book market in the 1990s. Akunin's postmodernist engagement with Russian and world classics to a certain extent reconciled Russian intellectuals with the drastic change in readers' tastes and publishers' preferences. After completing an article on Akunin's detective novels in 2003, I turned to other scholarly projects and stopped following his output closely. In 2015, when Ben Sutcliffe invited me to give a guest lecture on Akunin's* The Death of Achilles *at Miami University (OH), I realized two important things. The first one was that in the seventeen years since* Azazel' *appeared, Akunin became a unique phenomenon in contemporary Russian culture, a highly successful writer who would run one ambitious literary and cultural project after another. The second realization was that surprisingly, apart from individual articles and a few academic theses on Akunin, the Akunin phenomenon had received scarce scholarly attention. It was high time to look at Akunin's impressive output in its entirety. Given how prolific the writer is, I believed that inviting scholars who had worked on various individual aspects of the Akunin's oeuvre was the best way to initiate such discussion. Together with Stephen M. Norris, who, I knew, had met the writer, I co-organized two conference panels on Akunin in 2016. Several papers presented at the conference eventually became the backbone of the present volume. I am glad that the journey of looking at Akunin's work from an academic perspective, which began for me in 1998, has continued to reveal that the writer's experiment in creating Russian belles-lettres and essentially demonstrating how Western marketing models can work in Russia has been so successful. Indeed, the Akunin phenomenon makes it clear that popular literature may be entertaining and witty and yet raise serious questions pertinent for today's Russian society.*

What's in a Name? Boris Akunin and Grigorii Chkhartishvili

STEPHEN M. NORRIS

The writer named Boris Akunin was born on 1 April 1997. Or perhaps 1 February 1998. Or maybe even 1 May 1998. Regardless, he celebrated his twentieth birthday by 2018. He was also nearly named after a famous Soviet leader.

On that April 1997 day, as his creator, Grigorii Chkhartishvili would later write, "I suddenly realized that I would write a novel."[1]

Chkhartishvili's father had recently died and he was on his way to the cemetery. Chkhartishvili, known in intellectual circles for his editing of the journal *Foreign Literature* and for his translations of Japanese authors into Russian, had just finished a serious work of scholarship, *The Writer and Suicide* (*Pisatel' i samoubiistvo*).[2] A study of literary suicides completed at the time of his father's death and in the midst of post-Soviet crises took its toll: the book, Chkhartishvili would write, "Absolutely crushed me with its weight."

On that April trip to the cemetery, Chkhartishvili, who had recently read Dostoevsky's *Diary of a Writer*, was struck by a passage from 1876 about a young Muscovite who shot himself in the Alexander Gardens. Like Dostoevsky, Chkhartishvili was moved by this passage. He wrote about the moment when all of these events collided:

> Suddenly I saw a very clear picture.
>
> A bench, with a young, adorable girl and a solid woman of middle age. A young man approaches the bench, says something (the words cannot be comprehended), then takes a revolver out of his pocket, turns the drum, puts the barrel to his temple, and shoots. The man falls dead, the girl faints, the woman does not fall, and instead opens her mouth and silently screams. All of this is strange, yet fun. I cannot explain why it is fun. Somehow all of this overlapped, in that bus to the cemetery, and formed some sort of change of energy, which demanded a release.
>
> The main thing was that I really wanted to know what the young man had said and what it all meant.
>
> That same day I started writing a novel. Six weeks later it was finished. I called it *Azazel'*.[3]

The story captures the essence of Chkhartishvili's plans for a literary career and the creation of a pseudonym. The novel mentioned appeared in print in 1998 and did indeed open with a young man, Petr Kokorin, committing suicide in the Alexander Gardens in front of a beautiful young woman. The shocking action sets in motion a police investigation. Because the suicide seems to be a straightforward case, a twenty-year-old detective named Erast Fandorin is assigned to it. The preternaturally gifted Fandorin instead uncovers a vast conspiracy. The novel, published on 1 February 1998 (perhaps another birth day for Akunin), initiated a series starring Fandorin, published by the Moscow publisher Zakharov. Fandorin would die in the last novel in the series (or did he?), published exactly twenty years to the day later.

Azazel' only sold six thousand copies. The next three books in the series, all published in 1998, also sold modestly. With the fifth Fandorin novel, *Special Assignments* (*Osobye porucheniia*), which appeared in 1999, the series became a bestselling one – the previous four books, including *Azazel'*, became literary sensations.

In 1999, just two years after his birth, Boris Akunin became famous. At the time of his new-found fame, no one knew who he really was. Soon after, Chkhartishvili outed himself and began to stir the pot about the relationship between the mild-mannered former literary editor and his pseudonym. Chkhartishvili stated in 1999 that they were not the same person. The two wore different glasses. Akunin preferred a nineteenth-century style and that century's habits. On the website launched to promote the new-found fame of Akunin, the author's portrait does not entirely resemble Chkhartishvili's, his creator.[4] When Chkhartishvili first started they were not the same person, he declared Akunin was born on 1 May 1998 (why that date was chosen was not made entirely clear).[5] Over the years, however, the two became more and more entangled.

It turns out Akunin was nearly named Molotov. In a 2006 interview with an American newspaper, Chkhartishvili (or was it Akunin?) admitted: "In the beginning I was thinking about taking the name Molotov because of the Molotov cocktail and because of my books being sort of a combustible cocktail of highbrow and lowbrow literatures." Molotov, however, "was a historical figure who invokes so little sympathy. Akunin was much better."[6]

The story helps to explain the chosen pseudonym and why so many critics have focused on it. "Akunin" means "villain" in Japanese. Chkhartishvili knows Japan well and is fluent in the language, having studied in Tokyo in 1977–8. "B. Akunin," the shortened form of his creation, also conjures associations with the nineteenth-century anarchist, Mikhail Bakunin. In taking the name, Chkhartishvili indicated his creation, the author Boris Akunin, would act in the fashion of the Molotov cocktail, blowing up readers' expectations and perhaps even acting as a villain in his own stories by following his own rules. These notions were fuelled by readers and critics alike, who would attribute the luck Fandorin seemed to enjoy to Akunin's textual interventions. Sister Pelagia, Akunin's other early literary protagonist, also benefitted from circumstances that some interpreted as the author's willingness to intrude into the narratives he created. When Akunin (or was it Chkhartishvili?) wrote the film scripts of two of his popular Fandorin novels and changed the endings, the notion that "Akunin" was as much a part of the texts he wrote only deepened.

Because Boris Akunin became more famous than Grigorii Chkhartishvili, the latter became more and more conflated with the former in interviews and popular perceptions. Thus, when Chkhartishvili initially declared he was not the same person as Akunin, it is likely he was deliberately playing with his audience. In their study on Akunin as a celebrity, Brian James Baer and Nadezhda Korchagina argue that Chkhartishvili "worked very consciously – and self-consciously – to establish his authorial persona" to the extent that both Akunin and Fandorin became celebrities.[7] In part, they argue, Chkhartishvili's decision to adopt a pseudonym and to keep his identity secret played a major role in fuelling interest in the new author and in making him a celebrity. He also made Akunin "into an alternate persona, suggesting a conscious play with the notion of celebrity façade."[8]

Akunin created two more writers, both revealed in January 2012. One was Anatolii Brusnikin, published under the name A.O. Brusnikin, an exact anagram of Boris Akunin. The other was Anna Borisova. Both lived to be just over four years old. When he announced their deaths, Chkhartishvili, writing under his more famous pseudonym, stated that he had secretly created a project named "Authors" because the name "Akunin" had already become something of a straightjacket. To write something new, in a language that was not like Akunin's, required the creation of two more personas. The first, Borisova, was an author through which Akunin "imagined what it was like to be a woman and to look at the world through a woman's eyes."[9] She was educated, with a rich husband, and had grown-up children. Borisova took up writing "partly from boredom" and "partly because she wants to share her thoughts and feelings that had accumulated over the years." Chkhartishvili wanted to write "more serious" literature that was not necessarily aiming at market success, although he admired and envied Ludmila Ulitskaya for achieving both. Borisova wrote three novels under this name and even had an author's photo published that later was revealed to be a computer-generated mashup of Chkhartishvili and his wife, Erika.[10]

Akunin's second creation was Brusnikin, a persona made so that the author could write a historical novel "without the detective intrigue."[11] Brusnikin also gave Akunin the chance to "look at Russian history from an unusual side," that of a Slavophile-like patriot. Akunin imagined Brusnikin as a quiet museum worker, but also as part of a larger commercial project. Working with AST, his publisher, Chkhartishvili developed an aggressive, expensive marketing campaign to announce a new literary talent. One million brochures with the first chapter of Brusnikin's novel, *The Ninth Saviour* (*Deviatnyi Spas*), were laid out in shops around the country.[12] Boris Akunin even provided a blurb for the new author. Brusnikin's second novel followed a completely different, yet equally well-planned, advertising campaign; namely, no ads at all. *The Ninth Saviour* was set in the era of Peter I; *A Hero of a Different Time* (*Geroi inogo vremeni*), a riff on Mikhail Lermontov's classic, was also set in the 1830s. Both sold well. Brusnikin's third and final novel, *Bellona*, set in the Crimean War, appeared posthumously, after Akunin had revealed himself as Brusnikin.[13]

All of the above is a way of explaining two important facts about the author known as Boris Akunin. First, his creator, Grigorii Chkhartishvili, deliberately blurs the lines between his "real" persona and his pseudonym, giving interviews as Akunin and writing his extremely popular blog under that name. His revelations that he was also Borisova and Brusnikin were made as Akunin on his blog. This blurring only intensified after the revelations, when new editions of the Borisova and Brusnikin novels appeared with Boris Akunin's name on them. It further deepened after Chkhartishvili began writing "serious" fiction in 2012 using a hyphenated name, "Akunin-Chkhartishvili."[14] The effect is that one is never sure who is speaking for whom and how seriously one should take any statement from "Akunin" or "Chkhartishvili," which may be precisely the point.

Second, as is clear from Akunin's comment above, the entire Akunin-Borisova-Brusnikin oeuvre was deliberately imagined to be an artistic and commercial project. That it came to be delivered in the fashion imagined and was even more successful than Chkhartishvili dreamt of is the subject of the next section, written by Elena Baraban.

The Akunin Phenomenon

ELENA V. BARABAN

Mostly under the pen name Boris Akunin, Chkhartishvili has published over sixty books, as series and individually. Editions of his bestsellers reach up to half a million copies.[15] What is the secret of Akunin's success? Concisely, it may be explained by the writer's perceptively filling in the book-market niche created by political, social, and economic circumstances surrounding the fall of the Soviet Union. By 1998, when Akunin published his first detective novels, Russian society had been experiencing a profound cultural shock. The abolition of censorship in 1989 brought the collapse of decades-long traditions in publishing and writing. No other genre manifested these changes as clearly as the detective story (*detektiv*).

Indeed, while crime fiction has been popular in Russia since the appearance of the genre in the nineteenth century, in the Soviet Union, due to ideological constraints, the number of published *detektivy* (a genre that did not readily fulfil the requirement of educating the reader about Soviet moral values) was limited by a certain annual quota. In other words, *detektivy* were popular but were not published in a variety, quantity, and print-run size that satisfied the demand for them.[16] In the twilight of perestroika, when ideological constraints were eased, the *detektiv* boom first hit Russia through translations of Western authors.[17] Yet within a few years domestically produced detective fiction became more popular.[18] Given the brutal lawlessness (*bespredel*) that accompanied the comeback of capitalism in Russia in the 1990s, Russian authors found plenty of inspiration for their hard-boiled thrillers and mysteries.[19]

The detective genre changed radically. Soviet *detektivy* that could focus on harmless economic crimes and feature a criminologist who, when bored, would knit a sweater at her workplace, gave way to quick-paced stories that contained serial killings, drug dealers, mafia, disillusioned veterans of the Afghan or the Chechen wars who became hit-men, and more.[20] Mysteries (like those by Alexandra Marinina) that traditionally placed "greater emphasis on the investigation" included more detailed depictions of crimes, while hard-boiled detective novels (practically unknown in the Soviet Union) "emphasized the crime as much as the investigation" and could be more fittingly described as action thrillers (*boeviki*, such as Andrei Konstantinov's novels).[21]

Despite these novelties, however, the post-Soviet *detektiv* ironically had the same problem as its Soviet predecessor: it was too close to reality and, as a result, it was not sufficiently entertaining. Whereas Soviet *detektivy* were not thrilling enough because they depicted a rather peaceful society with a low crime rate, post-Soviet detective novels failed as escapist literature. By offering depressing depictions of a Russia that was anyway universally recognized as bleak, they were too close to the culture of the era, known by the Russian term *chernukha* (which might best be translated as "dark" or "blackening"). Moreover, they lacked analytical depth and were often poorly written. Readers, in short, were ready for a story that would be amusing and yet relevant for understanding the current moment.

Akunin successfully fulfilled these expectations with his historical mysteries. His elegant and witty protagonist Erast Fandorin quickly became popular. Starting his career in 1876, Fandorin did not live in an ideal society, but his Russia was not chaotic either. In fact, the book series *Adventures of Erast Fandorin* (*Prikliucheniia Erasta Fandorina*, 1998–2018) ends with the protagonist's death during the chaos of the Russian Civil War, when Fandorin can no longer serve his country and is trying to emigrate.[22] Comprising thirteen novels and two collections of short stories and novellas, the writer's first and so far the most successful book series follows the detective Erast Fandorin from 1876 through 1920.[23]

Likewise, Akunin's second books series, *Provincial Mystery, or Adventures of Sister Pelagia* (*Provintsial'nyi detektiv, ili Prikliucheniia sestry Pelagii*, 2000–3),[24] is also set either at the end of the nineteenth century or in the first years of the twentieth century. While Erast Fandorin in some ways resembles Sherlock Holmes or Auguste Dupin, the protagonist of the Pelagia trilogy is a thirty-year-old nun who reminds the reader of Miss Marple.[25] Both protagonists find themselves in situations that somewhat resemble those of post-Soviet Russia. In both book series, the historical setting was thus to a certain extent used to provide commentary on Russia at the end of the twentieth century and in the first years of the third millennium.

Akunin's strategy of using historical settings for his stories as a corrective lens for looking at Russia became even clearer when he launched his third detective book series, *Adventures of Nicholas Fandorin* (*Prikliucheniia magistra*, 2000–9). The series has parallel plots. One is set in present-day Russia and follows the adventures of Erast Fandorin's grandson in contemporary Russia; the other concerns the adventures of Fandorin's ancestors in the seventeenth, eighteenth, and nineteenth centuries.[26] This witty emplotment paved the way for Akunin's next highly ambitious project: a multi-volume *History of the Russian State* (*Istoriia Rossiiskogo gosudarstva*, 2013–present) that consists of popular historiography and historical fiction.[27] As Akunin has explicitly stated, this project was inspired by his desire to understand why the Russian state has failed so many times and why it continues to stumble on the way to democracy.

Tapping into historical memory in order to grapple with the present has energized Akunin's entire oeuvre. The writer's engagement with history brings to mind Andreas Huyssen's famous thesis regarding the past that, through the use of reproduction technologies, "the explosion of historical scholarship and the development of museums ... has become part of the present in ways simply unimaginable in earlier centuries."[28] Akunin's desire to gain valuable insights into the current problems in Russia by providing a historical perspective sets him apart from writers whose fiction lacks such depth. By applying essentially the same lens of an (amateur) historian so consistently, Akunin, as he intended from the very start of his writing career, successfully created Russian belles-lettres, literature that would appeal to the majority of readers and yet is serious enough (although not, as he often reminds readers, too serious, for Akunin does not want to be saddled with the weight of a "great Russian writer").

Akunin's success is also predicated on the writer's original contribution to the debate about the "Russian path." After the collapse of the Soviet Union, a crisis in Russian national identity manifested itself in nostalgia for the past. While some expressed nostalgia for the Soviet past, others denounced the Soviet period and idealized pre-Revolutionary Russia. By setting his historical detective novels in the era of the last Russian tsars, Akunin avoided compelling comparisons between Russia's present and the Russia of the Soviet period. In fact, aside from two novels in his book series *Genres* (*Zhanry*, 2004–12),[29] Akunin avoided writing about the Soviet period. In order to discuss the Soviet era, Chkhartishvili (not Boris Akunin) launched his *Family Album* (*Semeinyi al'bom*, 2012–), a book series that so far has three "serious" novels, published under the dual pen-name Akunin-Chkhartishvili with no first name given.

Akunin appeared when the initial post-Soviet debate on Russian history was at its peak. Filling in the "blank spots of history" – as the process of historical rediscovery of the past was frequently described during the glasnost period – was crucial in the 1990s. The end of the Soviet era was a tragic "shattering of the dreams of modernity – of social utopia, historical progress, and material plenty for all."[30] The Soviet era was demythologized as a "no-time."[31] This rejection also concerned the Soviet way of depicting Russia's pre-Revolutionary history. At the same time, as David Remnick argued, "the Communist Party's myth-making machinery had been replaced ... by Russian nostalgia for a pre-Revolutionary utopia that never was."[32] The myths about a "wonderful pre-Revolutionary Russia" and "people's well-being" before 1917 conferred on the past a wholeness that had never existed.[33] By contrast, Akunin wittingly evaded taking sides in the nostalgia battles of the 1990s. Instead of embracing either "Red patriotism" or "White patriotism" (to borrow Tatiana Glushkova's terms), Akunin, in a classical postmodern practice of reshuffling simulacra (surfaces), put on a mask of nostalgia for the pre-Revolutionary period while being rather critical of that past.[34] Akunin's detective novels and his *History of the Russian State* do not express nostalgia for Russia's pre-Revolutionary past. Rather, they are an attempt to understand which historical factors contribute to the setbacks on Russia's path to democracy today.

Akunin's success is grounded in part on the writer's witty use of postmodernist techniques of quotation, allusion, and pastiche in his fiction. Rather than a random reshuffling of fragments of pre-existent texts (as claimed by Fredric Jameson in his influential work on postmodernism),[35] Akunin makes quotations and allusions from classical Russian literature into *historical* details, relevant for his overall vision of Russia. The postmodern style of Akunin's projects (novels, plays, blogs, and computer games) provide a relevant response to a cultural situation in Russia today. The element of playfulness in the writer's co-optation of literary and cinematic classics (domestic and international) enriches the reader's experience.

It is not accidental that the majority of scholarly articles on Akunin focus precisely on the writer's postmodernist techniques, including ludic intertextuality, pastiche, and parody. Akunin's engagement with postmodernism, however, needs to be regarded in a historical perspective, since, after all, intertextuality is as typical of modernist writing as it is postmodern. On the one hand, Akunin's early work lends itself easily to postmodernist interpretations. On the other hand, the appearance of Akunin's work in the late 1990s and early 2000s signals the need to differentiate between his novels and earlier works by Russian writers such as Dmitry Prigov and Vladimir Sorokin, who had been viewed as postmodernist by scholars such as Boris Groys, Mikhail Epstein, Alexander Genis, Slobodanka Vladiv-Glover, and Mark Lipovetsky.[36] As Eliot Borenstein aptly notes, whereas Epstein, Genis, and Vladiv-Glover deal with "discrete postmodern phenomena (in particular, the works of the conceptualists and late Soviet deformations of language)," Lipovetsky examines many trends of Russian postmodernism. In his interpretation, which focuses on Russian postmodernism from the 1970s to the 1990s, Lipovetsky draws mostly on Francois Lyotard's observation regarding postmodernists' "distrust of metanarratives" and Jean Baudrillard's notion of simulation play. Fredric Jameson's discussion of postmodernism as a phenomenon of late capitalism was significantly less relevant for Lipovetsky because of the Soviet-era roots of Russian postmodernism.[37] Indeed, Jameson's critique of postmodernism in a capitalist society could not be very useful in an examination of literary works that were written against the grain of socialist realism.

The situation, however, changed with the comeback of capitalism to Russia after 1991. The radically changed economic and cultural situation defined new manifestations of postmodernism in Russia. Instead of inscribing themselves into elitist high culture, the postmodernist techniques of the 2000s were incorporated into a colourful and far less sombre production of belles-lettres that, right from the very start, was conceived of as not a commercial product. In other words, if one is to examine Akunin's oeuvre in the framework of postmodernism, one necessarily has to draw on Jameson's notion of late capitalism as well as his (and also Slavoj Žižek's) critique of globalization and the new globalized popular culture.[38] Thus in the example of Akunin's fiction (at least part of his impressive output), we are dealing with a type of postmodernism that is closer in spirit to American pop art, a more Western type of postmodernism that is explicitly non-elitist and seemingly apolitical. The same could be said of Akunin's (self-described) amateurish history series, one that clearly aims for a wide commercial market. This type of postmodernism lends itself to analysis in the framework of Jameson's critique of popular literature as "surrendering" to the market.[39]

One of the crucial appeals of the Akunin phenomenon is its multimodality. Besides writing in different genres and styles, having run several literary projects, and disseminating his oeuvres through a variety of traditional and digital channels, Chkhartishvili has also spliced up his creative identities into Boris Akunin, Anna Borisova, Anatolii Brisnikin (to have the last two welded back into Akunin), and Akunin-Chkhartishvili. This radically ludic component of using a variety of bigger and smaller projects, styles, and pen names is rather new in Russian literature. While in the West some writers, when publishing books in a style or genre that is different from their "regular" literary niche, have long used as many as ten pen names, contemporary Russian writers normally limit themselves to one, maximum two, recognizable pen names. However, instead of rushing to interpret Akunin's playfulness with pen names as a sign solely of postmodernity, one can remember that a vision of literature as a game, a masquerade during which one can put on many masks, one after another, was well established by Anton Chekhov, who had more than fifty pen names. In other words, while the critic may be tempted to view the Akunin phenomenon, along with its multi-modality and numerous social media avatars and pennames, in light of the theory of postmodernism, one needs to be cautious about creating a meta-perspective on Akunin. It might end up being a straitjacket.

Last but not least, one of the primary means through which Akunin engages with his readers and employs his witty techniques is his savvy use of social media. Unlike any other writer in Russia, Akunin has created a blueprint of successful contemporary interaction with his fans, critics, and readers. Akunin has successfully created several participatory interactive platforms that, as the media theorists inform us, produce an illusion of the consumer's inclusion in the creative process. No other writer in Russia has embraced contemporary technology with such intensity and with such impressive results for promoting his creative identities and their creations.[40] Furthermore, Akunin's media usage also turned him more towards politics and ultimately to his current status as an "exile," as the next section will explain.

Posts and Politics

STEPHEN M. NORRIS

When you open Boris Akunin's first official website, akunin.ru, you enter a different world, for you are greeted with a picture of a pince-nez, stamps that you might associate with an old library, and the name "Boris Akunin" along with "Writings" (*Sochineniia*). The entire page manages to conjure up the nineteenth century, the era of Erast Fandorin. Only when you read the fine print do you realize the trick that has been played: instead of a stamp declaring this to be a "complete collection" (*polnoe sobranie*) of the author's works, a phrase any Russophile would know from the voluminous tomes associated with the literary greats, you are instead told this is a "full *interactive* collection" (*polnoe* interaktivnoe *sobranie*, emphasis added). You have to click to continue, and therefore be reminded you are in the twenty-first century.

From the beginning, Boris Akunin made use of new media and new technologies to develop his project and to connect with his readers. The author's use of websites, a LiveJournal blog, and a Facebook page (among other media outlets) have helped him cultivate his fan base: they provide a prime example of what Henry Jenkins has called "transmedia storytelling" and "convergence culture."

In his influential work, Jenkins traced examples of "convergence," or "the flow of content across multiple media platforms, the cooperation between multiple media industries, and the migratory behavior of media audiences who will go almost anywhere in search of the kinds of entertainment experiences they want." This sort of coming together, Jenkins notes, brings consumers, fans, and creators into a "participatory culture."[41] Akunin's readers take part in the project by commenting on his blog posts, using his interactive website, and creating sites of their own devoted to his works. In doing so, as Elisa Coati has argued, the internet has acted as an important tool for "different levels of interactivity" among Akunin's fans, one enhanced by the medium's "playful nature," which in turn echoes the author's style.[42]

Akunin's Fandorin series gained an internet component in 2000, when the author collaborated with the award-winning graphic designer Artemii Lebedev to create the website. The site allows readers to download Akunin's novels, but also acts as a visual complement to them: visitors can look at a portrait of the author as a nineteenth-century gentleman, read about the history of Moscow and Russia in the era of Fandorin and Sister Pelagia, view maps from that century, and much more. Readers of Akunin, in other words, can immerse themselves in the worlds he created on the pages of his books by taking virtual tours of the past on the pages of the website. Fans can also connect his authorial projects through this web portal, downloading not just the Fandorin and Pelagia series but also the Nicholas Fandorin books and his rewriting of Chekhov's play *The Seagull* (*Chaika*). Visitors can also read Akunin's *Fairy Tales for Idiots* (*Skazki dlia idiotov*) on the site.

The website, as Coati notes, allowed Akunin to "establish contact with his readers" and to develop his celebrity status in the new Russia.[43] Not surprisingly, given the interactive, playful pasts Akunin cultivated in his writings, his fans developed sites of their own, most notably fandorin.ru, a "virtual museum" developed by a reader that expands on the contexts found in the pages of akunin.ru (Akunin linked to the Fandorin site after it was created). The fan site encourages visitors to take virtual journeys, to "follow Mr. Fandorin through the streets and squares of St. Petersburg and see the same places, just as they appeared in the late nineteenth century and were pictured on antique photos, postcards, and paintings."[44] Users have organized actual walks, taken part in online debates about Akunin's projects, and produced two physical books that explore Fandorin's world (*Fandorin's Moscow*, a 2008 book by Andrei Staniukovich, and *Akunin's Moscow*, a 2008 work by Maria Besedina).[45] At the heart of the Akunin project and its success, in other words, is the creation of a "knowledge community," to borrow from Jenkins once more, where collective production, debate, and circulation of meanings take place between the author and his readers.[46]

The Akunin website acted as a first stage in this community development. Neither the author nor Lebedev, the website's creator, added to the site after 2003, even though it remains accessible. Instead, in January 2010, using the popular Russian social media platform LiveJournal, Akunin launched his "Love for History" (*Liubov' k istorii*) blog, allowing him to interact even more with his readers. The site, as Natalia Erlenkamp notes in her chapter in this volume, served as a place for true dialogue between the author and his readers. Akunin tested out ideas for projects, answered questions, and even developed polls that allowed fans to participate in the creation of future Akunin projects. It was on this blog that Akunin announced he was Borisova and Brusnikin, and announced their virtual deaths.[47] It was on this site that Akunin announced himself as a "new Karamzin" and with it, the genesis of his history series.[48] It was on this site that Akunin announced he "was now a writer" after all and not just a belletrist, recounting the development of his "serious fiction" under the name Akunin-Chkhartishvili.[49]

Not long after he debuted his blog, Akunin also created a Facebook profile, first under the name "Boris Akunin" and then under the hybrid name "Akunin-Chkhartishvili." On a 2014 post to his blog, Akunin noted that reading Facebook darkens his mood while reading Live-Journal brightens it, for the latter allows for more colourful, frivolous reading. He pledged to divide his social media posts according to his moods, keeping his political statements to Facebook and literary projects to LiveJournal (he has not always succeeded).[50] Before he made this pronouncement, Akunin had used his blog to announce his political opposition during the December 2011 protests against the Duma elections. In a post entitled "Why does everything in this country," Akunin wrote:

> I Could Not Sit Still
>
> Why does everything in this country have to be like this?
>
> Even civil society has to wake up when it's most inconvenient for the writer. I went away to the French countryside for some time in peace, to write my next novel. But now I can't concentrate. I guess I'm going home. That's 500 kilometres behind the wheel – and then wish me luck getting on a flight. I hope I do make it and get to see the historic occasion with my own eyes and not via YouTube. But the reason I am writing this post is that I have been asked to warn all those who don't yet have this information: THE PROTEST WILL TAKE PLACE IN BOLOTNAYA SQUARE (not in Revolution Square).[51]

This post marked an important moment in Akunin's life (that is to say, "Akunin" as a creation, but in Chkhartishvili's life, too). From 2011 onward, "Boris Akunin" was no longer just a popular writer who carefully managed a literary project; he was now "Akunin-Chkhartishvili," a celebrity who sought to use his connections with readers to articulate anti-Putin political stances.

ELENA V. BARABAN

The writer's celebrity status, as Stephen M. Norris indicated above, has been reinforced by his political activism. In August 2008, he criticized Russia's military campaign against Georgia in South Ossetia.[52] In 2012 he became one of the founders of the League of Voters that organized opposition protests against Vladimir Putin's re-election as Russia's President.[53] When asked how he reconciles his own liberal beliefs with the beliefs of his most popular protagonist, Erast Fandorin, who is a statist ("a nineteenth-century version of a KGB man"),[54] Akunin explains that he is essentially not against a well-organized state. However, since the Russian state has never been run well, and, furthermore, since Russian liberals are often perceived as the opposite of statists, he is a liberal. Even if his own political activism might seem like a poor match for his hero's conservative patriotism, he sees no contradiction between how he writes and what he does as a public figure. Like Fandorin, Akunin (Chkhartishvili) is ready to serve his state as long as this service and the authorities' actions are in tune with his own understanding of what is right and wrong.

Regardless of the complexity involved in distinguishing Akunin as a statist from Akunin as a liberal, Akunin's political activism has earned him the title of dissident, a reputation that has been solidified through numerous interviews with the writer.[55] Described as "a powerful voice in his country's opposition movement,"[56] since 2013 Akunin has settled in Western Europe as an expat. Feeling disappointed with the Russian public, he has announced that he would not return to Russia unless the atmosphere there changes and the majority of the Russian population stops supporting Putin.[57] While the flavour of dissent has helped to generate interest in his books both in Russia and abroad,[58] Akunin has, in fact, always positioned himself not simply as an author of entertaining novels that help to pass time on public transport, but also as a producer of hidden messages for those who can see beyond his novels' story lines. By means of literary projections, some of his novels set in the nineteenth century offer critiques of contemporary Russia.[59] A more explicit critique of the Russian state was offered in Akunin's *Fairy Tales for Idiots*, which, according to the writer, was not particularly successful. On the surface, it may seem that Akunin's "tinkering" with Russian classical literature and the underscored playfulness of his Erast Fandorin series, along with his claims that he has no concept of Russian history (he states he did not have a preconceived concept of the history of the Russian state when he began writing his historical series), all fit into a project that shuns overarching truths. However, Akunin's projects do not quite illustrate the postmodernist stance that, since there are no overarching truths, everything is up for grabs. Beneath a façade of entertaining literature lurks a tangible ideology that, ironically, seem to clash with Chkhartishvili's political position. Given the outlook of his most attractive protagonists, Akunin may be confronted with questions similar to those posed by the important contemporary author Ludmila Ulitskaya, namely the questions of an impossible combination of the writer's personal political position and the views of his heroes, which seem to agree with neoconservative policies of President Putin. Despite the tremendous appeal of Akunin's most prominent protagonist, Erast Fandorin's patriotism might be an involuntary match for the patriotic stance of the heroes of patriotic novels of the 1990s.[60]

Currently, Akunin believes that in Russia the current historical period is "black-and-white," and thus his political position had to be stated clearly and explicitly.[61] In September 2015, however, he wrote

on his blog that after living abroad for a year he no longer wanted
to write about politics because people's positions on contemporary
political matters had become fixed, resulting in angry online exchanges.
"I think," he wrote, "that the time for politics in Russia is over."[62] For
now, Akunin remains an expat, as he describes himself, occasionally
engaging in politics via his Facebook profile.

Akunin and Scholars

ELENA V. BARABAN

As soon as Akunin's first books appeared, the critical discussion of
his work became heated. The critics' assessment was polarized: some
celebrated Akunin's seeming postmodern playfulness and the rich
intertextuality of his narratives,[63] and some were enraged by Akunin's
"tinkering" with (Russian) classics.[64] Inadvertently, however, even
disparaging articles by the critics of the calibre of Marina Adamovich
testified to the significantly better quality of Akunin's *detektivy* in comparison to what had been available on the Russian book market.[65] For
the last twenty years, Akunin has kept readers and critics intrigued by
introducing new literary and historiographic projects, writing in different genres, turning to film scripts, releasing some stories as computer
games, and maintaining the writer-reader communication via social networks and blogs. The academic community has obliged by turning from
initial reviews of Akunin's books to more formal studies of his works
including their style, language, ideology, and commercial success.

Not counting hundreds of reviews and biographical sketches, to date
there have appeared two monographs on Akunin. Natalia Bobkova
examines Akunin's use of postmodernist techniques in the example of
Erast Fandorin and Sister Pelagia book series.[66] Co-authored by Tatyana
Snigireva, Aleksey Podchinenov, and Aleksey Snigirev, the book *Boris
Akunin i ego igrovoi mir* (2017) examines Akunin's playfulness, his *History
of the Russian State*, as well as the chronotopes of his other works.[67]

The majority of these focus on Akunin's use of postmodernist literary devices and his interaction with a variety of cultural traditions and
genres.[68] Following the publication of Akunin's *Seagull* (2000), scholars
of Chekhov examined Akunin's input into the Chekhovian discourse[69]
and compared his re-writing of Chekhov's play in the detective genre
with its reinterpretations by other contemporary authors.[70] Likewise,
Akunin's "Hamlet. A Version" ("Gamlet. Versiia") in *Comedy/Tragedy*
(*Komediia/Tragediia*, 2002) was examined not only for its literary techniques but also for its political subtext.[71] Akunin's two-volume *F.M.*

(2006), his rewriting of Dostoevsky's *Crime and Punishment*, awaits a similar inclusion into the Dostoevsky discourse.[72] Besides these aspects, scholars looked at Akunin's work from the perspective of narratology,[73] gender studies,[74] genre studies,[75] film studies,[76] historiography, and linguistics.[77] Several articles examine Akunin's game poetics.[78] Some studies examine the artistic time and space in Akunin's fiction.[79]

Since in the present volume there is no article dedicated to the novels published under the pen-name Anna Borisova, it may be worthwhile to outline possible academic approaches to discussing Borisova's three novels, *There... (Tam...,* 2008); *The Creator (Kreativschik,* 2008); and *Seasons (Vremena goda,* 2011). Borisova was Akunin's secondary project. Upon publishing *Seasons,* the author (through his Akunin blog) announced that he would no longer write under the pen name Borisova. This project was subsumed by Boris Akunin: Borisova's novels were later republished with an explicit indication that they were part of Akunin's literary project "Authors." The font size for the pen name Anna Borisova was significantly smaller than the font size for Boris Akunin.

Anna Borisova's three novels are different even from Akunin's historical fiction: they are about present-day Russia and Russians, with only *Seasons* having substantial historical sections. Given the fact that *Children's Book for Girls (Detskaia kniga dlia devochek,* 2012) written by Gloria Mu on the basis of Akunin's script, was criticized for its misogynistic images of girls, a gender studies approach can be productive in examining Borisova's novels.[80] "Women's Fiction" by Akunin draws on the established genre features. The reader associates women's novels with spirituality and sentimentality. Borisova's oeuvre is essentially popular philosophy in soft covers, which provides spiritual guidance of the sort that may be found in women's magazines or magazines on healthy lifestyles. At the same time, Borisova's novels are different from Russian women's fiction. According to Benjamin Sutcliffe, the essential characteristic of Russian women's prose is its engagement with the description of everyday life, which translates as the life, unhappy or happy, of a family. In Borisova's books, by contrast, family is never central for any of the main and even secondary characters. Unlike fiction by Ludmila Ulitskaya, Ludmilla Petrushevskaya, Olga Slavnikova, and also women writers in Russia who specialize in mass literature (for example, Tatiana Ustinova and Daria Dontsova), the characters in Anna Borisova's novels are not family-oriented.[81] Family ties are much less important than in women's prose. In *The Creator,* for instance, the heroes who listen to the Devil are almost devoid of family ties. Typically, a married woman on her way to pick up her daughter from the nursery school "forgets" her duty and would like to listen longer to the strange man she has just met.

In Akunin, unlike more typical examples of so-called Russian women's prose, there is no room for *byt*, for the everyday. He just changes the gender of the protagonists who are preoccupied by the same issues that have preoccupied his male protagonists. In this sense Borisova's prose is not quite psychologically subtle. It is a genre prose based on the motifs of fairy tales. In the Fandorin series, women are often depicted as irrational, impulsive, moody, and inconsistent. Those who are independent are tragic figures (business women, escort women, mistresses, revolutionary fanatics).

While a great deal has been written about Akunin's remarkable output over the last twenty years, the majority of this scholarly work has been in Russian and has been devoted either to specific works or specific themes within his works. Our project aims to be the first sustained attempt in English at evaluating the project as a whole.

The Project for the Akunin Project

STEPHEN M. NORRIS AND ELENA V. BARABAN

In tune with the subject, this volume was carefully planned: we wanted it to be playful, creative, and different from the typical scholarly volume. To that end, *The Akunin Project* has involved Grigorii Chkhartishvili from the start. It begins and ends with interviews conducted between the co-editors and Akunin, both touching on topics that run throughout this volume.

The Akunin Project is divided into six sections, each comprising two chapters. Part One tackles Akunin's postmodern techniques in his longest and most popular book series (so far), about Erast Fandorin, a secret agent in the service of the Tsars. In Part Two the discussion shifts to Akunin's shorter book series and their amateur detectives, Sister Pelagia and Nicholas Fandorin (Erast's grandson). The focus of the analysis here is Akunin's engagement with readers and his rewriting of Fedor Dostoevsky's *Crime and Punishment*. Part Three, "Buried Secrets and Historical Spies in Akunin's Works," explores intricate connections between Akunin's different book series and individual projects. Here one learns why Chkhartishvili writes about cemeteries, and about his use of spies as actors in history. With the first three sections of the volume primarily offering a discussion of Akunin's detective fiction and his postmodernist stylistic preferences, Part Four takes up Akunin's histories, his currently most ambitious project, launched in 2013. Two professional historians, including one of this volume's editors, offer critiques of this project, to which Akunin would no doubt respond by saying we have once again missed the forest by looking at the trees. The two chapters that form Part Five look at Chkhartishvili's side projects that appeared under new pen names and are written in styles distinct from the one typical of Boris Akunin. In this part one learns how Brusnikin (Akunin) engages in the practice of *stiob* (a particular form of parody), and how the Akunin-Chkhartishvili "serious novels" engage with Russia's revolutionary past. Finally, Part Six tackles the Akunin Project in its entirety, first by examining the writer's engagement with mass literature and then by analysing Akunin's deliberate use of cross-media marketing strategies.

With Chkhartishvili's permission, in the four appendices to the volume we also present five Akunin/Chkhartishvili writings never before translated into English, so that readers can delve into the worlds he has created beyond the Erast Fandorin and Pelagia series (both of which have been translated). The first translation begins with the beginning; namely, how a literary scholar named Grigorii Chkhartishvili more or less outed himself as the new sensation "Boris Akunin" in 1999, when he published an article titled "If I were a Newspaper Magnate." Appendix 2 features Akunin's general introduction to his *History of the Russian State*, where he lays out his rules for how he plans to write history, as well as his blog post that announces Boris Akunin as the "new Karamzin." Appendices 3 and 4 are excerpts from *The Spy Novel* (in Akunin's "Genre series") and from the novel *Ninth Saviour*, published under the pen name Anatolii Brusnikin. All of these translations complement the discussion of Akunin's work in the chapters that comprise the volume. Enjoy!

NOTES

1 Boris Akunin, "Fandorin XV," *LiveJournal* (blog), 21 April 2015, https://
   borisakunin.livejournal.com/146185.html?thread=69961481. Unless otherwise indicated, all translations are by the authors.
2 First published in 1999 and republished in 2008. See Grigorii Chkhartishvili,
   Pisatel' i samoubiistvo (Moscow: Zakharov, 1999).
3 Akunin, "Fandorin XV."
4 See Brian James Baer and Nadezhda Korchagina, "Akunin's Secret and
   Fandorin's Luck: Postmodern Celebrity in Post-Soviet Russia," in *Celebrity and Glamour in Contemporary Russia: Shocking Chic*, ed. Helena Goscilo and Vlad Strukov (London: Routledge, 2011), 75–89.
5 See Anna Zhebrovskaia, "Prilozhenie k Fandorinu," Tema, 20 January 2007,
   http://tema.in.ua/article/1598.html.

6 "The Death of Achilles: A Fandorin Mystery," San Diego Reader, 11 May 2006, https://www.sandiegoreader.com/news/2006/may/11/death-achilles -fandorin-mystery/#.

7 Baer and Korchagina, "Akunin's Secret and Fandorin's Luck," 76.

8 Ibid., 80.

9 Quotes are from the blog post announcing the authors as Akunin. In *Echo Moscow*, it appeared under the name Boris Akunin: "Proekt 'avtory': Anna Borisova," 12 January 2012, https://echo.msk.ru/blog/b_akunin/847938 -echo/. In the journal *Snob*, it appeared under the name Grigorii Chkhartishvili: https://snob.ru/profile/5232/blog/45102.

10 Borisova's novels include *Tam ... (Over There ...*, 2007), *Kreativshschik (The Creator*, 2009), and *Vremena goda (The Four Seasons*, 2011), all published by AST (Moscow). The current editions of these novels all come with Akunin's name one them.

11 Boris Akunin, "Proekt 'avtory': Anatolii Olegovich Brusnikin," 13 January 2012, https://echo.msk.ru/blog/b_akunin/848329-echo/. Under Chkhartishvili's name: https://snob.ru/profile/5232/blog/45157.

12 See in this volume Yekaterina Severts' translation of the first chapter of *Deviatnyi spas (The Ninth Saviour)* as well as her analysis of this novel.

13 Brusnikin's novels, *Deviatnyi Spas (The Ninth Saviour*, 2007), *Geroi inogo vremeni (A Hero of a Different Time*, 2010), and *Bellona* (2012), are all published by AST (Moscow).

14 See Elena V. Baraban's chapter *"The Family Album*: Ordinary People in Extraordinary Circumstances," in this volume, on the novels published under the pen-name Akunin-Chkhartishvili.

15 Stephen M. Norris, "Boris Akunin," in Willard Sunderland, ed. *Russia's People of Empire: Life Stories from Eurasia, 1500 to the Present*, ed. Willard Sunderland (Bloomington, IN: Indiana University Press, 2012), 327–38. Akunin's individual books often sell 200,000 copies in their first week of release.

16 Because of this artificially created imbalance between demand and offer, established Russian literary journals would boost their subscriptions by announcing they were planning to publish several *detektivy* in a given year.

17 Anthony Olcott, *Russian Pulp:The Detektiv and the Russian Way of Crime* (Lanham, MD: Rowman & Littlefield, 2001), 7.

18 In the early 1990s, foreign works comprised some 70 to 80 per cent of all detective fiction being published in Russia. By 1998, however, translated detective novels accounted only 20–30 per cent. See O. Vronskaia, "Na podstupakh k 'Zolotomu pistoletu,'" *Literaturnaia gazeta* (22 July 1998): 13.

19 See Eliot Borenstein, *Overkill: Sex and Violence in Contemporary Russian Culture* (Ithaca, NY: Cornell University Press, 2008).

20 Zinaida Kirbit, one of the three protagonists in the film series *Sledstvie vedut znatoki* (Experts Conduct the Investigations, 1971–89), would knit at

her work place. The twenty-four episodes of *Experts Conduct the Investigations* were based on Olga and Alexander Lavrov's scripts and produced by the First Channel of the TsTV (Central TV of the USSR). One of the episodes – "Iz zhizni fruktov" (From the Life of Fruit) – was about selling vegetables and fruit on the black market. The last two episodes were released in Russian in 2002 and 2003 but the old investigating team would no longer fit post-Soviet reality.

21 Tzvetan Todorov, "The Typology of Detective Fiction" in *The Poetics of Prose*, trans. Richard Howard (Ithaca, NY: Cornell University Press, 1977), 43.

22 See more on the last novel in the Erast Fandorin series in Elena V. Baraban, *"The Family Album,"* in this volume.

23 Three novels – *Azazel'* (*The Winter Queen*, 1998), *Turetskii gambit* (*The Turkish Gambit*, 1988), and *Statskii sovetnik* (*The State Counsellor*, 1999) – were made into films.

24 The series consists of three novels: *Pelagiia i belyi bul'dog* (*Pelagia and the White Bulldog*, 2000), *Pelagiia i chernyi monakh* (*Pelagia and the Black Monk*, 2001), and *Pelagiia i krasnyi petukh* (*Pelagia and the Red Rooster*, 2003).

25 See more on this book series in Claire Whitehead's essay "The Temptation of the Reader: The Search for Meaning in Boris Akunin's Pelagia Trilogy," *Slavonic and East European Review* 94, no. 1 (January 2016): 29–56, republished in a slightly edited form in this volume.

26 This book series is composed of four novels: *Altyn-Tolobas* (2000); *Vneklassnoe chtenie* (*Recommended Reading*, 2002); *F.M.* (2006); and *Sokol i lastochka* (*The Falcon and the Swallow*, 2009).

27 So far, six volumes of non-fiction books in this book series have appeared and three more volumes are planned. See more about this project in the excerpts from Boris Akunin's blog "A New Karamzin Has Appeared" (2013) and "General Introduction" to the *History of the Russian State* series (2013), translated for this volume by Stephen M. Norris, in Appendix 2. See also the chapters by Ilya Gerasimov and Stephen M. Norris on Akunin's *History of the Russian State* in this volume.

28 Andreas Huyssen, *Present Pasts: Urban Palimpsests and the Politics of Memory* (Redwood City, CA: Stanford University Press, 2003), 1.

29 This book series so far consists of five books. *Shpionskii roman* (*The Spy Novel*, 2006, examined in this volume by Stephen M. Norris) and *Qvest* (*Quest*, 2009), both published by AST (Moscow), are the only ones that are set in Soviet Russia.

30 Susan Buck-Morss, *Dreamworld and Catastrophe: The Passing of Mass Utopia in East and West* (Cambridge, MA: MIT Press, 2000), 68.

31 Stanislav Govorukhin's documentary *Tak zhit' nel'zia* (We Can't Live Like This, 1990) helped destroy public belief in Soviet ideals. The title was borrowed from a monologue by a satirist Mikhail Zhvanetskii, one of

many that served the purpose of propelling the politics of glasnost and destroyed the old system of values. The shock experienced by Russians during radical critique of the Soviet value system is captured by Nancy Ries in her book *The Russian Talk: Culture and Conversation During Perestroika* (Ithaca, NY: Cornell University Press, 1997).

32 David Remnick, *Lenin's Tomb: The Last Days of the Soviet Empire* (New York: Vintage, 1994), 523.

33 Stanislav Govorukhin's 1992 documentary *Rossiia, kotoruiu my poteriali* (The Russia We Have Lost) became very influential in the 1990s' popular idealization of tsarist Russia. Academic publications with a distinct nationalist flavour also contributed to a critique of the Soviet period and the establishment of a new myth about tsarist Russia. See, e.g. the following collection of articles: Iu. S. Kukushkin (ed.), *Russkii narod; istoricheskaia sud'ba v xx veke* (Moscow: TOO "ANKO", 1993). Nikita Mikhalkov's 1999 film *Sibirskii tsiriul'nik* (The Barber of Siberia), with its nationalist agenda is another example of idealization of the Russian imperial past. In 2000, Mikhalkov opened the 22nd International Film Festival in Moscow with Gleb Panfilov's film *Romanovy–ventsenosnaia semia* (The Romanovs – the Sovereign Family). Panfilov's film propagated the same Russian myth about the prosperous pre-revolutionary past and continued the tradition of the post-Soviet glorification of Russian monarchism. Likewise, the book *Nikolai II: Zhizn' i smert'* (Nicholas II: His Life and Death) by Edward Radzinskii (Moscow: Vagrius, 1997, 2000, 2003) and the media campaign surrounding the burial and then the canonization of the Romanov family in 2000 also added to the idealization of Russian monarchy.

34 Tatiana Glushkova, "'Elity' i 'chern' russkogo patriotizma: Avtoritety izmeny," *Molodaia gvardiia*, no. 11 (1994) and four more instalments of the article in *Molodaia gvardiia*, nos. 1, 2, 6, and 7 (1995).

35 Fredric Jameson, *Postmodernism: The Cultural Logic of Late Capitalism* (Durham, NC: Duke University Press, 1989).

36 The most important works in this regard are Boris Groys, *The Total Art of Stalinism*, trans. Charles Rougle (Princeton, NJ: Princeton University Press, 1992); Boris Groys, ed., *The Total Enlightenment: Conceptual Art in Moscow 1960–1990* (Frankfurt: Hatje Cantz, 2008); Mikhail Epstein, *After the Future: The Paradoxes of Postmodernism and Contemporary Russian Culture* (Amherst: University of Massachusetts Press, 1995); Mikhail Epstein, Alexander Genis, and Slobodanka Vladiv-Glover, *Russian Postmodernism: New Perspectives On Post-Soviet Culture*, ed. Slobodanka Vladiv-Glover (New York: Berghahn Books, 1999); Mark Lipovetsky, *Russian Postmodernist Fiction: Dialogue with Chaos*, ed. Eliot Borenstein (Armonk, NY: M.E. Sharpe, 1999).

37 Eliot Borenstein, "Editor's Introduction: Postmodernism, Duty-Free," in Lipovetsky, *Russian Postmodernist Fiction*, xvi.

38 Jameson, *Postmodernism.* See also Žižek's explanation of mass culture as the bearer of postmodern techniques and ideas: Slavoj Žižek, "Intrduction: Alfred Hitchcock, or The Form and its Historical Mediation", in *Everything You Always Wanted to Know about Lacan (But Were Afraid to Ask Hitchcock)*, ed. Slavoj Žižek (London: Verso, 1992), 1–2.

39 Fredric Jameson, "Globalization and Political Strategy." *New Left Review 4* (July–August 2000), https://newleftreview.org/issues/II4/articles/fredric -jameson-globalization-and-political-strategy.

40 On how a variety of digital and social media employed by Akunin has contributed to Akunin's commercial success, see Natalia Erlenkamp's chapter in this volume.

41 Henry Jenkins, *Convergent Culture: Where Old and New Media Collide* (New York: New York University Press, 2006), 2–3.

42 Elisa Coati, "Time and Space Games on Akunin's Virtual Pages," *Digital Icons: Studies in Russian, Eurasian, and East European New Media* 5 (2011): 50.

43 Ibid., 51–2.

44 Quoted in ibid., 58.

45 Andrei Staniukovich, *Fandorinskaia Moskva* (Moscow: Zakharov, 2008); Mariia Besedina, *Moskva akuninskaia* (Moscow: Folio-SP, Olimp, 2008).

46 Coati also makes this connection: ibid., 64.

47 See "Authors: Anna Borisova, " *LiveJournal* (blog), 11 January 2012, https://web.archive.org/web/20120622144924/http://borisakunin.live-journal.com/50686.html.

48 "Novyi Karamzin iavilsia, " *LiveJournal* (blog), 20 March 2013, https://borisakunin.livejournal.com/94544.html.

49 "Ia stal pisatelem, " *LiveJournal* (blog), 23 May 2012, https://borisakunin.livejournal.com/63290.html.

50 "I eto ser'eznoe delo nel'zia poruchat' nikomu," *LiveJournal* (blog), 4 February 2014, https://borisakunin.livejournal.com/122243.html.

51 Post from 9 December 2011, https://borisakunin.livejournal.com/45529.html. The post appears in this translation in Masha Gessen, *The Man Without a Face: The Unlikely Rise of Vladimir Putin* (New York: Riverhead Books, 2012), 285–6.

52 See, for example, Kseniia Larina, "Rossiia i Gruziia: Esli u nas obshchee budushchee?" *Ekho Moskvy*, 16 August 2008, www.echo.msk.ru/pro-grams/kulshok/534013-echo.phtml.

53 The writer's reputation as "a powerful voice in his country's opposition movement" has been solidified in numerous interviews with the writer. Charles Clover, "Russia's Protest Movement Gets Organised," *Financial Times*, 18 January 2012, https://www.ft.com/content/f482927e-41f8-11e1 -9506-00144feab49a?mhq5j=e5; see also Alexei Navalny and Boris Akunin, "The Akunin-Navalny Interviews," OpenDemocracy, 11 January 2012,

https://www.opendemocracy.net/od-russia/alexei-navalny-boris-akunin /akunin-navalny-interviews-part-i; Sally McGrane, "Boris Akunin: Russia's Dissident Detective Novelist," *The New Yorker*, 27 July 2012, https://www .newyorker.com/books/page-turner/boris-akunin-russias-dissident -detective-novelist.

54   See "Ludmila Ulitskaya i Grigorii Ckhartishvili. Podslushivaem pisatel'skie razgovory," Youtube video, 41:31, 11 May 2017, https://www .youtube.com/watch?v=NChl1yIGzMk, 28:00–33:00. Boris Akunin and Ludmila Ulitskaya discussed their views on literature and politics at the London-based club Open Russia (Otkrytaia Rossiia), which was founded by Mikhail Khodorkovsky as part of a larger Open Russia project. See more on the issue in Elena V. Baraban's chapter *"The Family Album"* in this volume.

55   A teaser in the *Financial Times*, for example, reads: "Russia's dissident detective novelist talks about oligarchs, angering the Kremlin and why even peaceful revolution could lead to Russia's collapse." John Thornhill, "Lunch with the FT: Boris Akunin," *Financial Times*, 1 March 2013, https:// www.ft.com/content/77f7ca96-80d4-11e2-9c5b-00144feabdc0?mhq5j=e5.

56   Charles Clover, "Russia's Protest Movement Gets Organised," *Financial Times*, 18 January 2012, https://www.ft.com/content/f482927e -41f8-11e1-9506-00144feab49a?mhq5j=e5; See also Navalny and Akunin, "Akunin-Navalny Interviews"; McGrane, "Boris Akunin."

57   "Boris Akunin: V Rossiiu ne vernus' ...," YouTube video, 18:20, 19 April 2015, https://www.youtube.com/watch?v=cprXLtFgcRk.

58   Although, according to market analysis, Akunin's books are by far less popular in translation than in the original.

59   Akunin welcomes such interpretations. See, e.g., Elena V. Baraban, "A Country Resembling Russia: The Use of History in Boris Akunin's Detective Novels," *Slavic and East European Journal (SEEJ)* 48, no. 3 (2004): 396–420. For Norris's interpretation of one of the passages in a Sister Pelagia novel, see Stephen M. Norris, "Boris Akunin," in Sunderland, *Russia's People of Empire*, 332–3. According to Norris, in one of his numer-ous interviews Akunin states: "The problems that Russia faced at the end of the nineteenth century are essentially the same problems we have in Russia today. I don't want to go on at great length about the political and economic aspects of these problems. That's not really the point. Right now there is an ongoing debate in my country about which values deserve the highest priority: whether individual values need to be emphasized, or whether we should return to social and collective interests. Last century, Russia chose an answer to this question that led to the tragedies of the twentieth century. Now we find ourselves at a similar crossroads, but we don't know yet which road will be taken this time" (333).

60 For more on the convergence of the views proposed in Russian mass culture of the 1990s and 2000s and the neoconservative policies promoted by Putin, see Boris Dubin, "Ispytanie na sostoiatel'nost': K sotsiologicheskoi poetike russkogo romana-boevika," in *Slovo–pis'mo–literatura* (Moscow: NLO, 2001), 218–42. See also Boris Dubin, "O banal'nosti proshlogo: Opyt sotsiologicheskogo prochteniia rossiiskikh istoriko-patrioticheskikh romanov 1990kh godov," in *Slovo–pis'mo–literatura*, 243–61.

61 Boris Akunin's interview with BBC Russian Service: "Boris Akunin: V Rossiiu ne vernus' … ," YouTube video, 20:31, 19 April 2015, https://www.youtube.com/watch?v=cprXLtFgcRk, 3:00–4:00.

62 "Kak ia provel leto," *LiveJournal* (blog), 7 September 2015, https://borisakunin.livejournal.com/148593.html.

63 Vyacheslav Kuritsyn was one of the first critics to welcome Akunin. Some claim that by writing positive reviews of Akunin's novels on his website *Sovremennaia russkaia literatura s Vyacheslavom Kuritsynym*, Kuritsyn made Akunin famous. See, for example, Vladislav Gorin's interview with Kuritsyn: "Vyacheslav Kuritsyn. Chelovek, kotoryi proslavil Akunina," ETV (Ekaterinburg TV), 15 March 2016, https://ekburg.tv/programmy/summa_mnenij/2016-03-15/vjacheslav_kuricyn_chelovek_kotoryj_proslavil_akunina. Aware of his reputation as a person who has helped to make Akunin famous, Kuritsyn starts his review of the novel *Vneklassnoe chtenie* (*Recommended Reading*, 2002) by stating his admiration for Akunin's work: http://old.russ.ru/krug/news/20020718_kur.html.

64 Marina Adamovich, "Iudif' s golovoi Oloferna: psevdoklassika v russkoi literature 1990kh," *Novyi mir* 7 (2001), http://www.nm1925.ru/Archive/Journal6_2001_7/Content/Publication6_3740/Default.aspx.

65 It is unimaginable that detective writers such as Daria Dontsova (although the overall print runs of her books are comparable to those of Akunin) would merit a discussion by Marina Adamovich or Pavel Basinskii. See Baskinskii's mixed review of *Almaznaia kolesnitsa* (*The Diamond Chariot*, 2003): Pavel Baskinskii, "Kosmopolit suprotiv inorodtsa," *Russkii zhurnal*, 31 December 2003, http://www.russ.ru/pole/2003-Pavel-Basinskij-ob-Almaznoj-kolesnice-Borisa-Akunina.

66 N.G. Bobkova, *Funktsii postmodernistskogo diskursa v detektivnykh romanakh B. Akunina o Fandorine i Pelagii* (Ulan-Udė, Russia: BGU izdatel'stvo) 2015.

67 T.A. Snigireva, A.V. Podchinenov, and A.V. Snigirev, *Boris Akunin i ego igrovoi mir* (St. Petersburg: Aleteia, 2017).

68 The earliest articles that demonstrated this approach are: Baraban, "A Country Resembling Russia" and Andrei Ranchin, "Romany B. Akunina i klassicheskaia traditsiia: Povestvovanie v chetyrekh glavakh s preuvedomleniem, neliricheskim otstupleniem i epilogom," *Novoe literaturnoe obozrenie* 67, no. 3 (2004): 235–66.

69   See, for example, O. Glebova, "Chekhovskaia 'Chaika' v kontekste
     sovremennoi populiarnoi literatury: 'Chaika' Borisa Akunina," *Opus #
     1-2: Russkii memuar. Soavtorstvo,* ed. G. Mikhailova, N. Arlauskaite, and
     A. Dvoeglazov (Vilnius: Vilniaus universiteto leidykla, 2005), 203–16; O.
     Isakova, "'Chaika' B. Akunina i nekotorye problemy poetiki postmod-
     ernizma," *Molodye issledovateli Chekhova* 5 (2005): 53–64; O.A. Mal'tseva,
     "Situatsiia intertekstual'nosti v piese B. Akunina 'Chaika,'" *Vestnik Oren-
     burgskogo gosudarstvennogo pedagogicheskogo universiteta* 5 (2001): 216–22;
     V.V. Savel'eva, "'Chaika' B. Akunina–'chisto angliiskoe ubiistvo,'" *Russkaia
     rech'* 6 (2002): 36–41; T.S. Zlotnikova, "Chekhovskii diskurs khudozhest-
     vennykh praktik XX veka," in *Sovremennye transformatsii rossiiskoi kul'tury,*
     ed. I.V. Kondakov (Moscow: Nauka, 2005), 467–80; Lyudmila Parts, "Boris
     Akunin's Postmodern Čajka," *Russian Literature* 82 (2016): 37–47.
70   V.B. Shamina, "Chekhovskaia 'Chaika' v interpretatsii T. Uil'iamsa i
     B. Akunina," *Russkaia slovesnost'* 6 (2007): 2–6.
71   E.S. Demicheva, "Postmodernistskie interpretatsii gamletovskogo siuzheta
     v sovremennoi russkoi literature," *Izvestiia Volgogradskogo gosudarstven-
     nogo pedagogicheskogo universiteta. Seriia: Filolologicheskie nauki* 2 (2007):
     120–4; Elizabeth Richmond-Garza, "Detecting Conspiracy: Boris Akunin's
     Dandiacal Detective, or a Century in Queer Profiles from London to
     Moscow," in *Crime Fiction as World Literature,* ed. Louise Nilsson, David
     Damrosch, Theo D'haen, and Thomas Oliver Beebee (New York: Blooms-
     bury Academic and Professional, 2017), 271–89. See also Richmond-Garza's
     chapter in this volume.
72   See Zara Torlone's reading of this novel in this volume.
73   See Claire Whitehead's chapter in this volume.
74   Mariia Litovskaia, "Maska i dusha: Soznanie zhenshchiny XIX veka v
     proze B. Akunina," in *Zhenskii vyzov: Russkie pisatel'nitsy XIX – nachala
     XX veka,* ed. Evgeniia Stroganova and Elizabet Shore (Tver', Russia: Liliia
     Print, 2006), 61–74; Irina Savkina, "'Taste the Difference': The Children's
     Book for Boys and The Children's Book for Girls in Boris Akunin's 'Genres'
     Project," *Routledge Russian Studies in Literature,* 52, no. (2016): 190–204;
     O.E. Verkhoturtseva, "Tipologiia zhenskikh obrazov v romanakh
     B. Akunina," *Uchenye zapiski Shadrinskogo gosudarstvennogo pedagogicheskogo
     instituta* 9 (2005): 53–62.
75   M.A. Dorofeeva, "Traditsii zhanra uta-monogatari v romane B. Akunina
     'Almaznaia kolesnitsa,'" in *Sovremennaia russkaia literatura: Problemy
     izucheniia i prepodavaniia v 2 chastiakh,* vol. 2., ed. by M.P. Abasheva,
     V.E. Kaigorodova, and N.B. Lapaeva (Moscow: Izdatel'stvo Moskovskogo
     universiteta, 2005), 57–9.
76   Yana Hashamova, "Looking for the Balkan (Br)other: The National Gaze
     in Dzhanik Faiziev's *The Turkish Gambit,*" *Russian Review* 74, no. 2 (2015):

211–29; Robert Mulcahy, "A Not-So-Thrilling Thriller: Adapting Boris Akunin's *The State Counsellor,*" *Studies in Russian and Soviet Cinema* 7, no. 3 (2013): 311–35.

77 N.V. Danilova, "Traditsii i innovatsii B. Akunina v sozdanii antroponimicheskogo prostranstva romana '*Azazel',*'" in *Russkii mir v dukhovnom soznanii narodov Rossii,* ed. N.K. Frolov (Tiumen', Russia: Vektor Buk, 2008) 38–41. See also N.N. Menkova, "Iazykovaia lichnost' Borisa Akunina," *Voprosy fililogicheskikh nauk* 1 (2004): 7–9; Natal'ia Nikolaevna Men'kova, "Iazykovaia lichnost' pisatelia kak istochnik rechevykh kharakteristik personazhei: Po materialam B. Akunina: Avtoreferat dissertatsii kanditata filologicheskikh nauk" (Moscow: Rossiiskii universitet druzhby narodov [RUDN], 2005); R.P. Dronseika, "Prostranstvenno-vremennye aspekty proizvedenii B. Akunina," in *XI Pushkinskie chteniia: materialy mezhdunarodnoi nauchnoi konferentsii 6 iunia 2006 goda,* vol 2., ed. T. Mal'tseva and V. Skvortsov (Saint Petersburg: Izdatel'stvo Leningradskogo gosudarstvennogo universiteta im. A.S. Pushkina, 2006), 147–52.

78 Ch. De Lotto, "Literaturnye igry, ili igra v literaturu B. Akunina," in *XX vek i russkaia literatura: Alba Regina Philologiae: Sb. nauchnykh trudov k 70-letiiu G. A. Beloi,* ed. V.I. Tiupa (Moscow: RGGU, 2002), 302–15. Tang Shi has also published several articles on this aspect of Akunin's novels. See, for example, Tang Shi, "Features of Game Poetics in 'The Death of Achilles' by Boris Akunin," *Vestnik Rossiiskogo universiteta druzhby narodov: Seriia literaturovedenie* 22, no. 4 (2017): 614–26.

79 See, for example, I.A. Ostrenko, "Vremia i mesto v 'Detskoi knige' B. Akunina," in Mal'tseva and Skvortsov, *XI Pushkinskie chteniia, vol. 2,* 68–72.

80 Gloria Mu, *Detskaia kniga dlia devochek (po stsenariiu Borisa Akunina)* (Moscow: AST, 2012).

81 Benjamin M. Sutcliffe, *The Prose of Life: Russian Women Writers from Khrushchev to Putin* (Madison, WI: University of Wisconsin Press, 2009). See also Benjamin Sutcliffe, "Documenting Women's Voices in Perestroika Gulag Narratives," *Toronto Slavic Quarterly* 3 (2003), http://sites.utoronto.ca/tsq/03/sutcliffe.shtml; "Publishing the Russian Soul? Women's Provincial Literary Anthologies, 1990–1995," in *Soviet and Post-Soviet Review* 1 (2006): 99–113; Tat'iana Taiganova, "Roman v rubishche: O romane Svetlany Vasilenko 'Durochka,'" *Druzhba narodov* 6 (2000): 184–94; Yelena Tarasova, "She Who Bears No Ill," in *Half a Revolution: Contemporary Fiction by Russian Women,* ed. and trans. Masha Gessen (Pittsburgh: Cleis, 1995), 96–126.

2 Interview with Grigorii Chkhartishvili (Boris Akunin)

Note: The 2015 Havighurst Center for Russian and Post-Soviet Studies' annual Young Researchers' Conference was held at the Villa Virgiliana in Cuma, Italy. The conference began with an interview between Stephen M. Norris, Professor of History at Miami University, and Boris Akunin, the bestselling Russian author. Below is a transcript of the interview, transcribed by Emily Walton, a 2016 graduate of Miami University. The original transcription has been further edited.

Stephen Norris: This conference is called "Writing the Past, Righting Memory," a play on words that gets at serious subject matters; namely, the ways that Russian historians, writers, scholars, and officials have tried to write new histories after 1991 and address important historical legacies. These are also the implicit goals of your ongoing project, *The History of the Russian State*. I have several questions about it but I'll start with a broad one: What are your goals in writing this history, and how do you plan to "use Occam's razor in order to reveal what really happened," as you state in the introduction to the first volume?

Boris Akunin: Well, hello everybody. I'm happy to be here. Yes, this is my first time in this part of Italy and I have never participated in an event like this in my life, so it is a new experience for me; that's why I did not want to make a speech or a lecture, because it is not usually my kettle of fish. I am not the one who speaks – I am normally the one that writes. Talking about this new project of mine, *The History of the Russian State*, I should say that this is something that I have wanted to do for a long, long time. The main goal is not just to deliver a message to the public, it is something I want to do for myself because I have been living for many years in my country and I feel that I do not understand it properly. Russia is still a country of unpredictabilities for me.

This country keeps surprising me, recently more than ever. In order to understand it, I thought that I have to go to the very beginning.

As those of you that have studied Russians know very well, our favourite question is *Kto vinovat'?* (Who is to blame?). We have two almost sacred questions, both even became titles of classical novels. One is *Kto vinovat'?* The other is *Chto delat'?* (What is to be done?) Russians are never really interested in what is to be done, they are more interested in who is to blame. I grew up hearing this kind of talk ever since I was a kid. Everybody around me had been trying to figure out who was to blame because everybody agreed that life was terribly wrong. Things were not going the right way. This view is also a very Russian trait: Russians seem to be either absolutely unhappy with their life or absolutely euphoric about it. When I was young, the first general idea was that it was Stalin who was to blame. He spoiled everything and we had to go back to Lenin. That is what my parents used to say in the 1960s. Then we discovered that no, it was Lenin who was to blame. Then we discovered that no, it was the Romanovs who were to blame because the country was not well-ruled under them and they were not able to save this country, so it was their fault. But no, it was not the Romanovs, it was Ivan the Terrible who was to blame. No, it was not Ivan the Terrible, it was Ivan III who created this state. No, it was the Tatars. Well, everybody liked that idea and Russia accepted the Tatars because we have a lot of them in Russia today. I thought that I had had enough of this and I had to go back to level zero and to explain everything to myself.

I discovered that first of all, Russian history, probably more than any other history, is full of myths and lies. In Russia, historical science existed for a very short span of time, a part of the nineteenth century and a part of the twentieth century. Before, it had been practically non-existent, because it was only Nikolai Karamzin who invented it in a serious way at the beginning of the nineteenth century. During the twentieth century history became so full of ideology that it became no longer a science but a kind of propaganda. Soviet authorities used history in order to create myths for pedagogical purposes, so that young people would be proud of their great ancestors and their great country. I thought then and I still think now that this is an awful misconception. History is not about being proud. History is like an instruction manual, how to "use" your own country. It should be something such as: don't put your fingers in here or else you will be hit by electricity. If you want to achieve this do this and this and do that. History should be about that which you have to know. You have to know the truth. You have to know that if a country succeeded in something it was because of this and this and this. If there was a defeat we have to know everything about it: why it happened, what didn't go the right way. I wanted to write this sort of history.

This is something I believe that in our time no professional historian can do in general, because a professional historian is usually a specialist in quite a narrow field or someone who wants to create a new concept and build a new theory just to try to prove it. When you try to prove this theory, it is almost impossible to evade the temptation to push forward evidence that only supports the theory and to push down evidence that does not. My history is not like this. From the beginning, I had no preconceived conception. I didn't want to prove anything to anybody. I just wanted to understand what is true and what is probable among all the facts that I have been taught at university and that I learned in studying history. I wanted to go step by step along this ladder. Little by little I would be able to understand and explain to my readers what this Russian state is like.

I should say that my book in Russian is not called "A History of Russia" but "The History of the Russian State." It is a political history, a history of power, a history of relations between those in power and the people. It's also a history of a country written by a writer, not by a historian, which is not a new thing. Some of you have read the wonderful books by Isaac Asimov, who was known mostly as a science fiction writer but who also wrote histories. And now in the UK, for example, the novelist Peter Ackroyd is publishing a new volume of his history of England.[1] These books do not contain long commentaries and have no footnotes; nothing, in other words, to frighten off normal, peaceful readers. They are not meant for students nor for scholars; they are meant for people such as my wife, who claims to be uninterested in history. I want them to be interested in history. That is why these volumes of Russian history are also supported by a series of historical novels, which in turn create a history of Russia seen through the eyes of one family that has been living in Russia for 1,000 years. These historical novels are mostly about the history of human relations and the history of love: it is 1,000 years of love. In the novels I can run free with my imagination, with what I cannot write in my nonfictional histories. Of course, it's also part of a publishing scheme, because we were expecting most readers to buy just my historical adventure novels and hopefully to get hooked by them, to get interested in what was actually happening during this period and then to go to the book shop and buy the non-fiction volume, which is quite expensive because there are a lot of illustrations. The most difficult thing here is not the facts, which are more or less well known, but how to calculate the right balance of heaviness and lightness, of entertainment and seriousness, to avoid losing the reader's attention. I had to work on this formula when I was preparing the first volume. With the second volume I made it just a bit lighter. Now I am finishing the third volume and I understand that the second one was just a bit too light. Now I'm putting more "heaviness" in the third. So that's how it works.

Norris: Speaking of the third volume, I assume it's going to be on Ivan the Terrible and his period. Can you give us a sense of what you are going to argue in it, what will be heavier, and what in general you are planning?

Akunin: The first volume, which was entitled *A Part of Europe*, covers the period before Russia was conquered by the Mongols in the thirteenth century. The second part is about the Tatar-Mongol period and it's logically entitled, *A Part of Asia*, because Russia was a part of a vast Asian empire in the thirteenth, fourteenth, and first half of the fifteenth centuries. The third volume is called *Between Asia and Europe*. It starts in the mid-fifteenth century, with Ivan III, and ends at the beginning of the seventeenth century, during the *smutnoe vremia*, or the Time of Troubles. By my calculation we are currently living in the early years of the sixth Russian state. The first Russian state was the pre-Mongolian state, which began between Novgorod and Kiev and then moved to Vladimir before it collapsed when the Mongols conquered it. For two hundred years afterwards there was no Russian state, it was just a dominion of the Tatar Horde. My third volume is therefore about the second attempt at building a Russian state. It was started by Ivan III in the middle of the fifteenth century, and proved to be very successful, but in the end it failed and ceased to exist in the beginning of the seventeenth century, when the country was conquered by the Poles. There would be a third Russian state in the seventeenth century, then a fourth created by Peter the Great when the state had to be rebuilt and moved even closer to Europe. Then there was the fifth state, the Soviet empire. And now we are living in the sixth state, the post-Soviet one, which as it seems is not going too well right now.

Norris: How many of these states will you narrate?

Akunin: There will be nine volumes in total and I will stop in 1917.

Norris: Why stop then and not cover the Soviet state, particularly after the appearance of the very controversial history written by Alexander Filippov that referred to Stalin as a great state builder?

Akunin: Oh I'm not interested in that and nobody's really interested in it either, the book was just something meant to receive part of the state budget. It's in no way important. Why am I stopping in 1917? Well, you see my main task is to make sure that I am distanced from the events I am describing. I am not for this part or for that part, I try to be neutral. And I think that if I start to describe the events of the twentieth century after 1917 I feel I wouldn't be able to stay objective because it is too close to me personally. The Soviet era passes through the history of every family, mine included. I feel as though I wouldn't be able to cover it the right way, so better not to cover it at all. I should say, however, that I have found another way of describing the history of the past one hundred years in Russia. Since it is emotional, and since I cannot stay objective, I thought I would try to tell the story with the help of fiction, where you don't have to be objective. So I am now working on a series of serious novels, which is something new for me. Up to now I have only written entertainment. Just for a change, I wanted to publish a typically Russian serious series of thick, heavy, gloomy, and depressing novels. I wouldn't care about sales and bestseller lists at all, I would do it just for myself. They would be novels the way I always wanted to write, what we might call impolite literature. I wouldn't try to be polite or entertaining.

Instead, in these new works I would press my problems on my readers. I wouldn't care about the charter you make before writing a detective novel. Inhaling, exhaling, you have to keep rhythm. So here you have to go like this, then do this, then this, before this. You have to count the length of this chapter, and this part of the book should be that long, and here it only has to be three pages long. In my new project there will be nothing of this kind. If I want to describe a dialogue that is important for me, it can go on for twenty pages. I don't care. This is this kind of novel like *Doctor Zhivago*. I hate this book, but okay this is something. And I was also thinking of the sort of dusty, thick albums of family photographs that our grandmothers have. What intrigues me most is that there are people with faces that do not exist any longer. Their expressions, everything about them. Many family members who look at these photos do not even know who they are. There is a mystery to them. They are somehow related to your family but nobody knows how, because grandmother and grandfather are dead already and nobody will tell you who they are. When you also look at class photographs of, say, a gymnasium in 1915, or even a Soviet secondary school in 1939, the same thought occurs. You look at those young faces and you try to figure out what happened to each of them, because it is Russia and because this is the twentieth century. You know deep down that most of the boys were either killed or imprisoned and most of the girls were probably never married or were widowed. And you try to guess, looking at them, what happened to each of them. So, I called this series of novels *The Family Album*, and it is built on these notions. I focused on a photograph, an old photograph, and made a story around it. In 2012, I published the first novel, which is about the Civil War and the Revolution. Now I am finishing the second novel, which will be about the 1920s. I have no overall plan for this series, although I am usually very meticulous and make plans for decades ahead, at least when it comes to mass literature. Here I don't press myself. I just write it as it goes. So, if I ever finish, it will be my plan for the twentieth century. There may be ten novels, and if so, there will be a novel dedicated to each decade.

Norris: I want to shift focus for a moment and talk a little more about your previous projects, then return at the end to this family history you have just described. Again in *The Turkish Gambit*, Fandorin declares, "If you live in a state you should either cherish it or leave it. Anything else is parasitism or mere lackey's gossip." Varvara, who is his love interest in the novel, responds that a third way is for an unjust state to be demolished and a new one built in its place. Fandorin shoots back, "A state is not like a house, it's more like a tree. And it's not built, it grows of its own accord, following the laws of nature and it's a long business. And it's not a stone mason who is required," he says, "but a gardener."[2] I understand we should not read your fiction as a statement of your own philosophy, especially a novel written in 1998, but I'm curious, who might that gardener be today? Are there other possibilities aside from these three? Second, now that you've launched your own *History of the Russian State* series, how do you think the tree of Russia has grown under its own accord and what are the laws of nature it follows?

Akunin: This quote has been thrown back at me a lot! It is not me who is saying this. It is Fandorin who says it. Fandorin here is twenty-two years old. After that, and over the course of many novels, he has changed and his opinions have changed. I personally think that the state is not a tree. If it can be compared to something it would be a house. It has to be built and built according to a certain plan. I think that there is a difference between the notion of a country and that of a state. Now, a country is probably a tree – something that grows. But a state isn't. A state is something that is built by the people who create it. In most cases you can always name the architects of this state. This is true for the United States of America and for Russia. For example, now we are still living in a building the foundation of which was created by Ivan III in the fifteenth century. We are still living within its basic dimensions. I believe now that if we do not change it, this model of authoritarian rule will be recreated again and again and again no matter who wins. Tomorrow liberals will chase away Putinists and after ten years the building will again be something like it is now. So it's the foundation that is wrong and we have to change it.

Norris: As you have stated in several interviews, you initially planned the Fandorin series that made you famous as a response to the pulp mystery in the 1990s. According to one tale, you initially got the idea because your wife was reading a pulp fiction novel on the subway and had covered it up with a Dostoyevsky cover or something like that.

Akunin: No, just with brown paper.

Norris: Just with brown paper because she was embarrassed to read the pulp fiction of the 1990s. You wanted to write something explicitly more middlebrow, more elegant, more intelligent. In the end you have almost completed the Fandorin series. I think you're going to write two more? Is that right?

Akunin: One more. [Note: Akunin published his final Fandorin book in 2018.]

Norris: One more. In the end you have used this series to rewrite the history of the late tsarist period in Russia and rewrite it for an audience in post-Soviet Russia. Looking back, what do you think the Fandorin series helped to articulate about the Russia that was lost, that period of tsarist history?

Akunin: I didn't really intend to rewrite Russian history or to recreate a myth of Russian history. This series is ultimately not about history, it is about literature. I am fascinated not by the history of tsarist Russia, but by the people from a time when Russian fiction was great. Russian literature is the best thing to happen to my country: it is also the greatest gift Russia gave to mankind. Literature is something where Russia is second to no other country. If we talk about the Russian novel, about Russian literature they are – in all seriousness – not so much playing with history, they are about something else, something bigger. I do love most classical authors. I also dislike some of them. Russian literature is very much about life itself, about being alive ... it is not "classic" per se. Classic is something meant for a museum. I believe that as soon as an author becomes a "classic" and is treated like one it means he or she is dead. If you want to argue with him, if you want to mock her, if you want to deride him, it means he or she is still alive. I have been very heavily criticized for my rewriting of Chekhov's play *The Seagull*. But it means he is still alive to me. Or Dostoyevsky – I wrote a detective novel called *F.M.* and it's a remake of *Crime and Punishment* because Dostoyevsky irritates me a lot. It means, though, that he is alive. He is not an icon to me, he is not a statue. I admire him but sometimes – I also hate him. To me this is what literature is about. This view is very individual: I cannot read Cervantes, for example. I respect him, but he does not touch me in any way. Absolutely not. Shakespeare is alive. I am not moved by Moliere, but Chateaubriand is alive for me. Again, it is very individual and it doesn't have to be the same for everyone. My relations with literature are very private. I forgot what we were talking about ...

Norris: The Fandorin series and how you have rewritten the past. Because in the end it is as much a historical series as it is a mystery one, and it attempts to rewrite the past from just before the Russo–Turkish war all the way through the Revolution–a crucial period in Russian history.

Akunin: Well, I wouldn't advise anybody to study history by Fandorin novels! That would be a bad idea. Even if we talk about their historical elements they should be understood with caution, because I write for my contemporaries and there are a lot of deliberate mechanisms in there just for fun, just to make people smile. History is in one sense not important for me within the series. At the same time, everything I describe in those novels could have happened. This is a must. They must be a version of history that is possible. Sometimes it is not really plausible, but still it is technically possible. It is possible that the Russian army was stuck in Plevna because there was a gifted Turkish spy who provoked the army to undertake a useless siege instead of going straight to Constantinople. There is a mystery to the actual event. No one can adequately explain why, after their initial success, the Russian army stayed at Plevna and why tens of thousands of lives had to be lost there. Why not leave a smaller detachment to undertake the siege while the rest of the army could go on? This is a mystery to me, so I found an explanation for it in *The Turkish Gambit*. I have another novel, *The Spy Thriller–Shpionskii roman*. It is really impossible to explain how in 1941 Hitler could surprise Stalin with his assault. How could he possibly keep 190 divisions nearby, from the Black Sea to the Baltic Sea, and then attack the Soviet Union by surprise? There has to be a reason, so I offered one. Or I have another novel, which is called

Quest, about the Battle of Borodino in 1812. There is also a mystery in it. It was a very bloody battle between the French army and the Russian army and the French were winning. They were taking one position after another, albeit with a heavy loss of life, but still they were winning. The only thing that Napoleon needed to do was to send his old guard to attack and a final offensive would have been the absolute end of the Russian army. He didn't do it. Why didn't he do it? This is a mystery. He didn't do it and he lost the war and he lost his troops and eventually he lost everything. So, I created a quite fantastical version of events because I could not find a realistic version of them.

Norris: Your answer begs the question: Why is spying, why are conspiracies, the answer to explaining everything? Are you running the risk of writing a conspiratorial history of Russia?

Akunin: No, I don't believe in conspiriology in general. But I write about spies because they are so interesting to describe and because they create psychologically interesting situations where someone you think is your friend or your lover is actually your enemy and aims for your ruin. As a writer, these situations create the biggest dramas and the biggest tragedies. It can happen not only in politics, but in family life as well.

Norris: Speaking of conspiracies and the one involving Stalin in 1941, this conference is not one where we only seek to investigate the way things have been written about the past but the way things haven't been "righted" about the past. You recently conducted a series of very interesting interviews with Alexei Navalny and you broached the subject of Stalin, and whether or not Stalin had been properly dealt with in Russian history today. You suggested that Russia needs to drive a stake into the heart of Stalin's ghost. Navalny said that a ghost is a ghost and that the Stalin question is one for historians to solve, not current politics. This exchange made me think of Alexander Etkind's very interesting book *Warped Mourning*; in it, he also suggests that Russian society has not addressed the past forcefully enough, particularly the Soviet past. In his exploration of this theme, Etkind argues that one of the reasons for this failure is because "In Russia and Eastern Europe, novels, films, and debates about the past vastly outpace and overshadow monuments, memorials, and museums."[3] For him, the memory of the past is a hot and liquid one in Russia, rather than cool and crystalized, making it always unsettled. You, on the other hand, solely write novels and film scripts, so do you agree with this assessment? Or can novels, films, and debates produce a moral, more solid form of remembrance and in doing so maybe even drive that stake into Stalin's heart?

Akunin: Since you mention this dialogue with Alexei Navalny I should first say that although I disagree with him on many points, here I ultimately think that he was right. He said a very important thing, that there is no use arguing about Stalin because Stalin is alive as long as we still live in this sort of country. When we create a normal country Stalin will become obsolete, he will die by himself and no one will be interested in reviving him. It is true that during the perestroika era and in the 1990s there were a lot of novels, films, and non-fiction works that described all of Stalin's crimes. The problem is that, as we can see now, it did not produce any real effects because Stalin is still inside too many people's brains. There are too many examples of how many people's mental existences have not been changed. We are still living in the same structure devised by Ivan III, a structure that keeps on producing authoritarian rule, where the will of the ruler means more than the law. It is like this, of course, under Putin. It was like this under Yeltsin too, who is supposed to be a democrat and a liberal. He was also an authoritarian ruler. And this circumstance was not a coincidence; it was not something that happened because he wanted it to be like this and because the general logic of the state pushed him into it. His advisors pushed him into it, we all pushed him into it. This notion is really unpleasant to think about but it is true because we wanted him to be re-elected as president in 1996 no matter what and no matter what the cost because we were afraid of a Communist return to power. We were ready to look – actually to close our eyes – at some things we did not want to see. So Yeltsin's era ended in an authoritarian state; it ended, of course, in Putin. I think what we have to do is change the structure of the state completely and then nobody would even think of Stalin as an effective manager or whatever they call him these days.

Norris: The Navalny interviews came after you had done similar ones with Mikhail Khodorkovsky, but more importantly after you had become much more openly political. You may remember that when we first met in 2008 for an interview, you said to me that your major headaches were first traffic and then Putin – but that traffic was by far the bigger problem at the time. You also stated that you always saw yourself as a belletrist and wanted to write as one, not as a writer in the Russian sense, a *pisatel'*. What changed, specifically? How is it that you moved from traffic being your primary headache to Putin to being your primary headache?

Akunin: This move was a big disappointment for me because I always wanted just to be a writer, and when I heard the term "public intellectual" applied to me it made me shudder. I didn't want to be a public intellectual. I didn't want to be a *pisatel'* because this is a role I simply never wanted to play. I didn't want to be a Herzen, a Dostoyevsky, or a Tolstoy. I mean not just that I lacked their talents, but I lacked their desire to be a shepherd of the people and to show people the white and black, to move this piece here because it is the right move and to avoid this move because it is the wrong one, in other words to determine what is good and what is evil for other people. I just wanted to entertain. But Russia is such a peculiar country. You get into situations from which you cannot escape because otherwise you risk losing your self-respect and there is nothing worse than that.

Norris: Is the answer in media for you, at least in terms of change in society and maybe even changing the state? You have always been an avid blogger but you are now an even more political blogger and run one of the most-read blogs in Russia.

Akunin: I started my blog in 2010 and by then I was already a public intellectual, sadly, so it didn't make any difference.

Norris: Is this then the way to reform the state? There are some scholars who write that the blog sphere represents the best thing of a viable civil society in Russia today.

Akunin: No, this is something to let out the irritation that otherwise gets pent up. Sometimes you just have to let it go. There was a brief period in 2012 and 2013 when it seemed to me that blogs and internet forums actually did have a possibility to change the course of events. But because Putin and his team are so hopelessly stupid and ineffective they cost us this opportunity to live peacefully. Now there is no possibility for it. They are so proud that they crushed the opposition and its media outlets. What they did, however, was to crush the thermometer that showed how high the societal fever was. It doesn't mean that the problems have been solved. It certainly doesn't mean that the country is in good health, it's in much, much worse health and it will end badly. Their mistake and ours was there was at least one place to blow off steam. And now there isn't.

Norris: You have closed a lot of your projects. The Fandorin series has one more novel. The Pelagia series is finished. The *Brotherhood of Death* series is finished. The Nicholas Fandorin series is over. And you said you won't write using the names Anatolii Brusnikin or Anna Borisova anymore since you have been exposed as these authors too. You have begun to publish under the name Akunin-Chkhartishvili. So perhaps the last, best question is this one: Is the Akunin project over? "Boris Akunin," does he or it matter anymore?

Akunin: The Boris Akunin Project as entertainment is for all practical purposes over. There will only be one more Fandorin book to write and I am fed up with it [See note above]. It is not interesting to me anymore. I am getting older. I am getting, well, not wiser, but duller. As Pushkin said, "aging drives you into prose." It doesn't mean that I wouldn't entertain myself once in a while with writing something hilarious – if I have a good idea, why not? But my new project is this history series and this family album series. They are what make life interesting for me.

NOTES

1 Ackroyd published the fifth volume in his series in 2018: *Dominion: The History of England from the Battle of Waterloo to Victoria's Jubilee* (London: Thomas Dunne, 2018). The series began with *Foundation: The History of England from Its Earliest Beginnings to the Tudors* (London: Thomas Dunne, 2013). A planned sixth volume will bring this series to a close.
2 Boris Akunin, *The Turkish Gambit*, trans. Andrew Bromfield (New York: Random House, 2006), 54.
3 Alexander Etkind, *Warped Mourning: Stories of the Undead in the Land of the Unburied* (Redwood City, CA: Stanford University Press, 2013), 176.

PART ONE

Postmodern *Detektiv*: The Erast Fandorin Series

3 In Search of a Hero: Boris Akunin's *Death of Achilles*

ELENA V. BARABAN

The Death of Achilles (*Smert' Akhillesa*, 1998) is the fourth novel in Boris Akunin's first and most famous book series. Its protagonist, Erast Fandorin, is a talented sleuth whose career spans several decades, starting in 1876 and ending in 1920.[1] Born into an impoverished aristocratic family in 1856,[2] Fandorin begins his service in the police as a minor clerk in the 1870s and rapidly rises in the ranks following successful investigations of complex crimes and conspiracies. After distinguishing himself during the investigation of an international conspiracy in 1876, Fandorin helps Russia in its imperial overreach in the Russo-Turkish War 1877–8 by unmasking a French spy in the Russian Headquarters.[3] Following this military campaign in the Balkans, Fandorin becomes a diplomat. While on his way to Tokyo, he solves a series of murders on board the ship.[4] Six years later, in 1882, Fandorin returns to his native city of Moscow to serve as a deputy for special assignments at the office of the city's governor. In *The Death of Achilles* Fandorin investigates the murder of General Mikhail Dmitrievich Sobolev, Russia's national hero. The story line of this novel is based on rumours that began to circulate in Russia in 1882 after the sudden death of General Mikhail Dmitrievich Skobelev, Sobolev's historical prototype. In Akunin's novel, the general did not die of a heart attack, as was officially reported, but was murdered. It is further revealed that Sobolev was planning a coup d'état and was assassinated on the orders of the Tsarist family. Fandorin kills Achimas Welde, Sobolev's assassin, and retrieves from him part of the reward for killing the general. This sum – about 1 million rubles – in fact consists of the funds that Sobolev had collected for preparing a coup-d'état. Fandorin donates this money to the governor of Moscow for the noble cause of completing the construction of the "Temple," a major Orthodox cathedral in the city.

The three parts of the novel have unequal length: (1) Fandorin (180 pages); (2) Achimas (120 pages); and (3) White and Black (15 pages).[5] The first part concerns Fandorin's investigation of General Sobolev's death. The second is the assassin's biography. To underscore the idea that these parts are to be contrasted, in the Russian original they are printed in two different fonts.[6] The third and shortest part, with its fitting title, describes the final encounter of Fandorin and Achimas and the latter's defeat. Here the fonts alternate depending on whether the narration concerns Fandorin or Achimas.[7]

The unusual structure of *The Death of Achilles*, with almost half of the narrative being Achimas's biography, suggests that the figure of the assassin in this novel is more significant for understanding the story than is usual in a mystery. In addition to contrasting the characters of Fandorin and Achimas, with the first standing for law and the latter representing crime, Akunin's narrative also suggests contrast between Sobolev and Achimas. One the one hand, the title *The Death of Achilles* points to the death of General Sobolev, who because of his valour and military luck was enthusiastically described by his contemporaries as a "Russian Achilles." On the other hand, multiple allusions in the novel allow the reader to interpret the title as also applicable to Achimas. Many details of his upbringing remind the reader of Achilles's biography. Through an examination of Akunin's references and allusions to historical and fictional facts, figures, and texts, I demonstrate that both Sobolev and Achimas are Achilles figures. They are both courageous and seemingly invulnerable warriors who have known no defeats. Each of them, however, also has a weakness, an "Achilles's heel" that brings his demise. In terms of stylistics, the title of the novel is a historical reference when applied to Sobolev (Skobelev), although the reference to a popular description of Sobolev as Achilles is of course based on an allusion to Homer's text. When applied to Achimas, the novel's title is an allusion to *Iliad*.

I argue that in addition to producing an effect of irony and playfulness typical of Akunin's postmodern mysteries, in *The Death of Achilles* references and allusions to historical facts and literature serve the purpose of creating a commentary about the fate of a talented individual in Russia. Differing and sometimes incompatible interpretations of loyalty, patriotism, honour, and heroism shape the individual's relationship with the Russian state. Ultimately, the title of Akunin's novel is a pun, since both Achilles figures in this story – Sobolev and Achimas – fail as true heroes. In other words, fittingly for the postmodern style of Akunin's works, the title of the novel may be viewed as having a third meaning: Russia has no heroes like Homer's Achilles. The latter, as a hero who is physically and morally strong and who *consciously* follows his predestination to lay down his life for his people in a war with an external enemy, *is dead*. Unlike Homer's Achilles, Sobolev is a traitor and Achimas is an altogether selfish and antisocial individual whose ultimate desire is to own an uninhibited island where he could be "his own sovereign, his own police, his own court."[8] In both cases, the retribution for betraying or rejecting an (imperfect) society is inglorious death. Whereas Achilles dies like a hero on the battlefield in a war that is considered just by his people, Sobolev and Achimas are both removed as criminals. Akunin's novel asserts the triumph of an individual like Fandorin, who is ready for a compromise with the state. Fandorin, although understanding the imperfections of the Russian political and social system, remains loyal to the regime and works to protect the existing status quo.[9]

The Russian Achilles as Napoleon

An obvious Achilles in Akunin's novel is General Sobolev. The historical prototype of this character, General Skobelev (O.S. 13 Sept. 1843–25 June 1882), was famous for his victories in the Balkans during the Russo–Turkish War of 1877–8 and his conquests in Central Asia.[10] Considered a national hero in both Bulgaria and Russia, Skobelev was prominently commemorated in both countries.[11] His incredible popularity among Russian troops evoked comparisons with Alexander Suvorov (1730–1800), Russia's legendary military commander.[12] The Russian media of the second half of the nineteenth century compared him to Homer's Achilles. Like Achilles, Skobelev was a young military commander: he joined the army when he was eighteen. At the age of twenty he became an officer, at thirty-three he was major general, and at thirty-eight he was already a general.[13] For valour, he was awarded the highest military decorations in Russia: the order of St. George of the Fourth, Third, and Second Class.[14] Like Achilles, Skobelev had known no defeats. According to a popular rumour, a magic word that he had bought in Turkestan made him invulnerable like Achilles and thus, despite often being in the thick of the battle, Skobelev was never wounded seriously.[15] Like Achilles, Skobelev died young.[16]

The descriptions of Sobolev as Achilles[17] in Akunin's novel are thus historically grounded references. However, because by the time the story of the novel begins the general is already dead, the narrator's brief references to him as Achilles are not substantiated with more detailed depictions of his bravery, military talent, and popularity with the troops.[18] Instead, in Akunin's novel, the comparisons of Sobolev to

Achilles are consistently undermined. Following the first announcement of the general's death, Fandorin is puzzled by the tsar's telegram, which states that it would be difficult to find a replacement for Sobolev.[19] With historical accuracy, Akunin depicts the relationship between Alexander III and Sobolev.[20] The tsar views Sobolev as replaceable after all, which suggests less respect for a hero of Achilles's calibre than one would expect. In fact, already in *The Turkish Gambit* (*Turetskii gambit*), which focused on the siege of Plevna, Sobolev (Skobelev) appeared as a vain commander. To further indicate his insufficient reverence for Sobolev, the emperor does not attend the general's funeral. Instead, he sends his brother Grand Duke Kirill to Moscow. At the funeral ceremony, Kirill further undermines Sobolev's popular reputation as Achilles by suggesting that Sobolev must be compared not to Achilles but to Hector, who was noble and heroic and yet not invulnerable.[21] Although Hector, the leader of the Trojans, was the best warrior among the Trojans and the first-born son of Priam, the king of Troy, his status in the hierarchy of the Greek heroes is not as high as that of Achilles. Later it is revealed that Grand Duke Kirill (known also to Achimas as Monsieur NN) was in charge of organizing Sobolev's assassination and that he, as well as other members of the Romanovs, in fact viewed the general as a Russian Napoleon who wished to usurp the Romanovs' power.[22]

The comparison of Sobolev to Napoleon is also historically grounded. Indeed, the prototype of Akunin's character was compared to Napoleon. Initially, the basis for such comparisons was Skobelev's military genius and the troops' enthusiastic support of this commander. Later, however, Skobelev was described as a Russian Napoleon because of his political ambitions, which threatened to complicate Russia's relations with other European powers, especially Germany, and ultimately were to weaken the reputation of the tsarist family. After Skobelev had publicly expressed his nationalist pan-Slavist views in Paris in February 1882, less than half a year before his death, he was recalled to Russia. A few months later Skobelev briefly stayed in Moscow. In the early hours of 25 June 1882 (O.S.), Skobelev died of a heart attack in Hotel Anglia, in the room of Charlotte Altenrose (also known as Wanda), a singer and a courtesan.[23]

In Akunin's novel the perceptions of General Sobolev as Napoleon are crucial.[24] Sobolev is essentially a traitor who wished to usurp the power of the tsar by either becoming a dictator himself or placing "his" person on the Russian throne. His plans at empowering the Slavs at the expense of Germany and the Ottoman Empire would destabilize political situation in Europe. In order to save Russia from Sobolev while at the same time sparing Sobolev's reputation as a national hero, the tsarist family removes the general so that his death would appear to be of natural causes and, at the same time, would demoralize his co-conspirators. The latter would not forgive their hero that he died in the bed of a prostitute. While drawing on the rumours that began to circulate after Skobelev's death,[25] Akunin slightly alters the names of his characters' historical prototypes, thus suggesting that his story is but a fiction of the events that took place in 1882.[26]

Besides its storyline, the novel affirms Sobolev's defeat also in a subtler way. One of the subplots in *The Death of Achilles* is the affirmation of the Russian state's victory over Napoleon. In the opening chapter, Akunin introduces the topic of financing the construction of a large Orthodox cathedral. Judging by the historical context, this is the Cathedral of Christ the Saviour, the tallest and one of the largest Orthodox churches in the world. It is significant that even before a messenger announces the news about Sobolev's death, Prince Dolgorukoi, the governor of Moscow, tells Fandorin that his biggest concern is to gather the money for completing the expensive church.[27] In a way, *The Death of Achilles* is about a successful solution of this financial problem, since the novel ends with Fandorin donating Sobolev's 1 million rubles to Dolgorukoi for the purpose of completing the "temple."

The irony embedded in this subplot becomes clear when one takes into a consideration that the Cathedral of Christ the Saviour was built in honour of Russia's victory over Napoleon.[28] On 25 December 1812, following Napoleon Bonaparte's retreat from Moscow, Emperor Alexander I signed a manifesto declaring his intention to build a Cathedral in honour of Christ the Saviour. The cathedral was to signify the society's gratitude to Divine Providence for saving Russia from Napoleon and as a memorial to the sacrifices of the Russian people.[29] Appropriately, the name of the church, which compares Russian warriors' sacrifice to the redemptive self-sacrificial Christ, implicitly points to the Russian victory over Napoleon, who was viewed in Russia as the anti-Christ, officially (by the Russian Church) and often popularly.[30] It took much money and time to complete this church. Over the course of seventy years, the project was supervised by four Russian emperors.[31] The Cathedral was consecrated on 26 May 1883, the day that Alexander III was crowned. In 1882, when the events described in Akunin's novel take place, the government was to finance the painting of the church's interior. In Akunin's novel, these final touches to the church were paid with Sobolev's conspiracy funds. Thus the Russian state's victory over Sobolev, "the Russian Napoleon," is also moral. Sobolev becomes a somewhat comical figure since he, a Russian Napoleon, had himself collected the funds to further glorify his country's victory over Napoleon.[32]

Importantly, Akunin's narrators do not justify Sobolev's Napoleonic ambitions. Sobolev is not depicted as a hero who cannot find his place following the assassination of Alexander II, the tsar who had conducted major reforms, led the country through successful military campaigns, and during whose reign Sobolev's career soared. The successor of Alexander II, Tsar Alexander III, is understandably dissatisfied with the general. He orders Sobolev to return to Russia after Sobolev's provocative speech in Paris in 1882, which could lead to diplomatic tensions with European powers. Overall, with his ideas about a unique path for Russia, Russia for Russians, and the dreams to expand Russian (Slavic) influence in Europe, Sobolev looks more nationalistic than the imperial family, a depiction that is once again grounded in fact.[33] His betrayal of the state looks especially immoral when one considers the fact that he had been generously rewarded, decorated, and glorified by Russia's emperors.[34]

The reader is thus prepared for a critical perception of the general. In this regard, the contrast with Homer's *Iliad* is significant. The general fails as a true hero. His understanding of patriotism does not imply protecting the existing political regime, although he supposedly conspires to remove the tsar out of patriotic considerations regarding Russia's future. By contrast, Achilles remains loyal to the Achaeans despite his disagreement with Agamemnon, the Achaeans' leader. In the opening of Homer's poem, Achilles feels hurt when Agamemnon, the Achaeans' commander-in-chief, makes an attack on Achilles's honour as a warrior and leader of the Myrmidons by demanding that Achilles give him Briseis, his beautiful concubine captured during one of the battles. Achilles's wrath and his withdrawal from the battle lead to many deaths among the Achaeans. Nonetheless, later, when the circumstances change following Patroclus's death and after the conflict with Agamemnon is resolved, Achilles returns to the battlefield.[35] His sense of duty to his community prevails. To be more precise, the conflict between Achilles and Agamemnon is a disagreement between two individuals, which does not lead to a revision of social and political structures among the Greeks. Achilles's actions are selfish in the sense that at the beginning of the *Iliad* he asks the gods to send defeat to the Achaeans as punishment for Agamemnon's wrongdoing. At the same time, though, he does not wish to replace Agamemnon as the leader of the Achaeans. Unlike Sobolev, he acts instead within the existing hierarchies. Ultimately, his actions are informed by his obedience to gods and his acceptance of his predestination to die young.[36] In Akunin's novel, then, the references and allusions to Homer's *Iliad* and to Napoleon serve the purpose of distinguishing Sobolev and Achilles, depicting Sobolev as incapable of the same kind of respect for the existing social and political order and loyalty to a community exemplified by the character of Achilles in the *Iliad*.

Cloning Achilles

When preparing the assassination of Sobolev, Achimas acts under the alias Nikolai Nikolaevich Klonov. The name Nikolai, which is doubled as the first name and the patronymic, and the root of the last name Klonov both suggest cloning. Since Achimas's biography has many details that allude to the character of Achilles as depicted in Homer's *Iliad* and in Greek myths, it is productive to view both Achimas and Sobolev (a "Russian Achilles") as Achilles's clones (albeit failing ones). Whereas, as one can assume, Sobolev would welcome comparisons of him to the Greek hero, for Achimas these would be irrelevant. After Achimas drops out of school and begins helping his uncle with the latter's criminal business, he feels excited: "This was real life, not learning chunks of ancient Greek from the *Iliad*."[37] It is ironic that whereas Achimas views the *Iliad* as useless fictions, Akunin's narrator establishes a close association between Achimas's life and the *Iliad*.

In Greek literature, Achilles is a hero, the son of Thetis, a sea goddess, and Peleus, the king of the Myrmidons. Although many heroes are born of the unions between mortal people and gods,[38] it was highly unusual for a god or goddess to *marry* a mortal. Thetis and Peleus get married because Zeus (and other gods who had been interested in the beautiful Thetis) wishes to make sure that he will not father Thetis's son, since it has been predicted that her son will be stronger than his father and therefore can potentially present a threat to the father's power. Like Achilles, Achimas Welde is also born into an unusual family.[39] His father, Pelef, is a Christian and a pacifist whose community has immigrated into Russia from Moravia via Prussia because they did not wish to enter military service and looked for a country where they would be exempt from serving in the army. Achimas's mother, Fatima, is a Chechen of Muslim creed and is much younger than Pelef. Like Achilles's parents, the parents of Achimas seem to be an unusual match. Their backgrounds are too different and, like Achilles's parents, they disagree about the way of raising their son. Peleus prohibits Thetis from making Achilles immortal by immersing the boy into boiling water, a procedure that no human would survive. Thetis then, keeping it secret from Peleus, makes Achilles invulnerable in all of his body except his heel by plunging him into the River Styx.[40]

Achimas's mother Fatima, like Thetis, conceals from her husband that she has been educating their son about life as it is understood in Chechen culture and Islam. Although when marrying Pelef she had converted to Christianity and therefore had to respect the views of her husband's community, including pacifism, tolerance, and acceptance of suffering, Fatima secretly teaches Achimas the code of honour typical of her people. According to Achimas, his "mother's god" tells him to use violence and arms in order to stand up for himself or his family. After his parents are killed, Achimas finds it liberating and empowering not to follow any particular religion. As he becomes older, he praises himself for not being afraid of death because he does not love anyone and has no family.[41]

Assonance in a number of the names that appear in Achimas's biography links this character to Achilles. Phonetically, Pelef is similar to Peleus and the name Fatima reminds one of *Fetida*, the Russian version of the name Thetis. The name Achimas sounds similar to the name Achilles. Moreover, although such etymology is purely fictional rather than based on onomastics, Akunin's narrator suggests that the name Achimas means the "brother of rage."[42] This interpretation of the character's name further links him to Achilles. The latter, in the opening of Homer's poem, is enraged because Agamemnon has taken away his concubine Briseis. Achilles's wrath lasts for a long time and is central for the storyline of Homer's *Iliad*.[43] The name of Centaur Chiron, who raised Achilles, is somewhat similar to the name of Chasan, Achimas's uncle who raised the boy. Furthermore, the names of Achimas's enemies during his school years are similar to the names that appear in the myths about Achilles. Achimas kills his classmate Kikin and school inspector Tenetov.[44] The last name Kikin is an allusion to Cycnus, a Trojan hero killed by Achilles.[45] The last name Tenetov sounds similar to the name Tenes, the name of Apollo's son killed by Achilles.[46] Thetis had warned Achilles that he should not kill Tenes; it was a mistake to do so. Apollo eventually avenges the death of Tenes by bringing death to Achilles.[47]

Several toponyms in the novel are also based on assonance that links Achimas to Achilles. When Achimas's family and fellow villagers have been brutally killed by Chechens, Achimas temporarily finds shelter in an orphanage for girls in the town of Skyrovsk.[48] In order to be admitted into this institution, Achimas disguises himself as a girl. The name Skyrovsk reminds one of Skyros, the island where Thetis tried to hide Achilles among young women so that he would not be drafted by the Achaeans.[49] Thetis's trick, however, does not save Achilles from going to war against Troy. Since the oracle has promised the Achaeans victory over Troy only on the condition that Achilles, the youngest and the strongest of the Achaeans' military leaders, would join the war effort, Odysseus the Cunning is sent to Skyros to fetch Achilles. Disguised as a peddler selling women's clothes and jewellery, Odysseus places a shield and a spear among his goods. When shown the goods Achilles instantly grabs the spear, thus revealing his identity. He then joins the Greek military campaign. In Akunin's novel, Chasan, Achimas's uncle, uses the same trick to find Achimas in Skyrovsk. He pretends he is a peddler who sells goods for women. He steps out of the room while leaving the goods for girls and his sword and secretly watches Achimas through a door crack. When left alone, Achimas instantly drops the jewellery and grabs the arms, thus revealing he is a boy. Chasan takes his nephew away and raises him in the mountains. This detail is yet another allusion to the myths about Achilles, since he was also raised in the mountains by Chiron.

Two more toponyms in Akunin's novel link Achimas's story with Achilles. The final battle between Fandorin and Achimas takes place at the Trinity Inn, which in Russian is *"Troitskoe podvorie."* The first part of the word *"troitskoe"* is similar in sound to the name "Troy." Fandorin and Achimas then wage their own small-scale "Trojan War." Part of their battle happens at the Swedish Gate that leads to the Inn's courtyard. In the Russian original the Swedish Gate is pronounced in an old way as *sveiskie vorota*, which is similar in sound to *skeiskie vorota*, the Scaean Gate at Troy, the location where Achilles was mortally wounded.

In depicting Achimas, Akunin explores the motif of invulnerability. In addition to portraying many dangerous situations that Achimas survives, the novel's narrator explicitly describes Achimas as "invulnerable."[50] Yet Fandorin finds Achimas's weak spot. Achilles was killed near the end of the Trojan War either by Paris, directed by Apollo, or by Apollo himself.[51] Achilles was shot in the heel with an arrow. Akunin draws on this detail when he depicts the death of Achimas. Like Achilles, Achimas has previously "never been wounded."[52] Fandorin's arrow pierces his leg above the ankle.[53] According to another Greek source, Paris shoots two arrows at Achilles. The first one hits Achilles's heel and the second one his chest.[54] In Akunin's novel, Fandorin wounds Achimas in his leg and then Fandorin's servant Masa fires a gun, wounding Achimas in the middle of his back.

Achimas as Achilles is different from Sobolev.[55] Although both Sobolev and Achimas are about the same age[56] and both used to be seemingly invulnerable and courageous warriors, Sobolev is a public figure whereas Achimas avoids serving any particular society. Sobolev sacrifices his personal interests and wealth for the sake of a public good, even if his understanding of what is best for Russia is considered a crime by the state. Achimas, on the other hand, is selfish and has lowly aspirations: money and the comfort that money brings. He never establishes close connections with other people, whether romance or friendship, and desires to withdraw from people altogether by settling on a private island.

Sobolev massacres people in battles in the name of Russia, whereas Achimas kills for money and is eventually bored when none of the crimes commissioned to him excite him any longer as a specialist in murder. He knows no love for a person, political party, nationality, country, or culture. Ironically, however, the same woman, Wanda, brings demise to both Sobolev and Achimas. Since Sobolev's weakness (his Achilles's heel) is his inability to balance his public and private life, he falls prey to a courtesan who resembles his estranged mistress. Seduced by Wanda, Sobolev is poisoned. Achimas, in turn, also becomes vulnerable when he is tempted by the idea of true love with Wanda. Having completed his criminal business in Russia, he had no reason to postpone his departure from Moscow by a day, but did so in hope that Wanda would travel with him. As soon as he allows his feelings to come to the surface, he makes a mistake and is immediately removed.

The absence of humanity in Achimas distinguishes him from Achilles. Whereas Achilles follows the advice of gods and is a semi-god himself, Achimas respects no religion and rejects the gods of the communities where he happens to live. Furthermore, although both Achilles and Achimas avenge the death of their loved ones, while Achilles is distraught by his best friend's death and mourns it profoundly, Achimas kills his family's murderers out of a sense of duty, as he is told to do by his uncle, but does not seem to mourn his family or suffer because they are no longer with him. Achilles also seems to be more humane than Achimas when he takes pity on his enemy (Achilles allows Priam, Hector's father, to take Hector's body for burial and agrees to postpone further attacks on Troy to allow the community time to mourn their hero). Achimas, however, spares no enemy and does not seem to regret even the death of a woman who has loved him and given her life for him.[57] As soon as Achimas spares someone who must be removed, he makes a mistake. In order to halter Fandorin's investigation, Achimas needed to kill Wanda. Having spared her life, and having stayed longer than necessary in Russia in hope Wanda could become his companion, he brings demise to himself.

Conclusion

The Death of Achilles is a skilfully crafted postmodern novel. In it, the Homeric subtext announced in the novel's title proves especially relevant for a discussion of the themes of patriotism, honour, betrayal, loyalty, and the relationship between the individual and the state (community).[58] The fates of the main characters in the novel – Fandorin, General Sobolev, and Achimas – are important for understanding the relationship between the state and the individual. The price of social and political stability in Russia is the removal of heroes. A revolutionary figure such as Sobolev is removed. His understanding of the true Russian path requires the destruction of the existing political order. Selfish individuals such as Achimas are used by the state as a tool to remove Sobolevs and are later removed too. The novel affirms the triumph of characters such as Fandorin, who are depicted as true patriots of Russia.[59] Fandorin balances between becoming a superfluous person and serving the imperfect state while being fully aware of the state's imperfections.

In Akunin's novel, the Russian state is portrayed as imperfect. In addition to the perennial problems with corruption, it is associated with age and illness.[60] One of the faces of the Russian state in the novel is that of Prince Dolgorukoi, Governor of Moscow. He is an old man who has false hair and needs to take care of his digestion problems[61] by keeping on a healthy diet and taking laxatives that he also recommends to people in his service. The image of this character is in sharp contrast with a dashing young general of thirty-eight years old. Nonetheless, the elderly governor general of Moscow prevails.

Ironically, even Moscow topography affirms the triumph of Dolgorukoi over revolutionary figures.[62] Skobelev was commemorated in many paintings and monuments.[63] The most significant Skobelev monument was erected in Moscow on Tverskaia Square, renamed Skobelev Square in 1912.[64] The monument was destroyed on 1 May 1918 by the Bolsheviks, who replaced it with the Soviet Constitution Monument. Skobelev Square was renamed Soviet Square.[65] In 1940 the Soviet Constitution Monument was dismantled. In 1947, to celebrate Moscow's 800th anniversary, the foundation was laid for the Monument to Prince Iurii Dolgorukii, the founder of Moscow, a distant relative of Prince Dolgorukov, Governor of Moscow in the 1880s. The monument was erected in 1954,[66] but the square was still called *Sovetskaia* (Soviet) and was renamed Tverskaia Square in 1993.[67] The history of the monuments on this square adds a new layer of meaning to the novel: the Dolgorukovs prevail over the dashing Achilleses.

NOTES

1 The Erast Fandorin series ends during the Russian Civil War two years after Fandorin's death as described in the novel *Ne proshchaius'* (*Not Saying Goodbye*; Moscow: Zakharov, 2018).

2 Exactly 100 years earlier than Akunin.

3 The events are described in, respectively, *Azazel'* (*The Winter Queen*; Moscow: Zakharov, 1998) and *Turetskii gambit* (*The Turkish Gambit*; Moscow: Zakharov, 1998).

4 The action in *Leviafan* (*Murder on the Leviathan*; Moscow: Zakharov, 1998) reminds one of Agatha Christie's *And Then There Were None* (New York: Dodd, Mead, and Co., 1940), another "hermetic" mystery that was originally published in Britain in the book format under the title *Ten Little Niggers* (London: Collins Crime Club, 1939). The story is familiar in Russia. It became especially popular after the release of Stanislav Govorukhin's two-part film *Desiat' negritiat* (*Ten Little Niggers*) by Odessa Film Studios in 1987. Furthermore, from 1987 through 2015, Christie's novel was translated into Russian six times. The first unabridged translation, *Ten Little Niggers* (*Desiat' negritiat*, 1989) by Larisa Bespalova, had twenty-eight print runs.

5 I refer to the pagination in the first paperback edition of the novel.

6 In the translation, however, the same font is used throughout parts one and two of the book. Boris Akunin, *The Death of Achilles: A Fandorin Mystery* (New York: Random House, 2006).

7 Here, the fonts also alternate in the translation of the novel.

8 Akunin, *Smert' Akhillesa*, 267.

9 In the later novels, Fandorin is depicted as being increasingly disillusioned with the tsarist regime. Yet, until the moment when he drifts into a coma due to a gun wound, he still defends the crumbling empire. When he comes back to his senses after the October Revolution, he realizes he can take none of the political sides in the Civil War.

10 British Field Marshal Bernard Montgomery lists Skobelev among the world's most talented, "skillful and inspiring" military commanders. See Field-Marshal Viscount Montgomery of Alamein, *A History of Warfare* (Cleveland: World Publishing, 1968), 266, 269. For more details on the popularity of Skobelev see Hans Rogger, "The Skobelev Phenomenon: The Hero and his Worship," *Oxford Slavonic Papers* 9 (1976): 46–78.

11 Skobelev is prominently featured in the panorama memorial of Pleven's Epopee 1877 and also in a number of monuments erected in Bulgaria and Russia (e.g., Moscow and Ryazan). See "Mikhail Skobelev," Wikipedia, https://en.wikipedia.org/wiki/Mikhail_Skobelev, accessed 25 July 2017.

12 S.L. Markov, "Pamiati M.D. Skobeleva," https://military.wikireading .ru/28045, accessed 25 July 2017.

13 A.P. Strusevich, "Predislovie k pervomu izdaniiu," in Petr Dukmasov, *So Skobelevym v ogne. Vospominaniia o Russko-turetskoi voine 1877–1878*, https://military.wikireading.ru/28051, accessed 25 July 2017.

14 S.D. Markov, "Pamiati M.D. Skobeleva," https://military.wikireading.ru /28045, accessed 25 July 2017.

15 "Mikhail Skobelev," Wikipedia.

16 Skobelev died when he was thirty-eight years old. Achilles was probably
    younger when he died (possibly about thirty years old), yet in the nine-
    teenth century the death of a thirty-eight-year-old man was considered
    premature.

17 See, e.g., Akunin, *Smert' Akhillesa*, 86, 106, 112, 124.

18 Many people who served under Skobelev's command wrote mem-
    oirs that depict him as an outstanding person, a true hero. See, e.g.,
    P.A. Dukmasov, *So Skobelevym v ogne. Vospominaniia o Russko-turetskoi
    voine 1877–1878 godov i o M.D. Skobeleve ego ordinartsa P.A .Dukmasova*
    (Moscow: Eksmo, 2015).

19 Akunin, *Smert' Akhillesa*, 61.

20 Alexander III hated Skobelev. See Rogger, "Skobelev Phenomenon."

21 Akunin, *Smert' Akhillesa*, 124.

22 The prototype of Grand Duke Kirill is Grand Duke Vladimir Alexan-
    drovich of Russia (1847–1909), a son of Emperor Alexander II of Russia
    and a brother of Tsar Alexander III of Russia.

23 In Akunin's novel, this woman is featured mostly as Wanda. Her "real
    name" in the novel is Charlotte Tolle. In the novel, Akunin plays with
    Wanda's last name, Altenrose, which means "an old rose." She performs as
    a singer in the restaurant Alpenrose ("rose of the Alps").

24 The first comparison appears in a British newspaper article published
    after the announcement of Sobolev's death (Akunin, *Smert' Akhillesa*, 61).
    Sobolev's mistress reveals the General's Napoleonic ambitions without
    explicitly comparing him to Napoleon (105) while already using the
    French version of his first name (Michel). Later she explains that Sobolev
    viewed himself as a Russian Napoleon and proposed she would agree
    to the role of his Josephine (Napoleon's wife) (178–9). The comparison
    is also made in the conversation between Fandorin and General Evgeny
    Osipovich Karachentsev, the head of Moscow police force (195–6). Further
    down, Grand Duke Kirill explains to Achimas that the Tsarist family and
    Russia as a state need to get rid of Sobolev, who is a Russian Napoleon
    and would lead Russia to a catastrophic war against Germany (275).

25 See, e.g. Anastasia Dubrovaia, "Chto zhe iavlaetsia istinnoi prichinoi gibeli
    generala Skobeleva?" *Trud*, 9 July 2013, http://www.trud.ru/article
    /09-07-2013/1296522_chto_zhe_javljaetsja_istinnoj_prichinoj_gibeli
    _generala_skobeleva.html; Andrei Sholokhov, *Zagadka smerti generala
    Skobeleva* (Moscow: Znanie, 1992), https://www.e-reading.club/bookreader
    .php/66537/Sholohov_-_Zagadka_smerti_generala_Skobeleva.html.

26 Besides Grand Duke Kirill, another member of the royal family who helps
    to organize Sobolev's assassination is Evgeny, Duke of Liechtenburg.
    The prototype of this character is Prince Evgeny Romanowsky, Duke
    of Leuchtenberg (1847–1901). He was married to Zinaida Skobeleva,

Countess de Beauharnais (1856–99), Skobelev's sister. In Akunin's novel she is depicted under the name Zinaida Soboleva, Countess Mirabeau. Another character who has a direct historical prototype is Captain Prokhor Akhrameevich Gukmasov, senior orderly to Adjutant General Sobolev (Peter Dukmasov [1854–96], Skobelev's senior orderly); Gukmasov also figured in Akunin's *The Turkish Gambit*. General Evgeny Osipovich Karachentsev, chief of Moscow police (General Evgeny Osipovich Yankovsky [1837–92]). The prototype of Governor of Moscow Prince Vladimir Andreevich Dolgorukoi is Prince Vladimir Andreevich Dolgorukov (1810–91), the Governor General of Moscow from 1864 until 1891. His assistants also appear in the novel under slightly altered and yet recognizable names (e.g., Vedishchev's prototype is Vel'tishchev).

27 Akunin, *Smert' Akhillesa*, 11.

28 The Cathedral of Christ the Saviour is a church in the centre of Moscow on the bank of the Moskva River. The Cathedral is 103 metres (338 feet) high and is the tallest Orthodox church in the world. Nicholas I, who succeeded his brother Alexander I in 1825, disliked the architectural style that his brother had selected for the church. A new design, reminiscent of the design of the Hagia Sophia in Istanbul, was commissioned to architect Konstantin Thon. Thon's design was approved in 1832, and a new construction site was chosen by the Tsar in 1837. The cornerstone was laid in 1839. On 5 December 1931, the Cathedral of Christ the Saviour was dynamited and reduced to rubble. It was rebuilt in 1990–2000. During the time of its rebuilding, the church was the centre of many disagreements and controversies.

29 Evgenia Kirichenko, *Khram Khrista Spasitelia v Moskve* (Moscow: Planeta, Kuznetskii most, 1992). The book annotation states that the cathedral was to commemorate the sacrifices and the outstanding heroism of the Russian people in their fight against Napoleon; see https://www.livelib.ru/book /1001143957-hram-hrista-spasitelya-v-moskve-evgeniya-kirichenko.

30 See, e.g. "Pochemu russkie verili, chto Napoleon – 'antichrist,'" *Russkaia semerka*, 11 March 2017, https://russian7.ru/post/pochemu-russkie -verili-chto-napoleon-a/.

31 Following the death of Alexander I, his successor Nicholas I commissioned a new design of the church and chose a new construction site. In 1860, during the reign of Alexander II, the cathedral emerged from its scaffolding. The church's interior was completed in the early 1880s, after the assassination of Alexander II.

32 Some passages concerning the construction of the Cathedral are projections of Russia's 1990s onto the nineteenth century. Akunin criticizes neo-imperial attitudes in Russia in the 1990s, the desire to reinstate Russia's greatness through pursuing grandiose projects such as the Second World War memorial on Poklonnaia Hill, the celebration of the 850th anniversary

of Moscow, or the rebuilding of the Cathedral of Christ the Saviour. In Akunin's novel the painting of the Temple is commissioned to a Georgian artist, Gegechkori, who is a "well-known scoundrel" according to the governor's councillors. The councillors believe that it is both "cheaper" and more fair to commission the painting to Moscow artists who can paint "as well as, or better than, the Georgian." Akunin attacks contemporary Georgian artist Zurab Tseretelli (who was indeed commissioned by Moscow mayor Luzhkov to paint the restored Cathedral of Christ the Saviour in the 1990s). For details, see Elena V. Baraban, "A Country Resembling Russia: The Use of History in Boris Akunin's Detective Novels," *Slavic and East European Journal (SEEJ)* 48, no. 3 (2004): 396–420.

33 See *Smert' Akhillesa*, 97, 105, 195–6. For more details on Alexander III's conservative policies following the assassination of his father by terrorists and on Skobelev's conservative views, see Rogger, "The Skobelev Phenomenon."

34 At the peak of Sobolev's popularity, his portraits were almost in each household in Moscow, and the mourning over Sobolev was more profound than that for Alexander II. Akunin, *Smert' Akhillesa*, 86–7.

35 Patroclus was Achilles's best friend. He led the Myrmidons in Achilles's place and was killed by Hector.

36 James A. Arieti, in his article "Achilles' Alienation in 'Iliad 9,'" states that when Achilles withdraws from battle and quarrel he does not at the same time withdraw from society. *The Classical Journal* 82, no. 1 (1986), 1–27, http://www.jstor.org/stable/3297803.

37 Akunin, *Smert' Akhillesa*, 200.

38 E.g., Herakles, Perseus, Bellerophon, Aeneas.

39 The last name "Welde" may suggest welding different things together.

40 Achilles was left vulnerable at the part of the body by which she held him, his heel.

41 Akunin, *Smert' Akhillesa*, 268.

42 Ibid., 185.

43 It is also a recognizable image in European cultures, which inspired a number of representations in literature and music.

44 Akunin, *Smert' Akhillesa*, 199–201.

45 "Cycnus (King of Kolonai)," Wikipedia, https://en.wikipedia.org/wiki/Cycnus_(king_of_Kolonai), accessed 27 July 2017.

46 "Tenes, " Wikipedia, https://en.wikipedia.org/wiki/Tenes, accessed 27 July 2017.

47 In *The Death of Achilles*, the murder of Tenetov is also depicted as Achimas's mistake. He was arrested and his uncle Chasan barely managed to save him from being put on trial and convicted of murder. See Akunin, *Smert' Akhillesa*, 228–9.

48 Ibid., 218–20.

49 Since Achilles was not one of Helen's former suitors, he did not have to join the war effort against Troy. According to the prediction, Achilles could either live a happy and long life or die young on the battlefield as a hero whose courage and strength would be unmatched and would become legendary. Thetis hid Achilles on Skyros Island because she wished for her son a happy and long life.

50 Akunin, *Smert' Akhillesa*, 172, 234.

51 Many scholars discuss a number of classical sources, including, for example, the works by Pindar, Ovid, Quintus of Smyrna, and Gaius Julius Hyginus, which depict Achilles's death at the hands of Apollo. See, for instance, Katherine Callen King, *Achilles: Paradigms of the War Hero From Homer to the Middle Ages* (Berkeley: University of Carolina Press, 1987), 52, 62, 135, 196, and note 70 on p. 296. See also Guy Hedreen, "Achilles Beyond the *Iliad*," in *Heroes: Mortals and Myths in Ancient Greece*, ed. Sabine Albersmeier (Baltimore: Walters Art Museum, 2009), 39–48, esp. 42.

52 Akunin, *Smert' Akhillesa*, 313.

53 Ibid., 355–7.

54 Several retellings of Greek myths mention that Achilles was shot with two arrows. See, for example, A. Kondrashov, *Kto est' kto v mifologii Drevnei Gretsii i Rima: 1738 geroev i mifov* (Moscow: Rippol Classic, 2016), 94. Most likely, Kondrashov's source of information is a frequently republished dictionary article by the renowned scholar of antiquity Viktor Noevich Iarkho: V. N. Iarkho, "Akhill," in *Mify narodov mira*, ed. S.A. Tokarev (Moscow: Sovetskaia entsiklopediia, 1980). Iarkho's article as well as the entire dictionary is now available online, at http://www.mifinarodov.com/a/ahill .html and http://ancientrome.ru/dictio/article.htm?a=491574902.

55 As mentioned earlier, even the font used for the part about Achimas is different from the font used for the first part of the novel.

56 Achimas was forty when he died, and Sobolev was thirty-eight.

57 Evgenia helped Achimas to rob her husband's treasury and was killed in order to allow Achimas to escape (*Smert' Akhillesa*, chapter 2 in Part Two).

58 These themes are also important in the novels examined by Stephen M. Norris in his chapter "Spying on the Past: Boris Akunin's History of Espionage," in this volume.

59 Akunin, *Smert' Akhillesa*. See chapter 2 in Part One (201); and the final chapter in Part Three (361).

60 Prince Dolgorukoi's assistant tells Fandorin of the problems in Moscow. Akunin, *Smert' Akhillesa*, 70–1.

61 Ibid., 12.

62 See Baraban, "A Country Resembling Russia," on Akunin's projections of the 1990s onto the historical scene described in *The Death of Achilles*.

63 The Monument to Pleven Heroes in Il'inskii Park in Moscow was created by sculptor Vladimir Shervood and opened on 11 December 1887. It was built on public donations of 50,000 rubles. A Skobelev monument was also erected in Ryazan, the main city in the Ryazan province where the Skobelevs had an estate.
64 The sculptor of Skobelev's equestrian statue was P. Samonov.
65 See http://ru.paperblog.com/sovetskaya-tverskaya-ploschad-437299/.
66 The sculptor was Sergei Orlov.
67 See http://gazeta.aif.ru/_/online/kids/131/57_01.

4 Rewriting Homer: Boris Akunin's Postmodern Approach

JUDITH KALB

The troubled world described by Homer remains strangely familiar.
Adam Nicolson, *Why Homer Matters*

"Odysseus now left the harbour and took the rough path / up through the woodlands and over the crest of the hills/ till he reached the place that Athena had told him about ..."[1] "But he never got there! He *disappeared!*"[2] The first sentence is from Homer's *Odyssey*, that millennia-old, quintessential epic of wanderings and homecomings, featuring the Greek fighter Odysseus making his way back from the Trojan War. The second phrases are from Boris Akunin's penultimate Fandorin novel, *Black City* (*Chernyi gorod*), which first came out in 2012. All three sentences, Homer's and Akunin's, appeared for the first time together in the pages of the French newspaper *Le Figaro* in 2008 as part of a series of continuations of Homer by various world literary figures (Ludmila Ulitskaya also participated).[3] Each author started with the same phrase and then began his or her own story or essay. Akunin's story, "The Hunt for Odysseus," became the springboard for his novel. How does Akunin rewrite Homer's text, and to what end?

Odysseus, Athena, Fandorin, and Dr. Dorn

In Homer's text, Odysseus, newly arrived on his home island of Ithaca, begins the process of reintegration into his pre-war life. His helper is Athena, the Greek goddess of wisdom, who recognizes in the crafty Ithacan king a kindred spirit of sorts. Athena has given Odysseus advice on how best to conquer the young men who in his long absence have taken over his holdings and attempted (unsuccessfully) to take over his wife, Penelope, as well. In Akunin's text, the year is 1914, and the setting is the Russian Empire on the verge of the First World War. Akunin's Athena is a double agent, a Bolshevik sympathizer reporting to the imperial police. She is also, we are told, unintelligent and completely devoid of divine qualities.[4] Athena has attempted to ensnare Odysseus, in Akunin's telling a terrorist whose paperwork reveals an acquaintance with a certain Lenin and a little-known Koba. Having provided Odysseus with a working gun and a perfect vantage point for assassinating the tsar, who is vacationing in Yalta, Athena expects to be able to catch the assassin red-handed before any harm is done. But she finds herself outwitted. Odysseus kills the hated chief of security instead; in fact, the chief was the intended target, and the imperial assassination plot was a red herring. And Odysseus, as we have heard, then disappears.

The "hunt for Odysseus" is now on. For our hero, Erast Fandorin, was one of the men attempting to stop Odysseus from his supposed attempt on the sovereign's life. Visiting Yalta at the invitation of the late Anton Chekhov's sister, Fandorin had been sitting, bored, in his hotel room, rereading Chekhov's *Cherry Orchard* and wondering yet again, we are told, why this gloomy play had been labelled a comedy. Suddenly, he had been interrupted by the head of the local government, desperately seeking his help: Odysseus was not where Athena had told him to be, the tsar's life was in danger, and Fandorin's expertise was required. Having failed to prevent a murder, however, Fandorin is furious at Odysseus and himself. Of course our James Bond-esque leading man cannot accept having been outwitted by Odysseus, and he sets out to find the elusive assassin. (As Akunin commented in his blog shortly before the novel appeared, Odysseus had stayed in his mind after *Le Figaro*, even as Fandorin demanded revenge for his humiliating failure to stop the terrorist. Thus the novel was born.)[5]

As Fandorin begins his investigation, he interviews Athena, who proves almost useless. The lone, crucial clue she provides is her memory of a conversation in which Odysseus mentioned "the black city."[6] When Fandorin receives a postcard from his estranged wife, Klara, a movie star currently filming in Baku, he realizes from the postcard that "the black city" is in fact Baku. Klara has asked Fandorin to send her a new warm-weather wardrobe she has ordered; Fandorin adds that into his plans for Baku and sets off with his servant, Masa, and the requested clothing. Once Fandorin and Klara are awkwardly reunited on her movie set, her weepy (and false) protestations of devotion to her husband make Fandorin feel as if the couple are in the fourth act of Chekhov's *Seagull*, when former lovers lament their present circumstances.[7]

Once again Akunin inserts Chekhov into his text, a literary move that deserves attention. For as it turns out, Chekhov is instructive here (as he so often is). As Akunin fans will know, Homer is not the only author Akunin has attempted to "complete." Indeed, in 2000 Akunin published a continuation of Chekhov's *Seagull*, like Homer's epic a classic text in no apparent need of revision; Akunin's play was staged in 2001.[8] But Akunin picks a new genre, for his *Seagull* is a murder mystery. Treplev does not commit suicide, as he does at the end of Chekhov's play; rather, he is killed, and the remainder of the play consists of a series of tableaux, each featuring a different, plausible murderer. The Hercule Poirot of the play is Doctor Dorn – who himself turns out to be one of the possible murderers. An animal rights activist, he objected to Treplev's habit of shooting things, including a seagull. "I have avenged you, you poor seagull," he proclaims to the stuffed bird in the play's final lines.[9]

Dr. Dorn is significant as well because of his name. It turns out that Dorn is an abbreviation of a longer, old Russian name, Fondorin or Fandorin. So, we surmise, Dr. Dorn may be a relative of Erast Fandorin, both men serving as sleuths in Akunin's created – and now merged – worlds. Treplev's stuffed seagull and Odysseus's homecoming have just come together. Recall now that at the beginning of Akunin's novel, Fandorin is reading Chekhov; he later imagines himself as a character in *The Seagull*. He also realizes eventually why *The Cherry Orchard* is a comedy: it is a play written by a very sick man "who suspects his sad life is about to end as a farce," who will soon die far away from home and be transported back home ignominiously.[10] Spoiler alert: at the end of this novel, Fandorin is shot in the head, and presumably killed, far away from home.[11] Fandorin and Akunin's Chekhov have now merged: character and author-as-character come together. Keep in mind that *The Seagull*'s Treplev is a writer. That writer dies, too; in fact, in Akunin's telling, he is murdered, and the murder is played and replayed on the stage eight times. But does Chekhov, too, fall victim to this carnage? And, by extension, does Homer? Does Literature?

Some critics, disturbed by Akunin's irreverent take on world classics, would argue yes. As Elena Baraban notes, critics have raced to "defend the Russian classics from which Akunin unabashedly 'borrows' images, phrases, ideas, and characters, and to protect Russian history from being retold by such an 'unscrupulous' individual as Akunin."[12] "It is not now, nor was it ever, 'necessary' for Akunin to rewrite the last act of Chekhov's *Seagull*, which is a perfectly well-written play," insists Marina Adamovich. Along with other critics, she points to the postmodern nature of Akunin's writing, intent on "deconstruct[ing] authoritative discourse," including that of the nineteenth-century Russian classics, tempting targets given "their established ethical and esthetic credos."[13] Indeed, Akunin's postmodern, deconstructive tendencies have been characterized as plagiarism, or as vampirism, or as the commercialization of the golden classics, or as "mass literature" that erroneously and dangerously suggests that anyone is capable of rewriting canonical texts.[14]

Yet others, meanwhile, maintain that Akunin's "play" in fact encourages rereading the classics: after all, his *Seagull* literally links the two texts (the published version has Chekhov's original play and Akunin's own offering as two halves of one physical book). Thus, as Lyudmila Parts writes, "the primary function of intertextual engagement – as a defense mechanism of cultural memory – is fully activated."[15] The author himself told interviewer Stephen Norris, "I have been very heavily criticized for my rewriting of Chekhov's play *The Seagull*. But it means he is still alive to me."[16] Meanwhile, Akunin's "relativism, multiple truths, and intertextuality," to borrow Baraban's concise characterization,[17] also may serve to bring out ideas about Russia's history and national identity. The debate over Akunin's motivations and effects is ongoing: does Akunin murder his literary predecessors, or resurrect them?

Homer and Russia

Akunin's treatment of Homer provides an interesting window onto this phenomenon. While many treatments of Akunin's intertextuality have focused on the Russian nineteenth-century classics, a turn to a classical – as in, taking part in the Greco-Roman tradition – author such as Homer permits the consideration of Akunin's relationship to this heritage and the place of Russian literature and history in relation to it. "Homer is on a scale that stretches across human time," writes Adam Nicolson.[18] But this very consideration brings us back to the earlier questions posed in this article: Does Akunin's ludic approach to literature even permit the pondering of such weighty issues? After all, characterizing the *Figaro* venture in his blog, Akunin wrote that he "like(s) such toys."[19]

Russian involvement with Homer did not begin playfully. In 1813, Sergei Uvarov, Minister of Public Education in the 1830s and 1840s and originator of the "Orthodoxy, Autocracy, and Nationality" doctrine, called on Nikolai Gnedich, librarian in the Imperial Public Library, to create a Russian translation of Homer's *Iliad* specifically in Homeric hexameters. For Uvarov and his contemporaries, Homer was seen as an important – and serious – element in Russia's attempts to join European culture. Indeed, the Russian language's ability to accommodate hexameters was meant to demonstrate Russia's status as cultural heir to Greece.[20] Gnedich worked on the translation from 1807 to 1829, and his *Iliad*, still the standard translation read by Russians, found an ecstatic welcome among his fellow writers. Pushkin documented the work's significance in his 1832 poem "To Gnedich" ("Gnedichu"), in which he characterized Gnedich's *Iliad* as a near-holy document, one presented to barbaric Russians who had a misguided concept of the divine; the parallel, explicitly drawn, was to Moses bringing his people the stone tablets.[21]

Russia had an *Iliad*, and now it needed an *Odyssey* as well. Vasilii Zhukovskii completed a translation of Homer's *Odyssey* in 1849; it, too, is still the standard Russian translation. But Zhukovskii considered his *Odyssey* to be not a translation, but his own work. As he did not know classical Greek, he worked from a line-by-line German translation. "In this chaotically exact translation, quite opaque to the reader, I had before me as it were all the raw materials of a building; all that was lacking was beauty, order and harmony." Zhukovskii created this order and harmony in his own language, producing what was widely seen as a rebuilding of Homer in Russian.[22]

Critics were once again ecstatic. Zhukovskii's work was "a re-creation, a restoration, a resurrection of Homer," Nikolai Gogol wrote, and then took his reaction yet further.[23] Gogol felt that *The Odyssey* would change Russia profoundly: authors would be restored "to the light," criticism would be rejuvenated, the Russian language would be purified, all would be educated about the ancient world, and conservative values would come to the fore.[24] After all, Gogol maintained, Zhukovskii himself, once he had become "a more profound Christian," had created not "a servile reproduction" but rather an instance of "the living word" so that "all Russia might accept Homer as its own!"[25] Yet again, a translation of Homer into Russian was a quasi-religious event.

One could say, then, that in the nineteenth century, Homer had a certain stature: ennobling, grand, patriotic, sacred. Russian writers who took on the project of translating (or interpreting) Homer for their contemporaries were seen as profoundly influencing their nation. And Homer, as Uvarov had made clear, was a key to Russia's acceptance on a European cultural stage. The inclusion of Akunin and Ulitskaya in *Le Figaro*'s rewriting of Homer's ancient epic could be read in this earlier context as Russia's having come of age, fully accepted as cultural heirs of the European past. For Akunin, however, who has insisted, "I didn't want to be a public intellectual. I didn't want to be a *pisatel'* because this is a role I simply never wanted to play,"[26] taking part in *Le Figaro*'s project was playing a literary game, and a subversive one at that. Unlike his Homeric namesake, there is no redeeming side to Akunin's terrorist Odysseus, no echo of the hero who misses his family and weeps over his long absence from home. Moreover, whereas in Homer's tale the end of the text stresses a divinely ordained return to the former order, a re-established home and family, Akunin's Odysseus compares himself to figures including Pugachev, Zheliabov, and Plekhanov – in other words, to revolutionaries. His goal is the violent end of the Russian monarchy.[27] Indeed, even as Fandorin hunts for Odysseus, Odysseus is immersed in his own "elephant hunt," as he pursues rather than bolsters the enormous body of the imperial Russian state.[28] A similarly destructive mission is assigned to other Homeric figures in Akunin's series: recall, for instance, Akunin's fumbling Athena, whose incompetence leads to an unanticipated political assassination.

Two *Iliads*, a new Hector, and ... How Many Achilleses?

Akunin also turns repeatedly to Achilles, hero of Homer's *Iliad*, the Trojan War epic that precedes the *Odyssey*. In the *Iliad*, the Greeks, under the leadership of Agamemnon, attack the Trojans of Asia Minor; their prince, Paris, has absconded with Helen, wife of Agamemnon's brother Menelaus. The Greeks fight the Trojans for nearly a decade, as heroes on both sides die in vividly described brutal combat. Feeling undervalued by King Agamemnon, Achilles sits out most of the action in the tenth year of the Trojan War. He is finally spurred to murderous rage by the death in battle of his companion Patroclus, whose death he will avenge when he himself murders the Trojan champion Hector. Achilles's dangerous anger is brought home to the reader from the epic's famous initial invocation: "Sing, goddess, the anger of Peleus's son Achilleus / and its devastation, which put pains thousandfold upon the Achaians ..."[29]

In Akunin's 1998 *Turkish Gambit* (*Turetskii gambit*), another army is besieging a city: this time the Russians are besieging the Turks in the town of Plevna. The Russians, of course, absorbed religion and literacy from the Greek Orthodox Church. The Turks inhabit the land once occupied by the Trojans. The attractive Varya Suvorova, Fandorin's love interest in the novel, may be compared to Helen, as men vie – and even die – for her affections. Akunin makes sure we are noting the Homeric references: the novel's Irish journalist, McLaughlin, chastises Varya for flirting, reminding her of the Trojan War.[30] More significantly, the Russian war hero Mikhail Sobolev (based on historical figure General Mikhail Skobelev) is referred to as the "Russian Achilles" throughout the text. He is "the resplendent Achilles," who does not forget his friends. He is "the invulnerable Russian Achilles ... who at the decisive moment had taken the risk of striking through Plevna, already deserted by the Turks, straight into Osman's unprotected flank."[31]

Sobolev and Achilles do have definite resemblances. Achilles has Patroclus; Sobolev has a devoted friend in his subordinate Perepelkin, who "wanted Achilles to belong to him and nobody else."[32] Early in the *Iliad*, Achilles complains that Agamemnon is treating him unfairly and with insufficient respect. When we first encounter Sobolev, he is complaining that he is undervalued by his superiors and has not participated sufficiently in glorious battles. Glory is crucial here: both men crave it, though Sobolev moves beyond the Homeric ethos by adding into the mix an overweening, daredevil dose of pan-Slavic nationalism. When Fandorin needs a leader who will act without his authorities' sanction, it is Sobolev he turns to; this is typical of the authority-flaunting Achilles as well.

At the end of the novel Sobolev advances to the outskirts of Constantinople, which he sees as key to asserting Russia's Orthodox, imperial glory. In this section of the text, Sobolev is called "Achilles" repeatedly by the narrator and by Varya, who is assumed (incorrectly) to be Sobolev's mistress. Homer's Achilles prizes the slave girl Briseis, whom Agamemnon takes from him at the beginning of the epic, thereby affronting Achilles's dignity as a successful warrior. One might suggest that Homer's ever-present theme of the abducted or captured woman is played out once again in the outraged Varya's arrest when she first arrives in the Russian military camp, where she is not initially trusted. This echoes in a sense the initial scene in which she meets Fandorin, where (despite his later assurances that he had known he would triumph) he makes Varya the winner's prize in a wager.

Sobolev's story continues in *The Death of Achilles* (*Smert' Akhillesa*), which begins with Fandorin's return to Russia from a stint in Japan. Fandorin is delighted to find that his fellow guest at the hotel he has chosen is Sobolev, by now a vastly famous, widely adored Russian hero. But Sobolev, alas, is dead, having expired quite ingloriously in the bed of a glamorous prostitute. Fandorin spends the rest of the novel proving that this death was in fact a murder, and furthermore one desired by the Russian monarchy. Sobolev's pan-Slavic aspirations were seen as a threat once he prepared to move into the political arena and came to see himself as a new Napoleon.[33]

A reader who is familiar with the preceding novel will understandably conclude that Sobolev, whom we know already as the Russian Achilles, is the title character of *The Death of Achilles*. References in the text support this reading. Several characters refer to Sobolev as Achilles. Prince Dolgorukoi laments, "After all, this is not just anybody: it is the hero of Plevna and Turkestan who has surrendered his soul to God. A knight without fear or reproach, deservingly dubbed the Russian Achilles for his valor."[34] And Fandorin refers to Sobolev once again as Achilles when he is describing the general's grandiose plans for Russia – and for his own glory.[35]

But among these references comes another one, this time to Sobolev not as Achilles, but as Hector, the Trojan hero slain by Achilles. The tsar's brother Kirill Alexandrovich makes a funeral speech for Sobolev, in which he proclaims:

> Achilles should not have been his name – oh no! Well protected by the waters of the Styx, Achilles was invulnerable to arrow and sword; until the very last day of his life he did not spill a single drop of his own blood. But Mikhail Dmitrievich bore on his body the traces of fourteen wounds, each of which invisibly advanced the hour of his death. No, Sobolev should not have been compared with the fortunate Achilles, but rather with the noble Hector – a mere mortal who risked his own life just as his soldiers did![36]

Can Sobolev be read as Hector? Insofar as the quotation goes, he can be: Hector is indeed mortal, while Achilles is part-divine, though both men enjoy divine protection and support in battle. Hector is adored, as is Sobolev (Achilles, who does inspire fierce devotion, is not a beloved figure but rather a feared and glorified one). Hector loves his wife Andromache; Sobolev does not love his wife, but Fandorin learns of a love affair of apparently true devotion between Sobolev and Ekaterina Alexandrovna Golovina, characterized (confusingly) as "the golden-haired lover of the deceased Achilles."[37] But more to the point, if Sobolev is to be associated at least at times with Hector, to whom does the Achilles of the book's title refer? Is there another Achilles in the text?

A likely candidate is Achimas Welde, the main character of the second half of the book, Fandorin's major antagonist, murderer of Fandorin's late wife and now of Sobolev as well. Achimas, whose name echoes in sound the Russian "Akhilles," has subtle links to Achilles throughout his life story. Connections begin with his parents' names, which again call to mind the Greek ones (Pelef and Peleus, Fatima and Fetida) and continue with places important in both men's lives (the Skirovsk convent for Achimas and the island of Skyros for Achilles; in both places the men disguise themselves as girls).[38] Both men dream briefly of a quiet life, then return to killing. And kill they do (though Achilles as killer decidedly lacks Achimas's cool restraint). The hired killer Achimas, we are told, has spent his life thus far on the "process of killing,"[39] while Homer leaves us in no doubt of Achilles' murderous prowess:

> As inhuman fire sweeps on in fury through the deep angles of a drywood mountain and sets ablaze the depth of the timber and the blustering wind

lashes the flame along, so Achilleus swept everywhere with his spear like something more than a mortal harrying them as they died, and the black earth ran blood.[40]

Most tellingly, both men, who had appeared uncannily untouchable, are killed by an arrow in the heel.

We have two Achilleses, then, in Akunin's retelling: a glory-seeking, emotional general, and a cold, controlled killer for hire. Homer's Achilles has been deconstructed, pieces of his identity used to suit Akunin's changing narrative needs. As Eugenia Gresta writes, Akunin "implants" elements of earlier texts "in his plots, and de facto deprives the material he chooses of its primeval meaning by using it arbitrarily in his prose."[41] Most significantly, however, as underlined in the novel's title, *The Death of Achilles*, either as Sobolev or as Achimas, Akunin's Achilles is, indeed, dead. Achimas kills Sobolev, one Achilles killing the other in a sort of literary suicide. Fandorin himself then fatally wounds Achimas.

Pairs and Elision

While Akunin gives us two Achilleses in his novel, the structure of the text suggests another pairing: Achimas and Fandorin, who are evenly pitted, long-time antagonists featured respectively in the second and first halves of the novel. Like Achimas, Fandorin controls his emotions and lives by his own code of honour. Also like Achimas, Fandorin combines stereotypically Eastern and Western traits and identities. Achimas is part German, part Chechen. Raised by his maternal uncle, who trains him as a killer, Achimas combines his "Germanic" restraint and calculation with a stereotypically "Eastern" focus on revenge, a heartlessly imposed warrior's code of honour, and fanatical dedication to killing. Fandorin, too, is a hybrid: though Russian by birth, his stint in Japan influences him strongly, both through his continued friendship with his servant and companion, Masa, and through the "Eastern" training, from physical conditioning to his efforts at mental self-mastery, that he carries out faithfully with Masa's encouragement.[42] And both men kill an Achilles, Achimas assassinating Sobolev, and Fandorin killing Achimas himself.

Unlike Sobolev, neither man appears very similar characterologically to Homer's emotional, glory-seeking Achilles. And yet Sobolev, too, is associated through his associations and his goals with a combination of East and West. Recall that Sobolev is labelled both an Achilles and a Hector: the two heroes of the Trojan War's opposing forces, Greek and Trojan, come together in one figure. Further, motivated by his fierce sense of Slavic nationalism, Sobolev seeks to capture Constantinople, "the eternal, unattainable dream of the Russian tsars," at last "uniting the Slavs from Archangel to Constantinople and from Trieste to Vladivostok" in a far-ranging geographic coup.[43]

Can one read significance into these pairings and geographic signifiers? Might Akunin be referencing Russia's longstanding debates about national identity, East and West? Is he pointing out that when Russia engages with the Greco-Roman classical heritage, issues of geographic and cultural identity inevitably surface? Or, more likely, is he parodying not only the stereotypes he employs, but also Russian literature's – and literary critics' – ongoing efforts to address them? As Sofya Khagi writes, Akunin's "irony is all-pervasive," and "pastiche and parody, nostalgia and its ironic debunking productively coexist" in his work.[44] His characters, in whom culturally constructed geographic identities merge, are examples of the author's postmodern elision of boundaries and signifiers, as differences merge and lose assumed significance in a new context.

Fandorin's pursuit of Achimas/Achilles throughout *The Death of Achilles* resonates in his determined pursuit of Odysseus in *Black City*, as Akunin's Russian sleuth once again takes off to track down a Homeric hero's latest incarnation. As in *The Death of Achilles*, the narrative is told both from Fandorin's point of view and from his quarry's: Odysseus's portions of the text are short, dense chapters in a different typeface from the rest of the book. Again, as with Fandorin and Achimas, the two are evenly matched. Both men are clever, resourceful, and committed to their respective values – though these values are admittedly very different. Both men are also violent, willing to kill for their ideals. Odysseus kills to bring forth his desired political revolution; Fandorin meanwhile comes to the realization that after years of fighting for what he thinks is right, he has concluded that killing is sometimes necessary.[45] Further, their juxtaposition inevitably calls to mind Homer's Odysseus, that crafty, home-seeking survivor-trickster lauded by the Greeks and excoriated by the Trojans for his ingenious Trojan horse ruse. And indeed, both men can be linked partially to this Homeric hero.

Akunin's Odysseus is assigned this name by the befuddled tsarist police unable to trap him, despite his own preference for pseudonyms taken from the names of birds (he is called Woodpecker later in the text). Nonetheless, when leaving a note for the hapless pursuers he has tricked, he signs himself "Odysseus," thereby signalling awareness of his tsarist sobriquet and mocking his hapless pursuers with his apparently superior (and inside) knowledge.[46] This latter-day Odysseus is, like his predecessor, a clever survivor, though his survival leads not to his eventual and long-sought homecoming, but to long-desired revolutionary unrest. Again like Homer's Odysseus, Akunin's Odysseus is a leader and an organizer, one who can manipulate others to get a desired result. A skilled fundraiser for the revolutionary cause, this Odysseus manipulates oil supplies and consciously allies himself with the Bolsheviks as the most likely group to advance his desired goal.

Fandorin, too, in ways resembles Homer's Odysseus. Like Homer's hero before his return to Ithaca, Fandorin is constantly travelling: mention is made of his previous travels in Serbia, of his familiarity with Constantinople, and of a summons to Austria (supposedly to stop the First World War from breaking out). Again like Odysseus, Fandorin constantly defies the odds: using wit, charm, and good luck, he has survived an absurd number of potentially lethal happenings. Furthermore, in *Black City* Fandorin takes on a crucial task of the epic hero: the descent to the underworld and return to the world of the living, which is referenced parodically several times in the text. Homer's Odysseus descends to the underworld in order to get information about his return home to Ithaca; it is in the underworld that he meets the deceased hero Achilles, who desperately wishes he could inhabit the life of the simplest farmhand rather than the kingdom of the dead. Fandorin's own descent begins when he is attacked upon his arrival in Baku: he falls between the train tracks, is threatened with a knife, but escapes upwards with no damage other than a ruined shirt. He then attends a party that occurs literally several levels underground, after which he is submerged in a vat of oil, from which he is then rescued. Later in the tale, Fandorin chooses to disappear for safety reasons and then to be "resurrected," surprising his wife and her new companion, who had assumed based on sensationalist news articles that he was dead.[47] The story arc of the novel, punctuated with dangerous adventures and the occasional sexually loaded dalliance with an exotic, beautiful woman, recalls the steps of the epic hero's journey, particularly that of Homer's Odysseus.

At the same time, however, unlike Homer's Odysseus, there is no *nostos*, or homecoming, for Fandorin. His wife, Klara, is no Homeric Penelope, attending to weaving for her household and avoiding other men; rather, she needs Fandorin to deliver her new wardrobe, and she remarries the minute she thinks he is dead. In addition, while Fandorin has Gasym, a young man supposedly helping him (echoes of Odysseus's loyal son Telemachus, who fights at his side during his reintegration into Ithaca), Gasym is actually loyal to the revolutionary Odysseus, whom he sees as a father figure. The Telemachus–Odysseus paradigm is transposed. Indeed, it is Gasym who will pull the trigger at the end of the novel, apparently killing Fandorin. The parodic visits to the underworld seem to end with death, not resurrection.

Thus Akunin has linked Homer's heroes to an ambitious, Napoleonic Russian general, a hired assassin, a revolutionary, and his own sleuth-adventurer. And while Akunin has referred to his Fandorin series as a "new epic,"[48] his melding of epic heroes and tropes with the detective-fiction genre once again bespeaks a postmodern bent. "High" and "low" genres come together in a textual blend that suggests the irrelevance of such generic categories, even as iconic characters from world culture are deconstructed and parodied.[49] As Gresta writes, "the Russian writer's sacrilegious manners turn the *sancta sanctorum* of world culture into a universe of experimentation."[50] It is worth noting in this context that while in high school Achimas Welde rejects "learning chunks of Ancient Greek from the *Iliad*" for "real life."[51]

Akunin plays with history and fiction as well, again adding an ironic twist. In a 21 November 2012 blog post, he announced that *Black City* would be published in three formats, one of which, an electronic version, would come with authentic historical illustrations the author had found to depict events described in his fiction. "Unlike 'paper' illustrations, where the artist draws characters and their surroundings ... electronic pictures show reality as it actually was. In this edition there are many photographs, lithographs, newspaper clippings of that period – no fantasy, all real. You can see the real Baku ... of 1914," the author claimed. He then added, "Using this format is best for someone who has an iPad, that way everything should work properly."[52] The reader's experience of early twentieth-century Russia is thus mediated through twenty-first century technology, as temporal categories come together, their individual significance undermined. Moreover, the photographs' artful placement in a constructed literary text ironizes the very concept of the unmediated "reality" that they supposedly convey.

Murdering Epic? Fandorin, Akunin, and the Reader

As we have seen, Fandorin can be paired with Homeric heroes and the modern-day characters associated, albeit piecemeal, with them. But there is a further pairing to discuss: the pairing of Fandorin and the reader. When Akunin brings Homer into the detective genre, he is doing more than levelling the playing field between epic and mass literature. He is changing the relationship between text and reader. While in ancient Greece the Homeric tales were recited, or performed, rather than read, in the modern period they have existed predominantly as literary texts. Reading the *Iliad* or the *Odyssey*, one may well be enthralled by the narrative, moved by the characters, and uplifted by the feeling of participation in a centuries-old ritual of Homeric appreciation. Detective fiction, however, requires a different sort of buy-in from the reader. For just as Fandorin is a sleuth, so too is the reader of detective fiction on a perpetual hunt for clues. As Claire Whitehead notes, "The reader, like her fictional counterpart, the detective, is implicitly asked to consider clues, listen to testimony and construct hypotheses that will lead to the unmasking of the criminals."[53] Immersed in *The Turkish Gambit*, *The Death of Achilles*, and *Black City*, the reader joins Fandorin in his respective quests. The reader, too, chases Achilles and Odysseus.

Whitehead writes further that "detective fiction emphasizes the reader's expectation, present in any genre, of participating in an exercise of meaning-making."[54] The reader seeks out clues and assumes that they hold significance. Analyzing Akunin's Pelagia series, Whitehead addresses the role of intertextual references in this process, and also notes the potential frustration for the interpretive reader of Akunin's work: the reader is "constantly tempted into acts of interpretation and meaning-making which repeatedly result in ludic dead-ends."[55] In short, then, is there a point to locating and interpreting potential Homeric references in Akunin's novels? Or do they function simply for show, to tease the reader into a thwarted and fruitless sense of accomplishment?

Certainly show, or theatricality, is a central theme of Akunin's *Black City*, from the references to Chekhov's plays and characters to the actual movie set on which Fandorin sees and interacts with Klara. Odysseus's initial interactions with Athena and the immediate threat he poses to the tsar are based in subterfuge, forming an elaborately planned and executed drama. Fandorin remarks repeatedly that Klara is playing roles, both on the set and off; indeed, he realizes, she may not know what is real and what is not. Fandorin's lover, Saadat Validbekova, covers her face in public but in private smokes, drinks, and whistles "The Merry Widow."[56] Gasym plays the role of devoted surrogate son to Fandorin, only to hold a gun to his head at the end of the tale. Role playing is central to the tale and to its Homeric resonances: characters play the roles of Homer's heroes, but in deconstructed, partial form. The crime in the text may be solved, the adventure laid bare. But a reader's attempts to interpret Akunin's Homeric references in order to render a glorious verdict on Russia's national identity or the significance of world culture in a Russian context fall flat. The author outwits us; he is both stage manager and director.

Recall now the linkage of Fandorin's and Chekhov's own deaths in *Black City*, as the sleuth and the writer merge. And recall the murder on perpetual repeat of the writer Treplev in *The Seagull* – and at the hands of Dr. Dorn. Fandorin/Dorn kills Achilles and Treplev. Odysseus masterminds killing Fandorin/Chekhov. What does all this killing mean?

It's almost Homeric: "the black earth ran blood." But there is no Homeric glory or magnificence here. Akunin belittles Homer's epic heroes, killing them off or transforming them into petty terrorists.

And yet, reading Akunin, we engage with the classics once more. They reassert themselves. Who, after all, is left standing at the end of Akunin's Fandorin "project"? Crafty Odysseus, that long-lived trickster, has outlived the heroic Fandorin. And the author, too, has survived, as Akunin, a modern-day Odysseus, takes aim at the past and the present. Part way through the Fandorin series, when asked by a fan what to expect from the series, Akunin responded, "I still haven't shot all my bullets into [my] defenseless readers."[57] Akunin, smart, creative, and crafty, is an Odysseus rather than an Achilles, manipulating and convoluting identities in Revolutionary Russia through the prism of the "classical" Homeric text. The author challenges us, intrigues us, infuriates us, spurring us to attempt untangling his webs of references and echoes, urging us to read and keep reading. This is one overarching message we can take from the text. Perhaps, then, despite the death of Achilles, Akunin hasn't murdered Literature after all. Literature – self-referential, witty, adaptable, inspiring, and enduring – is the ultimate Odysseus.

NOTES

1 Homer, *The Odyssey*, trans. Stephen Mitchell (New York: Atria Books, 2013), 175.
2 Boris Akunin, *Chernyi gorod* (*Black City*; Moscow: Zakharov, 2013), 5. Translations from this text are my own.
3 See Boris Akounine, "Chasse à Ulysse," *Le Figaro*, 28 July 2008, https://www.pressreader.com/france/le-figaro/20080728/281835754477603.
4 Akunin, *Chernyi gorod*, 18.
5 Boris Akunin, "Baikhua iundun!" *LiveJournal* (blog), 21 November 2012, http://borisakunin.livejournal.com/83054.html.
6 Akunin, *Chernyi gorod*, 27.
7 Ibid., 68.
8 Shortly thereafter came a version of Shakespeare's *Hamlet*; Akunin has revisited Dostoevsky's *Crime and Punishment* as well.
9 Boris Akunin, "Chaika," *Novyi mir* 4 (2000), http://lib.ru/RUSS_DETEKTIW/BAKUNIN/chaika.txt.
10 Akunin, *Chernyi gorod*, 6.
11 His death is not in fact a fait accompli, as we learn in the final novel of the series, *Not Saying Goodbye* (*Ne proshchaius'*, 2018).

12   Elena V. Baraban, "A Country Resembling Russia: The Use of History in
     Boris Akunin's Detective Novels," *Slavic and East European Journal (SEEJ)*
     48, no. 3 (2004): 398–9.

13   Marina Adamovich, "Judith with the Head of Holofernes: Pseudoclassicism
     in Russian Literature During the 1990s," *Russian Studies in Literature* 38, no. 1
     (Winter 2001–2), 87.

14   Magdalena Kostova-Panajotova, "'Chaika' Borisa Akunina kak zerkalo
     'Chaiki' Chekhova," *Deti Ra* 9, no.13 (2005), http://www.detira.ru/arhiv
     /13_2005/mkp_sht.htm.

15   Lyudmila Parts, "Boris Akunin's Postmodern Čajka," *Russian Literature* 82
     (2016): 39.

16   For the interview, see chapter 2 of this volume.

17   Baraban, "A Country Resembling Russia," 399.

18   Adam Nicolson, *Why Homer Matters: A History* (New York: Henry Holt and
     Company, 2014), 31.

19   Akunin, "Baikhua iundun!"

20   Marinus Wes, *Classics in Russia 1700–1855: Between Two Bronze Horsemen*
     (Leiden: Brill, 1992), 141–2.

21   A.S. Pushkin, "Gnedichu" ("S Gomerom dolgo ty besedoval odin ..."), in
     Polnoe sobranie sochinenii, vol. 3 (Leningrad: Nauka, 1977), 225.

22   Wes, *Classics in Russia,* 145; James West, "Vasilii Andreevich Zhukovsky,"
     in *Russian Literature in the Age of Pushkin and Gogol: Poetry and Drama,*
     Dictionary of Literary Biography, vol. 205, ed. Christine A. Rydel (Detroit:
     Gale, 1999), 377.

23   Nikolai Gogol, "The Odyssey in Zhukovsky's Translation," in *Selected
     Passages from Correspondence with Friends*, trans. Jesse Zeldin (Nashville,
     TN: Valderbilt University Press, 1969), 33.

24   Ibid., 37ff.

25   Ibid., 33.

26   See the interview in chapter 2 of this volume.

27   Akunin, *Chernyi gorod*, 235–6.

28   Ibid., 84.

29   Homer, *The Iliad*, trans. Richmond Lattimore (Chicago: University of
     Chicago Press, 1951), 59.

30   Boris Akunin, *The Turkish Gambit: A Fandorin Mystery*, trans. Andrew
     Bromfield (New York: Random House, 2005), 107.

31   Ibid., 147.

32   Ibid., 175.

33   For information on the historical figure on whom Sobolev is based,
     General Mikhail Skobelev, see Hans Rogger, "The Skobelev Phenomenon:
     the Hero and his Worship," *Oxford Slavonic Papers* 9 (1976), 46–78. Rogger
     discusses the theories surrounding Skobelev's death (66–8), including that
     of political assassination.

34 Boris Akunin, *The Death of Achilles: A Fandorin Mystery*, trans. Andrew Bromfield (London: Westfield and Nicolson, 2005), 15.
35 Ibid., 176.
36 Ibid., 111.
37 Ibid., 161.
38 For more on the parallels between Achilles and Achimas, see Elena Baraban's chapter in this volume.
39 Akunin, *Death of Achilles*, 240.
40 Homer, *Iliad*, 417.
41 Eugenia Gresta, "From Moscow to London and Return: Some Perspectives on Boris Akunin's *Erast Fandorin Series*," http://sites.utoronto.ca/tsq/55/Gresta.pdf, 3.
42 I am grateful to Mila Nazyrova for her inspiring comments on Akunin's geographical signifiers in response to a paper I gave on Akunin at the ASEEES Conference in Washington, DC, in November 2016.
43 Akunin, *Turkish Gambit*, 180.
44 Sofya Khagi, "Boris Akunin and Retro Mode in Contemporary Russian Culture," *Toronto Slavic Quarterly* 13 (2005), http://sites.utoronto.ca/tsq/13/khagi13.shtml, n.p.
45 Akunin, *Chernyi gorod*, 35.
46 Ibid., 14. Odysseus's actual name is a prosaic Ivan Ivanovich Ivantsov (18).
47 Ibid., 145, 195.
48 Aleksei Makarkin, "Rossiia, kotoroi my ne teriali: Boris Akunin sozdaet epos novogo tipa," Viperson, 28 April 2000, http://viperson.ru/wind.php?ID=557548.
49 Akunin claimed in an interview that he was "one of the first in the country to attempt to unite two genres – high and low. [Russia] had never had the intermediate link – entertaining reading for a demanding reader" (cited in Khagi, "Boris Akunin," n.p.).
50 Gresta, "From Moscow to London," 8.
51 Akunin, *Death of Achilles*, 207.
52 Akunin, "Baikhua iundun!"
53 Claire Whitehead, "The Temptation of the Reader: The Search for Meaning in Boris Akunin's *Pelagia Trilogy*," *The Slavonic and East European Review* 94, no. 1 (2016), 31. This article appears in a slightly edited version as a chapter in this volume.
54 Whitehead, "Tempation of the Reader," 31.
55 Whitehead, "Temptation of the Reader," 55.
56 Akunin, *Chernyi gorod*, 112–14.
57 Quoted in Georgii Tseplakov, "Talent and the Widow's Mite of Project Literature," *Russian Studies in Literature* 45, no. 2 (2009), 92.

PART TWO

Amateur Detectives: The Sister Pelagia Trilogy and Adventures of Nicholas Fandorin

5 Tempting the Reader into a Search for Meaning: Boris Akunin's *Pelagia* Trilogy

CLAIRE WHITEHEAD

For some two decades now, Boris Akunin (the pen name of Grigorii Chkhartishvili) has been the king of the Russian *detektiv* scene. He announced his arrival with the publication of *The Winter Queen* (*Azazel'*) in 1998, the first in a series of fifteen novels featuring the detective Erast Petrovich Fandorin. Seemingly not content with one such series, two years later Akunin published the first in a trilogy of novels starring a Russian Orthodox nun, Sister Pelagia, as the sleuth. And in the same year came a third detective series, in which the main protagonist is the British-born grandson of Erast Fandorin, Nicholas, who returns to contemporary Russia to trace his ancestors from the pre-Petrine era of Tsar Alexei Mikhailovich.[1] What all three of these series have in common, and what distinguishes Akunin's detective novels from almost all of the manifold others that have flooded the Russian market in the post-Soviet era, is their combination of detective genre and historical novel.[2]

This chapter focuses on the Pelagia trilogy of novels: *Pelagia and the White Bulldog* (*Pelagiia i belyi bul'dog*, 2000); *Pelagia and the Black Monk* (*Pelagiia i chernyi monakh*, 2001); and *Pelagia and the Red Rooster* (*Pelagiia i krasnyi petukh*, 2003). In the first of the three novels, Pelagia is sent by her bishop, Mitrofanii, to investigate the killing of three prize bulldogs that belong to his great aunt, who lives in the Zavolzhsk region. The demise of these three animals is then swiftly followed by the murder of five people: two members of the local Zyt tribe; the photographer, Poggio; and the dog's murderess, Naina, and her maid. Although it takes a while to disentangle these two criminal plotlines, Pelagia discovers that these human killings are the work of the henchman of the assessor of the Holy Synod of the Russian Orthodox Church, who has been sent to the region to promote Orthodoxy as "the one true faith." *Pelagia and the Black Monk* recounts how Bishop Mitrofanii dispatches various people (including Pelagia as the fourth, in her disguised alter ego as the secular Mrs. Lisitsyna) to investigate the apparently spectral appearances of the figure of a black monk at the monastery of New Ararat. Pelagia works out that it is the mad physicist, Lampier, who is behind the monk's appearances, because he is trying to warn people about the radioactive meteorite that is killing monks in the hermitage on Outskirts Island in the area. However, the ultimate criminal is unmasked as being Mitrofanii's first detective, Lentochkin, who is desperate to enrich himself by collecting the precious metal of which the meteorite is made. Finally, in *Pelagia and the Red Rooster* the initial investigation is aimed at unmasking the killer of someone pretending to be the "false prophet" or "would-be Messiah," Manuila. Pelagia's efforts to solve this mystery see her quickly become a target, however, and the novel then centres around parallel investigations: public prosecutor Berdichevskii's efforts to discover who is trying to kill Pelagia and why; and Pelagia's journey to the Holy Land to try to find and save the real Manuila. As will be discussed in more detail below, this storyline sees the nun-detective discover a cave that apparently functions as a wormhole in time linking the "present" moment of the plot with Jerusalem 2,000 years previously. Compared to the more popular Erast Fandorin series of novels, this trilogy has been relatively little studied to date. However, it is, in the opinion of the author of this chapter, the most sophisticated of Akunin's detective series in terms of its combination of stylistic devices (especially intertextuality and metatextuality), plots, and themes. To an even greater degree than the other series, the novels in this trilogy are composed in such a way as to actively complicate the reaction of the reader and her interpretation of the text and its possible meaning(s). Such complication may well help to explain the polarization in reaction to Akunin's detective novels, where some commentators consider them to be "stylish" and to represent an "intellectual" approach to the genre, while others accuse the novelist of vampirically "devouring" the Russian classics, of playing ideologically empty postmodern games, or, paradoxically, of anti-Russian extremism.

In spite of the fact that the figure of the author looms large in Akunin's literary universe, the reader and her experience also constitute a central component of his fictional texts.[3] Most critics agree that detective fiction in the "whodunnit" mode, of which the Pelagia novels are an example, is a genre that invites and reflects the active participation of its reader.[4] The reader, like her fictional counterpart, the detective, is implicitly asked to consider clues, listen to testimony, and construct hypotheses that will lead to the unmasking of the criminal. Moreover, detective fiction emphasizes the reader's expectation, present in any genre, of participating in an exercise of meaning-making: the obscured story of the crime – from which meaning (or truth) is temporarily absent – will be uncovered, and its full significance revealed, by the story of the investigation.[5] The reader envisaged in this chapter is one akin to Stanley Fish's "informed reader," whom he defines as being "neither an abstraction nor an actual living reader, but a hybrid."[6] This reader is initiated in the conventions of detective fiction as well as possessing a decent knowledge of Russian and world literature, and she approaches detective fiction actively, keen to participate, to uncover possible meanings and, ultimately, the "truth."

In the Pelagia trilogy, Akunin unmistakably invites this "informed" reader to use her abilities, not simply to solve crimes, but to decipher other, perhaps deeper or more significant meaning(s) in the fictional narratives. However, much of the novels' appeal and sophistication derives from the manner in which they play with the "contract between reader and author" by simultaneously inviting active reader participation and appearing frequently to frustrate it.[7] By means of this ambiguous dialectic between solicited activity and subsequently imposed passivity (through frustration), Akunin can be seen to illuminate the sort of assumptions and expectations that accompany the act of reading, and not simply in the detective genre. This chapter will consider the contradictory games that Akunin's Pelagia trilogy plays with the reader in three different, though related, interpretive spheres: historical reference, intertextual and metatextual reference, and the search for faith. The discussion will illustrate how Akunin employs certain conventions of detective fiction to tempt the reader to prove her "informed" or "model" status by trying to establish meaning(s) in the text. However, it will also show how the novels repeatedly insist upon the pre-eminent status of the author figure as arbiter of knowledge within the text by ambiguating signification. In so doing, the Pelagia trilogy intriguingly and provocatively straddles the line often used to define postmodern (detective) fiction: does ultimate responsibility for meaning-making lie with the author or the reader? Are the postmodern games in which Akunin indulges in the trilogy ultimately "empty" and devoid of meaning? Or are concepts such as meaning, knowledge and truth (not just in literature and art, but more broadly) nothing more than chimera by which the reader should not be fooled?

Pelagia's Meaningful Games with History?

The particular combination in Akunin's novels of detective fiction and historical setting is one of the distinguishing features of his work in the Russian context. Internationally, however, "historical crime fiction" is a widely recognized and popular subgenre.[8] Crime fiction's attraction to the use of historical setting can be traced to the parallels that exist between the figures of the historian and the detective. As Robin Winks explains, "The historian must collect, interpret, and then explain his evidence by methods which are not greatly different from those techniques employed by the detective, or at least the detective in fiction."[9]

Historical crime fiction also offers novel ways in which authors can fulfil the genre's demands for realism and verisimilitude in respect of temporal and historical setting. This is a game that Akunin clearly enjoys playing, although not always in a straightforward fashion. Moreover, as this chapter will demonstrate, the incorporation of historical reference into crime fiction implicitly acknowledges the subjectivity of history as a "discursive entity" that must be "read as a text."[10] Akunin's Pelagia trilogy, as will be discussed in the final section, also shows an understanding of the potential for historical crime fiction to have both an epistemological and an ontological dominant.

Our starting point, however, is an aspect ignored by previous critics of the subgenre: the manner in which Akunin's decision to write historical crime fiction permits him to exploit the "active reader" convention of detective fiction in original and intriguing ways. Unlike the Erast Fandorin series, whose temporal location is always clearly announced, none of the novels in the Pelagia trilogy are at any point explicitly or exactly dated. This means that, more acutely than in the first series, Akunin not only invites the reader to attempt to solve crimes, but also to decipher various historical references and allusions to situate the novels' action specifically in time. It should be emphasized here that it is not that the novels' temporal location cannot be established, but that the author asks the reader to actively construct this location for herself, rather than it being given. So, for instance, in the first novel, *Pelagia and the White Bulldog*, she is told that the hotel in the provincial town of Zavolzhsk is called "The Grand Duke" after Konstantin Petrovich, who stayed there during a tour 100 years previously. If the historically informed reader can recall that Konstantin Petrovich was born in 1779, and was unlikely to have been on an official tour before the age of fifteen, this will allow her to date the action of the novel to some point in the mid-1890s. Similarly, in the final novel, *Pelagia and the Red Rooster*, the eponymous heroine refers to the Dreyfus affair in France. Rather than just informing the reader that the novel's action takes place in 1896, for instance, by means of this reference Akunin encourages the reader to establish herself as an active presence in the text and in the construction of its temporal location.

The interpretive invitations extended by such references are reinforced by the use Akunin makes of the *roman à clef* technique of including in his fictional world barely veiled doubles of actual historical figures.[11]

Most of these figures are taken from the historical period depicted. In the first and third novels, for example, the criminal mastermind is the Procurator of the Holy Synod of the Orthodox Church, Konstantin Petrovich Pobedin, who is clearly intended to represent the historical Konstantin Petrovich Pobedonostsev, who occupied this same position between 1880 and 1905. Similarly, in *Pelagia and the Black Monk*, the head of the government commission sent to study the economic miracle of the monastery at New Ararat is one Count Litte, an obvious double of Count Sergei Witte who served as minister of finance in Russia from 1892 to 1903.[12]

On the one hand, such references help to characterize the implied author as sufficiently historically educated to be able to incorporate them. On the other, they reach out to an historically aware reader who is capable of situating them correctly. Each reference functions as an implicit invitation to the reader to join a community of "informed" readers – composed of those who decipher successfully – and who can then bask in a (perhaps limited) sense of their own intellectual worth at being such history buffs. Indeed, Akunin at times seems keen to encourage this sense of interpretive superiority in as many readers as possible by emphasizing the historical privilege of almost any twenty-first-century reader. In *Pelagia and the Black Monk*, for example, the narrator describes the symptoms exhibited by the monks at the hermitage on Outskirts Island where a meteorite fell some 600 years previously as being hair loss, dizziness, nausea, and impotence. Twentieth-century scientific discoveries allow the contemporary reader to recognize these as signs of radiation sickness in a way that, from their nineteenth-century perspective, neither Pelagia nor the criminal Lentochkin are able. The reader is thus, at least temporarily, placed higher up in the hierarchy of historical knowledge than the fictional-world characters.

However, these apparently encouraging gestures towards the informed reader prove to be misleading. Akunin's implied author uses them to dupe the reader into a belief in her superiority while in fact underlining her ultimate inferiority. For all the historical allusions and references that the reader may be able to identify correctly, she is actually left with a negative and vague, rather than a positive and specific, knowledge of the novels' temporal setting. She can really only ever say that the action is happening sometime after 1894 and probably before 1900.[13] One might argue that not knowing the exact temporal location of a novel's action should not be construed as a significant problem in the reader's relationship with the text or the implied author. In many instances, approximate knowledge of the historical setting of a work is sufficient. In Akunin's trilogy, however, I would argue that it does have an impact on the reader's standing in the text. The sense of superiority she gains from correctly deciphered historical references and privileged temporal location becomes inextricably bound up with, and undermined by, a feeling of inferiority vis-à-vis the implied author, the narrator, and the fictional-world characters. All of these figures presumably do know the exact date at which the action takes place, and therefore, in this regard, sit above the reader in the hierarchy of knowledge.

Crucially, the issue of the trilogy's temporal location assumes greater significance when one considers how the ambiguous relationship it constructs between the reader and historical knowledge is reflected in the type of access that the novels allow to the resolution of their criminal plotlines. That is, as with the historical references, the stories of crime in the trilogy invite the reader to take an active role in their interpretation and resolution, only for her to learn ultimately that this is quite impossible and her efforts are futile. The relationship thus established between historical reference and the stories of crime in turn poses questions regarding the epistemic quest undertaken by the reader. As the genre's conventions dictate, each of the three Sister Pelagia novels features all manner of twists and turns in the plot, false suspects, red herrings, and multiple but intersecting crimes and culprits. So, for example, in *Pelagia and the White Bulldog* the synodical assessor, Bubentsov, is characterized in such a way as to make the nun's accusation of him as the murderer seem entirely convincing; however, as will be discussed below, it is only during Bubentsov's trial that Pelagia reveals she was mistaken and unveils an entirely different culprit. Meanwhile, in the second novel in the trilogy considerable effort is made to arouse suspicion about the potential involvement of a character nicknamed "Captain Fracasse" in the disappearance of Lentochkin; the development of the novel proves, however, not only that this man is innocent but that no one other than Lentochkin is responsible for Lentochkin's disappearance. On occasion in these novels, the reader is allowed briefly to experience the sense of getting ahead of the investigator, Pelagia, in understanding the significance of clues or recognizing suspects. In *Pelagia and the White Bulldog*, for instance, the generically informed reader will recognize that the nun's accusation of Miss Wrigley simply comes at too early a stage of the novel for it to be correct. In *Pelagia and the Black Monk*, the use of multiple focalizers[14] in the first third of the novel means that by the time Pelagia is dispatched to New Ararat the reader already has the benefit of three earlier accounts not wholly shared by the detective. The reader therefore possesses knowledge about the suspicious behaviour of characters such as Brother Jonah and Lidiia Evgenievna Boreiko to which Pelagia is not herself party.

In spite of such fleeting sensations of privileged insight, on the whole, the mysterious plots of Akunin's trilogy are so convoluted that the reader is never able to get ahead of the detective. This, in fact, is the lesson taught by all detective fiction. The denouement of *Pelagia and the White Bulldog*, for instance, provides a particularly effective illustration of the passive status bestowed on the reader in the unravelling of the crimes. With an example of fine deductive reasoning, Pelagia persuades her boss, Bishop Mitrofanii, that it is Synodical Inspector Bubentsov who is responsible for the five murders. On the witness stand during Bubentsov's trial, Mitrofanii repeats this version of the story of the crimes almost verbatim and it is corroborated by details provided by Bubentsov's assistant, Spasyonny. And the reader, like all of the other listeners present in the courtroom, finds this account to be entirely convincing. However, when Pelagia then testifies (and proves with physical evidence) that, while the sequence of events surrounding the crimes is accurate, the actual culprit is Spasyonny himself, the reader is firmly put in her place and her previous efforts at deduction are made to seem hollow.

Although unusually emphasized in Akunin's trilogy, this configuration of the power relationship between the implied author, the reader, and the detective is actually relatively conventional for the genre. Peter Hühn's analysis of narrativity and reading concepts in detective fiction centres upon the idea that the criminal's acts can be compared to those of an author because they "write" clues which are then read by the detective. These roles thus become doubles of those played by the actual novelist and the reader. In considering the issue of the relative access to information (and solutions) enjoyed by these various participants in detective fiction, Hühn notes: "The real author (of the book) always makes it a point of honor to prevent the real readers from being able to read his presentation of the two stories before he permits them to do so. ... Whereas within the novel the detective invariably proves the superiority of reading over writing, the novelist very often (I suspect) succeeds in proving the reverse – the superiority of his or her writing over the novel-reader's reading skills."[15]

Whereas Hühn chooses to consider the reader's inferiority in a largely positive light (as protection against the illusory power of reading), Akunin's enacting of it functions as a more profound warning. And this warning is sounded precisely by the clear links that Akunin establishes in the Pelagia trilogy between the reader's attempts to decipher historical references and her desire to actively participate in the unravelling of the story of the crimes. They suggest that Akunin not only problematizes the act of reading, but that he also problematizes the nature of knowledge itself, particularly historical knowledge. Discussing his work *History of the Russian State* (*Istoriia rossiiskogo gosudarstva*) in a 2007 interview, Akunin makes clear the problematic nature of historical truth when he says: "no historian knows reliably what happened in the nineteenth century, therefore I can dream things up here as they come into my head."[16] The informed reader derives a sense of self-satisfaction from understanding the historical allusions, but she never arrives at definitive knowledge of an actual date. She attempts to "read" the crime alongside the detective, but is ultimately taught that she can never arrive at its true "meaning" without the aid of the detective and the author. Akunin's trilogy can, therefore, be considered to offer a warning, however implicit and ironic, against any sense of confidence or superiority that the reader might invest in a belief in the successful outcome of her epistemic quest.

A similar note of caution is sounded by the uncertainty which the reader confronts when she attempts to decide whether it is intended that she ascribe meaning or meanings to the trilogy's historical setting and, by extension, to history more broadly. The temptation to do just that is clearly evidenced by a considerable body of critical reaction to Akunin, which has polarized around the question of whether the setting should be viewed as nostalgic or anti-nostalgic. Some critics believe that the author depicts pre-Revolutionary Russia as an idyllic time of stability, order, and gentility.[17] Others disagree and argue that the Russia illustrated by Akunin is "definitely not attractive" or idealized.[18] Whichever side of the argument such critics take, their views express the conviction that there is a need to read meaning(s) into Akunin's use of historical setting. Moreover, many of the views expressed in this debate reveal a belief in the existence of an interrupted (or uninterrupted) process of historical development in Russia. It might be posited that the depiction of historical settings in the particular context of detective fiction necessarily implies a teleological view of history. As a genre which is especially "preoccupied with establishing linear sequences"[19] leading to an ultimate solution, detective fiction implicitly suggests that a certain point in the past leads to (or has something to reveal about) a given point in the present and in the future.[20] The Pelagia trilogy partially conforms to this teleological model by offering the reader resolved criminal plotlines, at least in the first two novels. And in a more specifically historical sense, it suggests teleology by illustrating a rural idyll which might, according to the nostalgics, still exist if the Revolution and Soviet period had not intervened and where, for the anti-nostalgics, the corruption of Zavolzhsk merchants is an early precursor to the post-Soviet experience of oligarchs.

On many occasions, however, elements of the trilogy's presentation of the past encourage a view of history as more circular, or at least elliptical, than linear and end-oriented. As in the Erast Fandorin series, the reader is repeatedly invited to identify parallels between the Russia of the 1890s depicted in the novels and that of the 1990s and 2000s. So, for instance, in *Pelagia and the White Bulldog*, the reader is informed that Bishop Mitrofanii had warned Governor von Haggenau upon his appointment that free elections should not be introduced too swiftly in the region for fear that the people, out of a lack of readiness, "will elect some tavern-keeper to be their governor if he rolls a couple of barrels of green wine out into the square for them."[21] Such a description is surely intended to prompt the reader to infer a reference to Boris Yeltsin's problems with alcohol during his presidency in the 1990s. Similarly, the illustration in the trilogy of the role played by the Holy Synod of the Orthodox Church in the promotion of an ethnic Russian national identity and the primacy of Orthodoxy calls to mind the post-1990 situation of the Russian Orthodox Church and its influence in state affairs. In the first two novels of the trilogy, the primary impulse between this use of historical parallelism appears to be ludic, in the manner theorized by Linda Hutcheon and Fredric Jameson. However, there are also times throughout, but particularly in the final novel, where it is intended more earnestly. Specifically, it is this use of parallelism, whereby one chronological moment mirrors, rather than brings about, another, that understands history as elliptical rather than linear. As such, Akunin's novels conform closely to Hutcheon's description of postmodern fiction as "suggest[ing] that to re-write or re-present the past in fiction and in history is, in both cases, to open it up to the present, to prevent it from being conclusive or teleological."[22] Moreover, this more open-ended vision of history becomes associated in the trilogy with an insistence, noted by previous critics, upon the existence of a multiplicity of potential historical truths rather than a single grand narrative.[23]

The Pelagia novels employ a variety of narrative means to illustrate this open-endedness. For instance, the first novel, *Pelagia and the White Bulldog*, lacks a clearly delineated opening: it begins with points of ellipsis as if its first lines are the continuation of a story started elsewhere. Furthermore, the final word in the novel is "and," followed by more elliptical points. This sentence is then completed by the first line of the second novel, *Pelagia and the Black Monk*, which also begins in ellipsis, as the description of the arrival of a desperate monk from New Ararat straddles both novels. Although *Pelagia and the Black Monk* is given a more definitive ending in terms of punctuation and the time lag between its action and that of the third novel, in fact the trilogy can be seen to move towards increasing open-endedness in terms of plot resolution. In the first novel, the reader is shown the conclusion of the court case against Spasyonny and informed that he is sentenced to hard labour for life. In the second, although Pelagia eventually unmasks Lentochkin as the principal criminal, the novel closes without his being arrested and sentenced by a court. The clear implication is that his punishment will be divinely poetic, because he is already in the advanced stages of radiation poisoning. The most obvious illustration of open-endedness comes, however, in *Pelagia and the Red Rooster*, in which the master criminal, Chief Procurator Pobedin, is identified but suffers no punishment whatsoever and Pelagia disappears into a cave in the Garden of Gethsemane never to be seen again.

In terms of expressing the notion of the existence of alternative histories, Akunin makes effective use of the multiple criminal plotlines in each novel, whose frustration of the reader's interpretive efforts has been referred to above. In *Pelagia and the White Bulldog*, although Pelagia is initially dispatched to investigate the death of one prized dog, the plot soon comes to feature five complexly related human murders in which the Holy Synod is implicated. In *Pelagia and the Black Monk*, the search for an explanation of the apparently spectral monk's appearances becomes bound up with an investigation of the legend of the meteorite and the deaths of the monks on Outskirts Island. And in the trilogy's final novel, the initial investigation into the murder of the false Manuila and the attempts on Pelagia's life give way to an exploration of the deeper mystery of the supposed prophet's identity and the nun's search for faith.

Furthermore, the performance of Akunin's narrator, most notably in the first two novels, functions as an implicit warning to the reader against the idea of investing too much trust in a single version of events, especially, although arguably not only, in the context of the fictional text. This voice initially appears to belong to a first-person narrator who, as a character in the fictional world, is able to describe Pelagia and Mitrofanii while in church with them. On occasion, the narrator explicitly comments on the restricted privilege to information dictated by this position when, for example, he admits to difficulties in identifying one of the nuns at the Transfiguration Day ceremony "at first glance from the back."[24] However, it is subsequently difficult to reconcile such comments with the omniscient access this same narrator appears to possess into the inner thoughts and feelings of the fictional-world characters: descriptions of Mitrofanii's unspoken musings as well as of the emotions that Pelagia experiences abound throughout the trilogy. The fluidity of the narrator's position vis-à-vis the diegesis is an effective tool for feeding the reader's suspense: while at times this voice is highly informative, at others it leaves gaping holes in her knowledge of events by either refusing to divulge details or by pretending not to know them.[25] In anticipation of remarks to be made in the following section of this essay, this uneven and unpredictable narrative performance is reminiscent of the voices employed by Nikolai Gogol in his fiction.[26]

However, such narrative unreliability can be seen not only to play intertextual games, but, in a more serious tone, to highlight what post-modernism considers the absurdity of a belief in a single-authored account of history and the impossibility of historical truth. Indeed, the narrator supplements such implicit acts of self-reflexivity on the status of historical knowledge with one explicit gesture that undermines its supposed value. In *Pelagia and the White Bulldog*, at the beginning of a section describing the various conversations on the administration of the Zavolzhsk region between Bishop Mitrofanii and Governor von Haggenau, the narrator informs the reader: "For those who are follow-ing our tale only in order to discover how it concludes, and who have no interest in the history of our region, it is permissible to omit this brief chapter completely. No damage will be caused to the elegant line of the narrative as a result."[27]

At such moments, the paradoxical position in which Akunin's trilogy places the reader in terms of her attempts to interpret the novels' his-torical setting and references is made absolutely clear. Conforming to Hutcheon's definition of "historiographic metafiction," it incorporates historical events and actors as if to imbue them with significance but simultaneously demonstrates a playful "self-awareness of history and fiction as human constructs."[28] As throughout the trilogy, the reader is here left wondering whether she should be earnestly engaging with the trilogy's problematized presentation of the historical past, or just enjoy-ing the literary and intellectual games being played out.

Pelagia's Games with Texts

The type of games played with the informed reader by the Pelagia trilogy's historical setting are mirrored and reinforced by its exploita-tion of intertextuality and metatextuality. Akunin's use of these de-vices prompts two interrelated questions. First, if they are intended to invite the reader to infer meaning, what are the possible interpretations suggested by their use? Second, do they simultaneously undermine any such invitation by implying that these meanings are primarily self-reflexive and parodic, rather than extending beyond the bounda-ries of the fictional text? Although the focus here will again fall upon the experience of the reader, it is worth noting that, to an even greater degree than the incorporation of historical references, the novels' use of intertextuality in particular shines a spotlight on the attributes of both the implied and actual author. The impression that they help create of Boris Akunin as an "erudite" author of detective fiction in the mould of Umberto Eco is a key contributory factor to the situation in which the persona of the author on the Russian literary scene overshadows the reputation of any of his individual works.

Elena Baraban does not exaggerate when she describes Akunin as "saturating his mysteries with allusions to literary classics."[29] The Pelagia trilogy certainly makes no secret of the fact that, albeit in a quite different manner to Edgar Allan Poe's "The Purloined Letter," which revolves around an absent and hidden text, it is "comprised of borrowed texts."[30] Akunin employs intertextuality on both a macro- and a micro-level, and the references can be either implicit or explicit. For example, at an implicit macro-level, the decision to make his investigators (Bishop Mitrofanii and Sister Pelagia) members of the church recalls examples from the Western canon of detective fiction such as G.K. Chesterton's Father Brown series, published between 1911 and 1936, the Brother Cadfael mysteries penned by Ellis Peters from 1977 until 1994, and crucially, given remarks to be made below regarding metatextuality, Umberto Eco's *The Name of the Rose* from 1980. Although such nods to the Western detective canon are significant, the majority of the intertextual references in the Pelagia trilogy are to works of Russian literature, and most frequently to those from the nineteenth century. On a macro-level, the first novel incorporates implicit intertextual references in its rural setting and genteel atmosphere to works such as Leskov's *Cathedral Folk* (*Soboriane*, 1872)[31] and Turgenev's *A Nest of the Gentry* (*Dvorianskoe gnezdo*, 1859). As its title makes obvious, the second novel in the trilogy references Chekhov's 1894 story "The Black Monk," among others. The religious or mystical plane in *Pelagia and the Red Rooster* calls to mind Bulgakov's *Master and Margarita* (*Master i Margarita*, 1966–7), while the title of Akunin's final chapter, "The Gospel according to Pelagia," as a near copy of Bulgakov's "The Gospel according to Woland," makes the association more explicit. The figure of Dostoevsky haunts the entire trilogy, making both implicit and explicit appearances on the level of language, character, and plot; and Gogol is implicitly referenced throughout by means of the narrator's performance. Furthermore, on a micro-level, the trilogy features hundreds of references, both implicit and explicit, to scores of works from the supposed "Golden Age" of Russian literature as well as to the classical European tradition. To name but a few (among those that this informed reader can recognize), there are references to Nekrasov, Derzhavin, Karamzin, Pushkin, Lermontov, Turgenev, Garshin, Tolstoy, Dante, Shakespeare, Pascal, Rousseau, and Gautier.

On the one hand, it is possible to view this aspect of the novels as generically conventional, given Hanna Charney's claim that intertextuality is "a hallmark of detective novels in general."[32] Nevertheless, the sheer number and variety of Akunin's intertextual references takes his use of the device beyond what might be considered the norm for this, or indeed any, genre. So what intentions for the reader's interpretive experience can be identified behind this intertextual saturation? Firstly, whatever the nature of the intertextuality, one of its primary consequences is to establish a "horizon of expectations" in the mind of the reader.[33] The references to Chesterton, Peters, and Eco, for instance, encourage the generically informed reader to expect that Akunin's novels might share certain features with these earlier works: perhaps an illustration of the mystical or metaphysical attitude that religious figures bring to the supposedly rational art of detection, or a depiction of the tensions that exist between the spiritual life and the more secular realm of criminal investigations. More simply, by implicitly alluding to writers such as these, as well as to Agatha Christie,[34] Akunin is arguing for the legitimacy and reputation of his own work to be considered on a par with these highly regarded forebears.

Secondly, as with the historical allusions, the many references to other texts lay down a challenge to the implied reader to test her literary knowledge against that of the author. If she is successful in identifying a good number of the implicit references, she is rewarded with membership of the imagined community of not simply "informed" readers, but Akunin's "ideal" readership. At the same time that this achievement creates the illusion of being (almost) on a par with the author, it also fosters a feeling of superiority over those readers whom she imagines are not as capable. However, this is a contest that no reader (apart from Akunin himself perhaps) can ever likely win. It would be impossible – as well as undesirable in terms of the act of reading – to attempt to identify all of the various references. The terms of the game being played between author and reader thus become somewhat disingenuous, and any sense of equality or superiority experienced by the latter is shown to be hollow.

Turning more specifically to the issue of which, if any, meanings can be read into the trilogy's intertextual references, a first possibility is that they are intended to function as additional "clues" for the active reader. The informed reader is invited to use her knowledge of the referenced texts in order to throw additional interpretive light upon the contents of Akunin's novels. These clues rarely if ever relate specifically to the story of the crime itself; that is, the reader who deciphers these clues is no closer to solving the crimes than any other. However, this reader is arguably rewarded with a deeper sense of the novels' potential significances. For example, the implicit allusions in *Pelagia and the White Bulldog* to Leskov's *Cathedral Folk* tempts the reader into equating Akunin's performance with Leskov's perceptive portrayal of the changes occurring in nineteenth-century rural Russia and his refusal to propound simple ideological tenets. The intertextual bridge built across to "The Black Monk" in the second novel suggests not only that a similar debate around questions of religious faith, scientific reason, and psychiatric health is being staged in both works, but also that the behaviour of Akunin's Lentochkin references the megalomania of Chekhov's protagonist, Kovrin.[35] And the references in *Pelagia and the Red Rooster* to Bulgakov's *Master and Margarita*, as well as to various of Dostoevsky's novels, reinforce the idea already present in the plotline that this is a work whose ambitions reach well beyond the conventional limits of a detective novel.

One broadly shared interpretation of Akunin's decision to adorn all of his detective series, not just the Pelagia trilogy, so liberally with intertextual references is that it seeks to associate the "mass" genre with the "high" classical literary tradition. Indeed, it is arguably this aspect of his work, more than its inclusion of historical references, that motivates the use of epithets such as "intellectual," "erudite," and "stylish," which are more commonly associated with "high" literature.[36] For many years scholarly criticism of detective fiction demonstrated an almost obsessive preoccupation with the relationship between "popular" but "low" detective fiction and "high" literature. In his critical writing, G.K. Chesterton, for instance, is typical of those who feel the need to invoke this perceived division when he argues that a "detective story [is] a perfectly legitimate form of art."[37] Although traces of this hierarchical paradigm persist,[38] since the 1980s there has been a welcome move towards considering such terms as nothing more than constructs which, according to Brian McHale, should not be reified and turned into pseudo-objects.[39] It is in this light that Akunin's use of intertextuality should be seen: rather than attempting to shift the "mass" genre of detective fiction into the space occupied by "high" literature or the "classical tradition," it is better considered to collapse and thereby demonstrate the redundancy of such literary categories.

A further, more original reading of the trilogy's use of intertextual reference, albeit one related to the question of literary hierarchies, would be to suggest that it invokes and interrogates the myth, and its consequences, of the Soviet reader as the *"samyi chitaiushchii v mire"* ("most active reader in the world").[40] This myth, as Stephen Lovell makes clear in *The Russian Reading Revolution*, can be reduced to two assertions: "First, that in the Soviet Union people read a lot and that they would read more as society progressed further towards Communism; and second, that the printed word was capable of uniting people and instilling in them the core values of Soviet society."[41]

The Pelagia trilogy invokes this myth because, as asserted above, by means of its intertextuality it appears to reach out to the informed reader and flatter her by reinforcing the idea of her vast literary knowledge. Indeed, by means of its determined, almost exaggerated, inclusion of such a high number of intertextual references, all of Akunin's work in this genre seems to suggest that Russian literature is one of the few, if not the only, literatures in the world that could put such "literary" detective works on the market. Akunin's intertextuality might thus be seen to function as an implicit reminder of the desire of the Soviet authorities to use literature to create a new reader and thereby inspire some sort of a cultural revolution. Is the reader therefore being prompted to view Akunin's particular approach to the detective genre as harbouring similar transformational aspirations?[42] Moreover, the flattening out of distinctions between "low" and "high" modes enacted in Akunin's trilogy is possibly intended to be a modern refraction of the situation that, Lovell suggests, pertained in the Soviet Union after 1932. Lovell argues that, after this date, the notion of a specifically proletarian culture was abandoned and what Soviet society was left with was "a truly 'middle-brow' culture which tried to preserve the 'high' values and relative cultural homogeneity of a bourgeois educated public (such as the English reading classes in the second half of the eighteenth century) with the scale of a mass public."[43]

Without wishing to categorize Akunin's trilogy as "middle-brow," his use of intertextuality certainly suggests a similar mixing of an "educated" and a "mass" public. By extension, this device then interrogates the manner in which the myth of the most active reader served, by means of a model of cultural unity and homogeneity, to conceal real sociocultural divisions and inequalities during the Soviet period.[44] Can the Pelagia trilogy therefore be considered to function as an implicit warning about the possible return to such homogeneity in the post-Soviet era, where the bestseller lists have frequently been populated by largely derivative detective novels? At the same time as it seeks to collapse distinctions between "high" and "low" by forcing a supposedly "low" genre out of mediocrity, Akunin's work can be seen, paradoxically, as an attempt to counteract the considerable uniformity in the work of other contemporary Russian detective writers.[45]

To some extent, the interpretations of Akunin's intertextuality advanced up to this point can all be viewed as rather "modernist," insofar as they attribute constructive meanings to its use. However, certain aspects of this device, as well as the trilogy's exploitation of metatextuality, caution against the validity of such interpretive assertions. Rather, they demonstrate that the meanings derived from intertextual and metatextual reference are, as with the historical allusions, far more elliptical and much less definitive, elusive even, than those suggested above. Indeed, these devices permit the trilogy to evince a playfully sceptical and parodic attitude towards the possibility or validity of the existence of any meaning that extends beyond the fictional text. First of all, as Sofya Khagi has claimed in relation to the Erast Fandorin series, the trilogy's use of intertextuality can be seen to embody the claim made by postmodern historicism that the past has been entirely effaced as a retrievable artefact and replaced by texts.[46] The Pelagia novels' status as works substantially composed of a variety of other literary texts undermines any claim that can be made for their extra-textual referentiality by enacting Fredric Jameson's assertion that "popular culture can now only refer to other cultural signifiers whilst reality outside pop art has entirely retreated."[47] Similarly, Akunin's use of both intertextuality and metatextuality is designed to ensure that the reader is kept aware of the texts' fictionality and of the notion of "art as device."

For instance, not only is the narrative voice in the novels unreliable, it is also ludically self-conscious and keen to point up, and reflect upon, its own performance. In what is clearly an implicit nod to the style of Gogol's narrators,[48] Akunin's storyteller frequently highlights the fictional illusion of the supposed simultaneity of action and narration through comments such as: "Before Sister Pelagia sets out for the estate of the general's widow Tatishcheva, we need to offer certain explanations concerning the local geography, without which anyone who has never been to Zavolzhsk will find it a little difficult to believe everything that occurred subsequently."[49]

Similarly, the narrator is often keen to draw the reader's attention to her expectation that he will perform his storytelling duties skilfully and reliably. He announces with some fanfare in the first novel that, in revealing why the photographer Poggio's exhibition did not take place, it is necessary "to take everything in the right order, because every little detail is important, even if at first sight it seems absolutely insignificant."[50] And yet, having made a show of this obligation, as we have seen above, the narrator is frequently unreliable: he breaks his own rules, jumbles details up, and occasionally leaves out important information altogether.

But it is not just the narrator who ironically reflects on the processes and status of literary fiction in the Pelagia novels. On repeated occasions, characters within the fictional world provide playful metatextual commentary upon the value of literature in a manner that interrogates the standing of Akunin's novels themselves. In *Pelagia and the White Bulldog*, for instance, during a description of the extensive contents of Mitrofanii's library, the reader is informed that the only type of reading the Bishop avoids is fiction, because it is "of little value."[51] Pelagia disagrees and claims that "since the Lord had implanted in the soul of man the desire to create, He was the best judge of whether there was any sense and benefit in the writing of novels."[52] Later in the same novel, the commentary concerns crime fiction more specifically as Mitrofanii criticizes Dostoevsky for making "his own task too easy when he had the proud Raskolnikov kill not only the repulsive old money-lender, but her meek, innocent sister as well."[53] This intertextual reference thus serves a metatextual purpose by encouraging the reader to think that Akunin's trilogy will not make the same mistake.

More acutely ironic comments on the ultimately elusive nature of literary representation are to be found in *Pelagia and the Black Monk*. This second novel features the character Lev Nikolaevich, whose name and patronymic are playfully shared with both Prince Myshkin from Dostoevsky's *The Idiot* (1869) and with Tolstoy. His introduction is shrouded in mystery: he tells Lentochkin that he used to be a patient in the psychiatric asylum and reveals a passion for the works of Dostoevsky. Without knowing whom she is actually observing, Sister Pelagia then witnesses this same man heroically retrieving a kitten with little thought for his own safety. Later on, having rescued her from an attack by Brother Jonah, he introduces himself to Pelagia as Nikolai Vsevolodovich, using the name and patronymic of Stavrogin from Dostoevsky's *The Devils* (*Besy*, 1872). It is in this guise that he attempts to force himself upon Pelagia and reacts extremely angrily to her revelation that she is a nun. She is saved by the arrival of Dr. Korovin, who then informs her that this man is, in fact, one Laert Terpsikhorov, an actor from St. Petersburg who, in the absence of any personality of his own, inhabits the last dramatic role he has played. Besides the various ludic nods provided by this network of intertextual references built around this character, he is also the source of important metatextual commentary. The fact of having a character in a literary fiction – Akunin's novel – presented as an actor who, initially unbeknownst to anyone, assumes the identity of a series of other literary fictional characters – Prince Myshkin, Stavrogin, and finally Makar Devushkin from Dostoevsky's *Poor Folk* (*Bednye liudi*, 1846) – functions as a highly effective expression of the continual self-reflexivity of literature. It is like a sort of hall of mirrors in which one literary figure generates another almost in perpetuity. As such, it implicitly suggests that the constant refraction of one literary text through another results not in any definitive interpretation, but in a sense of ever-deferred meaning.

Metatextuality and the Search for Faith

By far the most powerful metatextual image in the trilogy is that of the cave in the final novel, *Pelagia and the Red Rooster*.[54] This is also the image that most effectively expresses the notion of the temptation extended to the reader to find meaning, and the potential for the ultimate frustration of this quest. As such, it functions as a symbolic representation of the reader's experience of the whole trilogy, but most particularly of this third novel. The cave is presented as a potentially crucial element in both Pelagia's and the reader's quest for knowledge. Its first manifestation in the narrative is in rural Russia during the period that Pelagia accompanies the civil servant Sergei Sergeevich Dolinin in his efforts to identify the "false prophet": she enters it alone, having been told by a witness that it is from here that Manuila initially appeared. Subsequently, when Pelagia undertakes her trip across the Holy Land in search of this same man, the cave in the Garden of Gethsemane is established as the location most likely to provide solutions to the various mysteries the case involves. Indeed, when Pelagia first enters this cave in Jerusalem it is so as not to interrupt a conversation with Manuila, which she hopes will give her answers to the questions accumulated during her investigation. It is thus cast as some sort of potential end point, or denouement. However, not only are these answers not forthcoming, but over the course of the two following days both Manuila and Pelagia re-enter the same cave, each carrying a red rooster under their arm, and disappear, never to be seen again. Therefore, having seemed to offer the hope of some sort of final resolution, this cave ultimately appears to thwart any search for definitive meaning undertaken either by the fictional protagonist or by the reader. Pelagia does not learn whether this prophet is actually false or not; and the reader does not discover what eventually becomes of either character.

Moreover, both the cave in Jerusalem and the one in Russia, it is suggested, function as wormholes through time and space. When Pelagia enters the "Devil's Cave" in Russia, she finds herself trapped by a landslide and struggles to find a way out. When she does escape, she is surprised to find that, in spite of feeling that she has spent several hours in the cave, only half an hour appears to have passed. Pelagia's confusion is then exacerbated when she witnesses a man deliberately setting off the landslide that has trapped her and that she has previously heard from inside the cave. In a similarly irrational manner, it is suggested that Manuila has arrived in nineteenth-century Russia from the Jerusalem of Biblical times by entering the cave in the latter and exiting via the cave in the former. And his intention upon entering the cave in the Garden of Gethsemane is to attempt to return to his own time, some 1,900 years previous. Pelagia initially hopes to dismiss her experience as a dream, but gives up attempting to understand "what was inaccessible to reason,"[55] and instead turns to prayer. The interrogation of the nature of the fictional world enacted by the caves consequently lends Akunin's trilogy attributes identified as belonging to the metaphysical detective story.[56] The caves also function metatextually because, like them, the novels in the trilogy offer the reader what Pelagia calls an "opening from one world into another."[57] Moreover, as labyrinthine structures that refuse to reveal ultimate and definitive meaning, just like the library in Umberto Eco's *The Name of the Rose*,[58] they become the perfect image for a postmodern and metaphysical insistence on an absence of teleology or resolution.[59]

Yet, in spite of the various clues which this image of the cave provides to the ultimate elusiveness of knowledge, it nevertheless tempts the reader into an interpretive act which potentially reveals the trilogy's most profound meaning. One explanation for Akunin favouring intertextual references to Dostoevsky throughout the trilogy, and Bulgakov particularly in the final novel, is that these two authors most effectively indicate that the presentation of the Pelagia novels as detective fiction is the greatest of all Akunin's red herrings. In fact, their presence suggests that rather than being crime fiction solely, his work is intended to explore the question of the individual's journey towards religious faith. Most strikingly in *Pelagia and the Red Rooster*, but actually throughout the three novels, it is possible to view the heroine's actions not only as a series of criminal investigations but as a spiritual undertaking. From the very first moments of her introduction, Pelagia's suitability as a nun is called into question. We are told that her physical appearance is "quite shameful and impermissible for a nun";[60] she is extremely clumsy in her habit and is described as "not a nun, but a walking disaster with freckles."[61] Indeed, she is portrayed as being far more at ease with herself when she discards her habit and adopts the disguise of the secular Polina Andreevna Lisitsyna, as if this were her true identity. The issue of Pelagia's relative comfort in these two roles is not merely superficial but obviously linked to the conviction of her faith. Early in the third novel, in pleading with Mitrofanii to be allowed to continue with her investigative work, Pelagia makes it clear which of her two roles she thinks is the more useful and effective: "'You see, sir, when I see evil-doing triumph, and especially when someone innocent is accused ... Or someone is threatened by mortal danger ... It feels here' the nun pressed one hand to her heart – 'as if a little ember catches fire. And it burns, it will not let me be until truth and justice are restored. In keeping with my vocation, I ought to pray, but I cannot. Surely what God requires from us is not inaction and futile lamenting, but help – such as each of us is capable of.'"[62]

A while later, when Pelagia asks the bishop for permission to accompany Dolinin on his Interior Ministry investigation, Mitrofanii urges her to consider whether she would be *truer* to herself if she were not a nun. He suggests that her real *métier* is detective work and that to deny her God-given gift of solving human mysteries is sinful. She insists that she wishes to remain a Bride of Christ; but her justification is based on a desire not to break her vows, rather than a more rooted sense of the rightness of her calling.[63] Moreover, having reiterated her determination to remain a nun, during the course of her work with Dolinin, and not for the first time in the trilogy, Pelagia experiences sexual attraction towards a member of the opposite sex. Even when she gets to the Holy Land, Pelagia still appears to be a woman more drawn to reason than to faith. Travelling across the country and seeing what she knows are some of the region's most famous Biblical sites, the reader is told that Pelagia "was not really moved: although she muttered a prayer, it was mechanical, it had no soul. Her thoughts were too far away from the divine."[64]

However, the very intentions with which Pelagia sets out to the Holy Land signal something of a shift outside the realm of conventional detective fiction: she has not gone in search of a criminal (as has Berdichevskii in the parallel plot line) but is tracking a potential victim, Manuila, in an effort to prevent his death. And her journey across the Holy Land certainly comes to resemble something less like a detective's pursuit and more of a pilgrimage: as the novel reaches its climax, Pelagia moves not only geographically nearer to Manuila, but also closer to an acceptance of faith. As she waits for him to turn up at the Garden of Gethsemane on the appointed day, she has absolute trust in the fact that he will arrive. Not only that, but she also begins to recite a prayer to herself, almost unknowingly. No longer mechanical, the narrator now describes how "the act of prayer simply arose of its own accord, without any involvement of her reason."[65] That evening, Pelagia follows Manuila into the cave seeking answers to her questions. There, she witnesses him convert the assassin Yakov Mikhailovich, who has spent the entirety of the novel trying to kill Manuila under orders from Chief Procurator Pobedin. The following evening, having realized that he needs a red rooster to perfectly recreate the conditions under which he apparently travelled from the Jerusalem of Biblical times to 1890s Russia, Manuila enters the cave again and disappears. The very next day, Pelagia herself buys a red rooster and does the same: she leaves behind the earthly realm of criminal investigations and reason to enter another world in which she needs to walk towards the light of true faith. In so doing, she appears, therefore, to have followed the terms of Manuila's earlier plea to Pobedin: "I told him that the Church was quite unnecessary ... Everyone should follow his or her own path. Concerning God I told him that He had been necessary before, in earlier times, to instill the fear of God into people. But now something else is needed – not glancing over your shoulder at the wrathful Almighty, but listening to your own soul.[66]

Pelagia, the sceptical nun whose calling appears for so long to be towards the rational, quasi-scientific field of detective work, gives it all up and follows a man who believes he is the son of God to a spiritual, otherworldly realm. This realm might, according to various veiled allusions through the novel, alternatively or additionally be that of death.[67] Either way, the novel thus becomes not a work of detective fiction but a demonstration of the ultimate need for a higher, spiritual faith to replace the inadequacy of merely earthly preoccupations.

Or does it? In precisely the type of circular interpretive movement encouraged by the labyrinthine spaces and narratives of postmodern fiction, the reader is implicitly warned about the instability of this, and indeed any, attribution of meaning. Alongside the cave, the other symbol that looms large at the end of the trilogy is the all-important red rooster. It is this creature, the reader has been informed on multiple occasions, which is the crucial factor facilitating access through time and space to another world. Moreover, its real significance, she has earlier been told, derives from the fact that it is an early Christian symbol – predating the cross – used to represent the son of God. Thus, when Pelagia disappears into the cave in the Garden of Gethsemane, the red rooster under her arm appears to be the most eloquent expression of her commitment to faith. However, there is no evidence of such a meaning in sources outside the novel to substantiate such a claim. It therefore becomes Akunin's final joke at the informed reader's expense. She is repeatedly encouraged to ascribe value and significance to – or, in other words, to place her own faith in – a symbol which, in the final reckoning, proves to be utterly self-referential and ironic. As such, it functions as the perfect image of the entirety of the reader's experience throughout Akunin's Pelagia trilogy – one of temptation ending in frustration.

Conclusion

The games that the three Pelagia novels play with the informed detective-genre reader's quest for knowledge suggest that they are best viewed as examples of postmodernist metaphysical detective fiction. The trilogy actively acknowledges that detective fiction is conventionally designed, by means of its illustration of a detective in search of the solution to a crime, to tempt the reader into mimicking such behaviour in her epistemological quest for interpretation and meaning. The particular mixture concocted by Akunin of historical setting and countless intertextual references invokes the image, and invites the participation, of an especially informed and model reader. And yet, simultaneously, by "deliberately, flamboyantly, ironically ... doubl[ing] its precursors,"[68] the trilogy reveals the membership of any such group of select readers to be ultimately illusory. While not perhaps as profoundly ironic and subversive as Eco's *The Name of the Rose*, Akunin's novels nevertheless pose progressively more serious questions about the meaning of history, the nature of knowledge, the act of reading, and the mysteries of being. Like all metaphysical detective stories, the Pelagia trilogy can be most accurately considered to be works that, in the words of Kevin J.H. Dettmar, referring to James Joyce's story "The Sisters," "[lure] the reader into a specially designed trap: the reader reads like a detective a tale which cautions against reading like a detective."[69] Therein lies its sophistication and fascination.

NOTES

This chapter is a slightly modified version of an article originally published as "The Temptation of the Reader: The Search for Meaning in Boris Akunin's *Pelagia* Trilogy," *Slavonic and East European Review* 94, no. 1 (2016), 29–56. I am very grateful to the journal for granting permission for the publication of this updated chapter in the present volume. I wish to extend my thanks to the Uppsala Centre for Russian and Eurasian Studies (UCRS, now IRES) at Uppsala University, Sweden for an invitation to spend time with them as a guest researcher in October 2011. This brief period proved vital in allowing me the space and time to develop many of the ideas contained in the present chapter. Julie Hansen, Margaret-Anne Hutton, Bettina Bildhauer, and Boris Dralyuk all read drafts of this paper and made invaluable suggestions for its improvement. I am also grateful to Stephen Norris and Elena Baraban for their guidance in adapting the original article for inclusion in the present volume.

 1 The series so far includes four novels, *Altyn-tolobas* (*Altyn Tolobas*, 2001), *Vneklassnoe chtenie* (*Recommended Reading*, 2002), *F.M.* (2006), and *Sokol i*

lastochka (*The Falcon and the Swallow*, 2009). *F.M.* is examined in this volume in the chapter by Zara Torlone. Boris Akunin is also the author of the series *Zhanry* (*Genres*), which to date covers: children's literature, the spy novel, the fantastic, and quest. In 2007, Akunin released the first in a new cycle, *Smert' na brudershaft* (*Brotherhood of Death*), in which each of the ten novellas showcases a different cinematic genre. A number of his detective novels have been made into television serials and / or films and he has also worked on a theatrical adaptation of *Azazel'*.

2 *Azazel'*, the first Erast Fandorin novel, takes place in 1876, while the last one, *Ne proshchaius'* (*Not Saying Goodbye*, 2018), is set in 1918–22. The Nicholas Fandorin novels are the only series to feature a parallel timeline: Nicholas is situated in contemporary Russia while his ancestors are active in the late eighteenth and early nineteenth centuries. The rather more vague temporal setting of the Pelagia trilogy, and its consequences, are an issue to be discussed in the main body of this essay. Leonid Yuzefovich is the other notable Russian crime writer whose novels are set in the historical past: the series he initiated in 2001 features a detective who is modelled on Ivan Putilin, Chief of Police in St. Petersburg from 1866 until 1892.

3 Akunin is a media star and influential cultural commentator who is frequently interviewed about his work. He has also been an outspoken critic of Russian politics since 2008 and has been described as a Russian dissident writer.

4 Dennis Porter expresses this idea effectively when he states: "The relationship between an author and his reader that obtains in detective stories is that of a problem setter to a problem solver." *The Pursuit of Crime: Art and Ideology in Detective Fiction* (New Haven, CT: Yale University Press, 1981), 85.

5 The idea that detective fiction plots represent a search for meaning or "truth" is shared by many different critics of the genre. See, for instance: G.K. Chesterton, "A Defence of Detective Stories" (1901) in Howard Haycraft, ed., *The Art of the Mystery Story: A Collection of Critical Essays* (New York: Grosset and Dunlap, 1946), 4; Martin Priestman, *Detective Fiction and Literature: The Figure in the Carpet* (Basingstoke, England: Macmillan, 1990), 50; Peter Hühn, "The Detective as Reader: Narrativity and Reading Concepts in Detective Fiction," *Modern Fiction Studies* 33, no. 3 (1987): 453. Tzvetan Todorov argues that the story of the crime in detective fiction is *"l'histoire d'une absence"* (the story of an absence); see "Typologie du roman policier," in *Poétique de la prose* (Paris: Seuil, 1971), 12. Srdjan Smajic defines the detective's quest as "an epistemological adventure in which sense perception leads to knowledge of the truth": *Ghost-Seers, Detectives and Spiritualists: Theories of Vision in Victorian Literature and Science* (Cambridge: Cambridge University Press, 2010), 71.

6 See Fish, "Literature in the Reader: Affective Stylistics," in *Reader Response Criticism: From Formalism to Post Structuralism*, ed. Jane Tompkins (Baltimore: The John Hopkins University Press, 1980), 87. Alternative, but similar, notions of this figure include the "implied reader" (Wayne Booth, Wolfgang Iser), the "model reader" (Umberto Eco), the "super-reader" (Michel Riffaterre), and the "ideal reader" (Jonathan Culler).

7 George N. Dove, "The Detection Formula and the Act of Reading," in Ronald G. Walker & June M. Frazer (eds.) *The Cunning Craft: Original Essays on Detective Fiction and Literary Theory*, ed. Ronald G. Walker and June M. Frazer (Macomb, IL: Western Illinois University Press, 1990), 29.

8 Historical crime fiction is a popular subgenre with numerous practitioners, including: Umberto Eco in *The Name of the Rose* (1980); Anne Perry in her two series featuring Thomas Pitt (1979–) and William Monk (1990–), both of which are set in the Victorian era; and C.J. Sansom in his novels starring the lawyer Matthew Shardlake (2003–), who lives in Tudor England. For a discussion of other authors of historical crime fiction as well as the various types of historical crime fiction and the subgenre's relationship to postmodernism, see John Scaggs, *Crime Fiction* (London: Routledge, 2005), 122–43.

9 Robin Winks, ed., *The Historian as Detective: Essays on Evidence* (New York: Harper and Row, 1968), xiii.

10 Paul Cobley, *Narrative* (London: Routledge, 2001), 30.

11 In anticipation of remarks to be made later in this chapter, it should be noted that this *roman à clef* technique is also one favoured by postmodern works as a means of indicating the ontological instability of the fictional world. See Brian McHale, *Constructing Postmodernism* (London: Routledge, 1992), 153.

12 Akunin is not averse, however, to including more anachronistic *roman à clef* clues. In *Pelagia and the Red Rooster,* the well-known philanthropist bankrolling the rebuilding and repopulation of Sodom is George Sairus, a clear reference to the contemporary billionaire financier George Soros.

13 The potential pitfalls inherent in this type of negative knowledge are illustrated by Elena V. Baraban, who mistakenly identifies the temporal setting of the *Pelagia* trilogy as the 1860s: "A Country Resembling Russia: The Use of History in Boris Akunin's Detective Novels," *The Slavic and East European Journal (SEEJ)* 48, no. 3 (2004): 400.

14 The term "focalizer" is taken from Susan Lanser, *The Narrative Act* (Princeton, NJ, 1981), where she defines it as follows: "A focalizer may be what is usually called a "point of view" character", or s/he may be a more nebulous and silent presence in the text. In both cases the focalizer is the presence – the recorder, the camera, the consciousness – through whose spatial, temporal and/or psychological position the textual events are perceived" (141). The three focalizers in *Pelagia and the Black Monk* are

Lentochkin, the chief of police from Zavolzhsk, Colonel Lagrange, and the public prosecutor, Matvei Bentsionovich Berdichevskii.

15 Hühn, "Detective as Reader," 459, 464.

16 Anzhela Iakubovksia, "Boris Akunin: 'Ia blagodaren svoim kritikam,'" *WomanHit*, 12 May 2014, http://www.womanhit.ru/stars/interview /657461-boris-akunin-ya-blagodaren-svoim-kritikam.html; my translation.

17 Elena Diakova, for example, considers the novels to be set in the "*sam[aia] dostoin[aia] epokh[a] russkoi istorii*" (the most worthy era in Russian history) and the location of the Pelagia novels, specifically, to be the "*ideal'no upravliaemyi rossiiskii gorod*" (ideally governed Russian town) of Zavolzhsk. Elena Diakova, "Boris Akunin kak uspeshnaia otrasl' rossiiskoi promyshlennosti," *Novaia gazeta* 45 (2 July 2001), 23, https://novayagazeta.ru /articles/2001/07/02/11382-boris-akunin-kak-uspeshnaya-otrasl -rossiyskoy-promyshlennosti.

18 See Elena Rabinovich, "Detektiv napominaet nam, chto pochem," *Kriticheskaia massa* 1 (2002), http://magazines.russ.ru/km/2002/1/erab.html.

19 S.E. Sweeney, "Locked Rooms: Detective Fiction, Narrative Theory, and Self-Reflexivity," in Walker and Frazer, *Cunning Craft*, 4.

20 The existence of such linearity and teleology in detective fiction is witnessed by Dennis Porter's statement that "detective fiction is preoccupied with the closing of the logico-temporal gap that separates the present of the discovery of crime from the past that prepared it." Porter, *Pursuit of Crime*, 29.

21 Boris Akunin, *Pelagiia i belyi bul'dog* (*Pelagia and the White Bulldog*), 121 / 190. References to all three novels are taken, in Russian, from the collected edition published in Moscow by Astrel' in 2010 and, in English, from the Andrew Bromfield translations, published by Phoenix in 2007, 2008, and 2009. The first page reference is to the Russian; the second to the English.

22 Linda Hutcheon, *The Poetics of Postmodernism: History, Theory, Fiction* (London: Routledge, 1988), 110. See also Fredric Jameson, *Postmodernism, or, the Cultural Logic of Late Capitalism* (Durham, NC: Duke University Press, 1991).

23 Baraban, "A Country Resembling Russia," 399–400.

24 Akunin, *Pelagiia i belyi bul'dog* (*Pelagia and the White Bulldog*), 15 / 16.

25 For instance, the narrator never reveals to the reader the details of the "great grief and terrible suffering" endured by Pelagia before becoming a nun. In *Pelagia and the White Bulldog*, the reader is told that Pelagia leaves Mitrofanii's aunt's house for some reason and "returned in a state of great thoughtfulness" (86 / 133); but she is never told what prompts this state of mind. And in *Pelagia and the Black Monk*, the narrator feigns ignorance about the true identity of Pelagia's alter ego, Polina Andreevna Lisitsyna, even though this has been unambiguously established in the first novel.

26 Consider, for example, the narrator in Gogol's "Nos" ("The Nose," 1836) who opens the story with the announcement that *"neobyknovenno stran-noe proisshestvie"* (an unusually strange occurrence) has taken place in St. Petersburg, but who then digresses to give the reader various irrelevant and nonsensical bits of information (including how one of the characters' surname has been lost) and does not immediately reveal what this occurrence actually is. Throughout the story, the narrator switches unpredictably between exercising his omniscient privilege and leaving the reader guessing about the correct interpretation of events because of his refusal to provide full information. See Nikolai Gogol, "Nos," in *Sobranie sochinenii v shesti tomakh*, vol. 3 (Moscow: Khudozhestvennaia literatura, 1959), 44.

27 Akunin, *Pelagiia i belyi bul'dog* (*Pelagia and the White Bulldog*), 113 / 177.

28 Hutcheon, *Poetics of Postmodernism*, 5.

29 Baraban, "A Country Resembling Russia," 411. Baraban is far from the only critic to note and discuss Akunin's use of intertextuality. See also: T. Prokhorova and V. Shamina, "'Dekorator' Akunina, ili fenomen kollektsionirovaniia v proze postmoderna," *Voprosy literatury* 5 (2008): 185–200; Sergei Dubin, "Detektiv, kotoryi ne boitsia byt' chtivom," *Novoe literaturnoe obozrenie* 21 (2000): 412–14.

30 S.E. Sweeney, "Purloined Letters: Poe, Doyle and Nabokov," *Russian Literature Triquarterly* 24 (1991): 216.

31 The allusions to Leskov, albeit in the Fandorin series, have previously been noted by Andrei Ranchin in "Romany B. Akunina i klassicheskaia traditsiia: povestvovanie v chetyrekh glavakh s preduvedomleniem, liricheskim otstupleniem i epilogom," *Novoe literaturnoe obozrenie* 67 (2004).

32 Hanna Charney, *The Detective Novel of Manners: Hedonism, Morality, and the Life of Reason* (London: Associated University Press, 1981), 1.

33 H.R. Jauss, *Towards an Aesthetics of Reception*, trans. T. Bahti (Minneapolis, MN: University of Minnesota Press, 1982), 23. Jauss explains: "The new text evokes for the reader (listener) the horizon of expectations and rules familiar from earlier texts, which are then varied, corrected, altered, or even just reproduced."

34 The genteel rural setting of Akunin's trilogy calls to mind Agatha Christie's Miss Marple novels, as does Pelagia's penchant for knitting, a pastime shared by her English predecessor.

35 Akunin complicates this potential interpretation by giving the director of the psychiatric hospital in *Pelagia and the Black Monk* the name Korovin. This is an obvious mutation of Chekhov's character's name, which also implies an ironic undermining by its relationship to the Russian word *"korova"* (cow).

36 The title of Alena Solntseva's article in *Vremia* in December 2000, "Massovaia literatura mozhet byt' vozvyshennoi," is a clear expression of this view. See *Vremia* 182 (6 December 2000), http://www.vremya.ru/print/4196.html.

37 Chesterton, "A Defence,'" 4.

38 Evidence of the persistence of this division is provided by Joel Black,
for instance, who refers to the role played by one "low" work and one
"high" work in the introduction of the term "detective" in Britain in
the nineteenth century. See *The Aesthetics of Murder: A Study in Romantic
Literature and Contemporary Culture* (Baltimore: The John Hopkins
University Press, 1991), 42.

39 McHale, *Constructing Postmodernism*, 164.

40 I am grateful to Philip Ross Bullock for initially suggesting this potential
interpretation of Akunin's intertextuality.

41 Stephen Lovell, *The Russian Reading Revolution: Print Culture in the Soviet
and Post-Soviet Eras* (London: Palgrave Macmillan, 2000), 21.

42 In a 2011 interview with *Rossiiskaia gazeta*, republished in *Daily Telegraph*,
Akunin notes that the reader has "surpassed" his "boldest expectations"
by reading his novels in such numbers. He also argues that the popularity
of the Erast Fandorin novels can be ascribed, in part, to the reader's desire to be more like his literary hero and to Fandorin's positive attributes:
"I think Russia would be a much better place if more people were like
Fandorin." See Alena Tveritina, "Russian Literature: Interview with Boris
Akunin," *Telegraph*, 6 April, 2011, http://www.telegraph.co.uk/sponsored
/rbth/culture/8432287/Russian-literature-Interview-with-Boris-Akunin
.html, accessed 17 October 2014.

43 Lovell, *Russian Reading Revolution*, 16.

44 In *After the Future: The Paradoxes of Postmodernism and Contemporary Russian
Culture* (Amherst, MA: The Massachusetts University Press, 1995), 205,
Mikhail Epstein writes: "These attempts to homogenize Soviet society
created a new culture of mediocrity, which was equally far from both
the upper and lower levels of a highly stratified Western culture. In the
Soviet Union, this middling level was established even earlier than in
the West, and the levelling process provided the ground for postmodern
development."

45 The history of crime / detective fiction in Russia since its inception in the
early 1860s is relatively complex. The genre enjoyed considerable popularity in the late imperial era with many works becoming the most widely
read publications of their respective years. Under Stalin, however, with
the closure of private publishing houses that had printed such works, and
with the advent of Socialist Realism as the state-approved literary genre,
crime fiction effectively disappeared from the Soviet literary landscape. It
enjoyed something of a revival during the Thaw with the publication of
works such as Iuliian Semenov's *Petrovka 38* (1965). In the post-Soviet era,
liberalization in the literary marketplace allowed crime fiction to flourish
once again, with publishing houses able to count on considerable profits
generated by the genre thanks to the voracious appetite of the reading

public for such works. However, the rush towards financial reward by both individual authors and publishing companies has arguably compromised aesthetic standards, with many works appearing to be derivative and formulaic. The work of Akunin distinguishes itself, in terms of both nature and quality, from the detective series published by authors such as Daria Dontsova and Aleksandra Marinina.

46 Sofya Khagi, "Boris Akunin and Retro Mode in Contemporary Russian Culture," *Toronto Slavic Quarterly* 13 (2005), http://sites.utoronto.ca/tsq/13/khagi13.shtml.

47 Jameson, *Postmodernism*, 20.

48 In *Mertvye dushi* (*Dead Souls*, 1842), for example, Gogol's narrator occasionally encourages a belief in the simultaneity of the time of his act of narration and the time of the action in the diegesis that does not, of course, exist. In chapter 2 of the novel, for instance, the narrator states that he will use the time during which Chichikov and Manilov walk to the dining room to describe the latter character.

49 Akunin, *Pelagiia i belyi bul'dog* (*Pelagia and the White Bulldog*), 23 / 29.

50 Ibid., 138 / 217.

51 Ibid., 17 / 20.

52 Ibid., 17 / 20–1.

53 Ibid., 119 / 187.

54 A cave does feature in the second novel of the trilogy but is not as obviously linked to the idea of elusive meaning. In *Pelagia and the Black Monk*, the heroine enters the cave on Outskirts Island in pursuit of Lentochkin, who is collecting precious metal from the meteorite that has fallen into it. With its walls lined with the skeletons of monks who have previously lived and died there, the cave shares features with the ossuary in Eco's *The Name of the Rose*, which links the church with the Aedificium. It is a chamber of seemingly fantastical dimensions but does not pose the same ontological questions as the one described in the trilogy's final novel.

55 Akunin, *Pelagiia i krasnyi petukh* (*Pelagia and the Red Rooster*), 589 / 103.

56 In yet another potential intertextual reference, the phrase "metaphysical detective story" was coined by Howard Haycraft in 1941 to describe the plotting and intentions of G.K. Chesterton's Father Brown series. In terms that can be applied to Akunin's novel, Jeanne C. Ewert argues that "metaphysical detective fiction abounds with examples of other, unfamiliar universes and of the uneasiness produced when boundaries between universes are violated." "'A Thousand Other Mysteries': Metaphysical Detection, Ontological Quests," in *Detecting Texts: The Metaphysical Detective Story from Poe to Postmodernism*, ed. Patricia Merivale and Susan Sweeny (Philadelphia: University of Pennsylvania Press, 1999), 189.

57 Akunin, *Pelagiia i krasnyi petukh* (*Pelagia and the Red Rooster*), 585 / 98.

58 The intertextual reference to Eco is strengthened by the fact that, upon returning to Zavolzhsk, she reads a treatise on caves from Mitrofanii's library authored by Adalbert, whose other works were destroyed during a fire in a monastery – the fate that befalls the library in *The Name of the Rose*. Umberto Eco, *The Name of the Rose*, trans. William Weaver (San Diego, CA: Harcourt Brace Jovanovich, 1993).

59 McHale suggests that spaces such as labyrinths (Eco), libraries (Eco and Borges) and law courts (Kafka) are "typical of an entire postmodernist topology"; *Constructing Postmodernism*, 157. Charles Jencks argues that postmodern space "suspends normal categories of time and space, social and rational categories which are built up in everyday architecture and behaviour, to become 'irrational' or quite literally impossible to figure out." *The Language of Post-Modern Architecture* (New York: Rizzoli, 1984), 124.

60 Akunin, *Pelagiia i belyi bul'dog* (*Pelagia and the White Bulldog*), 15 / 16.

61 Ibid., 15 / 17.

62 Akunin, *Pelagiia i krasnyi petukh* (*Pelagia and the Red Rooster*), 522 / 23.

63 Ibid., 554–5 / 61–2.

64 Ibid., 721 / 260–1.

65 Ibid., 807 / 361.

66 Ibid., 842 / 405.

67 For example, the treatise on caves which Pelagia reads mentions "special caves" which connect "the fleshly world from the non-fleshly world and every soul passes through them twice: when it enters into flesh and when it leaves the flesh after death"; *Pelagiia i krasnyi petukh* (*Pelagia and the Red Rooster*), 598 / 114. Furthermore, Pelagia belatedly realizes that the heart-felt prayer she recites while waiting for Manuila is that "for the transition from the earthly life to the Eternal Dwelling" (ibid., 807 / 361).

68 Ewert, "A Thousand Other Mysteries," 179.

69 Kevin J.H. Dettmar, "From Interpretation to 'Intrepidation': Joyce's 'The Sisters' as a Precursor of the Postmodern Mystery," in Walker and Frazer, *Cunning Craft*, 156.

6 "A Little Theory": Boris Akunin's "Crime and Punishment"

ZARA M. TORLONE

In one of his public appearances, Grigorii Chkhartishvili (aka Boris Akunin) drew a distinction between two different ways Russian writers are received and perceived: one at home and one in the West.[1] He lamented that in the West there is always a lingering question looming over a visiting Russian writer: "Are you the next Tolstoy?" One, of course, can replace Tolstoy with another name that inevitably also occurs in the same context, that of Dostoevsky. In the national literature that gave the world these two writers, any novelist's worth is measured against them, and that is an impossible, if not to say a misguided, comparison. Akunin never claimed to be someone he knew he was not. Russian literature has always maintained a certain hierarchy: genres were divided into high and low, if not by the writers themselves then at least by their readership, in the best Aristotelean tradition. In that hierarchy, it is unclear where exactly the novel belongs, due to its "heterodox" forms,[2] but one point remains certain: Akunin has never thought of himself as the next literary genius, preferring to call himself a "belletrist," with its somewhat self-deprecating connotation. Elena Baraban adeptly summarized the controversy surrounding the quality of Akunin's literary oeuvre.[3] Blaming the writer for distorting Russian imperial history, xenophobia, Russophobia, and lack of "clear priority to any one view,"[4] Akunin's critics displayed uncertainty about his place in the highbrow literary tradition, ultimately entirely overlooking the changes in literary tastes, with the modern Russian reading public looking for literature that can entertain rather than always pose eternal philosophical questions – or perhaps even do both. This chapter does not aim to elaborate again on Akunin's worth as a writer, but rather offers a taste of one of Akunin's highly allusive novels, *F.M.*, in which Dostoevsky's existential contemplations become artfully and seamlessly woven into the fabric of a captivating mystery thriller. For

Akunin, Dostoevsky's novel presented an opportunity for the archetypal plot to be developed into the form of a bestseller appealing to a consumer of a pop culture. Akunin himself has always claimed that his "borrowing" from classic Russian literature in the creation of postmodernist mystery catered to the evolved tastes of Russian readers.[5]

The title of the novel stands for Fedor Mikhailovich (Dostoevsky), and thus immediately introduces high expectations. What prompts Akunin to "rewrite" the *sancta sanctorum* of the Russian classics, *Crime and Punishment* (1866), offering another version of it within his modern mystery novel? The answer seems to be obvious: in recent years Dostoevsky underwent a certain revival in Russia and has in fact become a darling of popular culture. Films and television series were developed based on his works: *Down House* (2001, dir. Roman Kachanov; 2002, dir. Vladimir Bortko), *Demons* (2014, dir. Vladimir Khotinenko), and *Brothers Karamazov* (first season made in 2008, dir. Iurii Moroz). There is a film, *Letter to a Husband* (2010, dir. Igor Nurislamov), about Anna Dostoevskaia (Snitkina), Dostoevsky's second and long-suffering wife, who as a young twenty-year-old woman married the forty-five-year-old troubled writer in an attempt to bring order and happiness to his life. For Akunin it was an opportunity to bring together his unabashed love for highbrow Dostoevsky with his strong dislike for popular mass culture.[6] The minotaur that emerged is *F.M.*

Akunin's interest in "revising" Dostoevsky is already apparent in his earlier works. In his novel *Pelagia and the White Bulldog* (*Pelagiia i belyi bul'dog*), one of the novel's characters, Mitrofanii, states:

> I think that the author [Dostoevsky] makes his task too easy when he forces the prideful Raskolnikov not only to kill the repulsive money lending hag, but also her mellow and innocent sister. Mr. Dostoevsky, it seems, got scared that the reader would not wish to charge the criminal only with the death of the moneylender: for why pity such a beastly creature? But God has no beastly creatures, he loves everyone equally. But if the writer were able to show the indignity of homicide using an example of the old hag alone – that is all together a different matter.[7]

Akunin also explains the main direction of his revision of Dostoevsky's canonical novel: "I do not like Raskolnikov, Sonia Marmeladova makes me yawn, but the detective, Porfirii Petrovich, provokes my great interest. Dostoevsky reports little about him, I want more, and Porfirii is my main hero."[8] Porfirii Petrovich, Dostoevsky's astute detective, indeed emerges as a central figure in Akunin's version, marginalizing even Rodion Raskolnikov, Dostoevsky's hapless student turned murderer.

In the following pages, I would like to offer two translated excerpts of *F.M.*, each accompanied by a brief interpretation, in order to illuminate Akunin's authorial intent and his masterful intertext.[9] A short overview of the plot of the novel will clarify its constituent parts and facilitate the appreciation of Akunin's virtuoso "playing with Dostoevsky," or in some instances even "playing Dostoevsky."

Akunin's fabricated "version" of *Crime and Punishment* as it comes out in *F.M.* was inspired by the fact that the novel was written at the request of the publisher, F.T. Stellovskii, to whom Dostoevsky owed money. Dostoevsky was in need of money because of his gambling problem, and he signed a rather short-sighted contract with Stellovskii.[10] Accordinging to their agreement, the writer sold the publication of all of his works in three volumes for a mere 3,000 rubles. In addition, he promised to write a new novel of at least ten print pages in length.[11] This contract clearly inspired the thesis of Akunin's novel. Stellovskii, according to Akunin, commissioned from Dostoevsky a mystery novel in which the protagonist was supposed to be the detective, Porfirii Petrovich Fedorin – the character who most interested Akunin in the novel, to such a degree that Akunin makes him an ancestor of his most famous detective, Erast Fandorin.

Akunin's *F.M.* consists of two texts: the main part of the novel, set in modern times, and the fragmented text of "Teoriika" – the supposed first version of Dostoevsky's *Crime and Punishment*. Both parts are detective stories. In the central narrative, which takes place in today's Moscow, Nicholas Fandorin, the descendant of Akunin's well-known detective Erast Fandorin, is looking for the lost (or stolen) parts of the first version of Dostoevsky's famous novel. In the version that he seeks, Porfirii Petrovich (supposedly an ancestor of both Erast and Nicholas), familiar from Dostoevsky's novel, is also trying to solve the mystery of several homicides in St. Petersburg. Both texts overlap by creating two different but complementary time and space frames, one occurring in Moscow at the beginning of the twenty-first century, the other in St. Petersburg in the second half of the nineteenth century.

The text-within-a-text is, of course, a familiar literary device to a Russian reader raised on *Master and Margarita*. The only difference in *F.M.* is that Akunin ascribes the inserted text not to a fictional character but to the greatest Russian writer, whose style and diction are highly recognizable to every even moderately literate Russian reader.

The excerpts of Akunin's *F.M.* translated here are illustrative of each of the plot lines in the novel and of Akunin's unique ability to manipulate the Russian language. The first excerpt reveals the character and intentions of Arkadii Sergeevich Sivukha (whose unfortunate name means "hooch" in Russian), the *deputat* of the Russian Duma, a self-made man with vast wealth amassed during the turbulent nineties who explains himself to Nicholas Fandorin. Sivukha is the driving force (financial and otherwise) behind the quest for Dostoevsky's lost novel. Wishing to be remembered as someone who brought back to the Russian people the lost work of their national genius, Sivukha's character and his impassioned soliloquy "On a Free Mason" ("*Pro vol'nogo kamenshchika*") enhance our understanding of the rise of the so-called *novye russkie* (the New Russians) in the nineties.

On a Free Mason[12]

How do I resemble the historical freemasons, Nikolai Aleksandrovich? Like them, I also value only two things: freedom and creativity. I had that slogan during my pre-election campaign on every poster and flyer. I always dreamt of being independent from everybody and of always building, creating. But nonetheless I always depended on those who surrounded me and I always built not what I wanted, but some sort of nonsense.

Do you know that in early childhood when a human character is formed, the best type of training is when you have some sort of a handicap,[13] and it does not even matter whether that handicap is real or imaginary? That is when you either break under its pressure, or, on the contrary, overcome the deficiency and then nothing scares you again. All of these stories are textbook stuff: blubbering Demosthenes, who learns to speak with the pebbles in his mouth, becomes a great orator. Or that athlete with a sick spine, who starts as an invalid and becomes the strongest man on earth. Et cetera, et cetera. In my case the handicap was ludicrous. Well, it seems that way now, but in my childhood, I thought that the fate was awfully unfair to me. One cannot live in the world with the last name "Sivukha"![14]

If you do have this name, then you have to plan to either live your life as some sort of a silly jester, or you turn your stupid name into what they call now a "brand." In order for the name "Sivukha" to begin to sound proudly, I had to put some real effort into it. But thankfully I had some predecessors.

The last name "Pushkin" also caused his contemporaries much amusement, the future sun of Russian poetry was teased as both "Chushkin" and "Khriushkin."[15] And Tolstoy Lev, isn't that funny? I read that his army buddies called him the "Skinny Tiger."[16] Or take the company "Dunhill," which made this smoking pipe. It sounds so super-aristocratic, but nobody even remembers that the name came from "Dunghill," "the manure pile."

I, Nikolai Aleksandrovich, in my early, gentle years was a dreamy and secretive lad. When I first read about the freemasons, I had a vision. I had in fact a very clear picture. As if I am standing on the top of a very high wall of some half-finished building, with a trowel in my hand. Beneath me is a giant city, the wind blows through my hair, and there is nobody around and I am laying the bricks and singing a song about builders of high-rises. Funny? Forty years and then some have passed since then, but nothing has changed. I stand high up on the wall with the trowel. Only there is no hair blowing in the wind.

Arkadii Sergeevich patted his either cleanly shaved or merely bald head and laughed. Throughout his monologue he was looking directly into the eyes of his interlocutor, and Nika [Nicholas Fandorin] almost physically felt that the *deputat* was doing his magic, weaving his verbal wizardry as if trying to pick up a girl. That is the eternal trick of the classic talkers – they engulf you with an intimate tone, pack you in the web of words. Well then, let him weave his web. The best way to learn about a client is to let him talk about his most beloved subject: himself.

On a Certain Force

But I always knew: before you earn the title of a free master, you have to endure a long tedious time in the role of an apprentice. But what does that mean? To live according to the regulations and rules of your workshop. I always lived like that, biding my time.

Everybody joined the Communist Party – so did I. Everybody left the Communist Party – I also left. Everyone hurried to sell computers – here I come. Everybody switched to the gas pipeline and investment portfolios – Sivukha was the first. Everyone is a thug – and I am a thug. Everyone stopped being a thug – I am the epitome of law-abiding. Everyone is a deputat – I am a deputat too. And please note, always from the ruling party, regardless of its name.

And I always did it better than the others of my kind. Because for them the money – or some lousy mandate – is the goal of life, but for me it is the means. Who are they? Dung beetles, but I am a free mason. When I become a master – I will build such things, the whole world will exhale. That is why my fate guards me, does not allow any injury.

I am approaching my main point here. I talked about this to very few people, but I will tell you.

Recently I began to suspect that everything is not that simple in my life. That I have some special mission that I need to fulfil. And everybody who stands in my way will not do well. Do not look at me like I am a psycho. I am not off my rocker. There is just some Force, and it is on my side. It is not a delirium – those are facts.

"Are you talking about God the Lord, is that it?" interrupted Nika, thinking: What times do we live in, when every hustler always imagines himself to be chosen by Providence?

Sivukha frowned. "I do not know. It is not for me to decide. But I will cite for you a couple of facts and you can come to your own conclusions."

The *deputat* looked back at his son, but he was not listening – busy shooting some extraterrestrial monsters on the screen, frantically repeating: "Yeeess! Yeess!" The bodyguard Igor was doodling something in the magazine – perhaps solving the crossword puzzle.

On a Certain Force (*Continuation [of Sivukha's monologue]*)

To start with, here is a story for you, which happened to me ten years ago, at the peak of the thug era. I had my own thug, his name was Shika. "A specialist in problem solving" – that is how it was called. I was paying Shika a percentage of my profits, and he, well ... he solved problems. I will not tell which ones exactly in order not to digress. No, really, I omit the details only to save time, I have nothing to fear. Not that I am crystal pure in the face of the law (among us, the 90s gold seekers, nobody is pure) – but I happen to belong to the ruling party; nobody will be digging into my past. Of course, all kinds of things happened, but my past pranks are much less interesting than what I am about to tell you.

In short, Shika and I had a conflict due to a misunderstanding. I assumed that he worked for me and received a compensation for his service, and he, as it came out, imagined that I was working for him and was paying him a toll. That is why we argued. And Shika, in my house, at my dining table, began to threaten me. He spat in a glass of wine, spilled it on the tablecloth. He loved dramatic effects and had a propensity for ornate expression. "I," – he was saying –"will destroy you, make you a zero. You will disappear without a trace, as if you never existed. You just wait." And he left slamming the door.

To be completely honest, I got quite scared – my "business partner" and his gang's reputation was serious. I sent Olezhka, my son, together with Igor to the dacha of my college friend, although I had not seen him for twelve years. I myself headed hastily to Shremetievo – and then to Czechia. From there, in order to muddle my trace, I took a car to Venice, rented a yacht, and sailed to the Greek islands.

I called Igor from Rhodes. Asked how things are. And Igor goes: "Come back, everything is fine."

Shika disappeared. Without a trace. Became a zero himself. Where to he vanished, why – to this day it is a riddle. And Shika's band got scattered.

I, as they say, crossed myself, and thought I got lucky. I kept living my life. And back then I never thought about The Force.

But incidents like that kept recurring. And that is when one has to be a total idiot not to start thinking.

For example, here is a plot. In 1998 it was, during the default. Right before 17 August I conducted some currency conversion. I exchanged a large sum in rubles for dollars, at the rate of six to one. And bam – all of a sudden one could not conduct an exchange even eighteen to one. The partner, who took my rubles, got very upset. And he was not just anyone, he was a deputy minister. Back then the high officials simply combined their service to the state with business; well, the other way around: the business with the state service. Now, of course, they are doing the same but not quite so brazenly. And the deputy minister started demanding his dollars back. I refused – what the hell? He started pestering me, and that is not child's play: tax audits, "costume shows" – that is when the police break into the office, force all the staff down on the floor face down, and turn everything upside down. And then all other sorts of joys. The bastard went as far as to initiate a criminal prosecution regarding some small episode in which, by the way, he directly participated himself. I called him, asking, "What are you, creep, doing?" Don't you believe in God, you who constantly drags himself around holy places? God will punish you for such lawlessness. "Give me back my dough," he goes, "then the prosecution will stop." At that time I did not have my deputat's mandate. So right after another interrogation they handcuffed me and off I go to Matrosskaia Tishina.[17] I sat there for three days – and then all of a sudden, they let me go. It comes out that my enemy was punished by God. Literally. That deputy minister was indeed extremely devout. During the day, he took bribes with abandon, abused his post like there was no tomorrow, but in the evening, he wore out his knees genuflecting in front of the crucifix. He had a special kind of crucifix, it was brought to him from the Urals as a valuable gift; it was made of malachite, and the Saviour was cut out of jasper. It weighed probably twenty kilos, if not thirty. And so, two days after my arrest, while he was praying, the crucifix somehow jumped off the top hook and hit him right on the top of his head. He fell to his death right away. How is that?

I am only telling you about the most dramatic of the events, but there were others. It was not once or twice that my freemason God has saved me. The moment I have a serious enemy who starts creating problems – that is it, he is gone. Some, like Shika, just disappeared, and that was it. One hundred per cent mysticism. Others had even more curious fates.

The last time the miracle happened was not long ago, in May. There were additional elections in the county under my mandate. Perhaps you remember – it made the newspapers. I had only one dangerous rival. By all accounts, I should have lost about five or ten per cent to him.

On the ninth, on Victory Day, he was sailing on his yacht at the Istra Reservoir. Please note, he was alone. And all of a sudden, his yacht becomes engulfed in fire. It was a good yacht, vintage, made from old English wood. First the fire spread to the sail, then to the deckhouse. My rival barely made it into the water. He did not drown, he had a safety vest, but of course it was only May, so the water temperature was no more than eight degrees Celsius. By the time they fished him out, thirty minutes had passed. He froze all to hell, no more elections for him. To this day he is moving around in a wheel chair, all crooked. But I was not too surprised. I knew: my freemason Force will come to the rescue. Do not get in the way of a free mason.

So how do you like my story?

Through this impassioned monologue we fully come to appreciate the character of Sivukha and the driving force behind his unbridled and, as it turns out later, dangerous ambitions. Sivukha has received little attention in critical literature, overshadowed perhaps by Nicholas Fandorin and even more so by Porfirii Petrovich. However, he presents a rather noteworthy figure, not only because he is crucial for the plot of the novel, but also because he is supposed to be the cliché of the Russian "brave new world." He is not an ordinary nouveau riche, although by his own admission he was rather adaptable to the constantly changing circumstances of post-Soviet reality. What is rather striking about both his character and his speech is the masterful combination of "high" and "low."

He is by all means what the Russians would call *"iz griazi v kniazi"* (roughly translated as "from rags to riches" but literally meaning "from dirt to dukes"), with a definite contemptuous connotation. The aristocratic Fandorin views him with disdain, despite his enormous ill-begotten wealth. At the same time, and in the best Dostoevskian tradition, there is more to this chameleonic money- and opportunity-grabbing thug. Sivukha's speech has the quality of a truly Russian *ispoved'*, or confession, and an almost religious awe for the supernatural power that supposedly guards him.

He firmly believes that he is in fact protected by some higher almighty "Force" (*Sila*), which he adamantly refuses to call God or Providence, or other known appellations, dismissing Fandorin's feeble attempts to put a familiar name on it. He believes in a higher power that chose him because he wants to see himself as a benefactor of his nation, even of humanity as a whole, as he strives to bring back to the masses the lost novel of the national literary genius. In this first encounter with him, however, he appears as a complex individual even to Fandorin, and wants to be seen as driven by selfless altruism and a sense of duty to his compatriots. From Sivukha's despair over his unfortunate name to his childhood dream of becoming a builder on top of the world, to the deputy's mandate (*deputatskii mandat*), Arkadii Sergeevich wants to strip himself of the repulsive garment of a "new Russian" and appear as a representative of a new generation of philanthropists whose cultural contributions will shape the legacy of the whole nation (as he claims: "Arkadii Sivukha returns to his fatherland and the world culture an unknown creation of the classic ... The funny name 'Sivukha' will be firmly tied to a great name, 'Dostoevsky'").[18] Of course, later in the novel it is revealed (spoiler alert!) that he had rather devious and lucrative ulterior motives and that "The Force" was none other than his murderous and developmentally challenged son Oleg. The selflessness is turned into self-serving arrogance, the altruistic high aspirations become nothing but lawless and vainglorious pursuit of fame. All of the crimes, puzzles, and misunderstandings connected with the quest for Dostoevsky's "lost" novel are resolved by the end of Akunin's novel: Sivukha is also revealed to be the legal heir to Stellovskii, Dostoevsky's venal publisher, and thus holds an inalienable legal right to the "lost version."

The language of Sivukha's "confession" is also rather revealing, especially for someone who (like me) has not lived in Russia since the nineties. The language is tremendously enriched (or impoverished, depending on how one looks at such linguistic developments) with numerous English neologisms, the product of the "free economy" era (*defolt* – "default"; *konvertatsiia* – "conversion"). Furthermore, Sivukha is prone to demonstrating that he is not a stranger to history and culture, comparing himself with Demosthenes and even Pushkin and regaling Fandorin with constant references to freemasons and their virtues and values, which in his presentation seem rather limited. Interestingly enough, however, Sivikha's speech patterns also reveal to Fandorin and to us, the readers, his low pedigree. His language is simple, paratactic; he uses a lot of colloquial patterns (although never curses), street phrases (*choknutyi* – "off his rocker"; *shibko* – "swiftly"), *chto zh ty, gad, delaesh'?* – "what are you, creep, doing?"). His language is clearly juxtaposed with Fandorin's "intelligentsia" usage, void of similar earthy phrases and preserved in its pure literary form. Fandorin is a character linked with the language of Dostoevsky's era, cultured, sophisticated, full of subordinate sentences, while Sivukha is firmly rooted in the new world of profit and commerce and his own unimpressive heritage, where the great writer's work is sought not for aesthetic reasons but for lucrative ones and where Fandorin looks as outdated as his literary detective predecessor, Porfirii Petrovich, would have: a remnant of a bygone era. The chasm that separates Fandorin and Sivukha is infinitely larger than one that separates Fandorin from Porfirii Petrovich, his legendary ancestor. But the confrontation between Nicholas Fandorin and Sivukha serves as an illuminating foil for the next excerpt from *F.M.*

This excerpt, *Teoriika* ("Little Theory"), is part of the finale of Dostoevsky's unfinished "alternative version" of *Crime and Punishment* and it contains the showdown between Porfirii Petrovich Fedorin and Arkadii Svidrigailov, who in this version of the novel is not only the familiar villain of Dostoevsky's novel but also the serial killer.

Chapter 15: A Russian Conversation[19]

The pain was so great that Porfirii Petrovich not only could not think of anything for a few moments, but shut his eyes and went as if deaf. That is why he could not see the horrible thing that happened. He only felt a slight movement of the air, and then something soft and heavy crashed to his feet.

The police commissioner, still crouching, opened his eyes. Zametov [his deputy] was lying right near him, face down, and from the top of his head, seeping through the carefully coiffed crown of his hair, dark blood was pouring, already forming a rapid trickle between boards.

"I did not want this." Porfirii Petrovich heard the voice that came from somewhere far. "He did cock the trigger at me, believe it or not."

The bones on Porfirii Petrovich's hand were broken, that much the court counsellor felt, but the pain lost its sharp edge, replaced instead by a strange numbness. The commissioner straightened up and looked at the horrible man, who was waving his bloody cane.

"I pity the boy,"[20] ruefully pronounced Svidrigailov, and added something extremely strange: "That definitely goes for me into minus."

"Murderer!" whispered Porfirii Petrovich, because he could think of nothing else to say, confused by the speed of the events that had just transpired. He was also sure that the sphinx on Svidrigailov's cane would not crash onto his own head.

"That is by all means an indisputable assertion." Svidrigailov laughed rather stiffly. "Perhaps you are even thinking that I will do the same to you? Not so. I should not have killed the lad either. It was the instinct of self-preservation that misled me. Indeed, I should have let him shoot."

He skillfully twisted his cane with two fingers and sat on the chair, where Luzhin had only recently sat. He pushed aside the stack of money with his hands covered with rings, leaned on his elbow, and yawned.

"I do not understand you ..." the commissioner said with difficulty, understanding only one thing – that his life for some reason was not quite over this minute.

"And who are you? A policeman?" The criminal was contemplating him with curiosity. "I, for example, am Svidrigailov, Arkadii Ivanovich, retired second lieutenant and a landlord from Riazan'. And what is your name?"

"Fedorin, Porfirii Petrovich," answered the court counsellor, and, in addition, stupidly bowed, as if this was an ordinary acquaintance, "I am the police commissioner for the Kazan' district."

"So you are in charge of solving the murders? Very smart that you staked me out here, very smart. I did not expect that. Perhaps you are very intelligent."

The landlord from Riazan' yawned again. It cannot be that he was bored, the commissioner had a passing thought, what kind of boredom can there be with two corpses here? Perhaps it is nervous yawning, a rather well-known medical fact.

"No, dear sir, I am not intelligent at all, I am, on the contrary, a real fool," said Porfirii Petrovich bitterly, because that was the honest truth.

But Arkadii Ivanovich did not quite understand him. "Are you referring to the fact that you acted too self-assured, when only two of you came here? But how would you know that I am such a person?" He showed his hairy fist, which was the size of an infant's head. "You would be fine arresting just an ordinary person with your weapons. But I am as strong as a bear. By the way, when I was young, I liked, when I was drunk, to fight with a bear and I would wrestle him down without much effort. In my army regiment, I had a nickname: 'Toptygin.'[21] It is indeed the truth: I am naturally gifted, very generously. I did put that gift to use but not in a good way. Why are you still standing?" Svidrigailov suddenly remembered. "There is no truth in standing. Take a seat."

He wanted to move another chair forwards but Porfirii Petrovich anticipated him. "That is all right. I can handle this." He sat a little bit farther in such a way that he could be close to the fallen revolver. The distance was only two steps. He could not move any closer without attracting attention.

"Am I allowed to ask what you intend to do now?" the court counsellor asked, thinking at that moment only about procrastinating.

"With you?" Svidrigailov was surprised, as if this question had not yet crossed his mind. "Well, I honestly do not know. I am also not quite sure about myself. That is, I do intend to undertake a journey, but am still indecisive about the details. Let's talk in the meanwhile. It has been a long time since I had a decent talk, especially with a clever man. Let me bind your hurt hand, so that it does not bother you."

He took out a handkerchief and very skillfully, almost without causing Porfirii Petrovich any suffering, bound his wrist. Then he shook his head:

"The bones are shattered. In one hour or so it will start hurting a lot. There is lead poured into the handle of my cane. I did that already in the village in order to strengthen my hand. I never thought it would be used for anything else." Arkadii Ivanovich moistened the napkin from a pitcher of water and wiped the bloodied sphinx. "Mysterious animal. Poses questions for humans, and if you cannot answer then off you go to the realm of Hades."

He loosened his tie and constructed something resembling a sling, into which with great care he placed the commissioner's hand. "That is fine. And now you and I will have a nice, unhurried talk, the night is still young. Because why couldn't intelligent people have a heart to heart, even amid this madhouse?" He nodded towards the two corpses. "And especially amid this madhouse. The whole of Russia is just that."

"You think so?" Porfirii Petrovich turned towards him, expressing great interest with all his appearance, but in reality getting closer to his gun.

If only he could distract this lover of "good conversation" by talking, he thought, and then somehow contrive a plan; it would not be enough to grab the revolver, he had to jump towards the wall before Svidrigailov would swing with his sphinx. "To be frank, I was not staking you out here" – he started the small talk.

"Then whom were you staking?"

"The student, Raskolnikov, Rodion Romanovich."

Svidrigailov seemed to be terribly intrigued by that announcement. "Raskolnikov? But, I beg you, why?"

"Well, here is the thing" – Porfirii Petrovich gave an embarrassed smile – "I imagined that those murders were not ordinary, not out of greed or revenge, but ... How can I express it? A crime of a new kind in accordance with the general crisis of religion and our epoch's influences. Like a fool, I assumed that there should be some necessary theory behind all this. And, unfortunately, here came along Rodion Romanych. He, in fact, does have one little theory, very curious. About humankind. Like, it is rather alright to kill all kinds of ordinary, good-for-nothing, little people, if, of course, it is for the common good and if the murderer himself is an extraordinary man. That is one thing. Another is that during the investigation the student was constantly in my way. He would pop up from this side and that side. And I did not even think of you at all ..."

It seems like it worked. The estate owner was listening with enormous interest, and he pushed his horrible cane into the floor and leaned his chin against the sphinx. What eyes, thought Porfirii Petrovich. He, this Arkadii Ivanovich, is the real sphinx: he poses a riddle and you can't dare not solve it.

"What did you do?" grinned Svidrigailov. "A clever man, and by all accounts experienced, you should read better into the souls. How can Rodion Romanovich be a murderer? Murder is a serious matter, and he only has fantasies. Most importantly, his heart is full of pity, unlike mine. Do you think that it is easy to strike a person on the head, even the lousiest one, with an axe or with this sphinx? Our soul lives in our head. Not here, as the poets figuratively declare" – he touched his chest – "but here, under the bones of the skull. You don't think so?"

Porfirii Petrovich, being a man of practical mindset, considered the question about the location of the soul a scholastic one, and did not volunteer an opinion.

"No," continued Arkadii Ivanovich, "for murder one needs a brute man, a man of action, an *arithmetical* [emphasis Akunin's] man. So you got duped with Rodion Romanovich. But you did guess correctly about a theory. I have a little theory, of my own invention. I do not strive to enrich mankind with it, and it is dangerous, but I approved it for myself and put it to use."

The counsellor already understood that he did not need to distract his interlocutor with talk, just not interrupt his own – it would be better for the plan. It was clear that the estate owner indeed had not talked frankly to anyone for a long time; that is why the words were pouring out of his lips in an unstoppable stream.

"For I, my dear, sir, who am I? An animal, and, furthermore, an evil animal. It is only the noble lion who kills his victim with one strike, and to death, and only because he needs to satisfy his hunger. But I always resembled a cat, who also needs to torture the mouse. I always had that inside me, lust coupled with cruelty. Bu there was another thing ... something. If I did not have that other thing, I would not have perceived myself as an evil animal, right?"

Strange sparks flared up in the unmoving eyes of Svidrigailov as he pronounced these words, and Porfirii Petrovich mentally cringed: Wow, dear man, your place is most likely not in the hard labour prison, or in the madhouse, where the violently insane are kept.

"Something happened in my life, not so long ago. You do not need to know. I will only say that I met a special young lady ... No, not important." Arkadii Ivanovich shook his hand, as if chasing away some apparition. "But please do not imagine that I somehow, as the writers put it, was re-born through this event to a new life. Not at all! I poisoned my wife, Marfa Petrovna, after that ... Why are you batting your eyes? Are you surprised at my confession? Why should I be secretive, if just in front of your eyes I did away with two people?"

"And you soon will send me right after them," the commissioner added to himself, again slightly moving his entire body in the intended direction. Only a little bit of distance remained, and then he would just need to capture a convenient moment, when the chatty murderer squinted or looked away.

However, Svidrigailov's eyes, while fogged up by memories, were still directly pointed at Porfirii Petrovich. "But at the time when I added to Marfa Petrovna's favourite cordial some Italian drops, I already had my little theory. Based on it I went ahead with a small loan."

"Loan?"

"Yes. My theory, if you may, is that before my departure for the New World, I have to add myself up to a zero. So that I can undertake my journey as pure as an infant. A newborn man, so to speak."

"I somehow stopped following you," the commissioner frowned, indeed becoming more and more confused by Svidrigailov's allegories. "What do you mean 'add up to a zero?'"

"It is rather simple, by means of simple arithmetic action. Let it be known that I am a big sinner," trustingly reported Arkadii Ivanovich, as if hoping to surprise his interlocutor with this revelation. "Not in the ordinary sense of human vices, anybody can do those. That is, of course, I fornicated and cheated and boozed. I wanted it all, so to speak. Everybody does those sorts of things, many people anyway. But only very, very few kill a living soul, and there is no forgiveness for that. Every destroyed soul in some sort of accounting book is counted as a giant minus. I have four of those minuses."

"Sheludiakova, Chebarov, Zigel'[22] ..." Porfirii Petrovich began to count.

But Svidrigailov got irritated and interrupted: "This has nothing to do with Zigel'! What kind of soul was Zigel'? I will at some point get to Daria Frantsevna, but I am talking now about something else. I already told you about my wife, Marfa Petrovna. I made her my own advanced payment, with the subsequent return on the loan."

"What?" The counsellor became confused again.

"You, listen, do not interrupt! That is, as it appears, my first minus. Well, not really, if we count in chronological order, then it is the third one. Even before my wife, I destroyed two living souls. Marfa Petrovna's murder was premeditated and committed out of passion, but the two others were just out of boredom and perversion ... Yes, now the arithmetic. Count yourself: for the mute girl, my servant, and Marfa Petrovna I paid with the old loan shark, Chebarov, and Daria Frantsevna. Mr. Luzhin" – he nodded at the corpse of Petr Petrovich – "I wanted to add for myself as a credit line, as a future pardon. He was indeed an absolutely awful example of a human being. But too bad, your deputy got in the way. That is all right though. It will be a wash. Therefore as of this moment I am completely pure and added up to a zero point zero. There was Arkadii Svidrigailov, but it was as if he never really was. As much dirt as he left behind, he cleaned after himself in the same measure."

Akunin's facility with Dostoevsky's diction in this excerpt deserves some special praise. The writer had to stylize the language of the "Little Theory" to make a credible version of Dostoevsky's first try at his famous novel. That stylization involved the verbatim use of the novel's text accompanied by virtuoso manipulation of its plot lines. The novel then presents, as two Russian scholars point out, "an eloquent example of mimetic intertextuality"[23] also palpable in Akunin's rewriting of Chekhov's *Seagull*. That intertextuality not only linguistically connects the modern writer to his predecessor, but also establishes familial connections between the detective of the "Little Theory," Porfirii, and his descendant in the central narrative of Akunin's novel, Nicholas, and with Akunin's principal detective, Erast Fandorin. Akunin has an intrinsic feel for the fabric of nineteenth-century language and employs archaisms (*bezobrazneiishii; starushonka; uiutets*) with an ease and familiarity that feed the reader's belief that the "lost" Dostoevskian text has been found. Akunin, however, is keenly aware that there can be no mere slavish imitation of Dostoevsky, and the reader is often startled by the anachronistic words and phrases that give away the modern provenance of the "Little Theory." This "modernizing" appears on the level of un-Dostoevskian words as well as the behaviour of characters.[24]

The archetypal criminal of "Little Theory," Svidrigailov, who, as pointed out before, serves as Sivukha's foil in the Dostoevskian part of the novel, also displays a spiritual quest for justice, seeking a balance between good and evil in the world whose wrongs he tries to rectify in his own warped way. When reading Svidrigailov's unfinished dialogue with Porfirii, one cannot help but think that in the best manner of a good detective novel it would make sense for him, and not the poor student Raskolnikov, to be the villain of the novel, the vicious axe murderer. Svidrigailov himself laughs at the idea of Raskolnikov as a criminal. According to him, the young man simply does not have what it takes. In this way Akunin reveals the simplicity of "Little Theory" as a detective story, emphasizing the complexity of Dostoevsky's novel, in which Raskolnikov, the most unlikely to kill, is in fact the murderer.

The showdown between Svidrigailov and Porfirii Petrovich remains unfinished in this "version" of Dostoevsky's novel. Feeling disgust about writing on demand for Stellovskii, Dostoevsky suddenly interrupts the narration, draws angry lines across the last paragraph, and stops in the middle of Svidrigailov's speech, adding beneath it: "I can't do this any longer! All of this is nonsense! That is not what is needed, not about that! And start in a completely different way!" What follows is the very familiar first paragraph of the actual *Crime and Punishment*.

With that abrupt ending of "Little Theory," Akunin passes his own judgment on his own attempt to "revise" Dostoevsky. The Dostoevskian text that Akunin invents is labelled as "nonsense" (*chush'*) by the great classic himself. Akunin, in turn, does not pretend to write as Dostoevsky and maintains a distance between his text and that of Fedor Mikhailovich. He also emphasizes on more than one occasion (from Dostoevsky's standpoint) that "Little Theory" is weak, faulty, and cannot claim to be a literary artefact. Akunin plays with the rumour about an alleged lost version of a novel that Dostoevsky, Akunin claims, burned upon his return from Wiesbaden in 1865.[25]

Akunin's attempt at rewriting/reviving Dostoevsky testifies to the boredom of twenty-first-century readers with canonical literary pieces. In *F.M.* Valia, Nicholas Fandorin's hilarious secretary, rather eagerly admits that she never read Dostoevsky, but when she lays her eyes for the first time on *Crime and Punishment* (in the "Little Theory" rendition)

she exclaims: "His writing is cool. I should read me some."[26] Her ignorance would be appalling if she were not a representative of the new
generation liberated from the oppressive demands of the Soviet school
curricula. Valia is a transgendered woman, and a martial arts champion
obsessed with fitness and consumerist trappings. She also is dauntingly
ignorant of Russia's great literary tradition, although she is eager to
be involved in tracking the "lost" version of the novel and even pretending to be interested in it. In order to obtain information about the
missing manuscript from Marpha Zacher, a sleek literary agent and
one of the suspects, Valia proclaims: "I am tripping from Dostoevsky"
(*Zalipaiu ot Dostoevskogo*), a statement that seems to have the expected
effect on the agent, who expresses eagerness to share the pages of the
manuscript with her.

Akunin himself stated that "If after the publication of my book, the
novel *Crime and Punishment* gets on the list of bestsellers, just like what
happened after the serial *Idiot* – the primary source's sales increased –
I will consider the mission of this project accomplished."[27]

There is little doubt that Akunin's novels have wider appeal among
the contemporary Russian public than Dostoevsky's, and that *F.M.*
managed to pique the interest of the Valia-like readership for the
original Russian classic. If anything, the novel definitely humanized
Dostoevsky and knocked him off the pedestal reserved for him by the
overzealous Soviet school curricula, where *Crime and Punishment* was
presented as the pinnacle of Russian literary achievement but the actual
author was completely hidden from the readership when it came to
his numerous faults and human nature. Fedor Dostoevsky in *F.M.* is
presented as an obsessive, perpetually indebted gambler who also has
certain unsavoury sexual propensities, if not to say deviations. There
is little if any trace of the highbrow philosophical ruminations and
religious pangs of Alesha Karamazov in a writer who is ready to make
a humiliating pact with a venal publisher for a little bit of money. The
Dostoevsky of *F.M.* is anything but the dull bust of a famous writer: he
comes alive, even becoming interesting and fascinating, in his question-
able lifestyle choices.

Furthermore, in the modern part of the novel Akunin "multiplies"[28]
Dostoevsky's characters. Raskolnikov, for example, has several counterparts in the narrative of modern Moscow: Rulet, the hapless drug
addict in constant need of a dose; Dr. Zits-Korovin, who sees himself
as intellectually superior; the *deputat* and mobster Sivukha, who seeks
glory in posterity. Luzhin similarly has his counterpart in the book
dealer Luzgaev, and the moneylender old hag turns into the greedy
Dostoevsky expert Eleonora Morgunova and the literary agent Marpha

Zakher. Even Sonia Marmeladova has a foil in the simple Sasha Morozova, a weak character prone to bad judgment.

Akunin's novel is an example of a highly literary, allusive work with remarkably versatile and exuberant prose. Essentially, Akunin had to write between two styles of Russian speech and prose as he moved between his two narratives, one Dostoevskian, the other rooted in present-day Russia.

By writing *F.M.* Akunin in a sense answered the tediously unfair questions about his being another Tolstoy or Dostoevsky. His "Little Theory" leaves the reader frustrated, in part because of its incompleteness. That being said, it is significantly more captivating to read in terms of its plot and character development than *Crime and Punishment* with its long philosophical and psychological subtexts. Svidrigailov, a purely evil criminal with a complex theory for murder, is what we, the readers, want. Raskolnikov as a murderer is indeed less intriguing, and in the manner of Aristotelean tragic catharsis provokes pity and fear stemming more from the circumstances of his miserable life than his misguided Napoleonic ruminations. Svidrigailov is akin to Arthur Conan Doyle's Dr. Moriarty, the criminal mastermind par excellence, who inspires awe but never pity. Furthermore, in both parts of the novel Akunin astutely captures Dostoevsky's thought about the inherent duality of every human being. When the introvert philologist Morozov (also in search of the "lost manuscript") receives a head trauma, he turns into a lustful, dirty, repulsive deviant. Sasha Morozova wants to save her family but spies on Nicholas Fandorin for Sivukha. Sivukha is a thug but also a loving and doting father. Similarly, even Svidrigailov defies the simple definition of pure evil: he supports Marmeladov's children and widow and his theory, as explained to Porfirii, is almost heroically motivated: to cleanse the earth of horrible monsters.

In his novels, Dostoevsky always explored the extremes of human nature, the unpredictability of human kindness and human evil. Both of Akunin's story lines clearly continue that exploration, thus making his *F.M.* a classic work in its own right.

NOTES

1 "Russian Writers and the World," YouTube video, 4:13, 1 May 2012, https://www.youtube.com/watch?v=0292VvE8w7M.
2 See D.M. Bethea (2002), "Literature," in *The Cambridge Companion to Modern Russian Culture*, ed. Nicholas Rzhevsky (Cambridge: Cambridge

University Press, 2002), 161–208. Bethea points out: "Russians writers have developed a reputation in the West for their eccentric understanding of literary form" (168). Bethea mainly discusses the puzzling shape of Russian novels, which Henry James (in reference to Tolstoy's *War and Peace*) called "loose baggy monsters."

 3 Elena V. Baraban, "A Country Resembling Russia: The Use of History in Boris Akunin's Detective Novels," *Slavic and East European Journal (SEEJ)* 48, no. 3 (2004): 398–9.

 4 Ibid., 397.

 5 Ibid., 397.

 6 M.A. Cherniak, "'Tvar' li ia drozhashchaia ili pravo imeiu': Prestuplenie i nakazanie' Borisa Akunina," 2014, https://cyberleninka.ru/article/n/tvar-ya-drozhaschaya-ili-pravo-imeyu-prestuplenie-i-nakazanie-borisa-akunina.

 7 Boris Akunin, *Pelagiia i belyi bul'dog* (*Pelagia and the White Bulldog*; (Moscow: Astrel', 2002), 155. All translations from Russian in this chapter are my own.

 8 Boris Akunin, "Bol'she vsego ia liubliu igrat'," Viperson, 22 May 2006, http://viperson.ru/articles/boris-akunin-bolshe-vsego-lyublyu-igrat.

 9 Boris Akunin, *F.M.* (Moscow: OLMA Media Group, 2006).

10 Ibid., 567.

11 This means *"uslovnyi pechatnyi list"* (a conditional print page), which is sixteen typed pages (with the interval 1,5). This novel then would have been around 200 double-spaced typed pages, which is a rather modest size for the novel that Stellovskii was asking Dostoevsky to write.

12 Akunin, *F.M.*, 283–90.

13 Here Sivukha actually uses the English word, pronouncing it in Russian manner: "gandikap."

14 Sivukha in Russian means "hooch."

15 Both names have a connection with different names for pig in Russian.

16 Tolstoi Lev in Russian is close to *"tolstyi lev,"* which means "fat lion."

17 Famous prison in Moscow the name of which in Russian means "sailor's silence."

18 Akunin, *F.M.*, 291.

19 Ibid., 597–611.

20 He is talking about Zametov, Porfirii Petrovich's deputy whom Svidrigailov just brutally killed.

21 Toptygin, often Mikhailo Toptygin, is a folkloric name for a bear. See Ushakov's dictionary at http://dic.academic.ru/dic.nsf/ushakov/1055754, accessed 25 September 2017.

22 Here Porfirii Petrovich lists Svidrigailov's murdered victims in the novel.

23 I.V. Kuzmicheva and I.A. Sukhanova, "Priemy stilizatsii v povesti "Teoriika" – "vstavnom" tekste iz romana Borisa Akunina *F.M.*," *Yaroslavskii pedagogicheskii vestnik* 4 (2014): 146.
24 See Kuzmicheva and Sukhanova, "Priemy stilizatsii," 149 for exhaustive linguistic comparison between the text of Dostoevsky and "Little Theory," as well as instances of character behaviour unthinkable for the nineteenth century.
25 Interview with the newspaper *Izvestiia*, May 2006; cited in Cherniak, "Tvar' li ia drozhashchaia," 4.
26 Akunin, *F.M.*, 194.
27 Cited in Cherniak, "Tvar' li ia drozhashchaia," 3.
28 The word is aptly used by Galina Rebel' in "Zachem Akuninu F.M., a Dostoevskomu Akunin?" *Druzhba Narodov* 21, no. 1 (2007): 3, 15.

PART THREE

Buried Secrets and Historical Spies in Akunin's Works

7 The Mysteries of Moscow: In Which Boris Akunin Impersonates a French Writer and Reveals a Buried Secret

ELIZABETH RICHMOND-GARZA

Introduction: In Which We Compare Chkhartishvili/Akunin to Kurosawa

Grigorii Chkhartishvili's oeuvre is prismatic, constantly refracting a virtuosic imagination so as to multiply identities and complicate perspectives. Although often engaged in writing genre fiction, like detective stories, his diversity and agility serve a more substantial purpose than merely diverting his readers; they allow him to critique contemporary Russian culture and politics. His light touch and picturesquely retro styles allow him obliquely, between two whimsically illustrated black-and-white covers, to create an aesthetic and even ideological resistance to the very notion of any single, dominant narrative in the public sphere. His works' polyphony alone defies the monologic impulses of current hegemonic structures. From the title pages onwards, his many pseudonyms suggest that a contemporary Russian writer can multiply and reinvent himself potentially *ad infinitum*. He invites us to look closely and differently at both the worlds he invents and, perhaps even more so, the ones he does not. Whether channelling Fedor Dostoevsky, creating computer games and blogs, reworking Shakespeare, or adopting the role of a sleuthing nun, Chkhartishvili proliferates his avatars and their settings, offering us double, triple, or quadruple takes on what we mistake for the familiar and ordinary.

Boris Akunin, perhaps his most beloved avatar and the creator of his most widely admired character, Erast Petrovich Fandorin, epitomizes his project while slyly citing the Japanologist credentials of the works' creator with his own Japanophilia. Fandorin's fin-de-siècle Moscow makes witty use of historical alterity to explore contemporary concerns, while at the same time breaking monologic narration so as to encourage readers' self-awareness and offer political commentary. With a dazzling array of intertexts, Chkhartishvili complicates each of his works, including the Fandorin novels, to heighten the amusement of his intelligentsia readership even as he sustains a persistent polyphony that resists being flattened into slogans or morals. It is hardly surprising that Vladimir Putin himself delighted in the novels' historical charm initially; but their complexity has caused him subsequently to reject not only them but also their author. Like Alexander Pushkin and Mikhail Bulgakov before him, Chkhartishvili achieves a combination of official admiration and precarity which only the recourse to genre fiction like fairy tales, orientalist fables, and science fiction can accord to inventive Russian authors in persistently authoritarian contexts. The fantastic spaces created by these popular genres promise narrative and ideological closure to so great an extent that it can become its opposite, allowing for the emergence of ironic and multiple perspectives as we readers question the sufficiency of any singular answer and are left instead to make up our own minds about what has transpired.

The Fandorin mysteries stand at the crossroads of two sibling genres, the crime novel and the detective novel. These two genres are as close as they are remote, taking the same subject, a transgression, but viewing it from opposing perspectives, yoking the deviance of the criminal with the conformity of the detective. They are mysterious, paradoxical, and therefore subversive. They are part of a tradition of phenomenologically innovative representations of crime, trauma, and suffering in the twentieth and twenty-first centuries, one that appears under two signatures, Boris Akunin and Akira Kurosawa, both of which are connected with Japan and with a complex narratological way of presenting crimes.

Kurosawa's most admired Japanese *jidaigeki* (period) film, *Rashomon* (1950), about a murdered samurai and his raped wife, is also a detective story and anticipates Akunin's strategic use of the past and narrative polyphony.[1] Akunin invokes the filmic intertext, however, before we even open the book with his nom de plume, Akunin – literally "bad (or as Fedor Dostoevsky might say, *zloi*) man" in Japanese. Japanese film buffs immediately recognize Akunin's quotation of the title of Kurosawa's 1958 film *Kakushi-toride no san-akunin*, marketed in English by Criterion as *The Fortress*, but distributed in the Soviet Union with a literal translation of the original as *Three Bad Men of a Hidden Fortress* (*Tri negodiia v skrytoi kreposti*), itself a crime story set in the historical past.[2] Starring Toshiro Mifune, Kurosawa's *Rashomon* is known for the explicitly polyglossic plot device of several characters (a bandit, a priest, the wife, another samurai, a woodcutter) providing alternative, self-serving, and contradictory versions of an incident that Akunin would call *nepriiatnyi*, were it an incident in one of his novels, on the way to its denouement.

Although the viewer is placed in the role of the detective, in many ways the film depends upon *not* resolving the multiple perspectives it presents, instead offering a view of the ways in which idiosyncratic accounts of the same apparent events can be made to serve different, dishonest, and selfish agendas. *Rashomon*, along with Kurosawa's 1955 quasi-documentary film *Ikimono no kiroku* (literally *Record of a Living Being* or *What the Birds Knew*, distributed as *I Live in Fear*) about atomic testing in the Pacific, complicates post-Hiroshima views of guilt and innocence after trauma.[3] He draws on the very phenomenological uncertainty that permeates the post-Kantian golden and silver ages of many literatures, including Russian. Such works in the crime/detective genre use polyphony to engage the reader and to create suspense, among which the most admired may be Orhan Pamuk's *My Name is Red* (1998).[4] They invite viewers and readers to inhabit different points of view without ever fully resolving them into a shared and stable meaning. Although we may finally learn "who dunnit," we remain suspicious of all versions of what might be mistaken for the truth.

Invoking Kurosawa's inventive film, and expanding Mikhail Bakhtin's account of the novel as inherently resistant to the monologic impulses of cinema (despite Walter Benjamin's concern with the tyranny of the camera), I would like to suggest that Akunin, the author of all the Fandorin mysteries, talks with himself and with us about a past that may never have existed, so as to entertain and dialogically provoke us to be active investigators of both Fandorin's Moscow and our own present-day Moscow.[5] He would like us to "reflect" on what has happened, in Svetlana Boym's sense of the word, holding off any impulses to construct monologic, shared or "restorative" narratives.[6]

Any of the Fandorin detective novels could provide evidence of an equally nostalgic and satirical project, but a pair of novels written on the edge of the Fandorin experience provide an especially innovative case, along with a gothic collection whose very form embodies what Robert Louis Stevenson's *The Strange Case of Dr. Jekyll and Mr. Hyde* only describes with its textual double life.[7] *She Lover of Death* (*Liubovnitsa smerti*, 2001) and *He Lover of Death* (*Liubovnik smerti*, 2001) appear together, although they do not need to be read together.[8] *Liubovnitsa* is presented from the protagonist's point of view, amplified with pseudo-documents that purport to be police reports, newspaper clippings, scraps of poetry, and so on. It is the story of a poetically ambitious young provincial woman, who runs away to Moscow with her boyfriend only to find that she is more devoted to the emerging gothic and decadent literary scene than he is. Sexual and literary escapades are encouraged by a secret suicide society, the Lovers of Death, whose failure to kill themselves gives way to an alarming string of "successes" that cause the members, each of whom is given a literary identity, to become anxious, especially when a mysterious Japanese prince joins the group. Although the novel includes Fandorin as a character, his point of view is more than balanced by the focalization of the narrative around the young poetess. *He Lover of Death* equally doubles the usual alignment with Fandorin's perspective by tracing the adventures of a young street urchin, Sen'ka, in the criminal world of Moscow, as he follows and eventually becomes entangled with the top gangster's paramour, "Death." Her fatal effect on men is registered by the trail of dead former lovers she leaves behind, even as her current lover wonders how long he will last.

The City as a Character: Akunin's Debt to a French Author and Doubled Narration

Both novels shift the focus from Fandorin, the expert investigator, to the city of Moscow itself as protagonist. They track the paths not only of the beloved super-sleuth but also of two other amateur investigators through a deadly city of the still-alive. The pair of novels, especially *She Lover of Death*, pointedly double their narration, a technique that the author compresses into a single volume about cities explicitly not designed for the living, that is to say about the great cemeteries of the world. In the standalone non-Fandorin volume, *Cemetery Tales* (*Kladbishchenskie istorii*, 2004), a series of short stories by Akunin is paired with Baedecker-like entries that introduce the reader to the great cities of the dead and their secrets written by Chkhartishvili.[9] Chkhartishvili mimics the style of famous nineteenth-century travel guides to the treasures of the world, while Akunin's short stories each have a central adventure, often tracking members of the Russian global diaspora as they roam from Tokyo to Jerusalem, from New York to Paris and London. The entries and stories do not have to be read together, but they are interlaced. These pairings and assemblages produce an interactive and dynamic subversion that contributes to the pleasure so many readers attach to this deceptively light-hearted oeuvre.

She Lover of Death's protagonist begins the intertextual play of the novel by reminding us from the start of the protagonist of Nikolai Karamzin's *Poor Liza* (*Bednaia Liza*), a young woman filled with naive sensual immediacy.[10] Liza's descendant, however, although she succumbs to the advances of not one but two reincarnated Erasts, survives them both in a doubling of the familiar Don Juan plot line. The literary reprise will be played out not in an early-modern Spanish past but in a scenario lifted from Eugène Sue's mid-nineteenth-century *Les mystères de Paris*, displaced to Moscow at 1900.[11] In the cemetery collection, like the author he invokes most consistently across his diverse writings, Akunin will conjure the ghost of Dostoevsky's heteroglossic narration from the apparent first-person confessional *Notes from Underground* (*Zapiski iz podpolia*, 1864) by taking the idea of *podpol'ie* quite literally.[12] It is this combination of historical displacement, multivocality, and sensational surface that Boris Akunin has perfected in these novels. Each of the Fandorin novels, but particularly *She Lover of Death*, is tenaciously dialogic. The novel is about a Russian detective (Fandorin) who sometimes impersonates a Japanese prince (Genji) in a storyline stolen from a French novelist (Eugène Sue) about an imaginary German aristocrat going undercover in the criminal *demimonde* of Paris (Sue's hero Rodolphe). All of the Fandorin novels draw upon Sue's themes and content, as Fandorin's elite profile and his tendency to act the dandy echoes Sue's protagonist, the mysterious and distinguished Rodolphe, secretly the Grand Duke of the fictional German kingdom of Gerolstein, now disguised as a Parisian worker. In Fandorin's world, it is the resistance to interpreting and assigning familiar and normative meaning that reveals the secret. As two of the surviving characters at the end of *She Lover of Death* note, life is a dream within a dream – in a Buddhist rather than Freudian sense, one with no meaning to plumb. Or maybe life is a nightmare, a haunting in a Parisian graveyard. In the end, we are no longer in the streets of any living city but rather in their respective cities of the dead, their cemeteries. A cemetery is a surface over what no longer is. Among these Akunin counts a Parisian one, Père Lachaise, which in his story includes an expat, New-Russian descendant of Shakespeare's gravedigger and the ultimate homeless exile, Oscar Wilde.

In the title of the chapter in which Fandorin first appears, in *The Winter Queen* (*Azazel'*, 1998), Boris Akunin describes Fandorin's new boss, Detective Ivan Frantsevich Brilling, as a modern "bad man"-of-the-future (*budushchego*).[13] Anticipating the *fizkul'tura*, absolute devotion to the cause, independence from familial loyalty, and efficiency of the ideal *homo sovieticus*, Brilling disparages the plot of the first Fandorin novel, in which he plays a central role, as "nonsense," premised upon "meaningless coincidences," and he explicitly compares this inadequate plot to a novel by Eugène Sue. From the inception of the Fandorin mysteries, Brilling, a cynical modern orphan, describes a world that might seem at odds with that of the equally orphaned detective, one where there is no sense, only mere happenstance, and Brilling connects this meaningless world with a certain French writer. At the core of Sue's 1842–3 runaway success *Les mystères de Paris* lies an uncanny portrait of a great city, styled as a socially fluid and threatening space, where the undercover German aristocrat Rodolphe and his two unlikely companions reveal, and sometimes resolve, the sufferings of a city no longer Romantic and not yet Decadent. Reviled by Alexandre Dumas for artistic reasons and Karl Marx for ideological ones, Sue's novel was tentatively admired by Edgar Allan Poe and Vissarion Belinsky.[14] Other writers, however, saw in it a source of inspiration and a resource for provocation, as its sensational style confounded good taste and serious literature, opening a space to present to its readership a portrait of those who are overlooked and silenced in official accounts of society. Sue anticipated the revolutions of 1848 and offered a gothic tour de force about the surface of a thing, rather than its depths, being what readers need to see.

The work was condemned as merely *frénétique*, feverish and delirious, and viewed as a failed reprise of the Romantic *frénétisme* of English Gothic and German *Sturm und Drang*.[15] Nevertheless, Sue's novel initiated a mode which certain Russian writers like Dostoevsky, who was introduced to Sue at the Academy of Engineers, embraced.[16] Sue made clear the ideological potential of developing the portrait of a criminal and threatening city, a city that is not what it seems, which persists today. At the same time, its quality, neither serious nor pure pulp, like Akunin's reimagining of Sue's novel, has often denied Sue sustained scholarly critical reception. Along with other inventive but far too delightful mystery writers such as Umberto Eco, Akunin and Sue both invite more sustained scholarship. Like Victor Hugo, whose *Les misérables* (1862) owes much to Sue, Dostoevsky actively read *Les mystères de Paris*, and the modern mystery writer Akunin channels Sue via Dostoevsky and writers like Gogol, whose projects make the city itself into a character, by presenting a portrait as much of St. Petersburg itself as of those who dwell there. For Gogol and Dostoevsky earlier, and now for Akunin, *frénétisme* is more than a flashy style, and he does not apologize for the flash. Akunin's heroine is flamboyant and melodramatic in every way, as are the other members of the Lovers, and they all seek and revel in that heightened emotional state, in a Moscow that they keep fantasizing is a dangerous and gothic setting. Akunin unabashedly refashions fin-de-siècle Moscow and the members of the society so as to allow the very egregiousness of the *frénétique* to operate as a resistance to restorative interpretive strategies that would consolidate and ground a shared and conventional view of how Moscow's youth should be spending their evenings today.

Frénétisme makes possible subversive interventions in moments of cultural strain and hegemonic consolidation, even to the point of showing that detectives themselves, along with police inspectors, journalists, and persons of influence, consistently err in their interpretations. *She Lover of Death* in particular, with its secret suicide society, naïve heroine, and narratological polyphony, like the wittily macabre portraits of global cities of the dead in *Cemetery Tales*, embraces Sue's excessive style in ways that have always pleased readers in Russia, while perhaps surprisingly appalling their leaders. As the most self-indulgently decadent plot of the Fandorin series, *She Lover of Death* confirms Brilling's quip. Extreme in its topic and themes, and filled with references to Parisian decadence, the novel places an inexpert outsider in a gothic underworld, for the decoding of which she needs our help. At the same time, the novel undertakes a pointed and exact critique of how crime, investigation, and truth function in today's Moscow. Picturesque though the Lovers' poetry readings are in their citation of Edgar Allen Poe's "The Masque of Red Death," performed by costumed characters bearing names from Shakespeare and the commedia dell'arte, the novel is more than a gothic diversion. Akunin's readers are being cued to recognize a social critique amidst all the macabre flourishes. Some of Sue's readers saw only *frénétisme*, while Dostoevsky and Chkhartishvili saw more. Vladimir Putin has turned out to be both sorts of reader. Initially seeing only the danse macabre, he later had to realize that the Akunin whose novels he initially enjoyed reading was created by the same person who had conducted three interviews about the "enemy within" with Alexei Navalny before the anti-government protests on 24 December 2011, and that Fandorin's exploits had always been more than entertainment.[17]

The Moscow Experience: In Which We Add Japanese Literature and Bulgakov to Our Understanding

Both *She Lover of Death* and *Cemetery Tales* may be read so dynamically and differently because they mirror Kurosawa's proliferation of versions of violence and death. They create an unexpectedly shared anti-establishment literary history that connects the classical Japanese author Shikibu Murasaki and Karamzin. If in a Russian context Akunin invokes the story of Karamzin's simply-born Liza, the story of the equally socially modest Muraski no Ue, Prince Genji's beloved in *The Tale of Genji*, is equally being cited from the samurai tradition to which Fandorin is devoted.[18] Akunin's country girl turned amateur detective meets up with a character – the detective Erast Fandorin in disguise – whose real name is the same as that of Karamzin's seducer, and whose name as one of the Lovers is Prince Genji. Akunin creates a transnational and trans-temporal chronotope based on a valid but unexpected parallel between a medieval Japanese romance and a Russian sentimental novella, in which the guise of Prince Genji allows Erast to remain *incognito*. More importantly, an ordinary young woman who pays attention is not only alive at the end, she solves the mystery. Indeed, the young woman is the central character for Akunin, as she was for Karamzin. The protagonist of the novel this time is not the stammering and princely detective, but instead Masha Mironova, a poetry-writing provincial who travels from Irkutsk to Moscow with aspirations of sophistication and romance. As she enters into the intertextual matrix that is the Lovers of Death, whose secret practices, improvised poetic experiments, and pseudonyms range dizzyingly across the global canon, we enjoy both the invention and the recognition that she experiences in her social, sexual and aesthetic encounters with members of the inner circle – with Prospero and Ophelia, with Caliban, as well as with an array of other fictional figures from the global early modern world, which range from Germany to Italy and Japan. Even before disguising herself and changing her name to Columbina, taking on the role of the clever servant that we recognize from the commedia dell'arte in hopes of becoming Harlequin's mistress, Masha is our point of entry into the novel, and we learn not to rely upon her fully as she is prone to fancy. With the novel's focalization consistently connected to her, we quickly become aware that she regularly and melodramatically misreads her situation, mistaking "sad and mysterious" Moscow for an Italianate gothic novel or a Shakespearean tragedy. Most notably, she repeatedly misunderstands the "signs," three of which would consign any given member of the suicide society to a longed-for and self-inflicted death, imagined as a mystical erotic consummation with Death (capital D) itself. Given the complexity of the text in structural terms, Masha's limitations are important.

Before we even enter the novel and its Poe-esque gruesome intrigues, Akunin highlights the text's intricacy and begins his phenomenological game. The fictional Akunin names and thanks two real people in his acknowledgments at the beginning of the text – Sergei Gandlevsky and Lev Rubinstein – for helping the fictional Gdlevsky and Lorelei Rubinstein write the poems that punctuate the entire text. Mimicking perhaps the defining *frénétique* novel (after Sue's own), Bram Stoker's *Dracula*, the first page of the novel heightens the metatextuality of the novel even before its opening sentence.[19] It purports to be an extract from a newspaper, with the byline "L. Zh," whose full name, Lavr Zhemailo, appears at the end of the chapter. The second chapter is equally explicit in its refusal to obey the rules of conventional third-person narration that we expect from a mystery novel. It appears to consist of pages from Masha's diary. Each subsequent chapter is also designated by its varying provenance, rather than its content, with intriguingly rather than substantively titled subsections. The chapters comprise a bricolage of letters, depositions, notes, poems, and textual fragments. The source of the information is highlighted and brought into question before we even begin to consider what is said, and the accounts are divergent, forcing us as readers to embark upon our own investigation with appropriate scepticism. Unlike most of the Fandorin novels, the master detective does not provide a reliable orientation from which to approach the crime, here a paradoxical one, since people who want to commit suicide keep showing up suspiciously dead.

Although all the Lovers in principle have joined the group to await the magic triple confirmation that they are to kill themselves, and each is profoundly disappointed when they are not chosen, initially no one gets the magic messages – and, therefore, no one dies. Around the time of Masha's arrival, however, the messages start coming through and the lovers start showing up dead, though whether by their own hand or as victims is unclear. Fandorin enters in medias res, but he is only a character in this scenario, not the master detective to whom we are accustomed. Although we remember his Japanese adventures, and therefore recognize him despite his disguise as Prince Genji, he leaves us to decode the situation on our own. We must piece together the solution based on an incomplete archive of partial accounts from people who do not entirely understand the events they observe and in which they participate. The ideological parallels of such a portrait of Moscow are clear, though never expressed explicitly. Fandorin is cosmopolitan, like the many people across the whole series of novels who converge not only from across the former Soviet Union but also from the Far East and Western Europe. Fandorin nevertheless finds his Moscow transformed by these strange new arrivals. Indeed despite being a native, even he appears alien. Apparently a member of the Japanese elite, Fandorin mirrors his readers, Muscovites who in 2000 were being encouraged by fashionable magazines to eat sushi at the real Sumosan restaurant in the Radisson Slavyansky Hotel near the Kiev Railway Station, a hotel notorious for gangster violence. Like Mayor Yuri Luzhkov's Moscow of 2000, with its many schemes and intrigues, Masha's new Moscow is very different from the one we first encountered with a teenage Fandorin in *The Winter Queen*. It is a glitteringly chaotic archive that challenges anyone who wants to locate the primum mobile to separate out what is merely theatrical *léger de main* or *focus* from what is real and deadly. Masha's task is to figure out who is killing the lovers, while at the same time clarifying what she wants herself from the Moscow experience: poetry, sex, love, excitement, and/or death. For the readers of the text, who watch real and imaginary gangsters on television and in the streets every day, the challenge is the same: to make sense of a dangerous new environment while discovering who they are and to what they aspire. In the last moments before the internet fully took over, conventional media in 2000 still played a central role. What was printed in the papers, said under one's breath, or observed at a public event comprised the data for trying to imagine what Moscow was and might be, and Akunin's text literally reflects the last moments in which this nineteenth-century way of finding out information was still dominant.

The nature of the events in question in the novel is both eye-catching and unimportant, a ruse adapted from Sue and the fantastical underworld that he created in 1842–3 for his hero Rodolphe. Akunin's journalistic opening reminds us immediately that Sue's novels were serialized in the *Journal des débats* by pretending to be an actual newspaper item. The article that opens *She Lover of Death*, "The Selfless Devotion of a Four-Legged Friend," reports the sensational image of a dog committing suicide by leaping out of a window to die with his master in Semionovskaia Street. The story repeats Sue's lurid and pathetic scenes of violence against animals, including dogs. The passage also suggests Russian intertexts, perhaps especially Mikhail Bulgakov's use of newspaper reports and official dispatches about the supernatural as part of the magic realist fabric of *The Master and Margarita* and his designing an entire novella, *Heart of A Dog*, around the abuse of a stray dog who is in every way superior to his human masters. The effect is not merely entertaining, nor is it simply an invocation of Russian authors. In Sue, Bulgakov, and Akunin, the explicit inclusion of mixed genres brings into question both the facticity of the reported events in this fictional world and the status of real-world journalism as telling the truth. Each time the narrative switches from journalism to third-person narrative, to first-person confessional, to embedded poem, to police report, and so on, the bright distinctions between these different genres is emphasized. Conflated as they may be in the novel, moreover, they are all part of a fictional world, and yet one which offers uncanny parallels to the real one.

A Textual *Podpol'ie*: In Which We Can See How Servants Help Us See Moscow

Like *She Lover of Death*, the first words of *He Lover of Death*, which introduce us to the criminal district of Khitrovka, follow Sue. Here Akunin very closely mimics the first sentence of *Les mystères* in focusing on gangster slang and naming, in both cases in relationship to a powerful and intriguing woman. For Sue, this local colour was part of the author's socialist project to reveal the injustice of contemporary society. Like Rodolphe, Fandorin can speak in argot, is remarkably athletic, and is an accomplished fighter. Fandorin shares Rodolphe's compassion for the underprivileged and his brilliant analytical mind, both of which allow him to move undetected and sympathetically between layers of society. Rodolphe also has companions: Sir Walter Murph, an Englishman, and David, a gifted black doctor, formerly a slave. Unlike Sherlock Holmes's sole companion Dr. John Watson or Rodolphe's pair of companions, many figures, often women, accompany Fandorin on his adventures.[20] Perhaps the most extended case is that of Varvara Suvorova, whom he rescues from marauders and with whom he partners to protect the Russian Empire from Ottoman intrigues in *The Turkish Gambit* (*Turetskii gambit*).[21] Additionally, there is a particularly exact alignment between the ethnically othered servants, David and Masa (Fandorin's servant), who in each case have the most intimate relationship with the detective but are also outsiders, removed from their respective origins in America and Japan.

Unlike Rodolphe, however, Fandorin does not have a privileged birth, and Akunin regularly invites us to see the metropole not through the eyes of entitled compassion but from the perspective of the homeless and displaced, the orphan (Brilling, Fandorin, and Sen'ka) and the runaway (Masha). *She Lover of Death* and *He Lover of Death* employ a strategy of defamiliarization, using a partial outsider to reveal what the insider may not notice. Rather than being hermeneutically conversant, these outsiders are forced to rely upon assessing what they actually encounter, based on the surfaces that present themselves rather than the depths that normatively might be presumed. Again and again, Sen'ka and Masha give us exact descriptions of rooms, streets, people, actions, and so on. Unfamiliar as they are with their new neighbours and neighbourhoods in Moscow, they can only describe rather than understand what they see. Both repeatedly are puzzled and have to look more closely to make sense of, for example, a fine lady in a carriage in Sen'ka's case and a secret door in Prospero's home in Masha's. In place of Rodolphe's dilettante humanitarianism, I would like to invoke here not only a Holmesian notion of detection, observation, and deduction, but to go further, suggesting the aptness of what Stephen Best and Sharon Marcus have called for: a move from symptomatic readings to surface readings.[22] Best and Marcus suggest a consequence of psychoanalysis and Marxism has been to create a practice of symptomatic reading which assumes that a text's truest meaning lies in what it does not say, what is hidden, secret, and below the surface in a kind of textual *podpol'ie*. These veiled, latent, and almost absent meanings are detectable only through the investigation and diagnosis of their irrepressible and recurring symptoms. Rita Felski also warns against a certain scholarly sleuthing that entails not only detection but also suspicion and judgment.[23] Akunin shares these concerns. Whether resisting plunging beneath or framing beyond, actual surface reading observes the complexity of literary or evidentiary surfaces that have been rendered invisible by symptomatic and suspicious reading. Sen'ka and Masha see what even Fandorin cannot: what is right in front of their eyes.

The idea of surface reading raises a paradox, however. If Akunin is interested in Moscow as it "really" is, then why does he write such a paradoxically conventional and at the same time dialogic series of novels? Why have Masha refer several times to Moscow as "City of Dreams" in the first ten pages of the novel, a phrase that might invite expert and hermeticist interpretation so as to bring us back to the real? Akunin appears to be abstracting Moscow and at the same time Westernizing it, using Paris as an inspiration and a matrix for his figurative move. He might be seen simply as transposing the project of a French author of sensational novels about the seamy side of urban life so as to mimic the leading exponent of the *roman-feuilleton*. *She Lover of Death*, however, does not copy Sue's novel; it embeds it narratively. The Sue-style novel is not the metanarrative; instead it is one of several polyphonic voices in the narrative. Masha is continually disappointed in her attempts to write her imagistic and predictably conventional sentimental diary, as are many of the other authors of the novel's intratexts, and the newspapers report the terrible events connected to the suicide society only incompletely. Masha and Zhemailo aspire to be like Sue, attempting synoptic melodramatic and journalistic interventions respectively, and both are disappointed and disappointing. Each repeatedly tells us that they would like to be better writers, and Masha explicitly says that she is disappointed with her poems and diary entries as she aspires to write and star in a decadent French-style mystery. The official narratives shaped as a cover-up for the Lovers of Death by their overlord, and equally the one invented by the press based on official reports, are not to be trusted. Akunin's pose, however, is something different; he is a collector of pieces of paper and scraps of evidence, an assembler of an archive providing only the minimal intrusion of titles and provenance to keep the materials in order. The archive is left to speak for itself, as may another weightier archive in Chkhartishvili's current project of compiling an eight-volume history of Russia.

The Author as Dissenter: In Which Sue and Akunin Become Strangely Alike

The gothic project of recording an overlooked past is one we recognize as diverting but also as ideologically engaged. From the images of tyranny and oppression in Horace Walpole's *The Castle of Otranto* in 1764 onwards, the project of recovering the past, even in the form of a fanciful work of gothic fiction, has complicated the present.[24] We wonder whether the guilty secrets of a mysterious past are so far removed from the present. Sue's original Rodolphe stories, although faulted for their melodramatics, were the first to present many of the historical social ills that accompanied the Industrial Revolution in France. They provided a record of what history was not recording. Sue himself was a committed citizen. He participated in the 1848 Revolution, was elected as a Socialist deputy for the Seine in 1850, opposed Louis Napoleon's coup d'état in 1851, and went into exile at Annecy, Savoy until his death as a dissident. Declared by Will Cathercart to be as popular as J.K. Rowling, as a result of a parallel invention of a magical world that appeals to readerly nostalgia for a chronotope of wizards and tsars, Akunin has become an almost equally unlikely opposition voice.[25] His voice has become insistent particularly since his opposition to Vladimir Putin has become more visible with his participation in protests beginning in 2011 and his comments about the 2014 annexation of Crimea, but the critique was always there, from his first Fandorin novels and certainly in *She Lover of Death*.[26] With an intersectional identity as Russian, Jewish, Georgian, and Japanophile, and a peripatetic life that could always have been called exilic even before his departure from Russia, Akunin resists being collected into either the coherent narrative of retrograde tsarist revisionism or the legacy of dissenting intelligentsia.[27] Akunin is a very unusual person, whose very complexity and hybridity epitomize the actuality of the diverse and multi-ethnic Russian empire, about whose past and for whose present he writes. He existentially defies monolithic notions of a homogenous national identity.

Rodolphe's professional and ideological eccentricity is balanced by Sue's portrait of him as a classically flawless man, unlike the unusual and quirky Akunin and in even more marked contrast with the antisocial and mysterious Fandorin, whose stammer and slightness are only the most visible of his deviations from the ideals and norms of *homo sovieticus*. While Rodolphe simply crosses a European border with his French impersonation while continuing to identify as German, Fandorin not only travels to Japan, but acquires habits, beliefs, and practices (ranging from language and diet to attire and martial-arts training) and a life companion. Like his home, he is no longer purely Russian, as he had been in his youth, and yet he is not an imposter. He is perhaps characteristic of one type of New Russian and occupies an interstitial space in the city, between the authorities and the subcultures. Rodolphe is a model for such in-betweenness. With the exception of his hero's sympathy for those less fortunate than himself, and the social critique that Rodolphe's adventures offer of Parisian society, Sue otherwise depicts the Parisian nobility as deaf to the misfortunes of the common people and focused on meaningless intrigues. For this reason, some, such as Alexandre Dumas, have considered the novel's ending with Rodolphe's retirement a failure, just as Akunin's coterie of aestheticist suicidal wannabees might be seen as narcissistic and irrelevant in a novel that ends with a petulant official report of the events by a Lieutenant-Colonel Besikov. Rodolphe goes back to his fictional home in the imaginary German State of Gerolstein to take on the role to which he was destined by birth, rather than staying in Paris to help the lower classes, just as Masha fails to kill herself and Fandorin goes on to another adventure. That adapting Sue to Russia would be especially problematic was anticipated by Belinsky, who condemned Sue at length as merely a local writer, guilty of unapologetic praise of the French people as the true inheritors of a cultural obligation for excellence.[28] Sue is accused of not ultimately being a friend of the people, but instead seizing the current moment and situation in France for self-aggrandizement, something which the blacklist of 2014 has accused Akunin of doing as well. In the summer of 2014, Akunin's witticisms returned to haunt their coiner, as friends of the Russian authorities elided Comrade Akunin with his fiction. With his name on the blacklist, Akunin found himself translated from popular favourite to menace, a double role he has been forced to play ever since.[29] In a memo from 30 March 2017, Akunin was officially designated as among those it was inadvisable to invite to the VI St. Petersburg international cultural forum. Like his French predecessor, Akunin finds himself both a friend and enemy of the people, and both local and foreign at the same time.[30]

Russian Prosperos: In Which Akunin Helps Us Understand Shakespeare and Fake News

Split as the evaluations are of Akunin as public figure, his indebtedness to Sue could invite further disparagement. However, Belinsky's dismissal of Sue as lacking potential for Russian reception elides the context that Russian literature has already given to the French author, whose texts created a matrix for authors like Dostoevsky and Gogol, even before Akunin. The character of Masha, especially, as another impoverished young would-be artist, invokes Gogol's "The Portrait" ("Portret").[31] Her character draws on Gogol, reprising the story of a young and penniless artist who enters a fantastical, dangerous, and puzzling urban world. In "The Portrait," Chartkov stumbles upon a terrifyingly lifelike portrait in an art shop and is compelled to buy it, and an account of a second young man's experience after buying it follows. This story of choosing talent over magic is filled with metaphors of valuelessness and gazing. It is a text about watching and being watched, where the inanimate portrait stares back and is as much of a dandy as the obsessive viewer. The deception of moneylenders in literal terms suggests that there may be other false currencies, especially Chartkov's pretentious lack of talent, in a world where the surface of the image, not the depths of what is represented, are valued, even if the image is ultimately lost. In the closing scene, at an art auction where the portrait is to be sold, when the audience turns to examine the portrait they find it missing: someone *must have* taken it while they were listening to the young man's story. There should always be a solution in a detective story, but in this St. Petersburg hallucination, they wonder if they had ever seen the portrait at all. In the very first diary section of *She Lover of Death*, Masha insists that Moscow is the City of Dreams, rather than rigid like St. Petersburg despite the myth to that effect.[32] Certain banal and literal things are real in Gogol's story: the money, the lack of talent and the final absence of the painting, and it is these banal truths that matter. The portrait does not symbolize anything; it simply is, or is not, present. In his precursor to Dostoevsky's *Crime and Punishment*, a novel Akunin repeatedly invokes in *F.M.* (2006) especially, Gogol creates an elaborate frame for the narrative, one that tests the limits of form as well as content. Akunin also embeds his narration, constantly inviting us to remain aware of who is reporting, not only what is reported. Unlike his precursor, however, Akunin does not indulge in suspense, nor does he leave his tale open-ended. We are made to wait for the revelation of who is to blame – ultimately, Zhemailo the reporter and Prospero – but we are given a solution. Zhemailo is not only a key informant, but also a victim and a serial killer, and people have been murdered. The complexity of the phenomenological game is never collapsed and the dialogic multiplicity is sustained, but deaths are real, as are fingerprints.

She Lover of Death remains structured in dialogic form to the very end, retaining the explicit diversity of perspectives, genres, and media that Akunin introduced on the first page, like his precursors Stoker and Kurosawa. It takes the form of the feuilleton, the anonymous urban light reading of the flâneur or *frant*, as a dozen people try to decode what is happening so as to clarify what it all means. The Doge Prospero manipulates and controls his determined acolytes, encouraging them to interpret every detail allegorically so as to avoid the naked truth. That the signs come in the German form of *Stirb* invokes the gothic predisposition of the German Rodolphe as well as the equally undercover expertise of other ominous figures (like Putin himself) who share a covert German past. Akunin is precise in his polyphony, attending to details like including historical costumes taken from Sarah Bernhardt's actual performances. The snake armlet from her celebrated performance of *Medée*, made famous by Alphonse Mucha's haunting poster, becomes a real snake called Satan that Masha wears as a startling fashion accessory. Whether we are reading about a piece of art-nouveau jewellery or a member of the Lovers, nothing and no one are what or who they seem to be in a world of recognizable archetypes attending a *ballo in maschera*. Neither Columbina nor her fiancée Caliban are who they pretend to be, and, of course, Fandorin himself is certainly not Genji. All texts and language itself are suspect in a novel filled with magic writing and haunted voices that speak German so as to inspire suicides. Rather than being symbolic, however, each death is revealed as merely a visceral horror rather than a personal hermeneutics of death.

Although the central story of Masha Mironova is familiar from the Sentimentalist tradition, the unfortunate provincial female victim who moves to the capital city and becomes involved with a dangerous subculture via her fiancé, she is anything but a cliché as she makes of herself a chameleon-like fashion tableau, one that nearly rivals Fandorin's flair for disguise. Indeed, hers is bolder, as it is champions aestheticism rather than claiming the functional utility of disguise. Whereas Fandorin's attire and mannerisms mask his true identity, allowing him to work undercover, Masha's elaborate outfits are just expressions of sartorial exuberance intended to catch the eye and delight. Indeed only one of her complex costumes has a practical purpose rather than revealing a deeper meaning. Her final outfit, intended for her exquisite suicide, does pull off its symbolic promise, but by means of an almost grotesque utility. Rather than allowing her the beautiful and sentimental departure from this world that she elaborately plans, as she leaps like the dog with which the novel begins from a window to her imagined death, she is saved in mid-air by an artificial angel on the façade of the building on which the elaborate fabric of her Pierrette costume snags. Suggestive as the image of the guardian angel is, it is the very pragmatic matter of the excessive fabric that is the actual rescuer of this young life left hanging ungracefully. The material reality of the costume, as just a piece of cloth, is what matters, not its aesthetic symbolic force. The costume and the artificial angel do save her life, but in a very pedestrian and literal manner.

Masha's awkward rescue emphasizes the subterfuge of the official narrative. Death, consummated or not, is awkward, improvised, and ordinary. Any promise of a beautiful heroism offered to Russia's youth, whether to Prospero's Lovers of Death or to the pro-Putin patriotic group *Idushchie vmeste* ("walking together"; founded in 2000 and, in 2007, absorbed into the nationalist youth movement *Nashi*, "our own"), should be viewed with suspicion and interrogated. Akunin's suicide club has much in common with Vladimir Putin's regime. Akunin in fact compares Putin to Prospero explicitly in his first conversation with Navalny, suggesting a connection of Putin with the Doge from the Lovers of Death, as well as with William Shakespeare's problematic marooned duke in *The Tempest*.[33] Both Prosperos create a world in which, in the name of saving lives and doing what benefits the community, they are complicit in murders and violence, and especially in the covering up of the truth of these crimes. An apparent benevolence masks a ruthless willingness to control and purify society, and a rigged game of Russian roulette obscures a conspiracy by suggesting that life and death are only a matter of chance. While Fandorin's fortuitous capacity to cheat death is a recurring theme in the Fandorin novels, in this case the Doge has rigged the game to be able to pick who dies himself. Putin and Prospero engage in what Svetlana Boym has called "restorative nostalgia," with its resistance to facts and its emphasis on "the return to origins and the conspiracy."[34] From his first presidential inauguration in 2000, Putin's semiosphere was managed by people like Nikita Mikhalkov, who summoned the dead from Imperial Russia, in both the inauguration broadcast and in his luxurious *jidaigeki* film *The Barber of Siberia* (1998).[35] Indeed Mikhalkov, as actor rather than director, had already connected Akunin and Putin, albeit in an ideologically very different manner, by playing the rather Putin-like character of Count Pozharsky in the film adaptation of Akunin's *The State Counsellor* (*Statskii sovetnik*).[36] Sadly, neither the live coverage of the inauguration, nor the panoramic vision of a young cadet's path from *zolotaia molodezh'* (golden youth) to exiled protector of the Siberian forests retained the Kurosawa-like complex narratological irony. By contrast, both Prospero and Putin's grand narratives of restoration are resisted by Akunin. Shakespeare's exiled duke and Russia's new leader each claim an absolute control, based upon fear and compliance that has been repackaged as protection and concern. Moreover, each ruler is ultimately resisted and undermined by those he imagines could never rebel. Within the novel, Masha's reflective nostalgia "dwells on the ambivalences of human longing and belonging and does not shy away from the contradictions of modernity."[37] Masha's and Akunin's resistance depends upon what Boym calls "commonplaces,"

the non-utterance of things that remain legible by involving a shared
network of prior meanings that go unnamed, and by paying attention
to the details that are right on the surface.[38]

Putin and Prospero, as well as most of the other characters in the novel
except Masha and maybe Fandorin, anticipate our new normal, which
is defined by the "post-factual" or "alternative factual," Kellyanne
Conway's coinages of 2016. With the word "post-truth" achieving the
alarming honour of being the Oxford Dictionaries' International Word
of the Year, Prospero's/Putin's post-2000 and Trump's post-2016 world
is the one in which we now live globally, one in which we try to assemble texts and evidence to render a threatening present intelligible. There
is, at least in Akunin's novel, a way out of this epistemological abyss:
evidence. For Akunin there is a specific type of surface in *She Lover of
Death* that does reveal the truth, and it is something entirely appropriate to a detective story: the fingerprint. The person who loves to kill
is caught by this surface trace. Whether your code breaker is Russian,
British, German, or French, the body insists that you look at the absolute surface at the undeniable trace that it has left. It is not the theoretical profile, but the print created by the body on the world that can tell
the truth. That truth is that death is not an alluring god/dess, but really
just a trap door, a gun, slit wrists, a strangulation, and only the naive
young woman can see simply enough to find the culprit. Only she (and
the professional spy/detective Fandorin), like the child in *Rashomon*, is
allowed to survive from among the Lovers of Death. By contrast with
post-factual inaugurations, directed by movie directors in Putin's case
in 2000 and attended by tens of thousands of people who do not show
up in photographs in 2017 for Trump, Akunin's Masha is not distracted
by the need to diagnose, cure, and narrate. Instead she is able clearly to
see and respond to concrete symptoms.

**Love for Cemeteries: In Which the Dead Tell Us Something about
the Lives of Cities**

Traces of the past provide the evidence to overturn false narratives.
Like so many existential tombstones, they persist, resilient despite
efforts to erase them and restore the shared nostalgic narrative. If we
return to what Akunin calls "beautiful" Paris we find more such markers of the dead event in a text where Akunin displaces Parisian gambits
to Moscow and sometimes writes about Moscow being displaced in
Paris. One of his loveliest and most curious books is about some of
the oldest and largest cemeteries in the world, ones which Chkhartishvili himself has visited and about which Akunin writes delightful short

stories. Among them he includes Père Lachaise Cemetery in Paris, that enormous hillside graveyard in the eastern part of the city where sensational outsiders like Oscar Wilde, Sarah Bernhardt, and Jim Morrison are buried. *Cemetery Tales* is a dialogue, between the author and himself, the philologist and the creator of fiction, about six necropolises, actual cities of the dead by contrast with *She Lover of Death*'s would-be cities of the dead, where the golden youth wish to pass from this life into a community beyond the grave. *Cemetery Tales* is already on the other side, already *podpol'ie*.

A kind of funereal travelogue in the form of a compact little book filled with photographs, which we could take along with us as we visit each cemetery, *Cemetery Tales* introduces each location with a non-fiction essay by Chkhartishvili, which is followed by an original short story that Akunin has imagined specifically for each place. Each story takes its inspiration from someone actually buried there and is illustrated in a style that pays homage to the setting; in the case of Paris the artist invoked is Wilde's friend and the illustrator of his play *Salomé*, Aubrey Beardsley. His collection of locales is distinguished and cosmopolitan. It tracks likely Russian, Soviet and post-Soviet emigration paths, with a notable Japanese addition: Don Cemetery (Moscow), Highgate Cemetery (London), Père Lachaise Cemetery (Paris), Green Wood Cemetery (New York), the Foreign Cemetery (Yokohama), and the Cemetery of the Patriarchs on the Mount of Olives (Jerusalem). Along with a vampiric Karl Marx in Highgate cemetery in London for example, one of the European undead who is encountered is Oscar Wilde. Wilde appears in Akunin's story about the expat Russian experience in the 1990s, in which émigrés are tasked with maintaining a cemetery which is both theirs and not theirs. As the character Pasha Lenkov maintains someone else's dead, and at the same time his (a number of Russian exiles are mentioned in the guide to the cemetery), he cannot resist the temptation to steal that past and, in robbing a famous exilic grave, discovers Oscar Wilde's ring, as well as his ghost and even his corpse. This surprising success in bringing to the surface a buried past quite literally sponsors a homoerotic adventure for a gravedigger, who is a philologist turned tomb raider.

In the preface to the book as a whole, Chkhartishvili and Akunin explain their project as being composed piecemeal, over the years. Rather like the documents assembled in *She Lover of Death*, it seems, our confidence in this book too depends upon its being assembled, not composed, upon its status as a dialogic collection rather than a monologic narrative. The pressure of those years at the turn of the millennium, our author says, has split him into two people: a popular entertainer of the public and someone more profound. Together *they* have a discovered a rather specific passion, *tafofilia*, or the love of cemeteries.[39] In a move that parallels but does not intersect with the Doge's minions, our "authors" have become the lovers of the *dead*, or as they exactly put it, the lovers of lost time and of the past. If the decadent and gothic young people of *She Lover of Death* are fascinated enough to imagine a romance with death him/herself, Chkhartishvili and Akunin wonder where another absent beloved might ever be found. They seek not a personal death in the future but the many mysterious dead that are already part of lost time. In this elegiac and Proustian tone, Chkhartishvili plays the role of Dr. Jekyll and introduces each locale, only to be followed by the Mr. Hyde detective story that is its uncanny double.

Both halves of this writing team share the same inspiration, the notion that what is most salient about a great city is not who lives there but who has died there. The preface confesses: "Do you know what seems to me the most intriguing in the inhabitants of Moscow, London, Paris, Amsterdam, and especially Rome or Jerusalem? The fact that most of them died."[40] He contrasts new cities like New York and Tokyo with the four ancient ones. For Chkhartishvili and Akunin, all great cities, especially ancient ones, are haunted, and (to cite their example) if you have not seen someone on Kuznetsky Most dressed in the Russian imperial style, you really have not seen Moscow yet.[41] Like so many countesses from Pushkin's novella *Pikovaia dama* (*The Queen of Spades*), the dead return, they outnumber us, and they take little interest in our minority presence: "If you want to understand and feel Moscow, walk around the Old Don Cemetery. In Paris, spend half a day at Père Lachaise. In London, go to the Highgate Cemetery."[42] Cemeteries for our "authors" are like Roland Barthes' photographs; they are the *punctum* that captures lost time and causes pain to the still living when we gaze upon them.[43] The nostalgia of the *tafofil* is reflective, not restorative, because as Boym notes, "it dwells in *algia* (aching), in longing and loss, the imperfect process of remembrance."[44]

Père Lachaise is a special place, where all the outsiders lie in a space appended to the imaginary that is Paris. D'Artagnan and Louis XIV shaped this chronotope in our mind, Chkhartishvili says, but within it he seeks the familiar, the Russian dead. Exiled, impoverished, and celebrated, various sorts of exiles are there, as permanent residents and as tourists (themselves abroad in temporary voluntary exiles) who snap their photos with those whom they admire, at least in more recent years creating necro-selfies with the beautiful dead. In fact, Chkhartishvili notes, the dead are not as beautiful as we need them to be, just as the suicides in *She Lover of Death* are less picturesque than Masha would wish. Proust's grave, for example, a simple black slab for someone who was an outsider by religion although not by birth, disappoints Chkhartishvili, until he recognizes that it is not Proust who was so remarkable but what he wrote. To go behind or underneath the text, to exhume the author and his meaning, is to take a risk. What lies beneath may not impress and may fail to account for what is on the surface. Death needs to be aestheticized, to be considered phenomenologically rather than to be understood hermeneutically. It can be marked and commemorated; it can even be an object of reflection when pieces of what was, like a gravestone, are presented to us. It can be civilized and memorialized, but it cannot be tamed or interpreted. The black slab of the gravestone is just a stone with a name written on it. Like a fingerprint, it bears the trace of the human as one of those small leftover things that mark the surface on behalf of what is no longer there. For Akunin, the past is something that can only be treated as a social and surface phenomenon, not as an existentialist or essential one. His dead take leisurely walks along the fashionable streets of central Moscow and escape from the grave, rather than speaking truths to us *iz podpolia.*

The detective short story with which Akunin complements Chkhartishvili's comments on the Père Lachaise takes its title from the obscene and necrophiliac request that the titular Salomé makes of the severed head of John the Baptist at the end of Wilde's play, when she asks him to kiss her on the lips. It concerns Pasha Lenkov, a Russian émigré trying to get by through taking the job of curating someone else's dead, of attending to, and literally stealing, someone else's past. Each cemetery is given a subtitle of the format "[name] Cemetery, or the [adjective] death," with Paris being "beautiful," Moscow "forgotten," London "polite," Yokohama "unexpected," New York "optimistic," and Jerusalem "not the least terrible." Like the provincial Russians in the paired novels *S/he Lover of Death*, who join secret and criminal secret societies, Akunin's protagonists are always out of joint. Whether seeking an extraordinary life, like Masha, or merely seeking to preserve life itself, like Sen'ka and Lenkov, each fictional character discovers that things are exactly what they appear to be. This is the terrible secret, and those who attempt to "go beneath the surface" as Wilde says in the preface to *The Picture of Dorian Gray* (1890) do so "at their own peril."[45] In the hermeneutic endeavour, we create alternative truths and enter the realm of the post-factual. The secret is that there are no secrets. Secrets are symptoms, not truths.

Certain things remain resiliently true, and they are often painful. The attack does happen in Kurosawa's film, but we are not sure about how. We are challenged to perform a careful curation of evidence, of someone else's sexual and violent past. We are only rescued by Kurosawa from this pessimism by a finale, the adoption of the child, which is tacked on, just as the escapade with Masha's costume at the end of *She Lover of Death* verges on the comic. In no way does her salvation by an angel attend to the brooding uncertainties that always attract Fandorin's attention and always seem to present themselves anew across the Fandorin volumes. The suspicion about all narratives, especially official ones, that Akunin adapts from Kurosawa has been called the Rashomon-effect, an instance of multiple conflicting accounts of the same event that cannot be resolved so as to find a single truth. It is the very search for a meaningful truth, however, that causes that effect. All that really matters is that the samurai is dead and his wife has been raped; Wilde and all the other fin-de-siècle writers buried in Père Lachaise are dead; Sen'ka and Lenkov are broke and hungry; someone left a finger print on the gun. That is all. It is only, Akunin suggests, when we resist the impulse to narrate, or when we over-narrate, as Varvara does in *The Turkish Gambit*, that the very inadequacy of stories to recover the past, together with their virtuosic attempts to do so, emerges. By carefully selecting the adjectives that describe the various cemeteries, words that only define them relationally, how they appear, and how they are viewed by the inhabitants of their cities, Akunin capitalizes on our desire to investigate and discover, while always frustrating it. He never quite gives us the truth, always keeping something back with his picturesque period prose, whether from dandies in 1890 or New Russians in 1990, and by holding us at arm's length with his eccentric and aloof protagonist. A tour de force of polyglossic layering, each of Akunin's texts asks us to dig deeper, only to reveal not a fundamental truth but another layer of deferred and buried meaning. As a master of suspense and narrative seduction, Akunin invites the same necrophilic, or perhaps more accurately the same *tafofilic*, encounter that Wilde's ghost provides to the thief. The strange pleasure of perpetually excavating a past that is always incomplete, along with an invitation to dig deeper for evidence, is not merely a guilty pleasure like reading sensational detective novels. Reflectively assembling and digging up the many discarded and lost pieces of the past is also a moment of underground resistance to all restorative nostalgias, especially on a national scale, whether in Revolutionary France or Putin's Russia, or today, wherever Akunin's work is being read.

NOTES

1 Akira Kurosawa, dir., *Rashomon*, film (Tokyo: Daiei Film, 1950).
2 Akira Kurosawa, dir., *Kakushi-toride no san-akunin/The Hidden Fortress*, film (Tokyo: Toho Co. Ltd., 1950).

3 Akira Kurosawa, dir., *Ikimono no Kiroku / I Live in Fear* (Tokyo: Toho Co. Ltd, 1955).

4 Orhan Pamuk, *My Name is Red*, trans. Erdag Göknar (New York: Alfred Knopf, 2001).

5 See Mikhail Bakhtin, "Discourse in the Novel," in *The Dialogic Imagination*, ed. Michael Holquist, trans. Caryl Emerson and Michael Holquist (Austin: University of Texas Press, 1982), 259–422; Walter Benjamin, "The Work of Art in the Age of Mechanical Reproduction," in *Illuminations*, ed. Hannah Arendt, trans. Harry Zohn (New York: Schocken Books, 1969), 217–51.

6 Svetlana Boym, *The Future of Nostalgia* (New York: Basic Books, 2002), xviii.

7 Robert Louis Stevenson, *The Strange Case of Dr. Jekyll and Mr. Hyde* (London: Longmans Green and Co., 1886).

8 See Boris Akunin, *Liubovnitsa smerti* (Moscow: Zakharov, 2001); Boris Akunin, *Liubovnik smerti* (Moscow: Zakharov, 2001), as well as the translations of these novels: Boris Akunin, *She Lover of Death*, trans. Andrew Bromfield (London: Weidenfeld & Nicolson, 2009); Boris Akunin, *He Lover of Death*, trans. Andrew Bromfield (New York: Phoenix, 2011).

9 Grigorii Chkhartishvili, *Kladbishchenskie istorii* (*Cemetery Tales*; Moscow: Zakharov, 2004).

10 Nikolai Karamzin, *Bednaia Liza / Poor Liza*, Russian texts series (London: Bristol Classical Press, 1998).

11 Eugène Sue, *Les mystères de Paris* (Paris: Librairie de Charles Gosselin, 1842).

12 Fedor Dostoevsky, *Zapiski iz podpolia. Sorabranie sochinenii v desiati tomakh* (Moscow: Khudozhestvennaia literatura, 1957).

13 See Boris Akunin, *Azazel'* (Moscow: Zakharov, 1998), and its translation: Boris Akunin, *The Winter Queen*, trans. Andrew Bromfield (New York: Random House, 2003).

14 Christopher Prendergast, *For the People by the People? Eugène Sue's Les Mystères de Paris: A Hypothesis in the Sociology of Literature* (Oxford: Legenda, 2003), 15 and 22–3; Carl Ostrowski, "Kindred Contemporaries: Lippard, Bird, Simms, Hawthorne, and Irving," in *The Oxford Handbook of Edgar Allan Poe*, ed. J. Gerald Kennedy and Scott Peeples (Oxford: Oxford University Press, 2019), 544; Vissarion Belinsky, "Thoughts and Notes on Russian Literature," in *Belinsky, Chernyshevsky, and Dobrolyubov: Selected Criticism*, ed. Ralph E. Matlaw (Bloomington: Indiana University Press, 1962), 25.

15 See Prendergast, *For the People*, 27.

16 Dmitry Shlapentokh, *The French Revolution in Russian Intellectual Life: 1865–1905* (Westport, CT: Greenwood Publishing Group, 1996).

17 Boris Akunin, "Interview with Alexei Navalny," *LiveJournal* (blog), 3 January 2012, https://borisakunin.livejournal.com/49763.html.

18 Shikibu Murasaki, *Tale of Genji*, trans. Royall Tyler (New York: Penguin Classics, 2002).

19 Bram Stoker, *Dracula* (London: Archibald Constable, 1897).

20 Arthur Conan Doyle, *The Original Illustrated Sherlock Holmes* (Secaucus, NJ: Castle, 1976).

21 Boris Akunin, *The Turkish Gambit*, trans. Andrew Bromfield (New York: Random House Trade Paperbacks, 2005).

22 Stephen Best and Sharon Marcus, "Surface Reading," *Representations* 108, no. 1 (2009): 1–21.

23 Rita Felski, *The Limits of Critique* (Chicago: Chicago University Press, 2015), 87ff.

24 Horace Walpole, *The Castle of Otranto*, ed. Nick Groom (Oxford: Oxford University Press, 2014).

25 Will Cathercart, "How Author Boris Akunin Became Putin's Nemesis," The Daily Beast, 25 April 2017, updated 10 August 2018, https://www .thedailybeast.com/how-author-boris-akunin-became-putins-nemesis.

26 Boris Akunin, "Boris Akunin: Russia Ruled by a 'Khan,'" interview with Zhanna Nemtsova, *Deutsche Welle*, 12 May 2016, http://www.dw.com/en /boris-akunin-russia-ruled-by-a-khan/a-19252850.

27 Stephen Norris, "Boris Akunin (Grigorii Chkhartishvili), 1956–," in *Russia's People of Empire: Life Stories from Eurasia, 1500 to the Present*, ed. Stephen M. Norris and Willard Sunderland (Bloomington: Indiana University Press, 2012), 331–4.

28 Joseph Frank, *Dostoevsky: The Seeds of Revolt: 1821–1849* (Princeton, NJ: Princeton University Press, 1979).

29 "Putinskie SMI opublikovali spisok vragov Rossii," *Glavnoe*, 19 August 2014, https://glavnoe.ua/news/n188000. See the English translation of the post in Joel Harding, "Putin's Media Published a List of Russia's Enemies," To Inform Is to Influence, 19 August 2014, https://toinformistoinfluence .com/2014/08/19/list-vrag-naroda-enemy-of-the-people/.

30 Ibid.

31 Nikolai Gogol', "Portret," in *Peterburgskie povesti* (St. Petersburg: Nauka, 1995).

32 Akunin, *She Lover of Death*, 14.

33 Akunin, "Interview with Alexei Navalny"; William Shakespeare, *The Tempest*, ed. Virginia Mason Vaughan and Alden T. Vaughan (London: Arden Shakespeare, Bloomsbury Publishing, 2011).

34 Boym, *Future of Nostalgia*, 13.

35 Nikita Mikhalkov, dir., *Sibirskii tsiriul'nik* (*The Barber of Siberia*), film (Moscow: Studio TriTe, 1999).

36 Filipp Yankovskii, *Statskii sovietnik* (*The State Counsellor*), film (Russia: Channel 1, 2005).

37 Boym, *Future of Nostalgia*, xviii.

38 Svetlana Boym, *Commonplaces; Mythologies of Everyday Life in Russia* (Cambridge, MA: Harvard University Press, 1995).

39 Chkhartishvili, *Kladbishchenskie istorii*, 3.

40 Chkhartishvili, *Kladbishchenskie istorii*, 4. Translations mine.
41 Chkhartishvili, *Kladbishchenskie istorii*, 5.
42 Chkhartishvili, *Kladbishchenskie istorii*, 7.
43 Roland Barthes, *Camera Lucida*, trans. Richard Howell (New York: Hill and Wang, 1980).
44 Boym, *Future of Nostalgia*, 50.
45 Oscar Wilde, *The Complete Works of Oscar Wilde* (New York: Collins, 1989), 17.

8 Spying on the Past: Boris Akunin's History of Espionage

STEPHEN M. NORRIS

If there is such a thing as a sense of reality ... then there must also be something that one can call a sense of possibility. ... The sense of possibility might be defined outright as the capacity to think how everything could "just as easily be," and to attach no more importance to what is than to what is not.[1]

Robert Musil

Books and spy movies like *The Sword and the Shield* took hold of my imagination. What amazed me most of all was how one man's effort could achieve what whole armies could not. One spy could decide the fate of thousands of people. At least that's the way I understood it.[2]

Vladimir Putin, *First Person*

In the popular imagination, spies and detectives are cunning, rational, and nearly omnipotent. Espionage activities therefore frequently provide the fodder for conspiracy theories: spies working behind the scenes, in other words, produce outcomes most do not truly see. Detectives (or opposing spies) also shape these outcomes, employing the same sort of guile as their adversaries. Even former spies encourage these perceptions: Vladimir Putin, a former KGB agent, noted in 2000 that he became a spy in part because of the way agents appeared on-screen, able to shape history decisively in ways entire armies could not.

These perceptions of espionage are at the heart of the Boris Akunin project. Akunin has employed his fictional talents to craft a particular history of espionage, one where his fiction (in spite of what Akunin often says in his interviews), has helped to provide new historical interpretations for the new Russia. Beginning with *The Turkish Gambit* (*Turetskii gambit*, 1998), which was written in the style of a *shpionskii detektiv* (spy mystery story) set during the Russo–Turkish War of 1877–8,

Akunin has crafted a series of spy novels that cross chronological eras. His *Spy Novel* (*Shpionskii roman*, 2005), part of his "genre series," recasts the buildup to Operation Barbarossa in 1941 through the activities of spies. He would further explore the realm of espionage in the Stalin era in *Quest* (*Kvest*, 2008), his novel that takes the form of a video game. And finally, his *kino-roman* (cinema-novel) series, *Brotherhood of Death* (*Smert' na brudershaft*, 2007–11) consists of ten novellas that narrate the intelligence rivalries between Russia and Germany in the Great War.[3] These projects appeared while Akunin was adapting his spy novels for the big screen: Dzhanik Faiziev's 2005 blockbuster *Turkish Gambit* was briefly the highest-grossing film in Russian history when it earned $18.5m in 2005, and Aleksei Andrianov's 2012 *Spy* earned a respectable $5m at the box office.[4]

Most of the early scholarly literature on Akunin's work focuses on one of three topics: the nostalgia for a lost Russia his novels tapped into, the intertextual elements to his various projects, or the ways Akunin/ Chkhartishvili the author plays with his audiences.[5] This chapter, by contrast, takes his novels and screenplays that employ spies as a more serious attempt to "do" history: that is, to offer a meaningful interpretation of the past where espionage helps to explain historical outcomes. It focuses on two case studies: *The Turkish Gambit* and *Spy Novel*. Both books sold well and were turned into popular films, ensuring that the revisions of the past in them reached a large audience. Ultimately, Akunin spies on the past in order to illustrate a history full of conspiracy theories, secret plots, and behind-the-scenes deals. In doing so, he rethinks history by creating a "sense of possibility" about the past, as the novelist Robert Musil suggests in the epigraph to this chapter, one where espionage plays a more visible role in the way history unfolds but also one that does not challenge historical outcomes. To understand how Akunin reimagines history through espionage, however, requires two brief history lessons, offered in the two case studies below.

Case #1: Historical Gambits

In which we rethink the events of the Russo-Turkish War of 1877–8 and, with it, how we understand the past

In April 1877, the Russian writer Fedor Dostoevsky decided that war could be a form of salvation. Writing in his diary with less spite than usual, he rejoiced at the news that Russian forces were once more being given the chance to fight against the Turks. Dostoevsky, always one to speak on behalf of everyone, wrote that if you were to ask every single soldier departing for the war, they "will tell you, as one man, that they are going to serve Christ and to liberate their oppressed brethren, and not a single one is thinking about seizing territory." He concluded that the present war was a sacred one that would both demonstrate Russia's mission in Europe and help to establish a future peace based on "truth."[6]

Dostoevsky almost certainly did not speak for every soldier, but his belief that the 1877 war against the Ottoman Empire was a sacred one was widely shared among the educated public. Pan-Slavists such as Mikhail Pogodin, Ivan Aksakov, and Nikolai Danilevskii had called on the tsar to unite all the Slavs living under Ottoman rule. These calls only intensified after the 1875 and 1876 revolts by Bosnians and Bulgarians and the subsequent massacre of over 30,000 Bulgarians at the hands of Ottoman forces. At first, Alexander II worked with other European leaders to end the crisis, but pressure at home, including Mikhail Katkov's editorials and popular images devoted to the brother Bulgarians, helped to force Alexander's hand (even his wife and son, the future Alexander III, pressured him to act). The newly founded Slavonic Benevolent Committee openly sent aid and irregular troops to the region. The tsar declared war against Turkey on 24 April 1877. It may have been the first war declaration caused by popular opinion.[7]

Once war was declared, Russian forces crossed the Danube, adopting a plan developed by General N. N. Obruchev that envisioned a lightning campaign aimed directly at taking Constantinople, and a small force of Russian and Bulgarian troops under the command of General Iosif Gurko gained control over the strategically significant Shipka Pass in the Balkan Mountains. Soviet historians would even praise these early stages as an outstanding example of "a complex strategic operation conducted on a broad front."[8] For the next five months, between July and December, the war was dominated by the Siege of Plevna (now Pleven, Bulgaria), where Turkish forces held out against their opponents and where 50,000 soldiers would die, of which 40,000 were Russians. The siege began after Gurko's successful capture of the Shipka Pass. Turkish troops, led by their best commander, Osman Pasha, left Vidin and headed to Plevna to fortify it. Russian forces, who had just taken Nikopol, also turned to Plevna, but the Turkish troops beat them there by six to eight hours on 7 July. A lengthy siege ensued. The tide turned when Alexander II and his brother, Grand Duke Nicholas, turned to Eduard Totleben, who had overseen the fortifications of Sevastopol during the Crimean War. Totleben studied Turkish defences at Plevna and recommended the Russians encircle it completely rather than attack, which was accomplished by 24 October. On 9 December, the Turks, exhausted from the siege, attacked, were driven back, and surrendered the next day. From that point on, the Russians enjoyed spectacular successes and pushed the Turks back to the village of San Stefano, located fifteen kilometres from Constantinople itself. The decisive battle was conducted by Mikhail Skobelev at the Sheinovo redoubts, a bayonet attack across open ground that one American historian has labelled "one of the nineteenth century's 'perfect battles.'"[9] In March the Turks signed a treaty, handing over their Bessarabian and Caucasian provinces to Russia, guaranteeing Serbian, Montenegrin, and Romanian independence, and creating a large Bulgarian state.

The war furthered the "Skobelev phenomenon," the celebrity-like status of the so-called White General, Mikhail Skobelev, who had first been lionized during the Central Asian conquests and who had heroically fought at Plevna.[10] From beginning to end, the conflict was broadly understood in Russia as a holy war to liberate the Orthodox Christians suffering under Ottoman rule. After it ended and Bismarck's Congress of Berlin took away Russian gains, this notion continued: using funds raised across the country, Vladimir Sherwood's Plevna Chapel opened outside Moscow's Ilinskii Gate on the tenth anniversary of the Turkish surrender. The memorial was not subtle, featuring an Orthodox cross on top of a Muslim half-moon along with various bas-reliefs depicting Russian heroism and Turkish perfidy.[11] Even in this memorial, though, the war followed a familiar script: it started as a war of liberation led by the tsar, and featured heroic leadership embodied by Skobelev and brave actions by the soldiers who besieged Plevna.

Yet what if the war had not unfolded according to plans drawn by military strategists, popular Pan-Slavist sentiment, or charges led by generals? What if the entire campaign and its events had resulted from a conspiratorial gambit designed to reveal Russia's imperial ambitions in the Balkans? What if, in short, the Russo–Turkish War of 1877–8 featured spies, not soldiers, as the primary actors in the drama? The war unfolded at a moment when Russia's security police (*okhrana*) underwent significant changes, reforms that continued during the leadership of Sergei Zubatov between 1886 and 1902. The *okhrana* expanded its surveillance capabilities, engaged in more systematic intelligence gathering, and increasingly developed an ability to distinguish between nonviolent opponents of the regime and violent ones. The policemen who served the system, in short, became more modern. At the same time, *okhrana* agents practiced methods of secrecy called *konspiratsiia*, which "meant discussing professional matters with no one outside the service, hiding the identity of informants even from one's superiors, and avoiding routine public appearances."[12] While the security police engaged in a fierce rivalry with the gendarmes and often proved unable to either infiltrate revolutionary groups or win over the populace, nonetheless the era was one where plainclothes surveillants, a mobile surveillance brigade, and secret informants were created and flourished in Russia. The result was the creation of a new generation of policemen.

This was the era of Erast Fandorin, Boris Akunin's most well-known creation. *The Turkish Gambit*, the second novel in the Fandorin series, is set during the war. In it, espionage activities play a decisive role in driving the plot. After volunteering to fight in the conflict, Fandorin learns about a Turkish spy who might be guiding the war's activities. Fandorin accepts a mission to expose the Turkish secret agent, Anwar-effendi, who can pass undetected in both Ottoman and Russian camps. The effendi's manoeuvres alter the course of the war: among his behind-the-scenes moves, he manages to change a coded message that warned of the Turkish forces gathering at Plevna to state that they were headed to Nikopol instead. Russian forces captured the unguarded town, only to be bogged down at Plevna. The siege, in other words, did not result from Turkish forces arriving earlier than Russians after both sides executed precise orders, but from espionage.

In the end (spoiler alert!), the spy turns out to be a French journalist, Charles Paladin, who has roamed through the Russian encampments and befriended General Sobolev (Akunin's fictional version of Skobelev). His last gambit, as he explains in the novel's denouement, was to play on Sobolev's vanity and get him to travel with a small detachment of troops first to San Stefano and then into Constantinople. The ambitious general, in the "elegant plan" constructed by the Turkish mole, would then be exposed and, with him, Russia's imperial ambitions to capture Constantinople, inevitably triggering a reaction in Europe. Just as Sobolev is about to lead a charge into the Ottoman capital city, Fandorin bursts in and reveals Paladin as Anwar-effendi. The last part of the gambit is foiled. However, the subsequent Treaty of San Stefano's punitive measures trigger the anticipated European reaction: the novel closes with a British press clipping that states that the British government "categorically refuses to recognize the exorbitant peace terms imposed on Turkey by the rapacious appetites of Tsar Alexander. The Treaty of San Stefano is contrary to the interests of European security and must be reviewed at a special congress in which all the great powers will take part."[13]

Akunin's narration of the war and its espionage activities offers commentary on the increasing number of clandestine groups and the possible consequences of so many unfolding conspiracies in Russia. Anwar-effendi, buying time while his gambit unfolds, tells his Russian captive:

I've noticed that, in your Russia, the revolutionaries have already started shooting occasionally. But soon a genuine clandestine war will begin – you can take the word of a professional on that. Idealistic young men and women will start blowing up palaces, trains, and carriages. And, inevitably, in addition to the reactionary minister of the villainous governor they will contain innocent people – relatives, assistants, servants. But that's all right if it's for the sake of an idea. Give them time and your idealists will worm their way into positions of trust, and spy, and deceive, and kill apostates – and all for the sake of an idea.[14]

Elaborating, Anwar-effendi declares that the world is one best understood as one where "a great game of chess is being played out, and I am playing for the white pieces." Russia is the black. When asked why, he responds:

Today, your immensely powerful state constitutes the main danger to civilization. With its vast expanses, its multitudinous, ignorant population, its cumbersome and aggressive state apparatus ... The mission of the Russian people is to take Constantinople and unite the Slavs? To what end? So that the Romanovs might once again impose their will on Europe? A nightmarish prospect indeed! It is not pleasant for you to hear this ... but lurking within Russia is a terrible threat to civilization. There are savage, destructive forces fermenting within her, forces that will break out sooner or later, and then the world will be in a bad way. It is an unstable, ridiculous country that has absorbed all the worst features of the West and the East. Russia has to be put back in its place; its reach has to be shortened. It will be good for you, and it will give Europe a chance to continue developing in the right direction.[15]

Anwar-Effendi, in short, explains that the entire war has resulted from his spy gambit. In his speeches he also offers an alternative history of Russian imperial ambition, the rationale for the war, and an explanation for the peace to come. In the end, the spy's version of Russia and her immediate future triumphs. His historical gambit has succeeded.

What conclusions can we draw from this first case of espionage and how Akunin plots it into history? Interestingly, the historical outcome in Akunin's novel does not change: the siege of Plevna still dominates the action in the war, Russian forces under Sobolev/Skobelev eventually win the day and nearly took Constantinople, the Turks sue for peace, the Treaty of San Stefano imposes harsh punishments on the Ottoman state, and European powers intervene diplomatically. In the film version, Akunin's script introduces a new villain, Ismail-bei, who controls the mole. The spy this time (second spoiler alert!) turns out to be Sobolev's attaché, Perepelkin (Fandorin suspected him in the novel). He is motivated by greed and by the desire to make England enter the war, but the result remains the same. History does not change in *The Turkish Gambit*; its causes do. That is one.

Akunin's plot allows for individual vanities, stupidities, intelligence, blunders, and other human behaviours to drive history. Sobolev is a particularly important figure in this rewriting of the past. *The Turkish Gambit* takes the general off his pedestal (or white horse) and presents him as vainglorious. Sobolev declares that "my true passion is ambition, and everything else comes second."[16] The general's vanity is something Anwar-effendi exposes (and, as we discover, he has been doing so during Sobolev's career, dating back to Central Asia). In his cover as Paladin, the Turkish super-spy suggests that Sobolev load up a train and head to San Stefano just to see Constantinople. Once there, it is the Turkish agent who plays on the general's ambitions, suggesting that the general need only take a single battalion to take the capital city, which he declares would surely be in panic. The idea of riding into Constantinople with flags flying and drums beating and then presenting everyone with a fait accompli proves too seductive for Sobolev (this is, it's worth noting, exactly the way Skobelev charged at Plevna and then Sheinovo). Yet in a sense, he is following emotions and habits of mind that drive the action of all of Akunin's characters: throughout the novel, perceptions and misperceptions drive the course of the war and the search for spies. Earlier, the breakthrough at Plevna occurred because Fandorin realized Anwar-effendi had planted a false rumour and the Russian secret policeman was able to get Sobolev to attack. *The Turkish Gambit* does not present the past as a series of events where people act rationally and where events unfold according to logic; instead, subterfuge, misunderstandings, vanities, and irrational behaviours can explain historical outcomes. That is two.

Akunin's vision of the past is one where spies and subterfuge, conspiracies and behind-the-scenes manoeuvring, produce the events of history. Anwar-effendi has allegedly changed laws in countries, assisted in assassinations, and created a propaganda campaign designed to transform Turkey's image in the West. He has also, according to one of Fandorin's colleagues, "managed to build telegraph lines, introduce horse-drawn streetcars in Baghdad, set steamships sailing up and down the Euphrates, establish the first Iraqi newspaper, and enrol pupils in a school of commerce" (these achievements are notably presented second-hand; others describe Anwar-effendi in these terms).[17] One man, in other words, has decisively altered the fate of a country.

In the war of 1877–8, historians typically state that Osman Pasha was sent by the Ottoman high command to reinforce Nikopol, but Russian forces reached it first and easily took it. Faced with a change in plans, Osman decided to fortify the nearby town of Plevna and could control all the routes into Bulgaria from there. In other words, the war unfolded not according to a clear plan, but the main agents driving events were officers, generals, and other military leaders. In Akunin's reworking, spies play the more significant role, working behind the scenes in order to draw the Russians into Anwar-effendi's gambit. That is three.

Espionage is a "high art" according to Fandorin,[18] yet in Akunin's rendering of history it is more than that. In the rare instances where historians have treated tsarist espionage seriously, their roles are presented as informational gatherers, through the stories of sensational cases of double agents (Evno Azev, for example), or for their failures to convince tsarist officials of impending disasters during the Great War.[19] Mark Kramer, in an introduction to a collection of essays on spying culled from the *Journal of Cold War Studies*, writes that "espionage and covert operations are notoriously difficult to study because intelligence agencies in all countries try to keep their own activities highly secret." Espionage in many ways remains "the missing dimension of historical scholarship," as Christopher Andrew and David Dilks argued nearly thirty years ago.[20] As a result of this lacuna, novelists have taken the lead in inserting spies into the past. Fictional spies tend to be almost omniscient creatures, supernaturally smart and with an ability to change the course of history single-handedly. Anwar-effendi is presented this way in Akunin's novel. In *The Turkish Gambit* (and, for that matter, the entire Fandorin series), Akunin fleshes out the personality of a secret policeman, his mindset, and people's reactions to him. Fandorin, however, often bumbles his way through events and follows false trails. Only as he gains experience does he become a better spy. What guides him in the early novels, particularly in *The Turkish Gambit*, is a sense of patriotism (he retains this belief throughout, even when he questions his state service in *The State Counsellor* [*Statskii sovetnik*, 1999]). In the opening sequence, a young woman (Varvara) who has left Moscow to come find her fiancé in Turkey is saved by a disguised Fandorin. When she later discovers his profession, Varya "gave a feeble gasp of amazement. She had taken Fandorin for a decent man – but he was a police agent! And he had even made himself out to be some kind of romantic hero, like Lermontov's Pechorin. That intriguing pallor, that languid glance, that nobly graying hair. How could she trust anyone after this?"[21] Fandorin, for his part, declares to his superior that "it is not you I serve, but Russia."[22] These reactions and responses remain throughout the series. Akunin's rewriting of history revises the Soviet-era narrative that viewed the *okhrana* as evil agents of the tsar and presents its employees as patriotic citizens serving their country.[23] At the same time, Akunin's spy is human, full of the foibles we would expect of humanity but not of fictional spies. That is four.

Case #2: What Stalin Knew

[Top Secret]

On 17 June 1941, Pavel Fitin, chief of NKGB Foreign Intelligence, sent a report to Joseph Stalin. The report was a clear one, with a clear thesis: "All preparations by Germany for an armed attack on the Soviet Union have been completed, and the blow can be expected at any time." The spy had received his news from an intelligence officer in the Nazi Air Ministry. Fitin's report was one of many sent by Soviet spies in the months before June 1941. All concluded that Hitler was planning an attack.

Stalin's response was equally clear. In the margin, the Soviet leader wrote to Vsevolod Merkulov, Fitin's boss: "Comrade Merkulov, you can send your 'source' from the headquarters of German aviation to his fucking mother. This is not a 'source' but a *dezinformator*."[24]

The reasons why Stalin ignored sound intelligence in June 1941 remain the source of much debate. Mark Kramer, in his assessment of the role of espionage in history, cites the Barbarossa debacle as a classic case of how intelligence reports failed to impact history. Kramer writes that even though the Soviet dictator "received excellent intelligence from numerous, multiple sources about the impending German onslaught ... he took no measures to prepare for the invasion. On the contrary, he regarded the intelligence as essentially disinformation that was deliberately trying to provoke some Soviet action. So, he disregarded it, even though it was the best intelligence one could possibly hope for."[25] In the most exhaustive account published about June 1941, David Murphy agrees. Murphy studied the available documents about the Nazi invasion and what Soviet security agencies knew. He concludes that the sources "establish without a reasonable doubt that the Soviet services were highly alert to this threat."[26]

Why did Stalin ignore his agents? Some scholars argue that the Soviet dictator had created a climate of fear and subservience that made massive errors of communication inevitable. The system Stalin created, in other words, was to blame. Others suggest that Stalin's passivity resulted from his knowledge that the Red Army was still not fully prepared to face the Wehrmacht in June 1941. In this scenario, Stalin was also to blame, for his purges had decimated the officer corps. Still others give Stalin more credit, arguing that the dictator believed Hitler knew he could not conquer Russia and that Nazi troop movements were a bluff designed to cover his intentions to invade Great Britain. Finally, the publication of Viktor Suvorov's 1987 book *Icebreaker* introduced yet another, more conspiratorial, element to the controversy by suggesting that Stalin was preparing for a pre-emptive strike against Nazi Germany and not prepared for a defensive war. Suvorov, the pseudonym of Vladimir Rezun, a defector to the United Kingdom, based his case on the maps and phrasebooks handed out to Soviet troops in 1941, which contained German locales and phrases. Although his arguments have been met with scepticism from historians, the icebreaker controversy still lingers.[27]

The question remains, however: Why did Stalin disregard intelligence reports in June 1941? What did he know?[28] Akunin's *Spy Novel* seeks to answers these questions. It is set between April and June 1941. Its protagonist, Egor Dorin, is a young NKGB agent who also boxes for Dynamo Sports Club (the official sports club of the Soviet secret services).[29] Born the day after the October Revolution (8 November 1917), Dorin is also the son of Bavarian immigrants to the USSR on his mother's side and speaks fluent German. Because of his linguistic abilities, Dorin is recruited by a higher-ranking agent, Oktiabr'skii, and tasked with exposing a German Abwehr agent named Wasser. The German, Dorin is told, is deeply embedded within the higher echelons of Soviet officialdom and apparently up to no good.[30]

Spy Novel recreates a Stalinist-era Moscow where espionage abounds. The Soviet capital is full of suspicion and fear. Plots are seemingly everywhere, and Soviet leaders must try to figure out which ones are real and which ones are bluffs. Akunin's narration recreates a historical atmosphere, one where, in the wake of the purges, everything has become possible. Moscow in 1941 is a place where the extraordinary has become ordinary, where conspiracies are now increasingly plausible.[31] The hyper-urbanization of the city, the plan to reconstruct it, Stalin's vision of Moscow as a true capital of worldwide socialism: all have been realized in Akunin's pages (one scene in the novel references the completed Palace of Soviets, a point emphasized in the 2012 film version *Spy*). In one sense, *Spy Novel* is a hyperreal version of the past. Its Moscow is, to use the words of Karl Schlögel, "an amorphous 'maximum city'" held together by a grand vision of its future and a fear of the mortal dangers that threaten it.[32]

Above all, Stalin's city is saturated with rumours. In one scene, NKGB officers, including Oktiabr'skii, meet with Lavrentii Beria, who has assigned them all roles based on characterizations of the USSR's major rivals. Oktiabr'skii plays "the German" and declares that the Nazis represent the main threat and will probably invade in late May or June 1941. A second officer takes on the role of "the Japanese" and outlines how two war parties exist in Tokyo, one with army generals pressing for a land war against the USSR and a second made up of admirals advocating for a surprise attack on the USA. Soviet spies, he suggested, should help pressure the Emperor to take the side of the admirals. "The American" spins a fanciful tale of how that country's leaders "set a goal for world domination." The first step was the Great War, when American machinations saw the financial centre of the globe shift from London to New York. The second phase was to be American attempts to get Germany to fight in the East and become bogged down there, eliminating both Nazi Germany and the USSR as potential rivals. "If we allow American agents to act without control in Europe," the NKGB officer concludes, "it will have serious consequences" (the others find this argument "too weak"). "The Englishman," a Senior Lieutenant named Matvei Kogan, states that a truce between Hitler and Britain is imminent: the British are exhausted from air raids, the Germans worn out from submarine warfare. Kogan lays out a power struggle within the British leadership between those wanting to carry on the fight against Nazi Germany and those wanting to settle a truce, allowing the Germans to turn east. Beria concludes the meeting by instructing all four to assume that their side's plots are the ones that will determine "the fate of the future war."[33] The scene illustrates an important point *Spy Novel* makes in its attempt to work through 1941: in the mindset of Soviet officials, a viewpoint passed down to their security agents, every political rival was plotting against the USSR. Trying to figure out which plot was more likely to be realized formed the basic problem to solve in the lead-up to June.

The real plot, of course, is the one initiated by Hitler. The novel opens with the German dictator meeting with two of his advisors. Hitler is enjoying his successes in Yugoslavia but wants to turn his attention eastward. German troops have been massing near the Soviet border but Hitler wants the Abwehr to throw the Soviet leaders off the obvious conclusion. His advisors protest, noting that the NKGB already knows about Barbarossa. Hitler is insistent: find out a way to catch the Soviet leaders by surprise or else Barbarossa will have to be called off. Once this can be guaranteed, Hitler's armies will need only ten days. The Nazi leader instructs his advisors to target "the Asians" within the

Soviet leadership. His advisors construct a plan where the Russians will see the forest, but not the wolves lurking within it. They plan a distraction by trying to turn attention to Britain. But mostly they decide that the "role of personality in history" (*rol' lichnosti v istorii*) might sway things.[34] To employ it, they hope to exploit the intelligence and counterintelligence units in the USSR. They select the only person for the job: an agent named Wasser.

As these decisions are being made in Berlin, others are prepared in Moscow. Oktiabr'skii shows up to watch Dorin box and recruits him for a dangerous mission. He needs, as he says, a man who is "sporty, quick-thinking, and, most importantly, with fluent German."[35] *Spy Novel*, like *The Turkish Gambit*, also features a love story between the protagonist and a woman who does not view secret policemen positively. Nadezhda, Dorin's love interest, was homeschooled by her father, a doctor who Dorin declares is "a fragment of the past."[36] Dorin initially hides his profession from Nadia and her father. When he reveals it, she cries, "You're a chekist? No! No! It can't be!" Dorin tells her that he carries a "hunting license" to "hunt the wolves that sharpen their teeth on our motherland," then declares that Nadezhda and her father are "Soviet people," "not any kind of enemy," and that Dorin and his fellow officers "take bullets, risk our lives to protect you!"[37] Nadia tells him to go away forever. In the end, however, she accepts him and his job. Like he did with Fandorin and the stereotypes of the *okhrana* in Soviet culture, Akunin in part rehabilitates the NKGB agent as a loyal, patriotic citizen in *Spy Novel*.

Dorin's relationship with Oktiabr'skii also provides Akunin with a chance to write about the nature of the NKGB and its converts. In one scene, as they are driving towards the Lubianka, the senior chekist tells his new protégé that he can ask him anything he wants about the notorious agency. Dorin learns that Oktiabr'skii had been purged but allowed to return, which prompts the young man to ask about 1937. The senior officer justifies his own purging by replying that the organs of state security are "like a surgeon's scalpel. They need to be sharp, sterile, and clean."[38] To engage in cutting out the bad, Oktiabr'skii implies, means risking occasional infection and understanding that some preventive surgeries are not warranted. Later in the conversation, Oktiabr'skii states that secret policemen need to be professionals, not politicians. Ezhov, he tells Dorin, was a "reptile," but a "very clever" one who "fancied himself a politician" and therefore overstepped his boundaries.[39] The current director (unnamed, but clearly Beria) is "a professional," "even more so than Iagoda." While he is cruel and hard and "by the nineteenth-century ideas of Tolstoy, Dostoevsky, and

Nadson a monster and a villain," the twentieth century has brought a new morality that Beria embodies: "everything for the cause is moral, everything that harms the cause is immoral."[40]

As the plot unfolds, Dorin first intercepts one of Wasser's accomplices, a Ukrainian radioman. Dorin assumes the Ukrainian's identity in order to lure the German agent out (much like Anwar-effendi, Wasser can seemingly blend in everywhere). When the Ukrainian, Stepan Karpenko, is asked to describe his German controller, he cannot give any details apart from how Wasser contacts him. After two more failed escapades, one that results in a busload of Soviet citizens being killed, Oktiabr'skii and Dorin begin to understand the sort of agent and plot they are up against, an "operation of exceptional significance."[41] The senior officer muses that it could be a terrorist attack or an assassination plot directed against Stalin, but concludes that the most damaging plot would be a clever disinformation plan to make everyone believe there will be no war in 1941.

After yet another attempt to snag the German, Dorin is taken captive. He believes Wasser is the woman who holds him prisoner for nearly a month while she sends out coded messages (there are several pages in the novel left blank and marked as *"zasekrecheno"* [top secret]). Dorin manages to escape on 12 June and make his way to the Lubianka, where he sees the woman who held him prisoner. When she is revealed as Iraida Petrakovich, a fellow agent, Dorin and Oktiabr'skii believe they have exposed the mole and inform Beria just in time. During Iraida's interrogation, however, it emerges that she too has merely been recruited by Wasser to do his bidding. In one last twist (spoiler alert!), Wasser is revealed to be Matvei Kogan, the high-ranking NKGB officer. It turns out Kogan is the son of an Abwehr general who was deliberately abandoned at fourteen as an orphan in the USSR. He eventually joined the NKVD and bided his time. As he tells his story, Dorin thinks "What cunning enemies the USSR has! How ingenious, far-sighted!"[42] Wasser, it turns out, had been planted in the USSR just in case he was needed.

Kogan's gambit has proven victorious. Oktiabr'skii is deemed a suspect for spreading false information about a German invasion that will not happen because Germany's "real" target is Great Britain. Dorin is told he has become "an accomplice in a monstrous provocation [*chudovishchnaia provokatsiia*] that aimed to push Germany and the USSR together, to start a war."[43] Oktiabr'skii is labelled "either a fool or a scoundrel" for falling for the ruse.[44] The novel closes with Kogan talking to Beria and Stalin. As the three talk, Kogan disables the secret police chief and reveals himself to Stalin as a German agent. He tells Stalin that he could kill him, but will not in order to prove his good intentions. He comes from Hitler to report "person to person" that the German chancellor does not plan to attack the USSR, for his "primary goal is the destruction of England."[45] The spy tells Stalin that "there will be no war before 1 January 1943." Wasser departs. When Beria wakes, Stalin tells him to call off the defensive plans. It is 12 June 1941.

The war comes, Akunin posits, not because of Stalin's lack of knowledge, but because of the way that knowledge is turned against him. The Soviet Union is a state saturated in spy games, one where its leaders constantly suspect everyone is up to something and where every event has a sinister subplot lurking beneath it.[46] Just like the end of *The Turkish Gambit*, history does not change in *Spy Novel*, only its causes do: agents, it seems in Akunin's fictions, can affect events behind the scenes, but the ultimate outcomes cannot change. June 1941, Akunin's novel suggests, came about because Nazi agents proved more successful in their gambits than their Soviet counterparts. In a sense, *Spy Novel* presents a counter-narrative to the famous Soviet-era novel and television series, *17 Moments of Spring*.[47] In that series, a Soviet agent named Maksim Isaev has infiltrated the higher echelons of the Abwehr under the name Max Otto von Stierlitz. He successfully prevents the Germans and Americans from signing a truce earlier in 1945, thus ensuring that the eventual Soviet-American victory would happen (watching the show prompted Vladimir Putin to express his admiration for spies and how "one man" could alter history). In Akunin's novel and the subsequent film made from it, *Spy (Shpion)*, Wasser out-Stierlitzes Stierlitz: he has been planted in the USSR for years just in case he could be useful.

Operation Barbarossa also succeeded as a surprise attack, Akunin suggests, because of Stalin's personality and the state he created in his image. Stalin established a system that specifically tasked the police with the struggle against "treason, spying, counterrevolution, terror, wrecking, subversive acts, and other antistate crimes."[48] *Spy Novel* presents the logical result of this policy: Soviet agents are told that espionage is everywhere, so they find plots lurking everywhere. The obsessive focus on spying at the heart of Stalinism also produced an unwieldy institution: by 1941, the NKVD functioned as a state security organization, a major economic administration, an investigative organization, a social policing force, and a domestic surveillance organization, necessitating the February 1941 overhaul that created the NKGB as a separate branch.[49] June 1941, *Spy Novel* argues, resulted in part from the institutional bloat and inter-institutional rivalries Stalin introduced. The atmosphere that the focus on spying created also meant that the Soviet leader would be prone to miss the real wolves lurking within the forest. In the end, Hitler and his spies beat Stalin at his own game. No wonder parts of the novel are labelled "top secret."

Conclusion: Plausible Worlds and Russian Conspiracies

Taken together, *The Turkish Gambit* and *Spy Novel* create a revised history of Russia between the 1870s and 1940s. This is a history during which the police and security forces become more modern and undergo several transformations. It is also a history where spying is no longer the missing dimension of understanding the past. If we spy on the past more carefully, as in *The Turkish Gambit* and *Spy Novel*, we can begin to place espionage into a larger understanding of how history unfolds. Akunin's focus on espionage ultimately creates a "plausible world" where spies, agents, informers, saboteurs, conspiratorial agents, and state officials are constantly suspicious of Western "provocations" that aim to destabilize the motherland and where Russian/ Soviet spies see themselves as patriots attempting to foil their foreign counterparts.[50] Akunin, for his part, has stated that he wants his works to be "a version of history that is possible," where he creates "fantastical versions of events because I could not find realistic versions of them."[51] Akunin's plausible worlds thus help readers imagine alternatives to the way historical events unfolded while preserving the outcomes of these events intact.

Akunin's spy histories are also accounts that, while shining a light onto conspiracies, manage to avoid tapping into conspiratorial imaginings of the past. In a recent article on the connections between alternative history and conspiracy history in Russia, Marlène Laruelle writes that "the conjunction between conspiracy theory and the rewriting of history makes up one of the main instruments for disseminating nationalist theories in today's Russia, theories based on a kind of postmodern, paranoid cultural imaginary."[52] In part, she posits, this turn occurred because the Soviet state frequently changed its interpretations of the past, most notably under Stalin (when the state oversaw a nationalist Bolshevik re-imaging that replaced in part the Marxist framework) and Khrushchev (when the state oversaw a de-Stalinization plan).[53] Thus, as Laruelle argues, the public encountered regular reversals of historical perspectives. The USSR's collapse only furthered these trends. Alternate history, as she writes, has flourished since 1991; as a result "there coexists a multiplicity of alternate and plural histories of Russia" where the actual paths Russia took have to be explained by conspiracies.[54]

A conspiracy theory, as one scholarly study of the subject notes, "can generally be counted as such if it is an effort to explain some event or practice by reference to the machinations of powerful people, who attempt to conceal their role (at least until their aims are accomplished)."[55] The attraction of a conspiratorial history to those who subscribe to it is that it removes contingency and unintended consequences from developing an understanding of events. Instead, conspiratorial agents orchestrate things from behind the scenes, thus imposing causality on complex happenings. "I don't believe in conspiriology in general," Akunin has stated, "But, I write about spies because they are so interesting to describe and they create psychologically interesting situations where someone who you think is your friend or your lover is actually your enemy and aims for your ruin."[56] In the end, Akunin's historical vision, as counter-intuitive as it seems, employs spies in order to impose stability on the past. In *The Turkish Gambit* and *Spy Novel*, Plevna is still besieged, the Treaty of San Stefano is still abrogated, and Stalin is still caught by surprise in 1941. As told by Akunin, the conspiracies around these events do not become the basis for alternate outcomes, nor do they remove contingency or unintended consequences from the equation. Perhaps the greatest trick Akunin conjures up by spying on the past is to play with conspiratorial history in order to create a plausible world.

NOTES

1 Robert Musil, *The Man without Qualities*, Vol. I, *A Sort of Introduction – The Like of It Now Happens*, translated by Sophie Wilkins and Burton Pike (NY: Vintage, 1996).

2 Vladimir Putin, et al., *First Person: An Astonishingly Frank Self-Portrait by Russia's President* (New York: PublicAffairs, 2000), 22.

3 Boris Akunin, *Turetskii gambit* (*The Turkish Gambit*; Moscow: Zakharov, 1998); *Shpionskii roman* (*Spy Novel*; Moscow: AST, 2005); *Qvest* (*Quest*; Moscow: AST, 2008). The novellas in the *Smert' na brudershaft* series are published by AST (Moscow). Chkhartishvili also wrote a spy novel using the pseudonym Anatolii Brusnikin, *Bellona* (Moscow: AST, 2012), which is set during the Crimean War.

4 Dzhanik Faiziev, dir., *Turetskii gambit* (*Turkish Gambit*), film (Moscow: Channel One, 2005) and Aleksei Andrianov, dir., *Shpion* (*The Spy*), film (Moscow: Studio TriTe and Channel Rossiia, 2012).

5 See, for example, Elena V. Baraban, "A Country Resembling Russia: The Use of History in Boris Akunin's Detective Novels," *Slavic and East European Journal (SEEJ)* 48, no. 3 (2004): 396–420; Sofya Khagi, "Boris Akunin and the Retro Mode in Contemporary Russian Culture," *Toronto Slavic Quarterly* 13 (2005), http://sites.utoronto.ca/tsq/13/khagi13.shtml; Elena Diakova, "Boris Akunin kak uspeshnaia otrasl' rossiiskoi promyshlennosti," *Novaia gazeta*

45 (1 July 2001), https://novayagazeta.ru/articles/2001/07/02/11382-boris
-akunin-kak-uspeshnaya-otrasl-rossiyskoy-promyshlennosti; Brian James
Baer, "Post-Soviet Self-Fashioning and the Politics of Representation," in
Putin as Celebrity and Cultural Icon, ed. Helena Goscilo (London: Routledge,
2012), 160–79; N. Potanina, "Dikkensovskii kod 'fandorinskogo proekta,'"
Voprosy literatury 1 (2004): 41–8; Andrei Ranchin, "Romany B. Akunina i
klassicheskaia traditsiia," *Novoe literaturnoe obozrenie* 67 (2004), http://mag-
azines.russ.ru/nlo/2004/67/ran14.html; Georgii Tsiplakov, "Evil Arising on
the Road and the Tao of Erast Fandorin," *Russian Studies in Literature* 38, no.
3 (2002): 25–61.

6   Available online in Russian at: http://az.lib.ru/d/dostoewskij_f_m/text
_0490.shtml#II.

7   I cover the war and the popular prints produced during the conflict in
Stephen M. Norris, *A War of Images: Russian Popular Prints, Wartime Culture,
and National Identity, 1812–1945* (DeKalb: Northern Illinois University Press,
2006), 80–106. The best account of the war in English remains W. Bruce
Menning, *Bayonets before Bullets: The Imperial Russian Army, 1861–1914*
(Bloomington: Indiana University Press, 1992), 51–86. The description of the
war in this article relies on Menning's.

8   Quoted in Menning, *Bayonets before Bullets*, 57.

9   Ibid., 76.

10   See Hans Rogger, "The Skobelev Phenomenon: The Hero and His
Worship," *Oxford Slavonic Papers* 9 (1976): 46–78. See also V. M. Mukhanov,
"Istoricheskie portrety. Mikhail Dmitrievich Skobelev," *Voprosy istorii*
10 (2004): 57–81. See also Elena Baraban's chapter in this volume.

11   For information on the monument, see K. G. Sokol, *Monumenty imperii*
(Moscow: GEOS, 1999), 161–3.

12   Jonathan W. Daly, *Autocracy under Siege: Security Police and Opposition in
Russia, 1866–1905* (DeKalb: Northern Illinois University Press, 1998), 6.

13   Boris Akunin, *The Turkish Gambit*, trans. Andrew Bromfield (New York:
Random House, 2006), 211. The novel is available in Russian at Akunin's
website: http://www.akunin.ru/knigi/fandorin/erast/turetsky_gambit/.

14   Ibid., 201.

15   Ibid., 202.

16   Ibid., 176.

17   Ibid., 40.

18   Ibid., 113.

19   See Daly, *Autocracy under Siege*, as well as Charles Ruud and Sergei
Stepanov, *Fontanka 16: The Tsars' Secret Police* (Montreal: McGill-Queen's
University Press, 1999); Anna Geifman, *Entangled in Terror: The Azef Affair
and the Russian Revolution* (Wilmington, DE: SR Books, 2000).

20   Mark Kramer, "Introduction," in *Spies: A Batch from the Journal of Cold War
Studies* (Cambridge, MA: MIT Press, Kindle only, 2015).

21 Akunin, *Turkish Gambit*, 37.

22 Ibid.

23 In a 1999 review, Roman Arbitman argues that the first two books of the series, including *The Turkish Gambit*, presented a "romanticization of the Third Section" that made his novels "an apology for the gendarmes." See Roman Arbitman, "Bumazhnyi oplom prianichnoi derzhavy," *Znamia* 7 (1999), http://znamlit.ru/publication.php?id=859.

24 This anecdote opens David Murphy's *What Stalin Knew: The Enigma of Barbarossa* (New Haven, CT: Yale University Press, 2005), xv.

25 Kramer, "Introduction."

26 Murphy, *What Stalin Knew*, xviii.

27 Viktor Suvorov, *Icebreaker: Who Started the Second World War?* (London: Hamish Hamilton, 1990). Among the few books that support this thesis is Constantine Pleshakov, *Stalin's Folly: The Tragic First Ten Days of WWII on the Eastern Front* (Boston: Houghton Mifflin, 2005). Pleshakov writes "it is now clear that Stalin was indeed preparing a preemptive strike against Germany," though in June 1941 "he was aware of the danger, but he continued to believe that Hitler would not be able to strike before the summer of 1942" (13). The majority of historians, including Murphy, David Glantz, Gabriel Gorodetsky, and John Lukacs, disagree, arguing that Stalin was not planning a pre-emptive attack. See Teddy Uldricks, "The *Icebreaker* Controversy: Did Stalin Plan to Attack Hitler?" *Slavic Review* 53, no. 3 (1999): 626–43. All of the scenarios for why Stalin ignored his agents in June 1941 are covered in Murphy, *What Stalin Knew.*

28 The most thorough collection of published documents on the subject, culled from Russian archives, is L.E. Reshin and V.P. Naumov, eds., *1941 god*, 2 vols. (Moscow: Mezhdunarodnyi fond "Demokratiia," 1998).

29 The NKVD had been split into two sections in February 1941, with the new NKGB exclusively responsible for intelligence and counter-intelligence activities.

30 Dorin's last name, he reveals, comes from the village of his ancestors, Dorino, where his grandmother's family, "Fon Dorin" lived – Oktiabr'skii asks if the name should be "Fandorin." Akunin, *Shpionskii roman*, 116.

31 Akunin's Moscow in 1941 is not unlike the city described in Karl Schlögel's magisterial history, *Moscow 1937* (Cambridge: Polity Press, 2012).

32 Schlögel, *Moscow 1937*, 53.

33 Akunin, *Shpionskii roman*, 98–107. All translations from Russian in this chapter are my own unless otherwise indicated.

34 Ibid., 18.

35 Ibid., 33.

36 Ibid., 48.

37 Ibid., 187–8.

38 Ibid., 56.
39 Ibid., 59.
40 Ibid., 60. Oktiabr'skii will later explain to Dorin that state security officers "live in cruel times and have to use cruel methods" (121).
41 Ibid., 195.
42 Ibid., 332.
43 Ibid., 357.
44 Ibid., 358.
45 Ibid., 391.
46 Hiroaki Kuromiya and Andrzej Pepłoński have argued that "Stalin deemed the strategic use of intelligence and espionage indispensable to political life," and that "Stalin's reliance on them reached staggering proportions." Using Japanese sources, they explore the espionage policies employed by the Soviet leader in the 1930s and conclude that Stalin's system embodied both "total espionage" and "total counterespionage" policies that included mass terror. See their "Stalin, Espionage, and Counterespionage" in *Stalin and Europe: Imitation and Domination, 1928–1953*, ed. Timothy Snyder and Ray Brandon (Oxford: Oxford University Press, 2014), 73.
47 Tatiana Lioznova, dir., *Seventeen Moments in Spring* (*Semnadtsat' mgnovenii vesny*), television series (Moscow: Programme One, 1973). I thank Margarete Zimmermann for suggesting the connections with *17 Moments*.
48 This is the language of the April 1935 statue that recodified the role of the political police. See David Shearer and Vladimir Khaustov, *Stalin and the Lubianka: A Documentary History of the Political Police and Security Organs in the Soviet Union, 1922–1953* (New Haven, CT: Yale University Press, 2015), 8–9.
49 Ibid., 13.
50 I borrow the term "plausible world" from Geoffrey Hawthorn's classic counterfactual history book, *Plausible Worlds: Possibility and Understanding in History and the Social Sciences* (Cambridge: Cambridge University Press, 1991).
51 Interview with Boris Akunin, 31 May 2015, Cuma, Italy.
52 Marlène Laruelle, "Conspiracy and Alternate History in Russia: A Nationalist Equation for Success?" *Russian Review* 71, no. 4 (2012): 566.
53 Ibid., 567. The term "national Bolshevik," which I use to summarize Laruelle's point, comes from David Brandenberger's *National Bolshevism: Stalinist Mass Culture and the Formation of Modern Russian National Identity, 1931–1956* (Cambridge, MA: Harvard University Press, 2002).
54 Laruelle, "Conspiracy and Alternate History," 579. Laruelle's article appeared as part of a special cluster in the journal devoted to conspiracy theories. See the introductory article by Stefanie Ortmann and John Heathershaw, "Conspiracy Theories in the Post-Soviet Space," *Russian Review* 71, no. 4 (2012): 551–64. For other scholarly analyses of conspiracy

theories in Russia, see Ilya Yablokov, "Conspiracy Theories as a Russian Public Diplomacy Tool: The Case of *Russia Today (RT)*," *Politics* 35, no. 304 (2015): 301–15 and "Pussy Riot as Agent Provocateur: Conspiracy Theories and the Media Construction of Nation in Putin's Russia," *Nationalities Papers* 42, no. 4 (2014): 622–36. Finally, Eliot Borenstein is live-blogging his ongoing book project on conspiracy theories in Russia, *Plots against Russia*: http://plotsagainstrussia.org/.

55 Cass R. Sunstein and Adrain Vermeule, "Conspiracy Theories: Causes and Cures," *Journal of Political Philosophy* 17, no. 2 (2009): 202. Cited in Ortmann and Heathershaw, "Conspiracy Theories in the Post-Soviet Space," 553.

56 Interview with Boris Akunin, 31 May 2015, Cuma, Italy.

PART FOUR

Rewriting the History of Russia

9 *L'état, c'est tout*: Boris Akunin's *History of the Russian State* and the National History Canon

ILYA GERASIMOV

Had Boris Akunin presented his *History of the Russian State* (*Istoriia Rossiiskogo gosudarstva*) book series as another oeuvre in his *Genres* project, historians would have had no reasons to complain. As part of the series, Akunin has written a typical "spy novel," a typical "children's book," and a "sci-fi novel," among others, so an "archaic historical treatise" seems perfectly appropriate for this experiment with popular literary genres. In this deliberately mimicked format, it would be only fitting to use a writing style reminiscent of old historians – perhaps in the voice of younger contemporaries of the founder of modern Russian historiography, Nikolai Karamzin (1766–1826). Written as a nineteenth-century text, it would therefore be understandable specifically why the book reflects a state of historical knowledge that can be dated back to the 1830s or 1840s. Produced in direct dialogue with Karamzin's *History of the Russian State* (the last volume of which was finished in 1826), such an archaic historical treatise would engage well with Akunin's previous books, underscoring the postmodernist, playful, multilayered, and intertextual nature of his oeuvre. Accordingly, the main protagonist and fictitious author of that historical treatise could become some Faddey Fingalin – uncle of one Erast Fandorin,[1] an acquaintance of Pushkin and Griboyedov, and no stranger to the head of the Third Section of His Majesty's Own Chancellery (Russia's political police of the time), Alexander von Benckendorff. This imagined plot would open up endless opportunities for developing secondary storylines, and would allow "Fingalin" to demonstrate how Karamzin's *History* (in its poetics and approaches to the past) was rooted in Russian and European realities and the mindset of the first part of the nineteenth century.

That epoch witnessed the dissemination of very particular ideas. First off, it was the high point of Romanticism, with its rediscovering of "the nation" in a new key. Understood as mobilized, revolutionary "people in arms" during the Napoleonic wars, the nation was now seen as a synonym for an organic "people's body" that had been living almost unchanged on its "national territory" for centuries. The ultimate purpose of the nation's eternal existence was the evolution of the "national spirit" to its absolute, as manifested through the development of the state. Popular topics in the literature of the epoch included a mystic bond of blood and soil, the perfection of state institutions by rulers of antiquity, and the youth of a people just entering the path of history leading to future glory.[2] Russia's first chief of gendarmes, Count Alexander von Benckendorff, perceptively summarized this hegemonic discourse of the epoch: "Russia's past was amazing, her present is more than splendid, and what concerns her future exceeds everything that the boldest imagination can envision; this is, my friend, the vantage point from which Russian history should be viewed and written."[3]

Of course, in this context one cannot but recall the first intellectual circles of Moscow Hegelianists (who perceived as a sacral revelation the pun "that which is real is reasonable"), or the famous triad formulated by the minister of popular education, Sergei Uvarov, in 1833: "Delving deeper into the subject in search of the elements [*nachala*] that are unique to Russia (as every land, every people have such a Palladium), it becomes clear that we have the three elements without which Russia cannot prosper, grow, and live: (1) The Orthodox faith; (2) Autocracy; (3) Nationality."[4]

Those scholars, who replaced references to "autocracy" with "the state" in this formula in the 1840s, conceptually revolutionized it by revealing the historical (and thus temporary) character of autocracy as only one of many possible forms of the state, now eternalized as the nation. In the early 1840s, Baron August von Haxthausen of Prussia visited Russia and discovered for the entire world (and Russian educated society in the first place) the mysterious Russian land commune that, presumably, had survived since prehistoric times and promised to bypass capitalism with its horrors of pauperization and exploitation.[5]

In short, such a *History of the Russian State* by Fingalin could serve as a comprehensive projection over the Russian historical realities produced by the main intellectual trends in post-Napoleonic Europe: French historiography of the Restoration period (François Guizot and Adolphe Thiers) and German philosophy of history from Herder to Hegel. It is this intellectual breeding ground that produced, by the end of the nineteenth century, the ideal of a nation-state, which was turned into reality during the 1930s by purging all alien elements from the "national body," whether that the proletarian revolutionary nation or the Aryan German nation. Such is the power of historical imagination:

people reconstruct the past and make history using the same set of ideas. Historians themselves can be liberal or conservative, archival rats, uninspiring writers, and dull lecturers. What they (we) are leaving behind is not a stack of facts reshuffled yet another time but new ways of imagining society (even if speaking of the past millennium). Historians of the early nineteenth century, including Karamzin, accomplished a major conceptual revolution when, in line with the newest political and philosophical ideas of their time, they rendered the historical process as the history of "peoples." In their view, a "people" evolves from the primitive stage to highly sophisticated ones, and culture is the "soul" of a people preserving their identity throughout centuries, while the state is the highest form of a people's self-expression – an external body that makes mortal humans into an immortal nation. As Karamzin put it: "The victories, conquests, and mightiness of the state have elevated the spirit of the Russian people and had a beneficial influence on their very language, which, when managed by a clever Writer's ability and taste, can match the best languages of antiquity and our time in its power, beauty, and pleasance. Their future fate depends on the future of the State."[6] Following in his footsteps 200 years later, Boris Akunin truncated this statement to a lapidary formula: "Russia is, first of all, the state."[7]

Karamzin died after reaching only the Time of Troubles (the early seventeenth century) in his *History*, but this was sufficient for his main accomplishment: he shaped the very structure of thinking about Russia's past (and, by the same token, its future). Karamzin's critics and followers have improved and elevated this structure to the state of a classic canon – the "scheme of Russian history." It is embedded in the subconscious of every graduate of Soviet and post-Soviet Russian high school: our ancestors were Slavs – Kievan Rus' – the Mongol invasion / shielding Europe from barbarism – gathering lands around Moscow – drive to the sea – Peter I and overcoming backwardness – the empire of serfdom – the patriotic war against Napoleon – Decembrists and the rise of the liberation movement – and so on. As Akunin describes the first part of this scheme: "The state, which today is called the Russian Federation, was conceived in Novgorod, matured in Kiev, but became a direct heir not to the Novgorod *veche* republic and Kievan monarchy, but a North-eastern principality – one of the offshoots of the disintegrated ancient Russian grand state [*derzhavy*]."[8]

Altering interpretations of individual historical episodes within this scheme cannot change the overall picture. Whether Ivan IV was a tyrant or a wise king (or whether Comrade Stalin was a murderer or an efficient manager) is irrelevant in the grand narrative, because what matters is not individual assessments but the very structure of the story and the language used to tell it.

We use a certain language of historical narration without noticing it or perceiving it as a "natural" and "objective" instrument for describing reality. The hidden influence of this language can be seen, for example, in the way we identify polities of the tenth to thirteenth centuries CE between the Carpathian Mountains and the Volga River. Karamzin's younger colleagues invented the term "Kievan Rus',"[9] which was unknown to the chroniclers of the epoch (who spoke of the "Rous Land") – and we do not hesitate to use this term today. Meanwhile, Kievan Rus' "naturally" implies that Moscow Rus' was its direct heir (one capital city gave way to another capital city), while "Malorossiia" (Little Russia, or Ukraine) was not, because it does not "rhyme" with "Kievan Rus'" and literally cannot be pronounced as a continuation of it. Equally "naturally," this invented term makes us perceive the existence of individual Rus' principalities as the tragic "feudal fragmentation" of the once whole and flourishing polity (a clear instance of the Romantic trope of the bygone golden age). If Rus' was one, how could different "Russian" states legitimately coexist? The next step was the conclusion that the initial (and hence authentic and legitimate) unity of the "Kievan Rus'" should be restored in the name of historical justice. Accordingly, Russia with the capital in St. Petersburg or better still, in Moscow, fulfils this historical mission. The millennium-long history of the "Russian people" – creator of the ancient "Russo-Slav" state,[10] should culminate in the creation of the truly national and "Russian" state. Given that "our ancestors were Slavs," this Russianness appears as a fairly rigid concept. After living for over 1,000 years on "their" territory, this "Russian people" is "autochthonous," while all the rest are newcomers. Following this nineteenth-century logic, the most consistent realization of the national historical mission would be an ethnic cleansing of any strangers from the ancestral territory. A compromise solution implies the elaboration of a special legal status for "minorities." According to this worldview, the state is an expression of the nation's ingenious creativity, the guarantor of the nation's survival in the past, and the protector against rival nations in the present. Admitting occasional "excesses" and "abuses" on behalf of the state does not change this general assessment: as the famous Soviet physicist, Petr Kapitsa, used to say, "One can be upset by his wife and lover, but not the government."[11] The state is of primary importance compared to any person, precisely because the nation is more important than an individual, and the state is the product of a nation's highest stage of collective self-cognition.

The "scheme of Russian history" begins with a pastoral image of blond and blue-eyed villagers and ends, invariably and inevitably, with official portraits of great leaders dressed according to the fashion of their time – in a cuirass, holding a sword, or in a semi-military tunic with a smoking pipe in hand. If we believe in the existence of a single "national body" on a "historical territory" 1,000 years ago, we are perceiving a modern nation in the same "tribal" (racial) categories of biological kinship and cultural uniformity. By itself, the past can determine very little, otherwise the future would have differed from it only by the fashion of dresses and the design of vehicles. Yet, the imagery of the past has the power of self-fulfilling prophecies. From the vantage point of the present, everything is in the past, and so we construct the outlines of the future by projecting forward our perceptions about history.

A person who looks non-"Slavic" should be concerned about his life in the centre of Russia's capital precisely because a gang of racist thugs who have spotted him were exposed to this scheme of Russian history at school and within popular culture and embraced the view of society embedded in it. If "our ancestors were Slavs," and the Russian Federation is really a direct heir of Kievan Rus', the only way the Russian nation can defend itself in the situation of economic crisis and encroaching multiculturalism is to restore the purity of the "national body" and the hegemony of the indigenous tribe on its ancestral land. For the same reason, criticism of the state should remain a taboo no matter what, or else the disintegration of the country and chaos will ensue (as during the time of "fragmentation," subsequently "recognized" in the Ukrainian "anti-Russian" Euromaidan). It is just that some people show more consistency and even intellectual integrity in pursuing their inherited worldview, unbound by formalities of political correctness (while hard times encourage the making of hard choices). For example, while the Austrian leaders of the Second International could have allowed themselves to be polite to the bourgeoisie at the turn of the twentieth century, after 1917, Lenin and Trotsky had already found that it was time to implement the Marxist worldview more consistently. They turned this worldview of society as something divided into antagonistic classes (some are inherently good, others irrevocably vicious) into the political practice of population cleansings. Likewise, Hitler did nothing that had not been developed from the worldview and social thinking of academically quite respectable nineteenth-century pundits from Germany, France, or Russia.[12]

Within Karamzin's scheme of Russian history, any political disagreements over interpretation are little more than differences in temperament: some people are more decisive and consistent, while others exercise self-restraint and, for ethical reasons, reject certain measures that logically follow from the view of the historical process that they share. Ivan the Terrible can be applauded by conservatives and chastised by liberals, but their conflict is framed by the shared premises of the common scheme of Russian history that sees Ivan as the founder of the centralized state fighting for Russia's "access to the sea." Only liberals believe that Ivan used the wrong methods, while conservatives argue that the important end excuses the means.

The real scholarly problem found beyond the constraints of this Karamzinian approach to Russian history is not the characterization of Ivan, but a set of inquiries questioning the very explanatory scheme itself: How do we even understand and employ the term "state" in the mid-sixteenth century? How did Ivan himself perceive his mission and his realm? How were the boundaries between "us" and "aliens" drawn in reality? These questions cannot be formulated in the language of the scheme of Russian history or expressed through its imagery, which means that they are irrelevant and simply non-existent in that context. But this also means that these questions cannot be addressed to the society of the twenty-first century: What is the state (and can we call the state a system of public offices of all levels privatized by their holders, as in the modern-day Russian Federation)? What is the purpose of living together in one country – who is native and who is foreign there? The answer is contained in the first chapter of the standard school textbook: our ancestors (and thus, descendants) are the Slavs, we live together because we are indigenous people on this land, and the state is the main purpose for our collective existence.

Our hypothetical Faddey Fingalin could have penned such an intellectual thriller about self-fulfilling prophecies of the past as reconstructed by modern historians. It would have allowed the real author to discuss such important topics as the exciting and deadly dangerous "Eros of the state" (Peter Struve's term),[13] the cult of populism, and the profoundly ahistorical perception of history by Romanticism, which has been preserved to this day by the still hegemonic "scheme of Russian history."

Alas, Boris Akunin took his mission as a historian too seriously – or, rather, the mission of a writer turned historian (such as Karamzin), which he openly admitted in his announcement of a new project in March 2013: "I have always dreamed about becoming a new Karamzin... . I began my literary career with the novel *Azazel'* [*The Winter Queen*] ... At that time, I already secretly cherished a megalomaniac plan: to reproduce Karamzin's trajectory and, starting with fiction, eventually arrive at writing a history of the Russian state ... Despite [my] degree in history ... I remain a writer [*belletrist est' belletrist*]."[14]

As a writer aspiring to follow in Karamzin's footsteps, he authored the historical treatise as Boris Akunin (the pen name used in most of his fiction writing), rather than Grigorii Chkhartishvili – his real name, which he reserves for nonfiction books and essays.[15] The very seriousness of his intentions made it imperative to identify himself as a fiction writer – Boris Akunin[16] – but otherwise, he refused to share fame with a fictitious protagonist-author. He thus missed an opportunity to keep a distance from the narrative and, consequently, the ability to conduct critical analysis. As a result, instead of a benign literary game, he produced a new edition of the scheme of Russian history, stylistically reworked for readers of the 2010s. Making the traditional narrative more readable, Akunin edited out many semantic nuances that, surprisingly, made Karamzin's archaic text more complex and ambivalent than the modern remake. The main distinction of the original was a radically new understanding of history offered by Karamzin. It became the foundation of all modern ideologies in Russia – anarchism and nationalism, liberalism and populism. Akunin has offered nothing new and has only driven *ad absurdum* key elements of the Karamzinian worldview.

The idea of the people (nation) as the main protagonist of history has lost any Romantic ambiguity and has become fully comprehensible to any subway rider reading a pocketbook. This "people" is now defined through ethnicity and expressions of the "national character" in the style of Hollywood films about Russia. The "state" too has lost its ambivalence (sometimes Karamzin used this notion in the old meaning of "domination," sometimes to denote the general idea rather than the actual political system). This ambivalence somewhat compensates for the anachronism of applying this category to early medieval primitive polities. To Akunin, the state unequivocally means the modern system of centralized administration, except that the names of offices were "ancient" 1,000 years ago. The language of the Romanticist writer Karamzin was organicist (presenting social institutions as animate living organisms), but it allowed the possibility of internal development (in time) and drama (of relationships). Akunin's language is no less essentialist (implying that even the most abstract notions are embodied in material "things"), but at the same time profoundly Soviet and even socialist realist in its poetics. The primitive structuralism of this language cannot analytically grasp the changing nature of political institutions throughout the centuries (everything is "the state") or the evolving perception of groupness (everybody is "the people"). This is such a stark contrast even to Karamzin's naive Romanticism, which acknowledged the development of "soul" (of the people or even the state)!

The Soviet essentialism that is so recognizable in Akunin's social imaginary was largely a product of nineteenth-century positivist sociology brought to its utmost. The old positivism itself had its roots, inter alia, in the Romantic and neoromantic historiography of the Bourbon Restoration period (including Karamzin's writings). But because Karamzin was writing two centuries ago and influenced a whole spectrum of ideologies of the latter period, and Soviet social science reached its peak only a few decades ago but has left no productive impulse whatsoever, Karamzin's *History* arouses much warmer feelings today than its modernized replicas. The only visible result of the Soviet type of social thinking was demonstrated during the breakdown of Yugoslavia and the Soviet Union, which unleashed dramatic confrontations between rigidly defined national groups. One could see everywhere the same ardent belief in the priority of an "indigenous nationality" on its "historic land" (be it the Serbs, Estonians, Chechens, Russians, Georgians, etc.) and the desire to have a "nation-state" of their own.[17] Whenever it was deemed inappropriate to physically exterminate the "aliens," they were "just" deprived of civic rights and the right to be regarded as "part of us."

Beyond these basic conceptual premises, it is senseless to discuss the historical value of Akunin's work: after all, a bellettrist cannot be expected to demonstrate historiographic competence. Besides, the responsibility for most of the blatant blunders in Akunins book should be attributed to the very scheme of Russian history that he carefully reproduced (in its early, mid-nineteenth-century version, before the correction of the scheme by Vasilii Kliuchevskii and even Sergei Solov'ev). Akunin's *History* is useful as a manual for college students majoring in history, and as a catalogue of statements and tropes that must be barred from usage once and for all.

For example, on the very first page of the book the author proudly declares: "I am not advancing any conception. I do not have any … I want to find out (or detect), how it actually happened."[18] At this point, it seems very suitable to introduce students to Akunin as an anti-textbook to Leopold von Ranke's German school of history of the 1820s with its programmatic claim of writing history *"wie es eigentlich gewesen war"* (as it actually happened), and explain to them why this approach has been criticized within the historical profession for the past century.[19] It also makes sense to inform students about some basics of post-structuralism, referring them to a classical, fairly old, and not too abstruse piece like Roland Barthes explaining why there can be no text "without a conception" built in (regardless of the author's intent).[20]

At an earlier stage, it is important to explain to students why we cannot apply the notion of the state unproblematically to medieval polities, without additional qualifications (and why the title of Akunin's chapter about the ninth century, "Everything Is Ready for the State," sounds absolutely fantastic).[21] And even before that, students must be warned against using terms such as "Asia" or "Europe" as meaningful categories. These notions structure the scheme of Russian history in its Akunin version: the period before the Mongol invasion is called "A Part of Europe," and after that "A Part of Asia."[22] Equally meaningless are notions of the "West" and the "East," which are only highlighted by Akunin's use of them: "Modern Russia is a fruit of the marital union between West and East."[23] These are terms of mental (imagined) geography that are completely meaningless unless reconstructed through the analysis of a particular historical epoch's rhetoric (when they are used, who used them, and why). They acquired familiar connotations of cultural superiority or backwardness only several centuries ago, and in this sense have no place in modern scholarship or teaching.[24]

It is of no less importance to demonstrate to students (or any readers) the impossibility of using analytical categories such as "ethnos," "nation," or "race" as characteristics of actual social groups – something that Akunin does routinely in his *History*, as these examples show:

So far, the numerous animist tribes representing a branch of the Arian race – Lithuanians, Baltic Prussians, Samogitians, Curonians, Latgalians, Semigallians, Yotvingians and others – did not show any political activity.[25]

The Russian nation in the modern sense has been in existence for [the past] four or five centuries.[26]

From the end of the eleventh century onward, particularly common were marriages to Cuman (*polovetskimi*) princesses, that is, representatives of not just a different nation but a different race.[27]

Everything is complicated when it comes to the name of our country and its titular ethnos.[28]

In the context of a certain research project, one can discuss a group *as* an ethnos or a nation – which means explaining some patterns of collective behaviour using these concepts. (Methodologically, this implies differentiating between categories of practice and categories of analysis.) It is understood that no clear boundaries can be drawn between the supposed ethnoses or even nations, particularly retrospectively, as archaeological artefacts are very ambiguous markers of a particular "ethnos" or even a language spoken by the people who left these artefacts. To suggest that a group might share a language, beliefs, and some degree of kinship at a particular historical moment is not the same as to claim that a stable endogamic "collective time traveler" preserved its coherent identity and demographic composition over the centuries. But even metaphorically, even as a joke, there is no place in a modern book for such nineteenth-century nonsense as "branches of the Aryan race," musings about the influence of the forest on shaping the difficult "national character" of the Russians,[29] as well as all the talk about the "titular ethnos" of "our country," the twelve-century-old "Ruso-Slavonic ethnos" and "four or five centuries" of existence of the Russian nation.[30] By themselves, these statements are non-scholarly (it is impossible in principle to prove the influence of the forest on forming a common stable psychological type of millions of people), which means that falsifying them is as unproductive and senseless as serious arguments against the concept of the "Yellow peril" or the "Jewish global conspiracy."

Since Akunin reproduces the state of popular historiography of the first half of the nineteenth century, it is not surprising that his *History of the Russian State* has accumulated all the clichés and misconceptions of that early period in the development of the historical profession. What is surprising about the book is not its low quality of history-writing, but that its author, a trained philologist and renowned detective-story writer, proves himself so insensitive to linguistic nuances and so indifferent to any intellectual intrigue. This insensitivity and indifference reveal themselves throughout the text, in important episodes and minor details. Thus, Akunin sees nothing strange about the tribe of the Polianians (literally, the Fieldmen) living not in grasslands, as he suggests, but in the forest zone,[31] while about the name of the Severians (which sounds to the modern Russian ear as "the Northmen"), he melancholically notes: "Inhabitants of the easternmost lands had acquired, somewhat puzzlingly, the name of the Severians ... There is no single opinion about the etymology of this name, but 'north' [*sever*] here clearly depicted not a cardinal direction but something else."[32]

If Akunin had solved this charade (as a detective-fiction writer and a philologist), he would have discovered either the Iranian roots of the Severians, or their belonging to the cultural-political world of the steppe.[33] Both versions, mutually quite compatible, discredit all "Russo-Slavic" fantasies and raise history from banal parable to analytical problem. Unfortunately, the author persistently avoids any additional analytical efforts, which at times produces a truly comic effect. Thus, retelling the story of the *Primary Chronicle* about the transfer of the seat of power to Kyiv by Prince Oleg, Akunin comments: "And so, Oleg declared: 'It should be the mother of Russian cities.' Apparently, this canonical phrase was pronounced in some Scandinavian dialect, in which the word 'city' is of feminine grammatical gender. In the Slavic, it would have been more natural to call Kyiv 'the father of Russian cities.'"[34] Even without consulting with specialists on the Old Norse language, and being unaware of the dependence of the Russian *Primary Chronicle* on earlier Byzantine sources, how could a philologist miss a loan translation of the Greek *"metropolis"* (mother city) as indicator of the centre of authority?

Equally puzzling is why Akunin so uncritically reproduces from the chronicles the official version of the story of Sviatopolk the Accursed, who allegedly murdered all his brothers except the triumphant Yaroslav the Wise.[35] One would expect a detective writer to be particularly sensitive to the conspicuous lack of logic in this story that has confused historians for a long time, to its inability to stand the classical test of *cui prodest* (whom does it profit)?[36] Yaroslav alone had the motive, the means, and no alibi, which allows anyone to advance a different interpretation of the events: no less convincing than the official version, it explains much more in the events of that time. Yet it seems that "deductive reasoning" is incompatible with the poetics of romantic history-telling à la 1830s, wholeheartedly embraced by Akunin.

While Boris Akunin certainly could have shown himself as a better writer in *The History of the Russian State*, it is not his fault that he proved himself a lousy historian. After all, he must have relied on the standard works of professional historians. He tried to make their material more colourful and humane, structured by the classical scheme of Russian history: founded by Karamzin, critically reworked by Solov'ev and Kliuchevskii, decisively nationalized by Ilovaiskii, shaped by Stalin's *History of the All-Union Communist Party (Bolsheviks): Short Course*, and refined to perfection by the academician Boris Rybakov. Paraphrasing one of Stalin's famous quotes, it may be concluded that "we have no other history for writers" yet. Akunin has demonstrated only what a nonprofessional can deduce from the mainstream history narrative. His book is not a crooked mirror but rather a magnifying glass that shows the main clichés of the old scheme in enhanced detail.

NOTES

This is a substantially reworked version of the article that was first published in Russian. See Ilya Gerasimov, *"L'état, c'est tout:* 'Istoriia Rossiiskogo gosudarstva' Borisa Akunina i kanon natsional'noi istorii," *Ab Imperio* 2013, no. 4

(2013): 219–30. The current version of the article appears in this volume with *Ab Imperio*'s permission.

1 Erast Fandorin is the chief protagonist of the most famous cycle of Akunin's detective novels set in the late nineteenth century. Stylistically, "Faddey Fingalin" fits this name (as thoroughly Russified yet distinctively foreign by origin), while, quite appropriately, sounding more "1830s" and openly hinting at a prominent public figure of the period – Faddey Bulgarin. "Fingalin" may sound pejorative in Russian (as "Mr. Bruise"), but it can also refer to Fingal, a protagonist of James Macpherson's *Ossian* (Ossian's father), as an homage to one of the most famous literary mystifications of all time, extremely popular in Russia. See the first extensive Russian translation (and note the title): *Ossian, syn Fingalov, bard tret'ego veka: gal'skie (inache Erskie, inache Irlandskie) stikhotvoreniia* (Moscow: Universitetskaia tipografiia, 1792). In old Russian social protocol, Macpherson's fictional author of Irish ballads would have been formally addressed as Ossian Fingalin (son of Fingal).
2 The classic introduction to the poetics of the early stages of professional historiography is, of course, Hayden White, "Romanticism, Historicism, and Realism: Toward a Period Concept for Early 19th Century Intellectual History," in *The Uses of History*, ed. Hayden V. White (Detroit: Wayne State University Press, 1968), 45–58, and White, *Metahistory: The Historical Imagination in Nineteenth-Century Europe* (Baltimore: The Johns Hopkins University Press, 1973).
3 Allegedly pronounced by von Benckendorff in the mid-1830s in connection with the scandalous *Philosophical Letters* by Pyotr Chaadaev. Quoted from M.K. Lemke, *Nikolaevskie zhandarmy i literatura, 1826–1855* (St. Petersburg: S.V. Bunin, 1909), 411. All translations from the Russian in this chapter, unless otherwise noted, are my own.
4 S.S. Uvarov, "O nekotorykh obshchikh nachalakh, mogushchikh sluzhit' rukovodstvom pri upravlenii Ministerstvom narodnogo prosveshcheniia," in *Russkaia sotsial'no-politicheskaia mysl': Pervaia polovina XIX veka* 1, ed. A.A. Shiriants and I.Iu. Demin (Moscow: Moscow State University, 2011), 304.
5 See S. Frederick Starr, "August von Haxthausen and Russia," *Slavonic and East European Review* 46, no. 107 (1968): 462–78.
6 N.M. Karamzin, *Istoriia gosudarstva Rossiiskogo* 1 (Moscow: Kniga, 1988), 63.
7 Boris Akunin, *Istoriia Rossiiskogo gosudarstva* (Moscow: AST, 2014), 3.
8 Ibid., 295.
9 See more in Igor Danilevskii, "Drevnerusskaia gosudarstvennost' i 'narod Rus': vozmozhnosti i puti korrektnogo opisaniia," *Ab Imperio* 2, no. 3 (2001): 157. According to the Russian National Corpus database, "Kievan Rus" was not mentioned in print until 1862, and the first major peak in its

usage is registered in 1876, when the popular history course *The Beginning of Rus'* by Dmitrii Ilovaiskii was published (https://clck.ru/Nm5XG). A prolific and influential author of history textbooks and a Russian nationalist, Ilovaiskii explicitly treated "Kievan Rus'" as the starting point of the national history of modern ethnoconfessional Russians.

10　For example, Akunin, *Istoriia Rossiiskogo gosudarstva*, 18, 40.

11　"Iz vospominanii Anny Alekseevny (zapis' i literaturnaia obrabotka E. Kapitsy)," in *Dvadtsatyi vek Anny Kapitsy: Vospominaniia. Pis'ma*, ed. E.L. Kapitsa and P.E. Rubinin (Moscow: Agraf, 2005), 351.

12　For a standard, if somewhat oversimplified, account, see Neil MacMaster, *Racism in Europe: 1870–2000* (Houndmills, UK: Palgrave, 2001).

13　P.B. Struve, "Otryvki o gosudarstve (1908)," in *Patriotica: politika, kultura, religiia, sotsialism* (Moscow: Respublika, 1997), 64.

14　Boris Akunin, "Novyi Karamzin iavilsia," *LiveJournal* (blog), 20 March 2013, http://borisakunin.livejournal.com/94544.html.

15　There is also a category of books signed by "both" personalities (Akunin-Chkhartishvili), such as the novel *Aristonomiia* (Moscow: Zakharov, 2012).

16　Consider, for example: "I am quitting as a detective story writer ... The multivolume project *The History of the Russian State* has become my main interest and the main direction of my work ... for God only knows how many years." Akunin, "Novyi Karamzin iavilsia." Later he specified that he would dedicate ten years to this project: Viktoriia Ivanova, "Boris Akunin perepishet istoriiu Gosudarstva Rossiiskogo," *Izvestiia*, 5 September 2013, https://iz.ru/news/556582.

17　For the standard survey of post-Soviet national historiographies, all exhibiting a strong nation-centred or explicitly nationalist bias, see K. Aimermakher and G. Bordiugov, eds., *Natsional'nye istorii v sovetskom i postsovetskikh gosudarstvakh* (Moscow: AIRO-XX, 1999).

18　Akunin, *Istoriia Rossiiskogo gosudarstva*, 3.

19　It should be noted that von Ranke himself was not as naive or presumptuous as many of his positivist followers who have embraced his motto, and its original meaning did not imply a complete recovery of the authentic meaning of past events. See Gertrude Himmelfarb, *The New History and the Old: Critical Essays and Reappraisals* (Cambridge, MA: Harvard University Press, 2004), 17.

20　For example, Roland Barthes, *S/Z: An Essay*, trans. Richard Miller (New York: Hill and Wang, 1974).

21　See Rees Davies, "The Medieval State: The Tyranny of a Concept?" *Journal of Historical Sociology* 16, no. 2 (2003): 280–300. Medievalists and historical sociologists may debate specific models of medieval statehood (usually non-territorial) or the very applicability of the concept to the premodern period, but nobody argues that the term even existed prior to around 1500 CE, or that the medieval state, in one or another understanding of it, is similar to modern institutions.

22 ·Akunin, *Istoriia Rossiiskogo gosudarstva*, 21. This geopolitical-civilizational divide remains central to Akunin's conceptualization of Russia's history in subsequent volumes of the *History*. Volume 2 was subtitled "Part of Asia" (*Chast' Azii*)' volume 3, "Between Asia and Europe" (*Mezhdu Aziei i Evropoi*); volume 4, "Between Europe and Asia" (*Mezhdu Evropoi i Aziei*); and volume 5, published in November 2017, "Asian Europeanization" (*Aziatskaia evropeizatsiia*).

23 Ibid., 345.

24 For the classic deconstruction of these tropes and the history of their elaboration as a powerful rhetorical device in the eighteenth century, see Larry Wolff, *Inventing Eastern Europe: The Map of Civilization on the Mind of the Enlightenment* (Stanford, CA: Stanford University Press, 1994).

25 Akunin, *Istoriia Rossiiskogo gosudarstva*, 59.

26 Ibid., 40.

27 Ibid., 347.

28 Ibid., 94.

29 Ibid., 21.

30 Ibid., 40.

31 Ibid., 15.

32 Ibid., 45.

33 See Boris Zhivkov, *Khazaria in the Ninth and Tenth Centuries* (Leiden: Brill, 2010), 138.

34 Akunin, *Istoriia Rossiiskogo gosudarstva*, 107.

35 Ibid., 198–205.

36 See I.N. Danilevskii, *Drevniia Rus' glazami sovremennikov i potomkov (IX–XII vv.)* (Moscow: Aspekt Press, 1998), 336–64.

10 An Instruction Manual for the Russian Nation: Boris Akunin's *History of the Russian State*

STEPHEN M. NORRIS

Note to Reader: In keeping with Akunin's desire that his works of history should serve as an "instruction manual for the nation," let me offer my own manual to his project on the history of the Russian state. Like must instructional guides, this one contains setup instructions, a safety warning, and FAQs. Careful readers will note that the sections consist of explanation followed by interpretations in the form of section "summaries."

1 Setup Instructions

In 2013, Boris Akunin published the first volume of his new *History of the Russian State* (*Istoriia Rossiiskogo gosudarstva*), billed in the press and by the author himself as a work in the tradition of Karamzin. The first volume, *A Part of Europe* (*Chast' evropy*), covered the ninth-century foundations of the first "Russian" state up to the Mongol invasions of the thirteenth century. The second volume, *A Part of Asia* (*Chast' Azii*, 2014), explored the Mongol period, and the third volume, *Between Asia and Europe* (*Mezhdu Aziei i Evropoi*, 2015), narrated the history from Ivan III to Boris Godunov. Akunin kept up his furious pace, publishing one volume per year. In 2016, Akunin followed up with *Between Europe and Asia* (*Mezhdu Evropoi i Aziei*), which covered the seventeenth century, and in 2017 Akunin published *Asiatic Europeanization: Tsar Peter Alekseevich* (*Aziatskaia evropeizatsiia: Tsar' Petr Alekseevich*). *Eurasian Empire – The Era of Tsarinas* (*Evraziiskaia imperia – Epokha Tsarits*) appeared in 2018, with *The First Superpower – Alexander the Blessed and Nicholas Unforgettable* (*Pervaia sverkhderzhava – Aleksndr Blagoslovennyi i Nikolai Nezabvennyi*) published in 2019. A final volume, which will cover the period up to 1917 and the collapse of the tsarist state, will appear in 2020.

Akunin's histories, like all of his projects, appeared with great fanfare and became bestsellers (the third volume was the number two non-fiction bestseller in Russia; the series has also been among the most-requested library books). The histories are complemented by fictional tales set in the period covered by the non-fictional works. *The Fiery Finger* (*Ognennyi perst*, 2013) contains three novellas: the titular story focuses on a Byzantine spy in ninth-century Rus, "The Devil's Spittle" (*Plevok diavola*) is set in Yaroslav the Wise's court, and "Prince Cranberry" (*Kniaz' Kliukva*) recounts the troubles of a young ruler near the wild steppe in 1205. *Bosch and Shelm* (*Bokh i Shel'ma*, 2014) has two novellas, one set at the time of the Mongol invasion and narrated from a Russian and a Tatar point of view, and the other a comical novella about a swindler around the time of Kulikovo. *Widow's Kerchief* (*Vdovii plat*, 2016), accompanying volume 3, has one novella set in the time of Ivan III and a second set in Ivan IV's era. *Sennight of the Three-Eyed* (*Sedmitsa trekhglazogo*, 2017), published in conjunction with *Between Europe and Asia*, again had two tales, one a detective story about a seventeenth-century Muscovite and a second, written as a play, on Peter the Great and his half-sister, Sophia. Most recently, *Nutshell Buddha* (*Orekhovyi Budda*, 2018) consists of stories about a Japanese monk who visits the Russia of Peter the Great and an orphan girl in the same era.

In the preface to the first volume, Akunin established the three features that guided the project, noting that readers should understand them before moving on. The first was that the books are written for people who have poor knowledge of Russia's history and want to understand it better (Akunin, somewhat tongue-in-cheek, stated that he received an education in history, has written several historical novels, but still understands the big picture badly, before letting his reader know that he has now read tens of thousands of pages about Russia's past and will in turn write thousands). Second, he has no general concept or theory of history. Akunin claims that historians who do offer a generalizing theory often leave out inconvenient evidence that alters their writings. Third, Akunin argues that his is not a national or country history, but a history of the state, and therefore is an explicitly political history, not a cultural or intellectual one.[1] His method, he explains in the introduction to the first volume, is to employ "Occam's Razor," cutting through myth to arrive only at the "most plausible" or "most likely" scenario for the past.[2]

What follows in the histories is fairly tame and, by Akunin's standards, fairly boring (to be fair, one should heed the author's first, second, and third warnings). Readers get Akunin's clever way of explaining how climate change affected Rus's early history (for anyone living at the time, he explains, it was a matter of life and death). Readers can read about, based on a number of previous histories, what early Slavs looked like. And readers can glean where "Russia" and "Russian" originate as terms. For anyone who does know Russian history well, or who longs for some sort of general concept about the meanings of the narrative, or who wants more than just rulers, kinship, and battles, this is not the project for you.

Summary:

Akunin's histories matter, though, in two broad respects. First, they are popular: they are sold everywhere and have sold well. The histories have been reviewed and discussed across a wide variety of media: radio programs, TV interviews, book reviews, LiveJournal discussions. Thus, Akunin's historical project has arguably become the most widely-read and widely-discussed history of the post-Soviet era. Regardless of whether or not readers heed his warnings or like his approaches, this new *History of the Russian State* should be taken seriously in part because it has appeared at a time when the current Russian state has become more and more concerned with the past and how it is written. Second, and perhaps more importantly, *The History of the Russia State* appeared at a crucial juncture in contemporary Russian politics and the author's own political stance. Akunin, who had long declared his wish to be a belletrist and not a writer, and who had long maintained an apolitical stance, decided in December 2011 to join the Bolotnaia Square protestors. Thus, his new historical project appeared at a time when Akunin had become a very vocal, and very prominent, critic of Putin's state. The author, who had maintained a second home in France, officially emigrated and moved to London as a result of his political stance. His works also came out as the Putin state, led in this regard by then-Minister of Culture Vladimir Medinskii (appointed in 2012), declared his opposition to Russophobia and his desire to combat historical "falsification." This confluence coloured the reception of the histories: many defended the author's attempts to write an "objective" history of the Russian state, while other called Akunin a falsifier of history.

That these two trends coalesced in the debates about the *History of the Russian State* project should come as no surprise. In what follows, however, this manual will provide would-be readers of the histories with some of the language of these debates and the ways that the author and his critics have described the project.

2 Safety Warning

A) Paper cuts, empty pocketbooks, and drowsiness are the most common safety concerns when reading the *Histories*. Drowsiness is less likely to occur when reading the accompanying novels.

B) For readers who would describe themselves as "Russian patriots," intermittent explosive disorder is a common side effect. Treatment might include therapy and/or medicine.

C) Professional historians may experience headaches and heart palpitations when reading the *Histories*. These can be overcome by reading the novels.

Summary:

Best to read the fictional accompaniments rather than the histories.

3 Assembly

Akunin on his project:

> Russian history, probably more than any other history, is full of myths and lies. In Russia, historical science existed for a very short span of time, a part of the nineteenth century and a part of the twentieth century. Before, it had been practically non-existent, because it was only Nikolai Karamzin who invented it in a serious way at the beginning of the nineteenth century. During the twentieth century history became so full of ideology that it became no longer a science but a kind of propaganda. Soviet authorities used history in order to create myths for pedagogical purposes, so that young people would be proud of their great ancestors and their great country. I thought then and I still think now that this is an awful misconception. History is not about being proud. History is like an instruction manual, how to "use" your own country. It should be something such as: don't put your fingers in here you will be hit by electricity. If you want to achieve this do this and this and do that. History should be about that which you have to know. You have to know the truth. You have to know that if a country succeeded in something it was because of this and this and this. If there was a defeat we have to know everything about it: why it happened, what didn't go the right way. I wanted to write this sort of history.[3]

Akunin elaborating on the histories he grew up with: "You know, before the Revolution, educated people knew Russian history better, because there were just better textbooks in the gymnasium. Soviet texts, which I studied, were simply monstrous."[4]

Akunin on the problems with historical writings for students now: "This concept of a single textbook does not inspire."[5]

Summary:

Akunin's rationale for starting the project responds to several historical contexts. What might be termed the "Soviet memory project," which ensured that history had to be subsumed under ideology, was something that the writer thought still needed to be undone. That this new project took place under new economic circumstances informed Akunin's desire to write a popular "manual" that readers could "use" (Akunin's genius in part rests with understanding market trends and PR). Finally, Akunin's works were meant to counteract the increasing politicization of the past taking place in Putin's Russia, including the ongoing debates about a single textbook for all Russians to read, one that was to be "patriotic" and one that critics charged would bring back the infamous Stalin-era *Short Course*. Akunin's project, whether he admitted it or not, was a response to the textbook controversy surrounding A.V. Filippov's 2007 *The Contemporary History of Russia, 1945–2006*, which controversially argued that Stalin was an effective "manager" and that the Stalinist system emerged out of a 500-year old "tradition" of power being concentrated in the hands of one autocratic ruler with a centralized administration. Filippov's history was justifiably criticized for its defence of Stalin and his policies, its selectivity, its tendentious conclusions, and its partisanship (among others). As a work of history, however, it also focused almost exclusively on high politics and leaders at the expense of ordinary people. It also ignored all recent historiography, instead choosing to engage in straw-man debates. *The Contemporary History of Russia* charts a short course (pun intended) of state history, endorsing the "great man theory" in order to judge rulers on whether or not they kept the state strong (as David Brandenberger recounts, Stalin was good, Khrushchev bad, Brezhnev good, Gorbachev bad, Yeltsin bad, and Putin the best manager of all).[6]

Although the Filippov book was not adopted, the quest for a "manual," for an instruction book for the new nation, has not been abandoned by the Putin state. Akunin's *History* aimed to win at this game. His attempt to assemble the past for present-day readers has generated a host of reactions (see FAQs below) and has provided new technical specifications for making a "manual for the nation," which is covered in the next section.

4 Technical Specifications

Akunin on his histories, in 2015:

> The first volume, which was entitled *A Part of Europe*, covers the period before Russia was conquered by the Mongols in the thirteenth century. The second part is about the Tatar-Mongol period and it's logically

entitled, *A Part of Asia*, because Russia was a part of a vast Asian empire in the thirteenth and fourteenth, and the first half of the fifteenth, centuries. The third volume is called *Between Asia and Europe*. It starts in the mid-fifteenth century, with Ivan III, and ends at the beginning of the seventeenth century, during the *smutnoe vremia*, or the Time of Troubles. By my calculation we are currently living in the early years of the sixth Russian state. The first Russian state was the pre-Mongolian state, which began between Novgorod and Kiev and then moved to Vladimir before it collapsed when the Mongols conquered it. For two hundred years afterwards there was no Russian state, it was just a dominion of the Tatar Horde. My third volume is therefore about the second attempt at building a Russian state. It was started by Ivan III in the middle of the fifteenth century, and proved to be very successful, but in the end it failed and ceased to exist in the beginning of the seventeenth century, when the country was conquered by the Poles. There would be a third Russian state in the seventeenth century, then a fourth created by Peter the Great when the state had to be rebuilt and moved even closer to Europe. Then there was the fifth state, the Soviet empire. And now we are living in the sixth state, the post-Soviet one, which as it seems is not going too well right now.[7]

Akunin on *rusoslaviane* or what to call the early peoples living in the first state: "We need a term to call the proto-national group that would later split into Russians, Ukrainians, and Belorussians ... To my ears, '*rusoslaviane*' sounds better than '*slavianorussy*.'"[8]
The first "Russian state," Akunin claims in his history, collapsed because the "central government was too weak": the state collapsed, but the "country [*strana*] still existed." The second state, from Ivan III to Boris Godunov, developed because of the survival of parts of the first in the "eastern half" of the former Rus' and the development of Moscow as its home base. This second state, as Akunin writes, retained aspects of the Mongol polity, making it a country "between Europe and Asia." Throughout Akunin stresses "the role of personality in history," Ivan III and Ivan IV in particular. It was under these two rulers, Akunin concludes, that a new concept of the state developed, one where the ruler himself became the state, making the term *gosudar'* the key one, and where the Russian tsar was a "patriarch," the "father," with "all the other inhabitants of the country his children." "In a patriarchal family the father is not guided by law and by their own ideas of whether they are correct; rather, it is expected that children are to be unquestionably obedient. Father-sovereign (*otets-gosudar'*) knows best, and if he is wrong he answers not to the people, but to God." Ivan the

Terrible, readers are informed, took these ideas to excess, leading to the collapse of this state.[9]

From the conclusion of *Between Asia and Europe*:

Rus' radically transformed itself [in this period]. It transformed from a relatively small country, which is easier to manage using traditional "Horde" [*ordynskii*] methods, to become a large, varied, economically complicated, multi-ethnic state. ... The founder of this state, Ivan III, saw Russia as a great patrimony [*votchina*] and did everything to ensure that his successors ruled in the same way. It has been said that in the Russian language the word "State" [*gosudarstvo*] was derived from "sovereign" [*gosudar'*], that is, the country was seen as something like the personal property of the ruler ... [But a] big government cannot govern well as an estate [*pomest'e*]. If, like Ivan the Terrible, a ruler shows too much insistence on adhering to direct manual control, he triggers a self-destruct mechanism. By the end of the period described here three serious diseases had evolved within the life of the state: undeveloped administrative systems, rudimentary laws, and an ever-increasing gap with the rapidly growing West; with the second and third problems being largely a consequence of the first. The historians of the nineteenth century added another problem and even considering it the most significant: a crisis of national morality [*krizis narodnoi nravstvennosti*] ... But this social and psychological instability, manifested so dramatically during the state's decay by 1605, was also the result of a deep internal crisis by a *poorly organized* state. It was "too Asian," "too Horde-like." Its primitive verticality of power could not function within the demands of the time. There were no real ministerial departments that could effectively regulate the different spheres of the state's life. There was no normal operating regional management structure. There was no full-scale set of uniform rules on which it could manage a huge area that contains millions of square kilometres. The entire, giant pyramid rested on one stem: the figure of the autocrat, who made all the decisions, even down to the smallest. If I could briefly formulate the main problem of this "second state," it consisted in the fact that the autocracy had not yet learned to share power. Any personal shortcomings of the sovereign, any aberrations of character, immediately became an illness that affected the health of the entire country.[10]

Akunin on professional historians: "They see the tree, its textures, its details, its height, but not the forest." His task: "to see the forest, to remain at a bird's eye view, not to get too close to the trees for fear of getting too interested in one of them." He follows, he told Sergei Buntman in an *Ekho Moskvy* interview, the principle of three Latin letters: "EID. E is for entertaining and exciting; I is for informative; and D is for deep." It's an approach, he acknowledged, that is something like *History for Dummies* (he referenced this set of works).[11]

Akunin on his task (also from his *Ekho Moskvy* interview): "From my point of view, the main problem of Russia is an ongoing, perpetual, eternal conflict between the state and the population ... Here, our state and people have always treated each other with distrust in our country. This is the root of all our problems. As long as there's this barrier to overcome, nothing will happen."[12] This, he argues he is not writing a history of Russian culture, an intellectual history, or a history of technological progress, but a history of the state, a history of power and politics.

Summary:

For anyone with even a passing knowledge of Russian historiography, this is all-too-familiar stuff. Akunin's histories revive (or repeat) the so-called "state school" (*gosudarstvennaia shkola*) of Russian history in the nineteenth century, one that, for all its variations, insisted on the notion that "Russian history" was a story that traced the evolution of how leaders built a state out of tribes (that being said, it is not as if Sergei Solov'ev, Konstantin Kavelin, Boris Chicherin, Vasilii Kliuchevskii, and others copied each other, so the "state school" is something of a misnomer).[13] Thus, one only needed to focus on princes, kings, tsars, and emperors. Akunin's histories do the same (and, it is worth noting, so too did Filippov's book). The "state school" enjoyed a renaissance after 1991, as part of what Gary Hamburg describes as a "broader pattern of ongoing national reorientation in which post-Soviet Russians are 'rehabilitating' the imperial past and rediscovering their heretofore hidden cultural links and affinities with the empire."[14] In many ways, Akunin's manual represents the perfect synthesis of the way the "state school" has been imagined, not the way historians in the nineteenth century actually wrote about the past. Chicherin, Kavelin, Solov'ev, and the others argued with each other as historians do (they agreed that the state mattered, but they disagreed on when it had first appeared, whether it was like European states, and the relationship between state and people); to say they only thought the state drove history is a misstatement.

For professional historians, Akunin's ideas about his structure are also all-too-familiar notions. Popular political history is old hat in the United States, but, if one wishes to be generous, is still something new in Russia. One conclusion, however much it causes headaches for professionals, is that Akunin's bestselling histories proves that Russia has become a "normal" country. Before turning to how "normal" the debates over his manual have been, first a brief note about other installation instructions.

5 Additional Information and Specifications

A) *Read the Novels.*

Akunin on them: "In these stories, I behaved quite irresponsibly. I fantasized. Because what happened in them no one knows for sure and it was harder to fight about them on historical forums and defend previous versions of history. I felt completely free in these stories. They are practically a fantasy, 'Game of Thrones', or something like that."[15]

B) *Problems with Additional Installation*: See FAQs Below.

6 Troubleshooting/FAQs

A) *Nationalist Critiques*: "It's not a study about a failed state, but a study of a failed Russian writer."

Perhaps the nastiest critique of Akunin's new project appeared in *Odnako* (November 2013), where conservative blogger and columnist Dmitrii Beliaev entitled his article "How Boris Akunin Falsifies History in *The History of the Russian State*."[16] The takedown did not just critique Akunin's use of historical facts and terms (though it did that); it also suggested the writer was a hypocrite, someone who "has enough money to buy a small house in France," who gets to charge 700 rubles per book (this figure is cited twice), and who engages in a Russophobic reimagining of the past that indirectly criticizes the Putin system, all the while making movies that are financed by First Channel. Beliaev, who also quotes criticisms of the project levelled by Eduard Chesnokov (a blogger, political poet, and pro-Putin commentator), concludes by reversing Akunin's conclusion: it's not a study of how Ancient Rus' can be considered "a failed state, as you think," but a case study of a "failed Russian writer."

Summary:

In this and other criticisms of Akunin's histories, we can detect what Masha Lipman has termed "Putin 2.0" culture: the abandonment in 2012, after the protests, of any official toleration of dissent. As Lipman writes, "State-controlled television channels launched a smear campaign against the protesters, condemning them as pro-Western, unpatriotic, and immoral. National television painted the West as evil and labeled liberals, gays, and recipients of foreign grants as subversive Western agents."[17] While the most well-known targets of these policies were Alexei Navalny and Pussy Riot,[18] Akunin, as these reviews indicate, became caught up in them too: his interviews with Navalny in 2012, just before the history series launched, also made these connections and explored the concept of the "Russian state."[19]

The "Russian writer" tag is a not-so-subtle dig, for Akunin, as the article explicitly noted, is just the pen name for Grigorii Chkhartishvili. In the interview that aired on *Ekho Moskvy* in January 2014, the author explained how criticisms of his work had increasingly become ethnocentric. Sergei Buntman, who conducted the interview, began by referencing the criticisms of the *History*. Akunin separated these criticisms into parts, acknowledging that professional historians might find his work unsatisfying (even while stating that he had his facts straight and employed professionals to check them); but professionals, he stated, are not "prone to histrionics." The loudest complaints, Akunin stated, come from the mouths of "professional patriots of the Russian land" (*professional'nye patrioty zemli russkoi*).[20] For this crowd Akunin is, as he argued, a "liberal," a "white-ribbon wearer" or opposition activist (*belolentochnik*), and "a Georgian." For these "professional patriots," Akunin's ethnicity disqualifies him from writing about "great Russian" history ("how dare your shashlik fingers touch great Russian history?" he joked). Buntman agreed with this sentiment, and asked instead who the books are for, to which Akunin replied the point was to generate interest in history among those who often find it boring, a "Russian history for Dummies."

B) *Professional Critiques*: "This is a profanity of history in the most literal sense of the word."

Summary

Igor' Danilevskii, a professor at the Higher School of Economics in Moscow, gave an interview for *Profil'* in January 2014.[21] Danilevskii characterized Akunin's first volume as "folk-history" (he used the English), which he defined as an amateur writing history full of his own views for laymen. The difference, Danilevskii stated, was that the amateur this time was Akunin, giving this folk-history a wider readership than others in the genre. Danilevskii, when asked by his interviewer whether or not Akunin's history had value of some kind, responded with a list of factual errors (Yaroslav the Wise did not introduce rotating rulers beyond father to son, or *lestvichnyi*), conceptual errors (Akunin did not seem to be aware of how the Chronicles were composed), and anachronistic errors (Akunin introduced an ethnicity, *rusoslaviane*, that had never been used before). He saved his most vocal criticism, however, for Akunin's methodology, which consists mostly of Akunin weighing the evidence and employing "common sense" to determine the most plausible version of what happened. Danilevskii decries this "presentism" and concludes that "this is a profanity of history in the most literal sense of the word." For Danilevskiii, it is clear that Akunin's understanding of the discipline ends with Leopold von Ranke, Kliuchevskii, and Solov'ev. As to why Akunin writes for a seventh to tenth grade reader despite his obvious intelligence (in Danilevskii's estimation), the professional historian responded: "it's a mystery to me."

Danilevskii's reward: he was conscripted by Akunin to fact-check the second volume.

C) *Journalistic Critique*: "'Boring' is the overall keyword of this Akunin project."

Vadim Nesterov, a journalist, concluded on a Lenta.ru review that "Grigorii Shalvovich returned to where he began, the work of a translator. Because, if we call a spade a spade, in the framework of the project 'History of the Russian State,' he has been copying the works of Kliuchevskii, Karamzin, in a more contemporary language. He does it very professionally, and in the end it turns out it is easy to read, but it is also a very boring text. 'Boring' is the overall keyword of this Akunin project. Paradoxically, but the new book by Boris Akunin is completely devoid of the most important quality of this author: a brilliantly constructed plot."[22]

D) *Book Fair Critique*: "Illiterate."

The seventeenth annual Russian Book Fair (March 2014) awarded its "Illiterate Honour" (*Pochetnaia bezgramota*) to Akunin's first volume for "the concentration of mistakes, inaccuracies, and speculation. It is amazing how the author, for example, decodes the Russian soul."[23] The main complaint: the term *rusoslaviane*.

E) *Other Critiques*.

Maia Kucherskaia, in *Vedomosti*, suggested in her review of the first volume that Akunin must be trying to study Russian history only to get the source material for his new sagas, the fictional stories.[24] Nikita Sokolov, editor of *Otechestvennye zapiski*, declared the histories themselves to be fiction, concluding that Grigorii Chkhartishvili is smart enough to write a history, but unfortunately he left the task up to Boris Akunin.[25] In *Literaturnaia gazeta*, Arsenii Aleksandrov concluded: "In one word, it is a project. A commercial one" (he began the review by stating "Boris Akunin is a solid brand" [*solidnaia torgovaia marka*].[26] Ilya Gerasimov, writing in *Ab Imperio*, places Akunin's project within the "canon" of historical scholarship from Karamzin through the Soviet era, which stressed a history of the "Russian people" occurring on Russian "historical territory." Akunin, it is clear, has not made the imperial turn, much less the cultural turn, or the social turn, or any turn.

F) *Readers' Critiques*: Mixed.

And what of the readers? Ozon.ru has sixty reviews posted online: readers rated it 4 out of 5.[27] Most liked the accessible style and Akunin's seeming objectivity. Those more critical tended to make statements similar to those quoted above.

"Stal' Aleksandr Nikolaevich" gave it 4 out of 5; he worried, as he posted, that Akunin's "liberalism" and "liberalism of the brain" (*liberalism golovnogo mozga*) would infect his history and pour more dirt onto Russian history, but found the book free from Russophobia and "objective."

"Anna" succinctly declared that "the book has nothing to do with history," is nothing like Karamzin, and "should be in the fiction section."

7 Application

In a *Deutsche Welle* interview with Zhanna Nemtsova, daughter of the opposition leader Boris Nemtsov, who was assassinated in 2015, Akunin spoke about contemporary applications for his histories. These quotes serve as appropriate conclusions for this manual.

When asked about a "law of history" and Russia "always being a step behind," Akunin responded:

> I've always been interested in the question of what defines the Russian nation. Why do we see the same disasters being repeated over centuries? Every attempt at liberalization ends with even greater repression. I assume that Vladimir Putin is not personally to blame. I think that when this man came to power, he didn't set out to do away with all our freedoms and become a lifelong dictator. He probably wanted to rein in the oligarchs and somehow deal with the separatists. He had moderate goals.
>
> But then the force of certain laws unfolded, and the same thing happened that has happened many times before in Russian history. If there were a peaceful revolution in Russia tomorrow, if Putin were toppled and a democrat came to power but just left everything as it is, then after a while, this democrat would turn into a new dictator. The vertical structure of the state means there's no chance to move in a different direction.

Nemtsova followed up by asking about the system versus an individual changing it. Akunin elaborated:

> It's astounding that in our history, not one reformer has taken on the foundation of the state as laid down in the fifteenth century by Ivan III, the ruler who brought the Russian lands together. He borrowed from the same principles used to create the Golden Horde. At that time, the

Russians didn't know a more effective system than that employed by Genghis Khan. Our country is still not ruled by laws, rather by decrees, like under the Great Khans. At the same time, it's a system where the state does not exist to serve the people, rather the people serve the state. There's no room in such a system for the rights of individuals. There are only personal privileges that depend on one's position within the structure and the degree of loyalty to the authorities. And in such a system, the secret police play a significant role.[28]

NOTES

1 Boris Akunin, *Istoriia Rossiiskogo Gosudarstva: Chast' Evropy – ot istokov do mongol'skogo nashestviia* (*History of the Russian State: A Part of Europe – From the Beginnings to the Mongol Conquest*; Moscow: AST, 2014), 3.
2 Ibid., 4.
3 For the full interview, see chapter 2 of this volume.
4 "Istoriia Rossiskogo Gosudarstva," interview with Sergei Buntman on *Ekho Moskvy*, 18 January 2014, http://echo.msk.ru/programs/netak /1238026-echo/?=top. Translations from the Russian in this chapter are my own unless otherwise indicated.
5 Ibid.
6 See David Brandenberger's discussion of the book: "A New Short Course? A.V. Filippov and the Russian State's Search for a 'Usable Past,'" *Kritika: Explorations in Russian and Eurasian History* 10, no. 4 (2009): 825–34.
7 For the full interview, see chapter 2 of this volume.
8 Akunin, *Chast' Evropy*, 2.
9 From the interview: see chapter 2 of this volume.
10 Boris Akunin, *Mezhdu Aziei i Evropoi: Ot Ivan III do Borisa Godunova* (*Between Asia and Europe: From Ivan III to Boris Godunov*; Moscow: AST, 2015), 374–5. Emphasis in original.
11 "Istoriia Rossiskogo Gosudarstva."
12 Ibid.
13 Gary Hamburg has argued persuasively that the "state school" is an invented concept, mostly created by opponents of the historians in question and then reinvented after 1991. Hamburg, "Inventing the 'State School' of Historians, 1840–1995," in *Historiography of Imperial Russia: The Profession and Writing of History in a Multinational State*, ed. Thomas Sanders (London: Routledge, 1997), 98–117.
14 Ibid., 98.
15 "Istoriia Rossiskogo Gosudarstva."

16 Dmitrii Beliaev, "O tom, kak Akunin fal'sifitsiruet istoriiu v 'Istoriii Rossi-iskogo gosudarstva," *Odnako*, 23 November 2013, http://www.odnako.org/blogs/o-tom-kak-akunin-falsificiruet-istoriyu-v-istorii-rossiyskogo-gosudarstva.

17 Maria Lipman, "How Putin Silences Dissent: Inside the Kremlin's Crackdown," *Foreign Affairs* 95 (2016): 42.

18 For more on Navalny, see Marlene Laruelle, "Alexei Navalny and Challenges in Reconciling 'Nationalism' and 'Liberalism,'" *Post-Soviet Affairs* 30, no. 4 (2014): 276–97; Jussi Lassila, "Aleksei Naval'nyi and Populist Re-ordering of Putin's Stability," *Europe-Asia Studies* 68, no. 1 (2016): 118–37. On Pussy Riot, see the articles in *Digital Icons* 9: http://www.digitalicons.org/issue09/.

19 "The Akunin-Navalny Interviews," Open Democracy, 11 January 2012, https://www.opendemocracy.net/od-russia/alexei-navalny-boris-akunin/akunin-navalny-interviews-part-i.

20 "Istoriia Rossiskogo Gosudarstva."

21 Igor' Danilevskii, "Predan'ia stariny glubokoi," *Profil'*, 21 January 2014, 40–2.

22 Vadim Nesterov, "Akunin i tishina," Lenta.ru, 24 September 2014, https://lenta.ru/articles/2014/09/24/borisakunin/.

23 Anastasia Skorondaeva, "Les russkoi dushi," *Rossiiskaia gazeta*, 2 March 2014, https://rg.ru/2014/03/26/yarmarka-site.html.

24 Maia Kucherskaia, "Na sluzhbe persta," *Vedomosti*, 21 November 2013, http://www.vedomosti.ru/newspaper/articles/2013/11/21/na-sluzhbe-persta.

25 Nikita Sokolov, "Istoriia Rossiiskogo Gosudarstva," Afisha, 6 December 2013, https://daily.afisha.ru/archive/vozduh/books/istoriya-rossiyskogo-gosudarstva-akunina-s-tochki-zreniya-strogoy-nauki/.

26 Arsenii Aleksandrov, "Istoricheskii tovar," *Literaturnaia gazeta*, 4 December 2013, http://www.lgz.ru/article/-48-6441-04-12-2013/istoricheskiy-tovar/?sphrase_id=256720.

27 See the stats on http://www.ozon.ru/context/detail/id/24193097/, accessed 19 October 2018.

28 Zhanna Nemtsova, "Boris Akunin: Russia Ruled by a 'Khan,'" *Deutsche Welle*, 12 May 2016, http://www.dw.com/en/boris-akunin-russia-ruled-by-a-khan/a-19252850.

PART FIVE

New Pseudonyms and Projects: Anatolii
Brusnikin and Akunin-Chkhartishvili

11 "Under the Wide-Branching Cranberry": *Stiob* and Allusion in Anatolii Brusnikin's *The Ninth Saviour*

YEKATERINA SEVERTS

A prolific writer of historical fiction and non-fiction, Grigorii Chkhartishvili is known for trying his hand at different genres, from the detective series that have brought him international acclaim to a survey of writers' propensity towards suicide or even a hybrid of crime novel and online quest. His impetus towards literary innovation goes hand in hand with a proliferation of identities and pen names, such as Boris Akunin, Anna Borisova, and Anatolii Brusnikin. The latter pseudonym appeared on the cover of his novel *The Ninth Saviour* (*Deviatnyi Spas*, 2007), set in the late seventeenth–early eighteenth century and named after a fictional icon which mysteriously protects the Russian royal house and endows it with sacred powers. The title, however, is a red herring. The eponymous icon, discussed in great detail in the opening chapter, vanishes from the narrative almost till the end, when its reappearance affords a minor culmination point. Central to the plot are adventures of three friends – a nobleman, Dmitrii; a priest's son, Aleksei; and a peasant, Il'ia – who seek purpose, fortune, and, not the least, love in the rapidly changing socio-political context. By examining their identities, whether immutable, as in Ilia's case, or prone to transformation, as with Dmitrii and Aleksei, the author meditates on the fate of the generation caught amidst Peter the Great's reforms and having to choose between the wholehearted embrace of the Western influence and clinging nostalgia for the traditional Russian ways.

In this chapter, I examine how in *The Ninth Saviour* the constant feature of Chkhartishvili's creative corpus – the masterful use of literary allusions – contributes to the aesthetics of *stiob*, an elusive genre of parody that subverts a particular narrative (usually a state-enforced one), while ostensibly mimicking its form and paying lip service to the values it promotes. In *The Ninth Saviour*, *stiob* may be identified through its key functions as delineated by Alexey Yurchak in *Everything Was Forever,*

Until It Was No More.[1] Firstly, the novel reveals over-identification with authoritative form, in this case, with the imperialist fiction that has colonized the contemporary Russian literary scene. Faithful to the representational ambivalence of *stiob*, *The Ninth Saviour* offers pastiches of imperialist fiction seemingly at face value, a technique which ingratiates it with its conservative readership. Although engaging in a game with his readers is a meta-narrative strategy typical of Chkhartishvili, in *The Ninth Saviour* he takes it to a new level by adopting an overtly Slavophile persona and, with the help of this previously unknown alias, undermines the readers' ability to produce a convincing interpretation of the novel.

In addition to identifying the staples of the imperialist discourse, *The Ninth Saviour* mixes them with the context of Dickensian melodrama, entirely unexpected and incongruous with the conservative tenor of the novel. In and of itself, homage to Dickens in a novel penned by Chkhartishvili is hardly surprising, given the overarching significance of Dickens's influence on Russian, Soviet, and post-Soviet literature.[2] The changes in the political and ideological landscapes of Russia did not affect the interest in Dickens, and, as Emily Finer observes in her assessment of his influence, "writers still assume Dickensian guises, in particular in postmodernist prose such as the detective stories of Boris Akunin."[3] However, what sets apart the use of Dickensian allusions in *The Ninth Saviour* is their contribution to *stiob*, as opposed to merely strengthening the detective plot or, in typical Chkhartishvili's fashion, winking to the erudite reader. By imbuing his ostensibly nationalistic text with melodrama imported wholesale from the Western canon, Chkhartishvili succeeds in recontextualizing the authoritative form and breaking down its hierarchical structure.

A New Pseudonym and the Problem of Interpretation

In 2007, the Russian literary scene witnessed the rising of a new star in the popular genre of historical detective and mystery, a genre which hitherto had been the almost exclusive domain of Boris Akunin. Now Akunin appeared to have a rival. *The Ninth Saviour*, a debut novel by an unknown author named Anatolii Brusnikin, had an initial run of 270,000 copies – an extraordinary number, considering that the publishing house AST caps a typical beginner run from 4,000 to 5,000.[4] Why would a leading publisher invest so lavishly in the first book written by, according to the author's blurb, a humble museum employee? Equally suspicious was the wide-scale advertising campaign that accompanied the publication: light-box stands sprung up in Moscow, displaying the

Palekh-style book cover and quotes from top-selling Russian authors: "Minaev is delighted; Dashkova is charmed; and Akunin is frustrated" (apparently by encroachment into his genre territory). These promotion efforts tipped off the reading public. Could it be, the suggestion arose instantaneously, that A.O. Brusnikin was a nom de plume of none other but Boris Akunin?[5] After all, Grigorii Chkhartishvili, whose detective novels had appeared under the pseudonym Akunin, had gained a reputation for masquerade imbued with postmodernist irony.[6] In the spirit of his fiction, he was prone to playing a guessing-game with the readers, who, like Akunin's famous detective Erast Fandorin, were charged with deducing Brusnikin's true identity. In 2008, when the reclusive author gave an interview to Ekaterina Krongauz and even produced a headshot, suspicions intensified: Brusnikin looked like Akunin's twin brother, photoshopped ever so slightly.[7]

As for the book itself, the plot, setting, thematic range, and choice of characters prove a close match to Akunin's bestselling historical fiction. *The Ninth Saviour* is set in the tumultuous period between the conclusion of Sofia's regency and the first decades of Peter's reign. Prior to 2007, Akunin had already digressed from the second half of the nineteenth century, the period associated with his heroes Erast Fandorin and Sister Pelagia, to earlier periods of Russian history. *Altyn Tolobas* (*Altyn-tolobas*, 2001), the first book in the series *Adventures of Nicholas* (*Prikliuchenia magistra*),[8] takes place partially in the reign of Alexei Mikhailovich, in close temporal proximity to *The Ninth Saviour*. In *Children's Book* (*Detskaia kniga*, 2006), Akunin shows his familiarity with tsarist history by transporting his time-travelling protagonist back to the Time of Troubles in the early seventeenth century and to the late nineteenth century. Thus, by virtue of its historical setting, *The Ninth Saviour* provides a logical continuity with these two Akunin novels. Moreover, just as in *The Coronation* (*Koronatsiia, ili Poslednii iz Romanov*, 2000), the potentates here glide along the margins of the narrative canvas, being mentioned but passing virtually unnoticed. The plot in *The Ninth Saviour* is focused on the lives of ordinary people. As the wheel of fortune spins, the destinies of Dmitrii, Aleksei, and Il'ia are altered and reshaped, yet they remain true to their friendship against all odds. The novel is bursting with courtly intrigues, international espionage, undercover investigations with a gratuitous disguise, vigorous action scenes, and unrequited romance – in other words, all the staples of Akunin's earlier novels.[9] The main storyline, centred on the search for the icon "The Ninth Saviour,"[10] is thematically connected to Akunin's *Altyn Tolobas*, where the object of the quest was the lost library of Ivan the Terrible. In both novels, the search for the artefact amounts to nothing. Rather, the detective plot functions as a magnet for the reader's attention, and as he holds his audience captive the author uses this opportunity to conduct his comparative analysis of the socio-political situation in Russia.

As if to bolster the speculations, Chkhartishvili never directly denied his connection to *The Ninth Saviour*. His recommendation on the novel's back cover reads as a rather smug confession: "I once wanted to write a novel from the Petrine epoch, but now I don't think I will, as I will hardly do a better job than Brusnikin." By the time he acknowledged Brusnikin as his alias in 2010, his authorship had long been an open secret. Explaining that he never tried "to write in a fundamentally different way," Chkhartishvili pointed to his "recognizable archaic style with some mead [*medovukha*] mixed in."[11]

Despite the popularity of *The Ninth Saviour* among the Russian readership, as attested by a good sales record and positive reviews on social media,[12] this page-turner did not strike a chord with the critics. An obvious reason for their disgruntlement, one that Chkhartishvili himself admitted to, was an "expensive, obnoxious campaign," which involved, among other things, free leaflets with the novel's first chapter offered at major bookstores "like samples of the new sausage or cheese at a supermarket."[13] But the advertising avalanche only partially accounts for the critics' disgruntlement. According to their consensus, the novel was deficient of Akunin's sparkling wit and subtle stylization; it was written too crudely, and the game of identities that unfolded around it was equally crude and unworthy of the master. For example, Evgenii Belzherarskii in *Itogi* decries the futility of Chkhartishvili's name-changing, as only the self-sufficiency of the text validates another literary mystification. With *The Ninth Saviour*, this was sadly not the case. Because the text itself was so underwhelming, any attempt at analysing its objectives – such as, for instance, a Slavophile revision of Peter's reforms – would be pointless.[14] Lev Danilkin, previously a champion of Akunin's postmodern technique,[15] also took a negative stance towards the novel, upbraiding Brusnikin for "the phenomenal number of coincidences" that propel his plot – in other words, for what the Russians aptly call "the grand piano in the bushes."[16] In addition to its structural and stylistic infelicities, the lack of authenticity in the novel seems to be the major point of contention. In her review in the journal *Znamia*, Kuznetsova describes the novel as "a quasi-historical mythography" that "dovetails into obscurantism, a fusion of Orthodox tradition and Kabbalah."[17] Alluding to the idiom *razvesistaia kliukva*[18] ("wide-branching cranberry"), meaning "fake, exaggerated, unauthentic," an anonymous reviewer from Info-Tses.Kz goes as far as to call the novel *raskidistaia brusnika* ("wide-branching lingonberry"), a play on the "author's" last name.

However, these and similar reviews reveal the shortcomings of applying the lens of conventional criticism to the text, which more so than the other works in Chkhartishvili's corpus exhibits postmodernist playfulness, the deliberate non-seriousness that simultaneously invites and rebuffs a straightforward reading. As Mark Lipovetsky posits in *Russian Postmodernist Fiction*, "Postmodernist play replaces avant-garde fragmentation with an unstable, conditional, illusory, yet nonetheless total and integrated playful involvement, consolidating the text's heterogeneous elements and codes."[19] Indeed, even a cursory comparison of Brusnikin's novel with its two modernist predecessors, Alexei Tolstoy's *Peter the First* (*Petr Pervyi*, 1934) and Dmitry Merezhkovsky's *Peter and Alexis: The Romance of Peter the Great* (*Petr i Aleksei*, 1905), reveal what Lipovetsky calls "antihierarchical, antiteleological, antistructural" logic of postmodernism. Whether exploring the ethical dimensions of the conflict between modernity and spirituality, or using Peter's reforms to legitimize Stalin's industrialization, Merezhkovsky and Tolstoy are equally invested in crafting a hierarchical structure of meaning. In contrast, Brusnikin's novel undermines any attempt at essentialism by deliberately yet light-heartedly commingling such distinct semantic spheres as Russian folklore, socio-cultural debates in contemporary Russia, and the melodramatic tropes of Charles Dickens.

In his inimical manner, discussed in detail by Elena Baraban in her article "A Country Resembling Russia" and Claire Whitehead in her chapter in this volume, Chkhartishvili reshuffles meanings on the level of allusions. By setting up a dialogue between his aliases, Brusnikin the Slavophile and Akunin the Westernizer, the author opens up two distinct channels through which allusions pour into the narrative space, where they converge without losing the distinct markers of their origin. This bricolage informs the novel's structure and, on the part of the reader, may result in misinterpretation of the novel as filled with preachy nostalgia or narrating an excessively simplistic, didactic story of friendship. Conversely, recognition of the intricate interplay of allusions accomplishes the same goal that Whitehead identifies in her analysis of Sister Pelagia novels, where, as elsewhere in Akunin's works, historical and literary allusions constitute a literacy test, giving (or denying) the reader access to the imaginary community of like-minded individuals who can keep up with the author's vast erudition. But inasmuch as *The Ninth Saviour* reflects Akunin's characteristic interplay of allusions, the quality and stylistic discrepancies of the allusions point to a different technique, which elicits a wider range of reactions as critics and readers attempt to pin down the message, or at least the political tonality, of *The Ninth Saviour*. How are we to interpret an historical mystery where some allusions are so apparent that they border on allegory, while others are so unexpected that they may pass under anyone's radar? And what to make of Brusnikin's staunchly imperialist stance, which he expresses directly by means of authorial asides and ventriloquizes through the voices of his characters?

In light of the rising popularity of neo-imperialist writing, which actively relies on reinterpretation of historical events, it would be tempting to read *The Ninth Saviour* as yet another example of revisionist fantasy. In his analysis of imperialist fantasy in *Post-Soviet Literature and the Search for a Russian Identity*, Boris Noordenbos lists some of its better known adepts, such as Eduard Limonov, Alexander Prokhanov, and Pavel Krusanov.[20] Their works, however, are the tip of the iceberg. I would argue that what sets the horizon of expectations for the contemporary Russian consumers of imperialist fiction are the historical action or time-travel novels published in scores by Eksmo and Astrel'-SBP (a branch of AST). Before they get picked up by the publishers, many of these novels appear on the free self-publishing website Samlib.ru, which gives amateur writers an opportunity to upload their texts chapter by chapter and receive immediate feedback from readers. The ubiquity of imperialist fantasy, with its fixed tropes and a large, well-established readership, provides a fertile ground for Chkhartishvili's experiment in *stiob*, which he carries out by producing a deadpan conservative reading of a particularly controversial period in Russian history.

The use of *stiob* deviates from Chkhartishvili's usual postmodernist technique, which in regards to reception creates a hierarchy of the readers based on their overall erudition, separating them into those who find pleasure in the game of allusions and those whose engagement with the text is limited to the detective plot. *Stiob*, on the contrary, is characterized primarily by its ambivalence, whereby the reader is given fewer, if any, clues as to the author's intention. In Alexei Yurchak's definition, *stiob* is "a peculiar form of irony that ... [requires] such a degree of overidentification with the object, person, or idea at which this *stiob* was directed that it was *often impossible to tell* whether it was a form of sincere support, subtle ridicule, or a peculiar mixture of the two."[21] The elusiveness of *stiob* is what keeps the reader second-guessing whether a book is naive or over-saturated with postmodernist playfulness to the point that its confusing nature takes over the meaning of the text. Analyzing the use of postmodernist techniques in the conservative, neo-imperial Russian genres of sci-fi and fantasy, Noordenbos points out the problem of deducing authorial intention in texts ridden with *stiob*, because unless we place a heavy emphasis on the author's political leanings these texts can be read as both conservative and postmodernist.[22] Specifically, he addresses the mixed reception of Krusanov's novel *The American Hole* (*Amerikanskaia dyrka*, 2005), as critics hesitated whether to accept the author's fervent anti-Western invective or dismiss it as *stiob*, and their interpretations were also informed by what they knew or suspected about the real or implied author and his political sympathies. The same inability to ascertain the tenor of the novel is also evident in the reception of *The Ninth Saviour*, where the author, like the Pied Piper, beguiles the readers with an idyllic vision of the "good old Russia" only to lead them, in his inimical manner, down an entirely different path, towards critical reflection on contemporary discontents.

Stiob through Reproduction of the Authoritative Form

Commenting on his decision to try on a different pen name, Chkhartishvili states: "I am myself a Westernizer, even a cosmopolitan (the same goes for Akunin). However, I wanted to study an opposite point of view, that of a '*pochvennik*,' a Slavophile ... He [Brusnikin] respects the culture of others but also loves and esteems his own. In short, I have no disagreement with this kind of patriotism."[23] Chkhartishvili's previous pseudonym Boris Akunin, a double pun on the surname of the famous anarchist Bakunin and the Japanese word for "evildoer," was a fitting choice for the genre of the detective novels that made him famous. As Stephen Norris clarifies, the ironic references to villainy matched Chkhartishvili's aspirations to disrupt the imperial narrative by causing "chaos and anarchy in the accumulated memories about the nineteenth century in particular and the baggage of the Russian imperial project over the centuries."[24] Likewise, the pen name Brusnikin is consistent with the old-world values it represents. In his study of parallels between the novels of Akunin and Nabokov, Viacheslav Desiatov traces the pseudonym directly to Pushkin's *Eugene Onegin*, where *brusnichnaia voda* (lingonberry water), a token of old-fashioned hospitality, is a favourite drink in the Larin household; nonetheless, it does not agree with the metropolitan dandy Onegin.[25] Alla Latynina also remarks that *brusnika* shares the habitat with *kliukva* (cranberry).[26] Thus the pen name itself illustrates the subtlety of *stiob*: it is revealing enough to raise a few red flags but, at the same time, is not too obvious to disenchant the reader of any notions of authorial sincerity. A direct reference to cranberries, with associated connotations, would have earmarked Brusnikin's novel as a satire. Such well-defined genre designation would inevitably lay down guidelines for the novel's correct reading, which contradicts the deliberately elusive aesthetics of *stiob*. To function as *stiob*, the novel must keep the reader trapped in an uneasy hermeneutic circle, where each conclusion may be overwritten by the next.

The patriarchal ring to the name Brusnikin promises a nostalgic vision of Russia, wholesome and untainted by Peter's violent Westernization. This pastoral image is captured in the brief introduction, where the pre-Petrine Russia is depicted as a nation knit together through piety and good will. More importantly, it is homogenous, "still undivided into two unequal halves dissimilar in thought, clothing, and even manner of speaking."[27] Its unity is epitomized by Mitia (Dmitrii, also called Mit'ka), Alesha (Aleksei), and Il'ia, who represent the three estates: nobility, clergy, and peasantry. Any class contradictions, inevitable in the conditions of serfdom, are glossed over, and the peasant boy plays with the landlord's son as an equal. Their harmonious coexistence, prescriptive rather than descriptive, will be disrupted early on in the novel, as a direct result of shifting power after Peter's ascendancy. When next they meet, the three friends, now grown, will be changed beyond recognition – Alesha into an Italian adventurist and sword master, Mitia into a nostalgic conservative, and Il'ia into a savvy inventor along the lines of Ivan Kulibin. Seen together, they serve as an illustration of what Yuri Lotman saw as the crucial societal change brought forth by Peter's reforms – the increased chasm between the peasantry and the nobles who, as a result of Westernization, lost their touch with the native customs, clothing style, and even language.[28]

The cultural landscape lovingly crafted in *The Ninth Saviour* stands in opposition to the land of misrule as witnessed through the eyes of Cornelius Von Dorn in *Altyn Tolobas*, one of those foreigners incapable of seeing past the austerity of a log house: "The edifice of their state, not all too harmonious but timbered soundly from ancient logs, lacked in comfort and terrified the foreigners with the austerity of its unpainted walls and indifference towards outward prettiness; yet the skill and common sense showed through its squat outbuildings, rugged buttresses, and warily narrow windows. The corners and beams were held together by braces without a single nail; the roof darkened but did not cave in, and the golden dome shone above, and on the cross perched Alkonost, the white bird of joy."[29]

The lack of basic accommodations, a bane to Cornelius, is dwarfed in comparison to the Russian spirit of perseverance. In his traditionalist discourse, Brusnikin reads the log *terem* (used here as a synonym for a large house) as a metonymy of *sobornost'*, or spiritual unity of the people, producing a peculiar description of the "edifice of state," at once a dwelling place and a church "with a golden dome." The hybrid of church and state seems to be borrowed directly from conservative rhetoric, flourishing in 2007 and even more vociferous at present. Pointing out the impact of Orthodoxy on Russian culture, ecclesiastic speakers in tandem with right-wing politicians advocate for the greater presence of the Church in the state affairs, including such secular spheres as public education, health care, and legislation.[30] Equally telling is the structure of the *terem*, with its corners and beams "held together by braces without a single nail" and the roof "which darkened but did not cave in."[31] Two buzzwords signal the conservative tonality of this description. "Braces" (*skrepy*) inevitably brings to mind the phrase "spiritual braces" (*dukhovnye skrepy*), a rhetorical commonplace in political discourse, especially if marked with religious overtones.[32] Prior to the novel's publication, it had been circulating widely in a variety of contexts, mostly related to Russia's domestic policy and religious identity.[33] Ever so sensitive to his discursive environment, Chkhartishvili captures and replicates this type of conservative vocabulary. The semantic charge of the word "braces" is heightened through its proximity to another political cliché, *prognut'sia*, which may be translated as "to cave in, to sag, to yield, to bend down, and to give in to pressure." Although in the quoted sentence it refers to the roof of the symbolic log house, its connotations extend beyond this down-to-earth image, forming a semantic network that encompasses the whole of contemporary Russian mass media.[34] Since 2000, this verb has been increasingly used in the press to characterize the political vitality of Russia in contrast to its international opponents.[35]

By stringing together two hallmarks of conservative rhetoric, Brusnikin taps into the aesthetics of *stiob*, which Yurchak describes as "overidentification" with the subject or "the precise and slightly grotesque reproduction of the authoritative form."[36] Although a distinct Soviet phenomenon, *stiob* did not become obsolete after the collapse of the USSR. Rather, *stiob* depends on the presence of clearly defined hierarchical structures that it reduces *ad absurdum* in the process of their replication. Analyzing its resurgence in the contemporary Russian context, Boris Noordenbos arrives at the following conclusion: "A part of the explanation lies in a widely observed tendency under Putin towards the gradual elimination of critical political voices, the increasing control over the media, as well as the invention of the new, officially sanctioned strands of patriotism. As these tendencies provide important backgrounds for the reactualization of stiob."[37] Not surprisingly, the quasi-folkloric style of the introduction to *The Ninth Saviour* eventually accrues the bureaucratic formulas of "religious and national sentiment," reproducing the authoritarian discourse in its totality.[38]

It is, perhaps, not coincidental that the book cover itself is designed to resemble a lacquer box, depicting several scenes from the novel in typical Palekh style. In *Common Places*, Svetlana Boym describes a lacquer box as a Soviet simulacrum, a type of pseudo-folk art reinvented after the Revolution by unemployed icon painters who put their techniques in service of the new doctrine.[39] "A perfect fetish of Stalinist culturization," as Boym calls it, a Palekh box parses and neatly packages Russian culture for consumption, channelling nostalgia by means of vaguely recognizable icon stylization. At the same time, its very existence attests to the destruction of its prototype as a result of the anti-religious campaign in post-Revolutionary Russia. A troubling palimpsest, a lacquer box attempts to salvage certain aspects of artistic tradition, but in doing so obliterates its authenticity and reinvents it along the lines of Social Realism.[40]

Fashioned as a model imperialist fantasy, *The Ninth Saviour* dramatizes a highly controversial era much like how the far-right discourse treats another problematic time period, the 1930s. In the novel, the institution of monarchy is absolved of responsibility for any political upheavals, while a scattering of evildoers bear the brunt of blame. Among these villains are corrupt officials, the inevitable foreign spies, and a handful of homegrown rebels who just happen to be funded from abroad. Faithful to the implications of the Palekh book cover, Brusnikin draws unmistakable parallels between Peter's epoch and Stalin's purges. Although there is not direct equation of Peter and Stalin – and Peter never actually appears in the narration – the second half of the novel deals with the secret police and suppression of conspiracies. This juxtaposition harkens not only to Stalin's regime, with its admiration for Peter the Great, but also to the renewed fascination with Stalin himself. An important phenomenon of the 2000s, it is proliferated through a variety of channels, including books and documentaries in praise of Stalin as well as proposals concerning the erection of Stalin monuments. Obsession with Stalinism in general and the secret services in particular is also an important feature of the imperialist fantasy, especially in the genre of alternative history. A whole subgenre of popular fiction is focused on the adventures of time travellers, or the so-called *popadantsy* – present-day Russians, mostly male, who by some fiat are transported to the past, where they succeed in changing Russian history for the better. The most popular destination is either Stalin's or Peter's Russia, as the presence of an external threat allows exploring historical revisionism to its fullest. Time travellers prove immune to any form of persecution and tend to side with the authorities. In a typical scenario, the time traveller uses his contemporary knowledge for the greater good, such as stocking Peter's fleet with battleships or blasting through

Panzers with the help of skills learned from the online game "World of Tanks." In this fantasy subgenre, the secret services, the NKVD and SMERSH, tend to function as benign entities, certainly not as dangerous as the German invaders or the omnipresent foreign spies.[41]

The positive image of Stalinism in this patriotic fantasy, not to mention paeans to Stalin in conservative media, is one of those alarming tendencies that *The Ninth Saviour* absorbs. Despite his claims that his novel criticizes "state coercion with the help of the special services,"[42] Brusnikin takes a sympathetic stance towards the secret police, at least in light of its alternative, increased Western influence on domestic affairs. In a telling scene, Il'ia confronts the rebel leader, the Bull (*Byk*). Their encounter, like the rest of the novel, is steeped in Russian folklore: for instance, the Bull's countenance, "flat face with the eyes somewhat slanted and set wide apart," marks him as a racial Other, perhaps a Mongol.[43] Contrasted with Il'ia, he is forced into the role of Nightingale the Robber, typically portrayed as a caricatured version of a Mongol invader. Ironically, his fairy-tale attribute of deadly whistling is transferred to Il'ia, who in his capacity as a police informant must carry a whistle. During the standoff, the Bull voices his grievances against the government in an attempt to explain his treason:

> "I just don't get it, laddie, what sort of man you are," said the Bull suddenly ...
>
> "A regular man, a Russian."
>
> "But I'm Russian too."
>
> "What sort of Russian are you, if you are working for the Swedes?" ...
>
> "And how come our torturers from Preobrazhenka are better than the Swedes and the English? At least they don't rack people, don't stick their tobacco-covered fingers into the Russian soul, and don't turn it inside out."
>
> Il'ia could not respond with the same eloquence, so he grumbled:
>
> "Our torturers are better because they do their best for Rus and Russian faith."[44]

One must keep in mind that Il'ia is the most level-headed character in the book, as opposed to the diehard conservative Mitia and the equally impassioned Westernizer Alesha. When he passively accepts totalitarian politics, Il'ia acts as a stereotypical peasant who unquestioningly submits to his elders and betters. At the same time, he provides a point of identification for conservative readers desensitized to the surrounding Stalinist agenda. The elusiveness of *stiob* in this passage is highlighted by the 2008 book review in *Neva*, in which the author compliments the novel for its "eternal values," citing Il'ia's appreciation of Russian torturers as one of these "sacred truths."[45] Another instance where the author calls attention to a problematic trend occurs towards the end of the novel, after the defeated villain is sentenced to Siberian exile along with his son. Interpreting this law, Alesha says matter-of-factly: "The son is responsible for his father. For if you are flesh of the flesh and blood of the blood, you must bear responsibility with that flesh and blood."[46] Alesha's explanation resounds with Stalin's aphorism, "The son is not responsible for his father," a phrase infused with morbid irony, considering the plight of the "enemies of state" and their families. In an equally dark ironic twist, Brusnikin turns the catchphrase inside out to reveal that the reversal of meaning in fact constitutes its true meaning.

Stiob through Re-Contextualization of Allusions

Chkhartishvili's experiment at reconstructing the semantic and stylistic ambiguity of neo-imperialist fantasy novels proves successful, as is evident from the range of readings his novel has produced. It is precisely the "pseudo-language" of the novel that offends Dmitrii Fedotov of *Literaturnaia Rossiia*, who reads it as the *stiob* that, as if to make matters worse, accompanies any representation of Russian Orthodoxy.[47] As the result, instead of being allegedly "national Orthodox" or "Russian Christian," the novel appears to the critic as the antithesis of nationalist writing – in fact, as an "anti-Christian" product. It is worth noting that in its stylistic register and, crucially, on the level of allusions, *The Ninth Saviour* displays the heterogeneity that, according to Lara Ryazanova-Clarke, is intrinsic to the post-Soviet Russian language as a whole. As an important qualitative change in the modern language, she lists the resurgence of previously obsolete vocabulary items, many of them directly related to the religious sphere in correspondence to the newly emergent role of the Russian Orthodox Church in Yeltsin's and now Putin's Russia. In iturn, the comeback of archaisms and other non-standard elements into the standard lexicon coincides with another linguistic current delineated by Ryazanova-Clarke – the liberalization of the Russian language in the public sphere.[48] The linguistic liberalization has a direct connection to *stiob*, as it leads to the formation of a meta-discourse consisting almost entirely of allusions, jokes, and wordplay.[49] Owing to its self-referential nature, this new language of public discourse displays the quality of *stiob* that Boym aptly terms "claustrophobic," concluding that "[there] is no world outside *stiob*; there is virtually nothing that cannot be recycled and familiarized through it."[50]

As early as its first chapters, *The Ninth Saviour* displays such properties of *stiob* as stylistic heterogeneity as well as the tendency to recycle and re-contextualize allusions. For example, the first chapter contains several major stylistic strands: the overtly nostalgic authorial narrative; the neutral speech of Alesha and of Mitia and his father, the landlord Larion Mikhailov; Il'ia's peasant dialect, albeit superficially stylized; and the florid conversation of the parish priest, who kowtows to authorities at any given opportunity. However, what seems like loyalist sentiment on the surface is subverted through incongruous allusions that emerge unexpectedly, in deadpan manner. Such, for example, is the self-referential mention of "the noble man" and his code of honour,[51] a recurring theme in all Akunin's novels about Erast Fandorin in his post-Japanese period. At the same time, by virtue of its ambiguity, *stiob* accommodates the opposite interpretation of *The Ninth Saviour* as a patriotic tale with an uplifting moral message. This is evident from the numerous reviews on such platforms as Otzovik, IRecommend, or LiveLib, and buyers' comments in the online stores Ozon and Labirint. To them, the appeal of *The Ninth Saviour*, apart from its intriguing plot, lies in the sense of an imaginary community it creates, which proceeds from immediately recognizable semiotic markers such as the plot devices and characters imported wholesale from Russian folklore.

While in the series featuring Erast Fandorin and Sister Pelagia Akunin rigorously tests his readers' erudition, Brusnikin seems to relax the rules of the game. The folkloric allusions in *The Ninth Saviour* are so transparent that many readers, their educational background notwithstanding, are afforded the joy of recognition. The three protagonists – the ingenious peasant Il'ia, the clever priest's son Aleksei, and the nobleman Dmitrii, chivalrous to a fault – bear an unmistakable resemblance to the three *bogatyri* of Russian folklore, Il'ia Muromets, Alesha Popovich, and Dobrynia Nikitich. To solidify this connection, Brusnikin makes Il'ia a paraplegic after an accident, only to remove his disability when he reaches approximately thirty, the same age when the folk hero Il'ia started walking.[52]

As young boys, three friends get entangled in a conspiracy that involves Princess Sophia's illegitimate offspring, barrels of gold, and the sacred icon *Deviatnyi Spas*, which lends its title to the novel. This initial catastrophe sends the heroes on their separate journeys to Moscow, and from there to Ukraine and Western Europe. After multiple reversals of fortune and dramatic changes of identity, the friends are reunited in Moscow, where they cooperate with the *Preobrazhenskii prikaz*, which in the novel functions as Peter's secret police. In the course of their service they come into confrontation with their antagonist,

Avtonom Zerkalov, whose conspiracy they accidentally thwarted almost two decades ago. Like the three heroes, this unscrupulous official also bears a telltale namethat fits into the overarching *stiob* modality of the novel. As an autonomous, self-governing individual, Avtonom is committed only to advancing his family fortunes and ensuring the future of his son Petrusha, an uncanny child who blooms into a psychopath. A further example of irony, Avtonom's last name makes travesty of *A Youth's Honest Mirror* (*Iunosti chestnoe zertsalo*), the famous etiquette compendium of the Petrine epoch. While the aim of this publication was to indoctrinate the young noblemen into the virtues of the new era, Zerkalov is neither morally upright nor an ardent supporter of Peter's reforms: as soon as the tide turns, he is willing to trade one sovereign for another. In his schemes, Zerkalov relies on the assistance of his faithful servant and henchman, the bloodthirsty dwarf Iakha Sramnov. Together with Sramnov, Zerkalov makes several attempts to gain possession of the icon, which according to the legend endows the ruler with legitimacy, and can consequently support a claim to the Russian throne.

Each evil act involves some type of harm done to Vasilisa, Sophia's illegitimate daughter. In Brusnikin's rendition of Russian folklore, she functions as an equivalent of a fairy-tale princess whose rescue affords a display of the hero's valour and strength. Aware of the fairy-tale connotations of her own name, the young Vasilisa fantasizes of being both "Vasilisa the Beautiful" (*Vasilisa Prekrasnaia*) and "Vasilisa the Wise" (*Vasilisa Predumdraia*): the former is saved by the prince, while the latter herself becomes the rescuer.[53] Predictably, at every stage of her life Vasilisa receives assistance from one of the protagonists – from Alesha as an infant, Mitia as an adolescent, and Il'ia as a young woman. Additionally, she plays the part of Pushkin's Sleeping Princess when the shock of abduction places her in a lethargic state for several months. In this context, the heroes, Il'ia above all, assume the function of the *bogatyri* brothers who chastely guard the princess's sleep. Towards the end of the novel Vasilisa also takes on the role of donor and, similar to her folkloric counterpart, gives each of the three protagonists a gift – a book, an ointment, and a pin. As expected, these items later prove instrumental in saving the heroes' lives. Other interactions between characters are likewise easily reducible to the functions Vladimir Propp made famous in his work on the fairy tale:[54] Romodanovskii, the head of the *Preobrazhenskii prikaz*, and Zerkalov alternate the roles of antagonist and dispatcher, while Petrusha, whom Vasilisa views as her primary rescuer, is a vivid example of a false hero.

In reproducing pastiches from either patriotic discourse or Russian folklore, Brusnikin's novel displays the "overidentification with the symbol" that Yurchak characterizes as the primary aspect of *stiob* aesthetics. Another aspect of *stiob*, according to Yurchak, relies on the decontextualization of symbols, or "the act of placing this form in a context that is unintended and unexpected for it."[55] The deadpan retelling of Peter's era as an heroic fairy tale accomplishes this task, but only partially. Such mythologization of the past, near or distant, is not uncommon in Soviet propaganda, whether we look at fairy tales about Lenin the trickster or the so-called *noviny* glorifying Stalin.[56] This trend persists in contemporary Russian pop culture. The self-obviousness of the folkloric references in Brusnikin's novel corresponds to the promulgation of heroic tales, or rather their watered-down, bowdlerized versions in the 2000s. A production from the same period, the 2006 animated film *Prince Vladimir* (*Kniaz' Vladimir*), constructs an unmistakably imperialist picture of the Kievan Rus'. Co-sponsored by the loyalist First Channel and the State Committee for Cinematography, it eliminates virtually all hints of Vladimir's atrocities or sexual immorality. The source of evil is external to the head of state: in the cartoon, it is personified by the outsiders, the Pecheneg Khan and the rogue pagan priest who orchestrates each of Vladimir's misdeeds. However, an even more successful venture was the animated franchise *The Three Bogatyrs* (*Tri bogatyria*), which premiered in 2004 with *Alesha Popovich and Tugarin the Serpent* (*Alesha Popovich i Tugarin Zmei*). The epic style of narration is mocked in the opening of *Alesha Popovich*, and the patriotic message is downplayed significantly. With its unbridled humour, *The Three Bogatyrs* chips away at the paradigm of "patriotic upbringing" while retaining its outward characteristics, such as the emphasis on defending the motherland against foreign hordes.

Unlike *The Three Bogatyrs*, *The Ninth Saviour* does not achieve a *stiob* effect by lampooning the familiar folkloric tropes. Instead, the decontextualization, or rather re-contextualization, of the heroic paradigm is realized in the novel by combining traditional Russian material with allusions to the Western literary tradition, namely, to the novels of Charles Dickens. The predominance of Russian folklore in the novel at once obscures these entirely unanticipated allusions and renders them starker, as the reader, lulled by the cozy *à la russe* storytelling, suddenly recognizes certain characters as Dickensian archetypes. In her study of Akunin's use of allusion, Baraban elaborates on Akunin's thematic indebtedness to Dickens, for instance in *He Lover of Death* (*Liubovnik smerti*, 2001), where he emulates Dickens's orphans and street urchins in the character of the juvenile thief Sen'ka Skorik.[57] Indeed, *He Lover of Death* is styled as a neo-Victorian novel, akin to Michael Farber's *The Crimson Petal and the White* (2002) and Sarah Waters' *Fingersmith* (2002). Set in a desolate urban landscape populated with professional criminals, young thieves-in-training, and teenage prostitutes, it seems to draw its inspiration in equal portion from Giliarovskii's Moscow sketches and Dickens's *Adventures of Oliver Twist*, *Bleak House*, and *The Old Curiosity Shop*. The form of this novel, marketed as a Dickensian mystery, corresponds unproblematically to its content. Equally expected is the reference to Dickens in *Altyn Tolobas*, when the street-smart journalist Altyn Mamaeva struggles with the name of Nicholas Fandorin, her new acquaintance: "I don't have the heart to call you Kolia ... What sort of Kolia are you, anyway? ... As for Nicholas, that's something from Dickens. So I'll call you Nika, okay?"[58] To Altyn, Nicholas's foreign-sounding name evokes an English novel, the of title which she can hardly recall on spot. However, more than just the name connects Nicholas Fandorin to the Dickensian literary tradition. With his fine manners, heightened sense of duty, and excessive self-consciousness that often lands him in trouble, Nicholas Fandorin is an English gentleman to the bone, a chip off the same block as Mr. Pickwick, Arthur Clennam, and, quite obviously, Nicholas Nickleby. In the unstable and unruly context of Yeltsin's Russia, this paragon of English gentility seems not only a cultural Other but an outright anachronism and, ultimately, an alien stranded from a different literary universe.

In *Altyn Tolobas*, the juxtaposition of a Dickensian trope with the reality of the "roaring nineties" augments Akunin's postmodernist game of bricolage, whereby new meanings are generated at the nexus of seemingly disjointed, incompatible parts. But inasmuch as Nicholas's English background invites the Dickensian connection, in *The Ninth Saviour* these allusions appear unexpected, if not outright far-fetched, leading to major epistemological confusion as the heroic landscape of the Russian folk tale is impregnated with Victorian melodrama. The incongruity of this juxtaposition constitutes the "performative shift" of *stiob*, in other words, its propensity to alienate "the constative meanings" associated with authoritative symbols, so that "the symbol could suddenly appear baffling or absurd."[59] By commingling two strands of clichés, taken from native folklore and nineteenth-century English novels, Brusnikin achieves this semantic explosion, voiding the authoritative image of its propagandistic charge.

In *The Ninth Saviour*, references to Dickens are as overt as allusions to Alexander Afanas'ev's fairy-tale collection; and if anything impedes their recognition, it's the fact that the author deliberately sidetracks his readers with the abundance of folkloric references. Unexpected as it may be, the familiar dramatis personae of Russian folk tales double as Dickensian characters: all these jilted spinsters, charitable men of property, and self-sufficient yet vulnerable orphan girls. Such is the case of Granny (Babin'ka), an old woman whose reclusive lifestyle and expertise in healing beg comparison with Baba Yaga. Rumour holds that she, by virtue of being a witch, shape-shifts into a beautiful maiden with the help of a magical ring stored in her secret forest dwelling. Inspired by these tales, the young characters follow Granny to the abandoned mill, a liminal location in Russian folklore. But instead of a magical transformation, they witness a change of another kind:

> A figure walked out from the gloom, dressed in a long iridescent dress, in a tall silver *kokoshnik*. A high-pitched voice drawled the tune:

> *Oh you, my sweetheart,*
> *My intended one,*
> *Here comes not the rosy dawn,*
> *Here comes your darling bride.*

> The Tsar Maiden? No, it still was Granny, who for some reason or other, donned an old-fashioned wedding attire.[60]

The bizarre image of a crone in bridal dress invites a comparison with Miss Havisham from Dickens's *Great Expectations* (1861). When the boy Pip first beholds her in her crumbling mansion, she seems "the strangest lady" on the account of her white gown made of "satins, and lace, and silks," white shoes, and a trailing white veil accompanied by bridal flowers.[61] Closer examination reveals that the wedding finery "has lost its lustre and was faded and yellow" and that "the bride within the bridal dress had withered like the dress." Miss Havisham's unkempt attire is mirrored in Granny's dress, which is described as "shabby, patched all over, while the headpiece [*kokoshnik*] looked dingy and time-stained."[62] The background stories of Miss Havisham and Granny show significant overlap, as both lost bridegrooms on their wedding day, the former being jilted and the latter witnessing her groom die from a lightning strike. Moreover, both crones perform the dual function of helper and antagonist after the manner of their prototype, the folkloric witch, who not only preys on the protagonists, but, depending on the tale, may offer counsel and healing. Initially, Pip views Miss Havisham as his fairy godmother, only to discover in due time that she did not, in fact, support him financially. Inversely, Granny seems a vengeful sorceress in the beginning of the novel but later reveals her caring side by nursing Il'ia back to health and instructing him in the ways of restoring his mobility. Significantly, the mode in which Il'ia's mobility is fully restored, as he jumps from his wheelchair to save the falling Vasilisa, bears resemblance to a scene from another of Dickens's novels. In *Little Dorrit* (1857), the hard-hearted Mrs. Clennam rises to her feet for the first time in years to seek out the title character and make peace with her.[63] In addition to the psychological shock that jolts the characters into motion, both texts mention structural damage to a building, but Mrs. Clennam's tumbling house is reduced in *The Ninth Saviour* to a collapsed balcony.

One more character with a Dickensian pedigree is Iakha Sramnov, who ranks among Chkhartishvili's most repulsive villains. Presented to the reader as a "stump of a man," this evil dwarf sports a large head in addition to long arms and an enormous member, which gives him the nickname "Bawdy" or "Obscene." After his career as a jester is cut short by a foreign rival, Iakha gets a job with the secret police and thus discovers an outlet for his sadistic proclivities: "Iakha had a talent for comprehending human flesh and where pain or joy are located."[64] Later he finds employment with Avtonom Zerkalov and becomes the nemesis of the three heroes and their beloved Vasilisa. Iakha's beastly appearance, combined with his rowdiness and alcoholism, makes him a twin brother of Daniel Quilp from Dickens's *The Old Curiosity Shop* (1841).[65] Like his literary successor, Quilp revels in tormenting his fellow creatures, whether it involves abusing his wife, taunting his mother-in-law, or belabouring boys with a cane. But the main target for his malevolence is Little Nell, who must flee London to escape from his schemes and sexual advances. Although in *The Ninth Saviour* the confrontation between Quilp and Nelly is couched in different motivations, its original erotic underpinnings are kept intact. In chapter 6, Zerkalov arrives with his retinue in Sagdeevo, the estate of Prince Miloslavskii, to search for the long-lost gold and mysterious icon. During their visit, Iakha harasses the nine-year-old Vasilisa Miloslavskaia and half-jokingly proposes marriage to her: "Well now, my beauty, have you made up your mind to marry me? We will spawn baby mice and hedgehogs."[66] Even as she maintains decorum, Vasilisa can hardly contain her disgust at Iakha's foul smell and filthy clothes – because he dreads water, the dwarf never bathes.

Both Iakha's paedophilic tendencies and Vasilisa's revulsion for him mirror *The Old Curiosity Shop*. Quilp constantly fantasizes about the "chubby, rosy, cosy, little Nell" and goes as far as to suggest she should be his second wife.[67] Even though the sexual threat Quilp poses is restricted to his lewd insinuations, critics have noticed the paedophilic connotations of his encounters with Nell, noting how these encounters combine "the implied incest of the January–May marriage" with other sexual transgressions and posit Little Nell "as a pornographic object."[68] Iakha's paedophilic desire for Vasilisa is presented in a more sensationalist light, quickly spurring from verbal harassment into potential rape and murder. Upon the orders of his master, he kidnaps Vasilisa with the intention of murdering the heiress, leaving Avtonom in sole possession of the estate. As he carries the frightened girl away from home, Iakha reveals her imminent fate: "[We are going to] dig a small hole," playfully he patted her stomach. "But first we must get married, as I promised you."[69] It becomes clear that the seemingly neutral "to get married" from the very beginning was a euphemism for sexual intercourse, which in Iakha's mind is inextricable from murder – hence, "digging a hole" encompasses the imagery of deflowering and a grave. Equally shocking is Iakha's gesture of patting Vasilisa's stomach, as it invokes an earlier scene when he performed a brutal C-section on Avtonom's wife, saving the newborn while butchering his mother. The sexual violence implied in Quilp's leering suggestions becomes Iakha's plan of action. But unlike Little Nell, who reacts to Quilp by trembling and shrinking, Vasilisa shows more willpower and becomes an agent in her own rescue, striking Iakha and rolling off his cart. The young heroine's encounter with the paedophile serves as a pivotal point in both novels, laying the grounds for the narrative development, whether it involves Nell's journey through the Midlands or Vasilisa's acquaintance with the friends, the kernel of the ensuing love plot. The ending of both novels reveals further similarities: both villains, the British dwarf and his Russian doppelganger, drown as a result of the final confrontation with their antagonists, the police in Quilp's case and Mitia in Iakha's.

In juxtaposing Quilp and Iakha Sramnov, Brusnikin not only appropriates Dickensian characters but also interprets them by applying the hermeneutics of a neo-Victorian novel. That which was merely hinted at in the nineteenth-century fiction gets identified, spun into narrative, and brought to the reader's attention. Seen in this light, Brusnikin's use of Dickensian allusions is not drastically different from *He Lover of Death*. Nonetheless, in *The Ninth Saviour* these allusions carry an additional function, because they surround the recognizable imperialist symbols with that very "unintended and unexpected" context that Yurchak sees as integral to *stiob* aesthetics.[70]

The interplay of allusions in *The Ninth Saviour* may be seen as another example of Chkhartishvili's inimical postmodernist game, whereby the author lifts his mask just long enough to wink at readers who share the same cultural background. At the same time, their function in the novel goes beyond the typical erudition test, because they simultaneously contribute to the rich fabric of the narrative and undermine its ostensible imperialist allegiance. As Baraban argues, under his pen name "Akunin" Chkhartishvili reads against the grain the post-Soviet nostalgia for imperial Russia by exercising ironic detachment in his presentation of bygone days. This irony acts as a safeguard against excessive nostalgia or any kind of essentialist reading, for it prevents the reader from conflating the novel with the actual, historical past. According to Baraban, "By introducing allusions from the 'past' to the present, Akunin creates an intertext that allows for a historical perspective on familiar problems."[71] Under the guise of Brusnikin the Slavophile, Chkhartishvili abandons subtle irony for *stiob* to draw attention to the rise of neo-imperialist discourse in the cultural scene of Putin's Russia. In resorting to *stiob*, he mirrors conservative rhetoric both in lavishing praise on the old world Rus', with its serene provinciality, and in validating Peter's secret police, whose excessive violence is blamed on the schemes of dishonest individuals such as Zerkalov or Iakha. At the same time, Brusnikin undercuts his own anti-Western stance through the decontextualization of authoritative discourse: dog-whistles from imperialist propaganda are imbedded into the folk-style narration, and the fairy-tale characters, who also double as the stock figures of Victorian melodrama, make chilling Stalinist references. The ability, or willingness, to interpret *The Ninth Saviour* as an exercise in *stiob* rather than a straightforward accolade to the Old Order rests entirely with the interpreter: as such, the novel acts as litmus test for the ideological affiliation of its readers.

NOTES

1 Alexey Yurchak, *Everything Was Forever, until It Was No More: The Last Soviet Generation* (Princeton, NJ: Princeton University Press, 2006).
2 Emily Finer points out to the role of the World Literature Translators Studio, which was fundamental "in positioning Dickens' novels at the center of the Soviet canon, less because it produced new translations than because it provided a forum where literary templates for a new Soviet novel could be created." "Dickens in Twentieth-Century Russia," in *The Reception of Charles Dickens in Europe: Volume 1*, ed. Michael Hollington (London: Bloomsbury, 2013), 107. The influence of Dickens, as Finer argues, is discernible in a variety of texts produced by Soviet writers, for instance the Serapion Brothers or Veniamin Kaverin, whose novel *The Two Captains* is modelled after Dickens's *David Copperfield*. Soviet interest in Dickens's literary legacy, fuelled in no small part by his official designation as an anti-capitalist writer, climaxed in the thirty-volume edition of his collected works, published in 1957–63. The typically large Soviet print run, 600,000

copies of each volume, allowed for the wide dissemination of Dickens's works, while the translations produced under the supervision of E.L. Lann, despite accruing criticism, continue to be republished in the present day.

3 Ibid., 118.

4 The online store Ozon provides this information about the novel's initial run and two additional runs (http://www.ozon.ru/context/detail/id /3593457/). The runs of debut novels in the similar genre of historical action (for example, in the AST series *Istoricheskii boevik*) are capped at 5,000 copies. Examples of these novels may be found here: http://www .ozon.ru/context/detail/id/229674/.

5 Anna Narinskaia voices this suggestion in her article "The Mysterious Pen-name," which appeared in November 2007, almost immediately after the book's publication. Her speculation is based on several factors, not in the least on the publisher's significant financial investment in promoting an unknown author. See Narinskaia, "Tainstvennyi psevdonimets," *Kommersant*, 19 November 2007, https://www.kommersant.ru/doc/826109. In her 2008 journalistic investigation "Brusnikin, Akunin, Someone Else?" Ekaterina Krongauz also makes an attempt to prove that Brusnikin is a yet another avatar of Chkhartishvili. See Krongauz, "Brusnikin, Akunin, drugoi?" OpenSpace.ru, 23 May 2008, http://os.colta.ru/literature/names /details/951/page1/. All translations from Russian in this chapter are my own unless otherwise indicated.

6 During the same period, Chkhartishvili was exploring the potential of another literary identity, Anna Borisova, who worked in the genre of religious and philosophical fantasy. Under this alternative pseudonym, he has written three novels: *Tam* (*Over There...*, 2008), *Kreativshchik* (*The Creator*, 2009), and *Vremena goda* (*The Four Seasons*, 2010, the title originally in English transcription), all published by AST (Moscow).

7 For the full interview, see http://os.colta.ru/literature/names/details/951 /page3/.

8 I am following Elena Baraban's suggestion for translating the series' title. For an explanation of this choice, see Elena V. Baraban, "A Country Resembling Russia: The Use of History in Boris Akunin's Detective Novels," *Slavic and East European Journal (SEEJ)* 48, no. 3 (2004): 412.

9 Shortly after the novel's publication, Elena Chudinova accused Brusnikin of plagiarizing her novel *Larets* (2004). Specifically, she claimed that Brusnikin appropriated such elements from her book as the historical setting (the eighteenth century), characters (three teenagers, girls in Chudinova's case and boys in Brusnikin's), and the mysterious artefact as the centrepiece of the plot. It is obvious, though, that the similarities are cursory and, if anything, should be treated as clichés that migrate from one historical novel to the next. A more likely influence on Brusnikin's book

is Nina Sorotokina's novel *Three from the Naval Academy* (*Troe iz navigatskoi shkoly*, 1991), about the adventures of three daring naval cadets in the 1740s. Sorotokina's manuscript was reworked into the screenplay of the TV mini-series *Naval Cadets, Charge!* (*Gardemariny, vpered!*), dir. Svetlana Druzhinina (Moscow: Mosfilm film, 1998), and, according to Leonid Parfenov, was named best film by Soviet viewers for two years in a row. Leonid Parfenov, dir., "Namedni 1989," episode of *Namedni 1961–1991: Nasha era* (Moscow: NTV, 1998).

10 The title is deliberately whimsical and thus difficult to translate. Instead of *deviatyi* (the ninth), the author refers to the *Spas* as *deviatnyi*, a numeral he coined for additional quaintness. However, in the context of the novel, this invented numeral functions exactly as its regular synonym: based on a complicated numerological backstory, the full title of the icon sounds like "*Chetyrezhdy Deviatnyi Spas*" ("Four Times Ninth Saviour"). Although it would be worth matching the title with a more fanciful numeral, for the sake of clarity I have translated it simply as "the ninth."

11 Boris Akunin, "Kak ia stal Anatoliem Brusnikinym," *Komsomol'skaia pravda*, 13 January 2012, https://www.kp.ru/daily/25816/2795601/. Since 2007, Chkhartishvili has written two more novels as Anatolii Brusnikin: *Geroi inogo vremeni* (*A Hero of a Different Time*, 2010), a tribute to Mikhail Lermontov's *The Hero of Our Time* (1840), and *Bellona* (2012), which takes places during the Crimean War. As a part of marketing strategy, the works of Anatolii Brusnikin and Anna Borisova were united into an umbrella project, "Authors" (*Avtory*), a successor to the project *Genres* (*Zhanry*), where Akunin tried his hand a variety of popular genres.

12 For example, *Deviatnyi Spas* boasts the rating of 4.2 out of 5 on the popular review site LiveLib.ru, a Russian equivalent of Goodreads.com. For the reviews, visit https://www.livelib.ru/book/1000289363-devyatnyj-spas-anatolij-brusnikin.

13 Akunin, "Kak ia stal Anatoliem Brusnikinym."

14 Evgenii Belzheraskii, "Zhili-byli *A i B*," *Itogi*, 10 December 2007, http://www.itogi.ru/archive/2007/50/9717.html.

15 For a summary of critics' responses to Akunin's novels, see Baraban, "A Country Resembling Russia," 412–13.

16 Lev Danilkin, "Pliaska golovoi i nogami," Afisha, 14 November 2007, https://www.afisha.ru/blogcomments/532/page1/, accessed 22 August 2017.

17 Anna Kuznetsova, "Anatolii Brusnikin. Deviatnyi Spas," *Znamia* 4 (2008), http://magazines.russ.ru/znamia/2008/4/ku28.html.

18 This idiom is all the more relevant to the pseudonym "Brusnikin" because it contains a reference to another literary mystification. The popular imagination ascribes this phrase to Alexandre Dumas, who in his Russian travelogue allegedly mentioned "resting in the shade of a wide-branching

cranberry." However, this attribution is false, as the phrase was put into use in the St. Petersburg theatre *Krivoe zerkalo*, as a satirical response to foreign misconceptions of Russia. This absurd, over-the-top reference first occurred in the 1910 parody *The Cossack's Love* (*Liubov' kozaka*), marketed as a French play but actually penned in-house. In the original, the idiom appeared as "under the wide-branching boughs of a centennial cranberry," but with time it was reduced to "the wide-branching cranberry." For more details on this idiom, see Konstantin Dushenko, *Slovar' sovremennykhtsitat* (Moscow: Agraf, 1997), 86.

19 Mark Lipovetsky, *Russian Postmodernist Fiction: Dialogue with Chaos* (Armonk, NY: M.E. Sharpe, 1999), 15.

20 See the chapter "Imperial Stiob: The Aesthetics of Chauvinism" in Boris Noordenbos, *Post-Soviet Literature and the Search for a Russian Identity* (New York: Palgrave Macmillan, 2016), 11–145.

21 Yurchak, *Everything Was Forever*, 250. Emphasis mine.

22 Noordenboos, *Post-Soviet Literature*, 118.

23 Akunin, "Kak ia stal."

24 Stephen M. Norris, *Blockbuster History in the New Russia: Movies, Memory, and Patriotism* (Bloomington: Indiana University Press, 2012), 77.

25 Viacheslav Desiatov, "Na beregu pustynnykh vod: Akunin, Pelevin i Nabokov v 2008 godu," *NOJ: Nabokov Online Journal* 3 (2009), http://www.nabokovonline.com/volume-3.html/.

26 Alla Latynina, "Semeinyi roman i kletchataia tetrad'," *Novyi mir* 12 (2012), http://magazines.russ.ru/novyi_mi/2012/12/l12.html.

27 Anatolii Brusnikin, *Deviatnyi Spas* (*The Ninth Saviour*; Moscow: Astrel, 2011), 6.

28 For an analysis of the impact of Peter's reforms on reshaping the lives of the nobility, see the chapter "Liudi i chiny" in Yuri Lotman, *Besedy o russkoi kul'ture. Byt i traditsii russkogo dvorianstva (XVIII–nachalo XIX veka)* (St. Petersburg: Iskussktvo–SPB, 1994).

29 Brusnikin, *Deviatnyi Spas*, 5–6.

30 The ever-increasing influence of Russian Orthodox Church has taken an alarming turn, as evident among other instances from the notorious trial over Pussy Riot in 2012. In his LiveJournal entry from 20 July 2012, Akunin expressed support for the three members of the punk group, encouraging his readers to protest against their imprisonment. "Devochki i medved'," *LiveJournal* (blog), 20 July 2012, http://borisakunin.livejournal.com/69605.html. He was equally critical of the 2013 amendment to Article 148 of Russian Criminal Code, which enforced a stricter punishment (a hefty fine or imprisonment for up to two years) for "public actions that explicitly defy society and are committed with the purpose of insulting religious belief" (http://www.uk-rf.com/glava19.htmla). As Akunin commented sarcastically, "Perhaps tomorrow, someone may feel insulted if I mention

in my blog that the history of the Russian Orthodox Church has many shameful pages, and the day after tomorrow, if I don't cross my forehead when passing by a church." "Zastav' dumaka," *LiveJournal* (blog), 25 May 2013, http://borisakunin.livejournal.com/101939.html.

31 Brusnikin, *Deviatnyi Spas*, 6.

32 This phrase was further popularized by Vladimir Putin. who used it on 12 December 2012 in his address to the Federal Assembly. Like many of Putin's other aphorisms, "spiritual braces" became a tenacious Internet meme and merited an entry in several online encyclopaedias, including the infamous Lurkmore. For examples of *skrepy* as an Internet meme, see http://lurkmore.to/Скрепы#screpy, http://www.wikireality.ru/wiki/Духовные_скрепы, and http://cyclowiki.org/wiki/Духовные_скрепы.

33 A search in the Russian National Corpus (http://www.ruscorpora.ru/) for the period from 2000 to 2008 shows the usage of the word *skrepy* in the religious and socio-political discourse. Some of the examples include the following (the translation of *skrepy* is given in cursive): "From the first steps, the faith and the Church have become the secure *braces* of the local life" (Bishop Iona Karpukhin, "Vystuplenie na torzhestvakh v sviazi s 400-letiem Astrakhanskoi eparkhii," *Tserkovnyi vestnik*, 10 November 2002); "While in the Soviet time this construction was held by the powerful ideological *braces* ... currently, in the absence of those *braces*, the whole construction is absurd (Vilen Ivanov, "Mezhnatsional'nye otnosheniia v krizisnom obshchestve," *Zhizn' natsional'nostei*, March 2014, 2000).

34 The verb *prognut'sia* as a token of resilience in the face of adversity was popularized as early as 1997, in Mashina Vremeni's song "Odnazhdy mir prognet'sia pod nas," with its catchy refrain "No need to give in to the fickle world, it'd better give in to us" (see http://mashina-vremeni.com/).

35 Among the results from a search in the Russian National Corpus are the following: "As expected, the once proud and haughty London *bent down* completely before Washington" (Mikhail Tretiakov, "Vashingtonoposlushnyi Bler," *Pravda*, 12 September 2002); "If Putin *bent down* before the Americans, he would by default lose his support in Russia" (Vladimir Vorsobin, "Politolog Dugin o politicheskoi elite," *Komsomol'skaia pravda*, 15 April 2003); "But the role of Ukraine remained unsavoury to the extreme: it was obvious that its top officials ... by *bending low* before the Americans aided this dirty affair" (Vladimir Filin, "Kto i kak "pomog" Ukraine postavit' strategicheskie rakety v Iran?" *Novyi region*, 29 November 2006).

36 Yurchak, *Everything was Forever*, 252.

37 Noordenboos, *Post-Soviet Literature*, 130–1.

38 Brusnikin, *Deviatnyi Spas*, 6.

39 Svetlana Boym, *Common Places: Mythologies of Everyday Life in Russia* (Cambridge, MA: Harvard University Press, 1994), 107.

40 In the collection of the Museum of Decorative-Applied and Folk Arts in Moscow, one may find such fine examples of propaganda in miniatures of peasants in the reading house, military parades on the Red Square, or young pioneers cheering at the successful landing of a parachute. A later example even features a cosmonaut who, like a fairy-tale hero, flies an airborne chariot harnessed with three dapper horses. For a comprehensive history of Palekh art and its influence on Russian national identity, see Andrew L. Jenks, *Russia in a Box: Art and Identity in an Age of Revolution* (DeKalb: Northern Illinois University Press, 2005).

41 For examples of patriotic fantasy about *popadantsy*, see the novels published by EKSMO in the series *Voenno-istoricheskaia fantastika* (https://www .labirint.ru/series/12274/).

42 In his interview with Ekaterina Krongauz, Brusnikin clarifies the ethical premises of his novel in the following way: "My novel shows that the fatal disease of state coercion with the help of special services is rooted in Peter's 'reforms.' The goal was to make Europe fear us, even though it may not respect or like us. And may our own people freeze with fear. ... We are stuck in the same trap even now." Krongauz, "Brusnikin, Akunin, drugoi?"

43 Brusnikin, *Deviatnyi Spas*, 343.

44 Ibid., 416–17.

45 Elena Zinovieva, "Dom knigi Zingera," *Zhurnal'nyi zal* 1 (2008), http:// magazines.russ.ru/neva/2008/1/zi21.html.

46 Brusnikin, *Deviatnyi Spas*, 479.

47 Dmitrii Fedotov, "Brusnichnyi spas ili durilka kartonnaia," *Literaturnaia Rossiia*, 4 July 2008, http://www.litrossia.ru/archive/item/2866-tratatest.

48 Lara Ryazanova-Clarke, "The Russian Media in the 1990s," in *Russia After Communism*, ed. Rick Fawn and Stephen White (London: F. Cass, 2002), 120.

49 Ryazanova-Clarke gives *yornichestvo* as a synonym of *stiob*, and takes a critical stance towards this cultural phenomenon: "As well as the bright and carnivalesque side of the change-asserting travesty, the *yornichestvo* can also display the cynical side. Irony, which has become a typical mode of the press, is often used indiscriminately, with no consideration for the topic." Ibid., 135.

50 Svetlana Boym, *The Future of Nostalgia* (New York: Basic Books, 2001), 154.

51 For instance, Dmitrii's father "wouldn't raise his voice at any woman, least of all at the royalty. In doing so, a man of honor disgraces himself." Brusnikin, *Deviatnyi Spas*, 14.

52 See V. Propp and B. Putilov, eds., *Byliny* (Moscow: Gosudarstvennoe izdatel'stvo khudozhestvennoi literatury, 1958), 64.

53 Brusnikin, *Deviatnyi Spas*, 177.

54 See chapter 6, "The Distribution of Functions Among Dramatis Personae," in Vladimir Propp, *Morphology of the Folktale* (Austin: University of Texas Press, 1968).

55 Yurchak, *Everything Was Forever*, 252.
56 For a thorough examination of *noviny* (Soviet *byliny* used for propaganda purposes) and the state-sanctioned "reinvention" of epic poetry in the 1920s and 1930s, see Frank Miller's article "The Image of Stalin in Soviet Russian Folklore," *The Russian Review* 39, no. 1 (1980): 50–67. For examples of folkloric rendition of Lenin's biography, see the chapter "Leninist Fairy Tales," in *Mass Culture in Soviet Russia: Tales, Poems, Songs, Movies, Plays, and Folklore, 1917–1953*, ed. James von Geldern and Richard Stites (Bloomington: Indiana University Press, 2007), 123–7.
57 Baraban, "A Country Resembling Russia," 401.
58 Boris Akunin, *Altyn-tolobas* (Moscow: Olma-Press, 2000), 144.
59 Yurchak, *Everything Was Forever*, 252.
60 Brusnikin, *Deviatnyi Spas*, 31.
61 Charles Dickens, *Great Expectations* (New York: Modern Library, 2001), 51.
62 Brusnikin, *Deviatnyi Spas*, 31.
63 Charles Dickens, *Little Dorrit* (London: Oxford University Press, 1979), 784.
64 Brusnikin, *Deviatnyi Spas*, 42.
65 Viacheslav Desiatov finds parallels between Iakha and the dwarf Fred Dobson from Vladimir Nabokov's short story "The Potato Elf." In Desiatov's interpretation, the description of the dwarfs has strong phallic connotations, and they both suffer from nightmares related to their past. "Na beregu pustynnykh vod: Akunin, Pelevin i Nabokov v 2008 godu," *NOJ: Nabokov Online Journal* 3 (2009), http://www.nabokovonline.com/volume-3.html/.
66 Brusnikin, *Deviatnyi Spas*, 194.
67 Charles Dickens, *The Old Curiosity Shop* (London: Oxford University Press, 1975), 73, 45.
68 Esther Godfrey, *The January-May Marriage in Nineteenth-Century British Literature* (New York: Palgrave Macmillan, 2009), 63.
69 Brusnikin, *Deviatnyi Spas*, 200.
70 Yurchak, *Everything Was Forever*, 252.
71 Baraban, "A Country Resembling Russia," 404.

12 *The Family Album*: Ordinary People in Extraordinary Circumstances

ELENA V. BARABAN

A New Pen Name for a New Book Series

In 2012, Grigorii Chkhartishvili published *Aristonomy* (*Aristonomiia*), advertised as his first "serious" novel and launching the writer's new book series, *The Family Album* (*Semeinyi al'bom*).[1] The sequels to *Aristonomy*, *Another Way* (*Drugoi put'*), *Happy Russia* (*Schastlivaia Rossiia*), and *Treasury* (*Trezorium*), came out in 2015, 2017, and 2019 respectively. *Aristonomy* is set in 1917–20; *Another Way* depicts Soviet Russia in the middle of the 1920s; *Happy Russia* is set in the tragic year 1937; *Treasury* is set during the Second World War. Written in the genre of the novel of ideas, each of the first three books has a twofold structure comprising a philosophical part and a fictional narrative. *Treasury* has three plot lines, one of which is mostly dedicated to theory of pedagogy.

In *Aristonomy*, a philosophical contemplation about the titular concept concerns the ability of an individual to develop his or her dignity. An aristonom is an aristocrat of spirit, a responsible, respectful, and compassionate person who is committed to self-enhancement, has discovered his or her talent, and can do something better than others. The more aristonoms there are, the better society becomes. This philosophical tractate is split into sections that serve as "theoretical" introductions to fictional sections that essentially form an adventure novel about Anton Klobukov, a young man who manages to develop aristonomic qualities during the two revolutions of 1917 and the Civil War. Trying to find his path in life, Anton switches occupations and political camps, leaves for Switzerland and then returns to Russia, and finally becomes a medic who wants to be helpful to people regardless of their ideology. While feeling appalled by people's brutality and occasionally regretting that he had not stayed in Switzerland, he adjusts to the circumstances of his life. In *Another Way*, the fictional sections recount a love story involving Klobukov, now a medical graduate student, and Mirra Nosik, an undergraduate student who aspires to be a plastic surgeon. Each narrative section is introduced by philosophical notes about the nature of love, presumably written, as was also the case with *Aristonomy*, by Klobukov.[2] Whereas *Aristonomy* tells about an individual's attempts at finding his or her place in the world, *Another Way* is about private life, and the role of love in the person's evolution. In turn, *Happy Russia* depicts life under Stalinism, which abruptly and often randomly destroys individuals and entire families. With Klobukov and his wife as episodic characters, the focus in the third novel is on Philip Bliakhin, an NKVD officer, who is to investigate the activity of a group of intellectuals who discuss how Russian society may be organized in the future.[3] The philosophical sections in *Happy Russia* are composed of the manuscripts written by different members of the group in the genre of (anti-)utopia. In turn, *Treasury* tells of a pedagogical experiment carried out on eight Jewish children in a ghetto. The other two story lines of the novel recount the war experiences of Anton Klobukov's son Rem and of Tania Lenskaia, a young woman who, although raised in Germany by a Russian Jewish mother and Polish father, identifies herself as a Russian and who, having escaped from the ghetto, finally crosses the front line to the Soviet Army.

The Family Album series is published under the pen name Akunin-Chkhartishvili (with no first name given). Having by and large avoided depicting the Soviet era in the works that he published as Boris Akunin,[4] Chkhartishvili deliberately chose a new pen name for the series, which begins with a depiction of the Revolution in a slow-paced philosophical novel and then focuses on the Soviet period of Russian history. As is typical of Chkhartishvili, a new pen name signals that he works in a different genre, style, and generally attempts to approach the task of depicting life from a new angle.[5] Besides the fact that the double pen name is suitable for the novels, which have a twofold structure, it also helps to communicate the idea that *The Family Album* is different from Akunin's *belletristika* (belles-lettres), typical of the stories in the Erast Fandorin series.[6] The new pen name and book series, however, do not indicate Chkhartishvili's farewell to popular literature. Concurrent with *The Family Album*, the writer continues to publish belles-lettres under the pen names Boris Akunin, Anatolii Brusnikin, and Anna Borisova.[7] This circumstance suggests that *The Family Album* should be examined in the context of Chkhartishvili's literary *projects*.

In what follows, I argue that on the one hand *The Family Album* is anti-Fandorin; but on the other, in this book series the writer continues to explore the theme that has been central to his Fandorin series and his *History of the Russian State*, namely the relationship between the individual and the state. In contrast to the Fandorin series, which features a popular romantic hero, *The Family Album* focuses on ordinary people who live through extraordinary circumstances. The protagonist of *Aristonomy* and *Another Way* chooses an internal exile as his escape from the Russian state, a move that neither Chkhartishvili nor his most popular hero Erast Fandorin chose for themselves.[8] By saturating *The Family Album* with allusions to Russian and Soviet literature and cinema, Akunin-Chkhartishvili invites the reader to compare his new project to earlier depictions of the Revolution, the Civil War, and Stalinism. Besides serving the purpose of de-glorifying the Soviet past, these allusions are also used by the writer to comment on the tradition of portraying the Russian intelligentsia (and Russian society in general) in terms of relationships between fathers and sons.

A Statist versus a Liberal, or a Farewell to Fandorin

In 2017, writer Ludmila Ulitskaya noted that, upon reading Boris Akunin's first books about Erast Fandorin in 1998–9, she thought that Fandorin was a statist, a nineteenth-century version of a KGB man (*[ka] gebeshnik*). She therefore believed that Akunin must be a statist too and was later puzzled when she saw Chkhartishvili among the liberals who protested against Putin's re-election in 2012. In response to Ulitskaya, Akunin explained that he might be viewed as a statist insofar that he is essentially not against a well-organized state that can do much good for its citizens. He is, however, against a poorly organized state and, since the Russian state has never been run well, and, furthermore, Russian liberals are perceived as opposite of statists, he is, of course, a liberal. With regard to Fandorin's position, Akunin revealed that Ulitskaya was not the only one to compare Erast Fandorin to a KGB agent. Furthermore, Akunin has been frequently asked if his popular hero was created in the image of Vladimir Putin.[9] Indeed, certain characteristics of Fandorin including patriotism, conservatism, and work experience in the state secret services, as well as knowledge of foreign languages, physical fitness, and love of martial arts could be employed by Putin's image-makers to describe the Russian president. Such comparisons, however, enrage Akunin.[10] This kind of emotional response by the writer suggests that even if his own political activism might seem like a poor match for his hero's conservative patriotism, he sees no contradiction between how he writes and what he does as a public figure. Fandorin, Akunin explains, is not a samurai who is always faithful to his master regardless of what the master does. While a samurai would make a perfect statist, Fandorin, instead, is a follower of Confucianism and is ready to serve his state as long as this service and the authorities' actions are in tune with his own ethics, his own understanding of what is right and wrong.[11] Indeed, as depicted in the novel *The State Counsellor* (*Statskii sovetnik*, 1999), Fandorin leaves his formal engagement with the Tsarist police, the Okhrana, in 1891, when he realizes that serving Russia alongside corrupt statesmen would contradict his beliefs. He therefore resigns from his position and leaves for abroad. In other words, Fandorin begins his career as a statist. Then, when living in Japan as a Russian diplomat, he becomes a follower of Confucianism, which emphasizes the individual's path to wisdom and to a certain extent frees the individual from serving a corrupt master. Confucianism presumably inspires Fandorin to abandon the government service when he feels disillusioned with the corrupt authorities in Russia. The question, however, remains as to whether, by leaving the government service, Fandorin ceases to be a statist.

In his conversation with Ulitskaya, Akunin did not explain why his hero would return to Russia in the 1890s in order to serve the state, and specifically the tsarist family, as a private secret agent. In this capacity, he is deployed during the coronation of Nicholas II, the Russo–Japanese War, and a workers' strike in Baku, which is organized by revolutionaries in the wake of the First World War.[12] If he had not been seriously wounded in Baku in 1914, Fandorin would have been dispatched to Western Europe with a secret mission of preventing the war, which, in the Russian authorities' opinion, would serve as a catalyst for a revolution in Russia. As Fandorin's servant Masa explains in *Not Saying Goodbye* (*Ne proshchaius'*, 2018), the last novel in the Fandorin series, if his master had not spent three years in a coma, neither the First World War nor the revolution(s) would have taken place. As *Not Saying Goodbye* depicts, Fandorin stops serving Russia, both as a government official and as a private detective deployed by the authorities for special missions, only after the collapse of the state in 1917. Essentially, Fandorin's allure as a hero is predicated upon his links to Russia. It is not accidental in this regard that the short stories and novellas that portray Fandorin's adventures outside of Russia following his resignation from the Okhrana police did not merit a novel-length narration and are generally less popular with the readers.[13]

In his conversation with Ulitskaya, Akunin also omitted the fact that for many years his most popular hero fought revolutionaries who either consisted of or were inspired by Russian (liberal) intelligentsia.[14] Although an intellectual, an erudite, and a passionate advocate of technological progress, Fandorin is not part of the Russian intelligentsia, which formed through its opposition to the Tsarist regime.[15] Fandorin, instead, is inclined to defend the regime even when recognizing its serious flaws. After the Revolution, Fandorin does not view Russia as suitable for living. He decides to continue his personal path to wisdom in Japan or in Europe, but perishes in 1921 before he can leave the country. Nevertheless, even between 1918 when he awakens from his coma and his death in 1921, Fandorin seems to be a statist. During these last years of his life he still looks for a political force capable of founding a viable state in Russia that, despite its shortcomings (as was the case with the Russian Empire), would give a chance for the individual's personal growth and well-being. Indeed, *Not Saying Goodbye* is structured around this search. The parts of this novel are titled according to the political forces that fought for power during the Civil War: "The Black Truth" (the anarchists in Moscow), "The Red Truth" (the Bolsheviks), "The Green Truth" (the anarchists in Ukraine), and "The White Truth" (the White Army). The fact that Fandorin does not find the Reds, the Whites, or the anarchists suitable to run the country does not turn him into a liberal. He simply decides that a different state, outside of Russia, would better meet his need of striving for wisdom. Not interested in exploring Fandorin's life in emigration, Akunin kills his hero. Besides the fact that completing the Fandorin series during the Revolution or the Civil War was the writer's original plan, the Civil War is a perfect time to remove Fandorin. Following the Revolution, there is no mission left for this character. As a romantic hero of an adventure novel, he dies together with the empire he has served. The Soviet state calls for a different kind of protagonist. In order to depict the latter, Chkhartishvili uses a new pen name, turns to a literary genre that he has not previously explored, and launches a new book series.[16] Although *Aristonomy* was published six years before *Not Saying Goodbye*, the chronological setting of both novels is the same. The story about Klobukov begins where Fandorin leaves, in the chaos of the Revolution and the Civil War.

Pragmatic Individualism as a Platform for Internal Exile

There is nothing new in Chkhartishvili's desire to depict the Soviet period while using a new writing style. In 1923, Vladimir Mayakovsky glorified the October Revolution for giving artists "new huge ideas that require new language!"[17] In his turn, in the context of post-Soviet revisionism of Soviet history, Chkhartishvili feels no enthusiasm about the Revolution and seeks to de-glorify it by further undermining its positive depictions during the Soviet period. Like many post-Soviet critics, he views the October Revolution as a catastrophe that threw

Russia hundreds of years back in political, social, and cultural development. Unlike many such critics, however, Chkhartishvili refuses to merely reverse the Soviet portrayal of the Revolution and the Civil War by depicting the enemies of the Bolsheviks as positive heroes. He produces a rather critical depiction of the Whites, the Reds, and the Russian intelligentsia and proposes a more favourable portrayal of an intellectual who, like Fandorin, advocates an evolutionary path of social development.

Unlike the novels about Erast Fandorin, *The Family Album* focuses on ordinary persons, devoid of romantic charisma and charm. Anton Klobukov, the protagonist in *Aristonomy* and *Another Way*, is a physically unattractive, wishy-washy individual. He tries to survive in a society in which he ended up living rather accidentally, because of the twists and turns of Russia's tragic history and, in part, because at crucial moments of his life he acted on impulse instead of rationally deciding what he wished to do in life.

Klobukov's pedigree is important to his transformation into a hero who, in his beliefs, follows in the footsteps of Fandorin. Although Klobukov is the grandson of a Decembrist and the son of a revolutionarily inclined *intelligent*, he is no heir to the ideals of Russia's liberal intelligentsia. As true representatives of the intelligentsia, Anton's ancestors openly protested against Tsarism and, having served long exiles in Siberia for their political views, became the regime's martyrs. Since Soviet power celebrated the Decembrists as forerunners of Bolsheviks, Klobukov takes advantage of his ancestors' political capital when he invites his girlfriend to visit an exhibition about the Decembrists in 1926.[18] Unlike his ancestors, however, Anton is ready to compromise with different social and political systems. He ends up adjusting to the Soviet state. Like Fandorin, he is an intellectual who detests revolutions and believes in progress through evolution.[19] Unlike Fandorin, however, he is an ordinary man.

The narrative about Anton begins in St. Petersburg, a month before the February Revolution. His father, Mark Klobukov, is a former university professor of law. In the end of the nineteenth century, Mark supported his radically minded students, lost his academic position, lived in exile in Siberia, and returned to Petersburg weakened by tuberculosis. To shorten his agony, he commits suicide on 27 January 1917. As his loyal partner, his wife also commits suicide, thus leaving seventeen-year-old Anton with a feeling that he has been betrayed.[20] The death of Anton's parents is symbolic: the Russian idealist liberal intelligentsia that has prepared the overthrow of tsarism dies before the Revolution, thus avoiding the responsibility for the chaos that ensues.[21]

His father's former students help Anton survive throughout the revolutions of 1917 and the Civil War. They represent various political factions among Russian intellectuals, including constitutional democrats, liberals, and Bolsheviks. At different life junctions, these characters become father figures to Anton. Each of them naively assumes that Anton shares his views. Anton, however, never commits to any one of their ideological camps. Instead, he eventually abandons his "fathers," although without betraying them. As if to illustrate George Jacques Danton's famous thesis about revolutions devouring their own children, Akunin-Chkhartishvili depicts how Anton's idealist "fathers" either destroy each other or are one by one destroyed by the historical forces unleashed by the revolutions that they themselves prepared.[22]

The protagonist's wishy-washiness ensures his survival. First, one of his father's disciples helps Anton become a government clerk under the Provisional Government. After the October Revolution, Anton is a random victim of the Red Terror. He is freed from a Bolshevik jail thanks to the interference of a Bolshevik, Rogachov, also one of his father's former students. Soon afterwards Petr Berdyshev, an ideologist of the White Guard and yet another former student of Mark Klobukov, helps Anton to immigrate to Switzerland. From there Anton runs the White Guard's monetary fund. Simultaneously, he studies medicine, focusing on anaesthesiology. Like the main hero of Maxim Gorky's unfinished novel *The Life of Klim Samgin* (*Zhizn' Klima Samgina*, 1927–37), Anton is bored abroad. On an impulse he returns to Russia. He arrives in the Crimea, where Berdyshev hopes to realize a plan that was later depicted in Vasily Aksyonov's novel *The Island of Crimea* (*Ostrov Krym*, 1979). Anton supports Berdyshev's idealistic plan, according to which the White Guard must temporarily stop attempting to reconquer all of Russia from the Bolsheviks and should focus instead on creating a democratic Russian republic in the Crimea. Although the distant future is described in rosy terms, the reality of the White Terror in Sevastopol appals Anton. The depictions of the White Terror that Anton witnesses remind the reader of the scenes from Nikita Mikhalkov's film *A Slave of Love* (*Raba liubvi*, 1976). The heroine of this film is Olga Voznesenskaia, a famous silent-cinema actress, who condemns the atrocities that the Whites commit. She is traumatized when she witnesses the murder of her admirer, a cameraman who was one of the Reds' secret agents.[23] In *Aristonomy*, Klobukov is likewise shocked when he witnesses the capture of a Red agent, which is reminiscent of Mikhalkov's film. By making this allusion, Akunin-Chkhartishvili suggests a comparison between the sensibilities of Klobukov and those of Voznesenskaia. This allusion affirms Klobukov's lack of the masculine characteristics that would be mandatory in a hero who would take sides in the Civil War. Instead, he is an effeminate witness of brutalities and condemns them first to his superiors in the White Guard and then to his seniors in the Red cavalry.

The novelty of the position proposed by Akunin-Chkhartishvili through his hero lies in his integration of the contrasting perceptions of the Civil War that are typical of Soviet representations of this war and its anti-Soviet or at least critical depictions. As a result, this character's behaviour is inconsistent. Klobukov tries to accommodate irreconcilable ideological positions. In Sevastopol, while helping the Whites' counter-intelligence to crush the Bolshevik underground, Anton accidentally meets Rogachov again and switches sides. He leaves the Crimea to join the Red cavalry.[24] He understands the social and political reasons for the Revolution and yet cannot embrace Bolshevik ideology.[25] He is appalled by the Reds' brutality towards their enemies, civilians, and each other and yet remains passive in his response to it. His passivity suggests a forced acceptance of reality and is akin to the acceptance of life by the protagonist of Boris Pasternak's *Doctor Zhivago* (1957).[26]

Indeed, like characters in Mikhail Bulgakov's *The White Guard* (1925), Alexei Tolstoy's *The Road to Calvary* (*Khozhdenie po mukam*, 1921–41), or Mikhail Sholokhov's *The Quiet Don* (1928–32, 1940), Anton finds himself first with the Whites and then with the Reds during the Civil War. Unlike the protagonists of these novels, however, Anton does not quite take sides in this conflict. He is not "a man of action," who possesses "skill, courage, dominance and determination" and who deals with a difficulty rather than avoids it.[27] On the contrary, Anton is a markedly non-heroic pacifist who would not take up a weapon or harm another human being. As if to continue Boris Pasternak's work in depicting an indecisive hero, Akunin-Chkhartishvili explores the figure of an ordinary person who is drawn in by history but cannot quite make history. In his article about Pasternak's novel, Dmitrii Likhachev noted that instead of a weakness Zhivago's indecisiveness becomes a sign of his moral strength.[28] A similar perception is also expressed in *Aristonomy*, both in the storyline of the fictional sections and through philosophical notes by the protagonist.

To ensure that he can live through the Civil War while switching sides, the narrator endows Anton with "peaceful" tasks such as writing a plan of how a future Russian republic in the Crimea might look like under Baron von Wrangel or serving as a medic in the Red cavalry. In *Another Way*, Anton admits he is effeminate. He "lacks the masculinity to be a surgeon"; his "life credo certainly has something effeminate," for he hesitates to resolve any pain-giving problems (*bol'nye problemy*) and limits his involvement by "pacifying the suffering that these problems have caused."[29] When in 1926 his girlfriend expresses nostalgia for the heroic time of the Civil War, Klobukov disagrees. For him it is much better to listen to his neighbours' petty squabbles over stolen rubber shoes than to live during a time when people "heroically" kill each other using machine guns.[30]

By making his hero a specialist in anaesthetics, Chkhartishvili once again suggests a comparison between Klobukov and Dr. Zhivago. For Yuri Zhivago, poetry becomes more important than medicine. In turn, Anton's love of anaesthetics (much needed in a traumatized society), photography, and philosophy all contribute to his escaping society's pressures.[31] As an avid photographer, he is a contemplative witness of the events; he takes pictures of those who take sides, perform "surgeries," and perish in the cruel world. Like Zhivago, Anton is a Hamlet type, to evoke the typology of heroes suggested in Ivan Turgenev's famous essay "Hamlet and Don Quixote" (1860).[32] According to Turgenev, Shakespeare's Hamlet inspired a series of depictions of contemplative moody characters who question what is right and wrong so much that it prevents them from taking action. The affinity between Zhivago and Hamlet is announced by the poem "Hamlet" that opens Zhivago's collection of poetry. Although there is no similarly explicit link between Klobukov and Hamlet, the chain of associations suggested by allusions in *Aristonomy* and *Another Way* connect Klobukov with "Hamlets" of the European literary tradition. Besides Zhivago, another Hamlet figure to which Klobukov is related is Gorky's Klim Samgin, mentioned earlier. The latter's views on Faust and Don Quixote seem to continue Turgenev's discussion and, at the same time, anticipate Pasternak's contrasting depictions of Hamlets and Fausts.[33] Samgin, who in his youth was part of the Russian liberal intelligentsia but gradually switched to more conservative views about Russia's path, is ultimately an advocate of rationality as opposed to active (busy) idealism. For better or for worse, Samgin seems to be an inspiration for Anton Klobukov, who embraces the idea of evolution after living through the catastrophic events of 1917–21.

As a Hamlet figure, Anton shares the narrator's ironic view of the "Don Quixotes" and "Fausts" (the Whites and the Reds) who killed each other during the Civil War.[34] The depictions of the Whites and the Reds, which border on caricature, help to justify Anton's withdrawal from society. Anton strives to become a better person regardless of the historical and political circumstances in which he finds himself. His position of (pragmatic) individualism forms the basis for his internal exile, typical of Soviet intellectuals.[35] He regards even the most tragic circumstances of his life rather lightly, as stepping stones for his spiritual development.[36] While being very different from the attractive, heroic, and romantic Fandorin, Anton, like Akunin's man of action, also perceives revolutions as harmful for individual and social development. Fandorin worked to prevent the Revolution while people like Klobukov's heroic ancestors prepared it. The descriptions of the horrors of the Revolution and the Civil War, which are presented in *The Family Album* as perceived by Klobukov, serve to endorse Fandorin's view of revolutions as causing social and moral degradation. Like Fandorin, Klobukov believes that evolution is a much better path for ensuring the individual's and mankind's progress.[37] By making a representative of the younger generation more conservative than the generation of his father, Akunin-Chkhartishvili creates a parody of Turgenev's novel *Fathers and Sons* (1862) and, furthermore, of the Soviet tradition of tracing the historical lineage of Bolshevism to the leaders of peasant rebellions, the Decembrists, Alexander Herzen, Nikolai Chernyshevsky, the People's Will, and the first Russian socialist democrats. Contrary to this trajectory of viewing each new generation as politically more radical than the previous one, Klobukov, in the course of his trials during the Revolution and the Civil War, arrives at conclusion that an evolutionary path for society's development is preferable to a revolution. While having the opportunity to become a Bolshevik and benefit from joining the winning side early, he instead withdraws into the strictly professional sphere of medicine. At the same time, he does not wish to become a victim of the Revolution by staying in the ranks of the White Guard. In this sense, Klobukov is not a true heir to his "fathers."

Snapshots of Fathers and Sons

The title of the series, *The Family Album*, captures Anton Klobukov's interest in photography and points to a distinct structural element: each fictional part in *Aristonomy, Another Way,* and *Happy Russia* opens with a photo.[38] Despite these connections, the title *The Family Album* may be viewed as an instance of the narrator's irony, since the novels comprising the series do not focus on any particular family. As mentioned before, Anton's parents are removed from the narrative in the opening of *Aristonomy*. Anton does not have siblings; no relatives are mentioned either.[39] Since he is freed from family ties, a story about him, unlike Pasternak's *Doctor Zhivago*, Alexey Tolstoy's *The Road to Calvary*, or Sholokhov's *The Quiet Don* (1925–40), is not exactly a family drama. Even though Yuri Zhivago is, like Klobukov, also an orphan, there is a crucial difference between the characters. Despite losing his parents early in life, Zhivago is, at least initially, close with his uncle and also has his adopted family, the Gromekos, as well as his childhood friends. While he gradually unties himself from these connections, as well as from his relationship with Lara and family life with Marina, by the end of the novel, *Doctor Zhivago* still depicts the disintegration of familial ties as a tragedy. Moreover, Yuri's half-brother Evgraf constantly attempts to re-establish familial connections even after Yuri's death. By contrast, the narratives about Klobukov lack a similar melodramatic element that would allow viewing the collapse of an individual family as a symbol of the country's collapse.[40] Consequently, the reader's emotional identification with Akunin-Chkhartishvili's protagonist is rather weak.

None of the characters in *Aristonomy* who play the role of either a paternal or a maternal figure (like Anton's common-law spouse Pasha) becomes Anton's new family. Even though *Another Way* is a romance novel, the family life of Klobukov and Mirra Nosik is briefly depicted only at the very end of the novel. Their family figures as a sideline in *Happy Russia*. In the end of this novel Mirra is killed by the NKVD. Klobukov does not know that she is dead; he is told she had been arrested and would be sent to the Gulag without the right of correspondence. There is no depiction of how Klobukov receives the news about his wife's arrest and how he responds to the advice to divorce her. There is no detailing of how their children experience the loss of their mother. In other words, the ending of *Happy Russia* confirms the pattern that the narrator established in the opening of *Aristonomy*: Klobukov cannot have a family. As soon as he acquires one, it is destroyed. Furthermore, the protagonist is never depicted as deeply mourning the death of his family members or his family's close friends. In *Aristonomy*, he thinks that ultimately his parents did well when they died before the Revolution. A similar comment is also made when Anton learns of the passing of the wife of one of his father's former students. He concludes that nothing much happened when this woman – who, after her son and husband had been executed, did not want to live anyway – died in her own bed. In the midst of the Red Terror, Anton decides, this was even a good death. As Klobukov gradually becomes less sensitive, his professional interest in anaesthetics acquires philosophical justification. In *Another Way* he feels sorry when he learns that Berdyshev died in Constantinople, but this news does not change anything in Anton's life or his worldview. It is noteworthy that Klobukov's perception of this piece of news is presented through the point of view of his girlfriend, and is mentioned in passing, at the moment when her real concern is that her boyfriend may be linked to the counter-revolutionary underground.[41] Nothing in *The Family Album* suggests the emotional intensity of scenes of death and mourning such as, for example, the death of Aksinia in Sholokhov's novel.

The comical rendering of the motif of fathers and sons is manifested in *The Family Album* in the storyline concerning Philip Bliakhin. Depicted in detail in *Aristonomy*, Bliakhin is compared and contrasted with Klobukov. Approximately the same age as Klobukov, Bliakhin also switches sides during the revolutions and, like Klobukov, sometimes does so accidentally. However, unlike Klobukov, who comes from the upper middle class, is well educated, and retains his decency through a series of trials, Bliakhin is the illegitimate son of a proletarian woman and is an uneducated, immoral mediocrity. Whereas Anton is "given" too many father figures when he cannot accept their point of view and yet never betrays any one of them, Philip is given no fathers. He is the illegitimate son of a prison guard who dies before fulfilling his promise of giving Philip the right to use his first name as Philip's patronymic. Bliakhin is Akunin-Chkhartishvili's parody of the orphan character from the Soviet literary and cinematic tradition.[42] The mocking of this tradition is revealed in Akunin-Chkhartishvili's allusion to the novella *The Red Imps* (*Krasnye diavoliata*, 1923-6) by Pavel Bliakhin, which depicted teenagers who helped the Reds take power in southern Ukraine during the Civil War.[43]

In order to survive in the cruel world, Bliakhin chooses a father figure suitable for a certain period of his life. To symbolically seal the connection, he uses the first name of his father figure as his patronymic. First he tries to deserve the patronymic of his biological father, Stepan. He tries to please his father as best he can in the hope that one day he can become Philip Stepanovich. After Stepan is killed, however, Philip becomes Philip Vladimirovich by choosing "uncle Volodia," his superior in the Tsarist police, the Okhrana, as his father figure. As "uncle Volodia" becomes unsuitable for the role of Philip's father following the October Revolution, Philip chooses a Bolshevik "father," Pankrat Rogachov, and, accordingly, uses the name Philip Pankratovich. Philip kills "uncle Volodia" when the latter threatens to reveal Philip's past in the Okhrana police to the Bolsheviks. In the 1930s, when he is once again blackmailed because of his former service in the Tsarist police, Bliakhin denounces Rogachov. The latter is consequently executed. After Philip's new paternal figure suffers a stroke and becomes "useless," Philip decides that he has matured enough to be independent and resolves to live an inconspicuous life, away from the prominent father figures who all perish sooner or later. While both Anton's and Philip's father figures die, Anton does not betray any of his paternal figures, while Philip betrays all of his "fathers."

The parallels the narrator draws between Klobukov and Bliakhin suggest that both characters are the everymen left after the true heroes have died. *The Family Album* thus may be viewed as Chkhartishvili's attempt to find a new approach to understanding the Soviet past. He depicts the Revolution and the Civil War as historical events that killed the heroes. Their place is taken by ordinary individuals who survive in extraordinary circumstances thanks to collaboration, compromise, or, in case of Bliakhin, manipulation and crime. These are the "sons" of the Revolution, who are by far less admirable than their "fathers," both those who prepared the Revolution and those who tried to prevent it from taking place.

The Family Album is unlikely to become as popular with the readers as the Erast Fandorin mysteries. Mixing genres while still maintaining his traditional playful approach of recycling and re-contextualizing ideas and images from earlier literary and cinematic tradition, Akunin-Chkhartishvili is less concerned with the reader's response to his literary experiments. Whereas at the end of 1990s Chkhartishvili created Boris Akunin to satisfy readers' yearning for belles-lettres and to prove that popular literature can be of good quality, in *The Family Album* Chkhartishvili explores a new type of relationship with creative prose and the reader. Less concerned with the reader, Akunin-Chkhartishvili is interested in exploring the ideas that Akunin could examine only to a certain extent. *The Family Album* is Chkhartishvili's more serious dialogue with Russian history and literature. It invites readers to look at the social and political catastrophes in Russia of the twentieth century from an everyman's perspective, without a need to glorify any one political camp. In view of the current authorities' difficulties with proposing a coherent view of the Revolution and the Civil War, such an attempt at reassessing Soviet history from an unheroic position may prove fruitful.

NOTES

1 Its original print run was 79,000 copies, which is considerably lower than the print runs of any one of Akunin's adventure novels. Yet it is still an impressive print run given contemporary publishing standards in Russia.

2 In *Aristonomy* and *Another Way* there are photos of the handwritten manuscripts for these philosophical notes, and the handwriting is the same in both novels.

3 A serial traitor with no morals, Bliakhin was one of the least attractive characters in *Aristonomy* and *Another Way*.

4 For more about this see Elena Baraban, "A Country Resembling Russia: The Use of History in Boris Akunin's Detective Novels," *Slavic and East European Journal (SEEJ)* 48, no. 3 (2004): 396–420.

5 For more about Chkhartishvili's reasons for using a variety of pen names, see "Boris Akunin raskryl svoi zhenskii psevdonim," *BBC News Russkaia sluzhba*, 12 January 2012, https://www.bbc.com/russian/society/2012/01/120111_akunin_reveals_pen_names.

6 Some self-printed editions of *Aristonomy* list two authors: Boris Akunin and Grigorii Chkhartishvili. In some of these editions, the title of the series is *Semeinaia saga*, which obscures Akunin-Chkhartishvili's intention to present the stories in the *Family Album* as reflections about photos that may be found in a photo album of a regular Russian family. Each section of the novel is preceded by a photo.

7 As a rule, in recent years Chkhartishvili works simultaneously on three books of different genres – a volume of his popular history of the Russian state, a book of belles-lettres that accompanies this historiography, and a "serious" novel set in the Soviet period. This work method suggests that the new book series must be viewed in the context of Chkhartishvili's other *projects*. In 2016, in his "Big Interview" with Evgenii Kiselev, Akunin explained that he writes his "serious" novels in France; he works on historiography for *The History of the Russian State* in London; and he writes adventure novels in Spain. See Evgenii Kiselev, "Bol'shoe interviu: Boris Akunin," Newsone Live, 28 October 2016, video, 32:51, https://www.youtube.com/watch?v=Dojkgu1GgMo.

8 The writer left Moscow and settled as an expat in Western Europe in 2013, and so far has no plans to return to Russia. See "Boris Akunin. V Rossiiu ne vernus'," *BBC Russkaia sluzhba*, 15 April 2015, video, 20:31, https://www.youtube.com/watch?v=cprXLtFgcRk.

9 See 28:00–33:00 in "Ludmila Ulitskaya i Grigorii Ckhartishvili. Podslushivaem pisatel'skie razgovory," *Otkrytaia Rossiia*, 11 May 2017, video, 41:31, https://www.youtube.com/watch?v=NChl1yIGzMk. Boris Akunin and Ludmila Ulitskaya discussed their views on literature and politics at the London-based club Open Russia (*Otkrytaia Rossiia*), which was founded by Mikhail Khodorkovsky as part of a larger Open Russia project.

10 Ibid.

11 Ibid.

12 As depicted in the novels *Koronatsia* (*The Coronation*, 2000), *Almaznaia kolesnitsa* (*The Diamond Chariot*, 2003), and *Chernyi gorod* (*Black City*, 2012), all published by Zakharov (Moscow).

13 These are several stories in the collection *Nefritovye chetki* (*The Jade Rosary*; Moscow: Zakharov, 2007) and the novellas comprising the collection

Planeta voda (*Planet Water*; Moscow: Zakharov, 2015). While the sales of each new book in the Fandorin cycle are very high, the popularity rating of a book may be different from its sales ranking. With 168,000 copies sold in 2015, *Planet Water*, for instance, was in the first position in book sales for that year: Tatiana Sokhareva, "Fandorin pobedil antiutopii. 10 samykh prodavaemykh knig 2015 goda," RBK Stil', 25 December 2015, https://style.rbc.ru/impressions/571638469a79472acdb34879. At the same time, many readers consider it to be the weakest in the Fandorin series. See, for example, Galina Iuzefovich, "Vse romany ob Eraste Fandorine. Kakoi samyi udachnyi? Reiting Galiny Iuzefovich," Meduza, 8 February 2018, https://meduza.io/slides/vse-romany-ob-eraste-fandorine-kakoy-samyy-udachnyy.

14 On the issue of Akunin's depiction of revolutionaries in Russia see, for example, Aleksandr Mikhailovich Lobin, "Istoriia i revoliutsiia v tvorchestve B. Akunina (na materiale tsikla romanov "Prikliucheniia Erasta Fandorina")," *Vestnik Viatskogo gorudarstvennogo gumanitarnogo universiteta* 10 (2014): 148–54, https://cyberleninka.ru/article/n/istoriya-i-revolyutsiya-v-tvorchestve-b-akunina-na-materiale-tsikla-romanov-priklyucheniya-erasta-fandorina.

15 See, for example, Melvin C. Wren, *The Western Impact upon Tsarist Russia* (Chicago: Holt, Rinehart and Winston, 1971), 144–52; Paul Miliukov, "Bezgosudarstvennost' intelligentsii," in *Intelligentsia i istoricheskaia traditsiia*, http://dugward.ru/library/milukov_p_n/milukov_p_n_intelligencia_i_istoricheskaya.html#a004, accessed 4 September 2018; Petr Struve, "Intelligentsia i revoliutsiia," in *Vekhi: Sbornik statei o russkoi intelligentsii* (Moscow: Tip. Sablina: 1909), 127–45, http://www.vehi.net/vehi/struve.html#_ftn1; A.A. Shiriniants, "O nigilizme i intelligentsii," *Obrazovatelnyi portal Slovo*, n.d., https://www.portal-slovo.ru/history/35437.php.

16 Akunin has no intention to continue his *History of the Russian State* beyond 1917, either. See more on Akunin's *History of the Russian State* in the chapters by Ilya Gerasimov and Stephen M. Norris in this volume.

17 *"Tol'ko Oktiabr' dal novye ogromnye idei, trebuiushchie novogo oformleniia."* See Vladimir Mayakovsky, "Tovarishchi–formovshchiki zhizni!" in *Polnoe sobranie sochinenii v trinadtsati tomakh*, vol. 12 (Moscow: GIKhL, 1959). Available online at http://az.lib.ru/m/majakowskij_w_w/text_0840.shtml.

18 See Akunin-Chkhartishvili, *Drugoi put'* (Moscow: Zakharov, 2015), 151.

19 As described in the novel *Another Way*, Anton, like Fandorin, loves technological innovations that make life more comfortable. He uses his self-made scooter to move around Moscow in the 1920s and builds a shower room in his apartment when other tenants have to rely on public baths.

20 In their commitment to the ideals of social justice, Anton's parents remind the reader of the idealistic characters in Nikolai Chernyshevsky's novel *What is to Be Done?* (1863). Chernyshevsky's novel inspired hundreds of young people (populist intelligentsia) in Russia.

21 *Aristonomy*'s fictional sections are written in the genre of an adventure novel. An orphan is a frequent protagonist of the adventure novel, for the absence of a family makes the hero mobile, thus allowing a writer flexibility in depicting society. It is hardly accidental that Erast Fandorin, Akunin's most popular protagonist, was orphaned at nineteen, approximately the same age that Klobukov lost his parents. See Boris Akunin, *The Winter Queen: A Novel*, trans. Andrew Bromfield (London: Random House, 2003), 7. By the time the action in *The Winter Queen* (in Russian, *Azazel'*) begins (1876), Fandorin is an orphan.

22 As depicted in *Happy Russia*, Rogachov, Anton's Bolshevik "father," outlives the others by more than a decade and perishes in the Great Purge.

23 This character was presumably inspired by Vera Kholodnaia, a star of early Russian silent cinema.

24 Scenes depicting pogroms and the brutality of the war are inspired by Isaac Babel's *Red Cavalry* (1926) and, to some extent, also by Mikhail Bulgakov's *The White Guard* (1925).

25 In *Not Saying Goodbye*, the last novel of the Erast Fandorin book series, Fandorin too understands well the reasons that had led to the Revolution. Yet he cannot accept the regime that the Reds were trying to establish after the Revolution.

26 See Dmitrii Likhachev's analysis of the novel in "Razmyshleniia nad romanom B. L. Pasternaka *Doktor Zhivago*," *Novyi mir*, no. 1 (1988): 5–22.

27 Margery Hourihan, *Deconstructing the Hero: Literary Theory and Children's Literature* (London; New York: Routledge, 1997), 95.

28 Likhachev, "Razmyshleniia," 7–8.

29 Akunin-Chkhartishvili, *Drugoi put'*, 97. Klobukov also explains that when he was little he disliked "boys' games" and liked to watch how the girls played; ibid., 101. All translations from the Russian are my own unless otherwise indicated.

30 Ibid., 149–51.

31 Only once in his life Zhivago admires the Revolution, as it resembled a surgery that was meant to cure society. He soon regrets this moment of feeling fascinated by the revolutionary violence. In Chkhartishvili's novel, Klobukov briefly admires the February Revolution and is horrified when living through the hardships and violence of the October Revolution and the Civil War.

32 I.S. Turgenev, "Gamlet i Don-Kikhot," in *Polnoe sobranie sochinenii i pisem v 30 tomakh*, vol. 5 (Moscow: Nauka, 1980), 330–51.

33 Faustian figures are condemned by Pasternak's protagonist and narrator.
The most prominent of the novel's Fausts is Pavel Antipov, Lara's husband, who became a ruthless revolutionary. Pasternak's contrast between
"Hamlets" and "Fausts" in post-Revolutionary Russia was grounded in the
writer's work as a translator. When working on *Doctor Zhivago*, Pasternak
was also working on his translations of Shakespeare's *Hamlet* (from the end
of the 1930s through the 1950s) and Goethe's *Faust* (1948–53).

34 Some depictions of proletarians are allusions to characters mocked in
Bulgakov's *The Heart of a Dog*. Anton's common-law spouse Pasha is a
former maid in his parents' house. After the October Revolution Pasha
becomes an activist in one of the women's departments. She is inspired
by the ideas of women's liberation (this section is a parody of Alexandra
Kollontai's theory of free love). When Anton is arrested by Bolsheviks,
Pasha visits him but she does not feel obliged to be faithful to him. She
picks up a new common-law partner, Comrade Shmakov. The latter's
description (associated with the topic of bathroom hygiene) and even his
last name are reminiscent of Bulgakov's *Heart of a Dog*. Another brutal proletarian in *Aristonomy* also has a last name starting with "Sh": Shurygin.

35 On internal exile, see, for example, Alexander Etkind, *Internal Colonization:
Russia's Imperial Experience* (Cambridge: Polity Press, 2011).

36 Some of the characters in the famous narratives about the Revolution (like
Vadim Roshchin in Alexei Tolstoy's *The Ordeal*, for example) could be
unconvincing but they were not switching sides for fun, out of boredom.

37 In *Aristonomy*, during a brutal pogrom in a village in Western Ukraine,
Anton witnesses how Khariton Shurygin, his "spiritual brother" (*bratukha*),
rapes a ten-year-old Jewish girl. Anton fails to stop this crime. Later, when
Khariton along with other Red Army soldiers is about to be executed for
this pogrom, Anton asks for Khariton's life to be spared. Rogachov disagrees, for should such misbehaviours persist a new glorious world would
not be built.

38 The idea of placing photos in the opening of a narrative section is inspired
by Chkhartishvili's recent interest in family albums. Several years ago he
asked his blog followers on LiveJournal to publish their family photographs
accompanied by a story about the people depicted in the photos.

39 This was also the case with Erast Fandorin, who as noted earlier became
an orphan early in his life.

40 For more on Pasternak's symbolism see Dmitrii Bykov, "Doctor Zhivago,"
Russian Studies in Literature 48, no. 2 (2012): 6. Bykov writes: "*Doctor
Zhivago* is a Symbolist novel written post-Symbolism. Pasternak himself
called it a fairy tale. And it had indeed 'made Pasternak its conduit'
because he was one of the few still standing; it had no choice but to appear
because someone had to conceptualize the past half-century of Russian

history from the standpoint of Symbolist prose, which was mindful not of
events but of their primary causes."
41 Akunin, *Another Way*, 222.
42 One prominent narrative like this is Nikolai Ekk's film *Putevka v zhizn'*
    (*Road to Life*, 1931).
43 The film *Neulovimye mstiteli* (*The Elusive Avengers*, 1966), dir. Edmon
    Keosayan, is based on Bliakhin's novella. I thank Mark Lipovetsky for
    his comment that Bliakhin as the last name of the character in *The Family
    Album* is an allusion to Pavel Bliakhin's depiction of the Civil War.

PART SIX

Boris Akunin as a Literary and Commercial Project

13 Socialist Realism Inside-Out: Boris Akunin and Mass Literature for the Elite

BRADLEY A. GORSKI

We have no knowledge of story and therefore we have contempt for story ... And we're proud of it. There's nothing to be proud of.

Lev Lunts, "To the West!" (*"Na zapad!"*), 1922

In 1999, Grigorii Chkhartishvili, Deputy Editor of the prestigious journal of literary translation *Foreign Literature* (*Inostrannaia literatura*), wrote an article playfully titled "If I Were a Newspaper Magnate." In the midst of the many dire prognostications of the demise of Russian literature appearing at the time, this article stood out for its light-hearted optimism. Chkhartishvili (who, the year before, had taken on the pseudonym B. Akunin) proposed a half-serious plan to save Russian letters from the current crisis. Given infinite money, wrote Chkhartishvili, a "glorious news-and-periodical life would begin under the trustworthy wing of my many-headed oligarchic eagle ... Russian literature would blossom."[1] Among other things, he went on, his empire would include a second *Foreign Literature*, an FL-2 completely devoted to entertainment: "Intellectual murder mysteries [*intellektual'nye detektivy*], provocative memoirs, literary games, and further amusements ... This is the contribution I can make to raising the culture of entertainment. I imagine FL-2 will have ten times the readers as FL-1."[2] A year earlier, in 1998, Chkhartishvili had begun to publish his own *intellektual'nye detektivy* – the adventures of Erast Fandorin, written under the pen name B. Akunin – which attracted even more readers and accomplished even more to "raise the culture of entertainment" than the imagined FL-2 ever could.[3]

In this essay, I argue that Chkhartishvili's purpose with his Fandorin detective novels is no less ambitious than the jocular aspirations that frame "If I Were a Newspaper Magnate": to create the conditions under which "Russian literature would blossom." Indeed, the wild success that he imagines for FL-2 is the central pillar of the rejuvenated Russian literature that he envisions in this essay. In fact, for Chkhartishvili, I argue, success is not simply a means to an end; it does more than attract a broad audience or provide ample monetary compensation for literary labour. Success as a concept, even as an ideology, becomes the central structuring principle in Chkhartishvili's multilayered literary project, which involves the creation of an explicitly successful authorial persona named "B. Akunin," and of his central hero, the unfailingly successful sleuth Erast Fandorin. Both of Chkhartishvili's creations are characters of extraordinary personal merit – intelligent, courageous, reliable, competent – and both are situated in literary worlds capable of perceiving, valuing, and rewarding their personal qualities with public markers of success – that is, in worlds constructed as reliable meritocracies.[4] In this way, Chkhartishvili's creation of Akunin and Fandorin does more than simply bridge the rift between genre fiction and the Russian literary heritage (filling the gap, as one critic puts it, between "Pushkin and pulp").[5] Chkhartishvili has also helped make success into an acceptable, and even prominent, conceptual category through which authors in post-Soviet Russia can understand and perform their own place in the literary field.

Indeed, "If I Were a Newspaper Magnate" suggests that importing an ideology of success into the contemporary literary landscape might help rejuvenate Russian literature. Chkhartishvili insists on the importance of attracting an enormous readership ("ten times" the size of a standard journal's), as if success itself were his overriding aim. A very specific mythology of success, in fact, informs Chkhartishvili's entire essay. Written in a jocular tone throughout, the article begins in a curious way: "If only I were not I, but the most handsome, intelligent, and best person in the world (and, of course, the richest) – in a word, Gusinskii-Berezovskii – I would immediately found a news-and-magazine empire."[6] Why, one might ask, does Chkhartishvili need to be a handsome, intelligent, and good person to found his empire – would not "richest" be enough? And what are the oligarchs Vladimir Gusinskii and Boris Berezovskii (neither of whom was known as a particularly handsome or good person) doing here? I would argue that the answers to these questions point towards an ideology of success similar to that which informs the creation of both B. Akunin and his character Erast Fandorin: extraordinary personal qualities should reliably translate into success. Notice how in this opening paragraph the composite oligarch Gusinskii-Berezovskii – whose real life analogues were seen as economically successful, but corrupt at best and more likely criminally suspect – turns into "the most handsome, intelligent, and best person in the world (and, of course, the richest)." The marker "Gusinskii-Berezovskii," meant to stand in for success writ large, when placed within Chkhartishvili's fantastical ideology of success becomes a signifier of all things good. In this way, the essay "If I Were a Newspaper Magnate" contains the kernel of an ideology in which success is reliably traceable to merit. Furthermore, in its jocular prescription for the crisis ailing Russian literature in the 1990s, the essay positions this vision of success – both economic and popular – at the centre of a grand restructuring of the literary field. The imagined success of Chkhartishvili's "news-and-periodical empire" not only reflects something about the quality of its productions, but also creates the conditions under which "Russian literature would blossom." Success both reflects actual merit and projects a better version of society. This ideology of success lies not only at the foundation of this essay; it also deeply informs Chkhartishvili's literary creations, B. Akunin and Erast Fandorin, and the fictional worlds they inhabit.

In what follows, I argue that Chkhartishvili's ability to combine mass and elite tastes and, in the process, to communicate an ideology of success to literary elites might be productively understood as "Socialist Realism inside-out." Like Socialist Realism, Chkhartishvili's Fandorin novels would bring together the needs of the elites with the communication strategies of popular fiction, joining ideological content with popular literature in a new way. Unlike Socialist Realism, however, Chkhartishvili would use irony, parody, and travesty to expose the devices of genre literature, and would set these devices against a backdrop woven from scraps of the Russian literary tradition. As such, rather than great literature aimed at the masses, Chkhartishvili would create mass literature aimed at the elites, a form analogous to Socialist Realism, but one that is inverted and intentionally exposes its seams.

To make this argument, I analyse the development of the literary field in the immediate post-Soviet decade. I argue that the divergent priorities of literary journals, on the one hand, and the book market, on the other, effectively pulled Russian literature between two opposing poles. I then turn to the first Soviet decade, the 1920s, as a somewhat unexpected historical antecedent.[7] I argue that Socialist Realism, along with other new forms, arose largely in response to a rift in the literary field, which can be seen as analogous to the 1990s literary crisis. Finally, I offer a close reading of Chkhartishvili's pseudonym "Boris Akunin" and of the first novel in the Fandorin series, *Azazel.*[8] I show how the creation of B. Akunin and Erast Fandorin – Chkhartishvili's "Socialist Realism inside-out" – helped reconcile the mass and elite poles of the post-Soviet literary field not only through the creation of hybrid forms that joined genre fiction and the classic Russian tradition, but also, and at least as importantly, through the dissemination of an ideology of success.

Russian Literature in Crisis: The 1990s

In 1990, the most prominent of the monthly periodicals known as "thick" literary journals, *Novyi mir*, reached a circulation of 2.7 million. The same year, *Literaturnaia gazeta* sold an average of 4.2 million copies an issue.[9] Interest in the serious literary fiction and poetry published in these outlets had never been higher in Soviet Russia – at least as measured by circulation numbers. This was the direct result of Mikhail Gorbachev's glasnost policies, which allowed for the publication, at long last, of previously censored literature.[10] Everything from Boris Pasternak's *Doctor Zhivago* to the previously suppressed poetry of Osip Mandelstam and Anna Akhmatova to Andrei Bitov's experimental novel *Pushkin House* appeared in rapid succession in *Novyi mir* and its competitors, *Druzhba narodov*, *Znamia*, and others. Readers, it seemed, could not get enough of the serious, difficult, and at times experimental literature of which they had been deprived for the previous seventy years. Such an optimistic conclusion, however, turned out to be unfounded: 1990 marked the peak of the so-called journal boom, and in the ensuing years, spanning the fall of the Soviet Union in 1991, circulations would drop even more precipitously than they had grown throughout perestroika. By 1993, *Novyi mir* would sell only 60,000 copies an issue, and would fall further in the following years to around a tenth of that number.[11]

Far from sparking a sustained interest in literary fiction and poetry, the spike in journal circulations turned out to be a temporary phenomenon, a momentary flood after a long dry spell. Furthermore, as Lev Gudkov has argued, this flash flood brought more long-term harm than good to the literary field for several reasons.[12] First, the legitimacy of literature during glasnost did not depend on critical consecration or even attention, but on a text's sacral status within the mythologized underground and/or suppressed literary tradition. "*Samizdat* and *tamizdat*," writes Gudkov, "invalidated criticism as a mechanism of organizing the literary process," because their aura of legitimacy, derived from their political rather than literary qualities, rendered "superfluous the agencies and individuals that had previously determined the success of a literary or journalistic debut, laid the foundations of a writer's reputation."[13] Second, the popularity of the suppressed texts created incentives for literary journals to devote the majority of their space to older poetry and prose, limiting the pages left for contemporary literature and criticism. Finally, the turn to past works meant that current literary production was all but ignored by the prominent journals, giving critics little new material for their work. As Gudkov points out, "Since the 'thick' journals snubbed the literary avant-garde and stockpiled nothing new (meaning reserves of intellectual understanding and analysis of current events or of liberal or 'contemporary' – which in this context are the same – values) and were bereft of spiritual fiber, they proved incapable of subjecting modern forms of literature (even those of the 1970s) to systematic consideration or of being an instrument of topical social criticism."[14]

As the floodgates of glasnost opened, the incoming tide overwhelmed and, to a large extent, washed away both current literary fiction and the concomitant critical apparatus. In Gudkov's words, "The journal boom of the late 1980s and the early 1990s 'wiped out' literary criticism as such, eliminating it as a distinct sub-system within the institution of literature with responsibility for upholding standards of literary quality."[15]

In the same year that journal circulation reached its peak, 1990, the publishing industry was fully liberalized.[16] No longer was the printed word legally the exclusive province of the state – anyone with a printing press could, and soon would, print and sell verbal material. While throughout the Soviet Union between 100 and 190 presses had operated at any one time, between 1991 and 1992, 456 licences were granted to new publishers, and by 1994, more than 6,500 publishers were registered and working.[17] As Birgit Menzel writes, "In 1991 only 8 percent of all book titles and 21 percent of total copies were released by private publishing houses; by 2002 these figures had risen to 66 percent and 87 percent respectively. Commercialization brought the end of the book shortage [that had plagued the late Soviet years], and the variety of available material increased massively."[18] This growth was largely driven by the profitability of imported mass or popular literature, usually from the West, and usually of several relatively stable genre paradigms: mystery, romance, thriller, and so on.

As literary fiction and elite criticism lost their relevance, mass literature grew, especially imported mass literature, leading to an enormous amount of public hand-wringing from critics about the state of Russian literature and of the intelligentsia more broadly. Natalia Ivanova wrote an early elegy to the era of the great Russian writer in her *The Death of the Gods* (*Gibel' bogov*, 1991), while the sociologist of culture Mikhail Berg argued in 2000 that the bifurcated post-Soviet literary field lacked a space capable of innovating new forms that were neither borrowed from mass genre tropes nor inherited from the past.[19] Grigorii Chkhartishvili's fictional project should be seen against the background of these trends. With B. Akunin and Erast Fandorin, Chkhartishvili explored the possibility of bringing the communication strategies of popular culture into contact with the Russian literary heritage in a way that helped to mend the growing rift in the literary field and to pull post-Soviet Russian literature out of its crisis.

Russian Literature in Crisis: The 1920s

Some seventy years earlier, in the immediate post-Revolutionary decade, a similar crisis faced the fledgling field of Soviet literature. Indeed, an examination of the Soviet 1920s reveals several productive parallels with the post-Soviet 1990s.[20] Beginning in August 1921, the New Economic Policy (NEP) allowed private firms to operate printing presses after a three-year state monopoly, while the Bolshevik censors and state control over the publishing industry remained relatively weak throughout the decade.[21] Though the central Bolshevik censor Glavlit was founded in 1922, it largely failed to control the output of private printing presses during the NEP years.[22] The influx of imported mass literature largely bypassed censors, while its popularity precipitated a critical crisis in the 1920s that was no less acute than its 1990s analogue, though the future orientation and ideological prescriptiveness of the post-Revolutionary decade gave the crisis a very different character. Nevertheless, warring factions – from the Russian Association of Proletarian Writers (RAPP) to the Proletkult to the Formalists to Left Front of the Arts (LEF) – all argued about the future development of literature, while the market was flooded with mass literature on a scale not seen before or since, at least until the 1990s.[23]

In a state-sponsored study carried out in workers' libraries in Odessa from 1926 to 1927, researchers found an "unheard of 'Americanization' of the working-class reader," who requested specifically American books at more than forty times the rate they did those by Russian and Ukrainian authors.[24] For the new socialist power structures, who saw mass literature as a product of Western imperialism, this preference for imported popular literature was problematic. The state would have preferred workers to read texts produced by proletarian authors, but it had no reliable mechanism to redirect preferences. Readers largely ignored the critical elite from throughout the ideological spectrum, and at the same time, elite criticism seemed to pay little attention to the popular reader. As Evgeny Dobrenko summarizes, "All polls of readers about criticism gave one and the same picture: criticism goes unread and sparks no interest; its proportional importance in readers' demands is insignificant. The generally recognized flowering of criticism in the 1920s, which was stimulated by the relative pluralism of the aesthetic programs and by the presence of the contending literary camps, ignored or overlooked the reader."[25] This impasse precipitated an unprecedented collection of qualitative and quantitative data on mass reading habits and preferences, which asked readers to step into the role of critics. As Dobrenko has shown, the result was a set of readers' priorities for literary fiction like "the plot should develop sequentially/logically," "it should be 'entertaining' and 'with adventures,'" "The narration should be simple," "written in understandable language," "without those futurism things," and so on.[26] Readers showed a distinct preference for the communication strategies associated with popular literature, rather than the avant-garde or elite literature produced by either the revolutionary or reactionary camps.

When the state-mandated literary mode, Socialist Realism, was developed, it stabilized the literary field not only by fiat, but also by bridging the gap between the demands of the new Bolshevik elites and the tastes of the masses.[27] In Katerina Clark's formulation, Socialist Realism was meant to "produce a literature that would be internationally acclaimed as literature [that is, satisfy the demands of the elite] yet remain accessible to the masses."[28] It did this by co-opting the styles and modes preferred by the general reading public for a literature that would "match in significance the place ... Marxism-Leninism occupied in the evolution of human thought."[29] In other words, it used communication strategies taken from the "realism" of popular fiction in an essentially rhetorical mode that communicated socialist values of the new Soviet elite.[30] Among Socialist Realism's major successes, writes Clark, was its ability to "popularize ideology, to disseminate it in a form both attractive and accessible to the masses."[31] Whether or not Socialist Realism truly managed to produce works that were broadly attractive and accessible, Clark's point is that it was both perceived and presented by the Soviet state as having done so.

If Socialist Realism successfully bridged the "gulf between high culture and popular culture" that plagued the 1920s, it was not the only effort to do so. Other literary projects attempted different modes of reconciliation. In a 1922 article in *Pravda*, Nikolai Bukharin called for a mass literature that would embody socialist ideals. Recalling that "Marx, as is generally known, read crime novels with great enthusiasm," Bukharin argued that the popularity of mass literature should not be condemned but was rather the result of the universal fact that "the mind requires a light, entertaining, interesting plot and unfolding of events." That interesting plot, however, could be filled with any ideological content. "The bourgeoisie knows and understands this," he concluded. "We do not yet have this, and this must be overcome."[32] Bukharin's call resulted in a new strand of Soviet popular fiction known as "Red Pinkertons," often written by anonymous Russian authors, that co-opted the characters, plot lines, and even settings of the popular American Nat Pinkerton novels and coloured them with a more socialist ideology.[33]

More originally, novels such as Marietta Shaginian' *Mess-Mend, or Yankees in Petrograd* (*Mess-Mend, ili Ianki v Petrograde*, 1924) and Viktor Shklovskii and Vsevolod Ivanov's *Mustard Gas* (*Iprit*, 1929) adapted and parodied various genre conventions from imported mass literature into their own original revolutionary plots and settings. Like Socialist Realism, these works deploy communication strategies from popular fiction to popularize apparently incongruent revolutionary Soviet content. They might be understood, adapting another Bolshevik phrase, as popular in form, socialist in content. Unlike Socialist Realism, however, these works use irony, mockery, and travesty to expose and even exaggerate the devices of genre fiction that they co-opt. If Socialist Realism brought together high and low culture by taking the demands of each equally seriously (leading to what Clark calls the characteristic "modal schizophrenia" of the genre), Shaginian and Shklovskii and Ivanov undermine the formula in order to expose and question its sources. In their irreverent alternative to Socialist Realism, these authors parody mass literature. They borrow plotting mechanisms, character archetypes, and genre conventions, and then amplify these elements in order to lay bare the devices of mass literature and question its content.

Within the first ten pages of Shaginian's *Mess-Mend*, for instance, the main character is abandoned by his parents, raised by a railway porter, and inherits a mysterious fortune. Shklovskii and Ivanov's *Mustard Gas* takes place during an international chemical war and includes a fugitive Russian sailor, a trained bear, and a beautiful girl, whom the Russian saves from certain death. As one critic puts it, "The authors of *Mustard Gas* mock ... pulp fiction. For plot twists, not only do [they] use 'deus ex machina,' but they do it in such a pointed and exaggerated way that it creates the sense of a phantasmagoria."[34] Parodying the forms and devices of mass literature allowed Shklovskii and Ivanov to borrow the entertainment potential of popular genres while attempting to raise the literary value of that fiction through ironic and self-conscious play.

Both Shaginian and Shklovskii and Ivanov very explicitly borrowed devices from imported popular literature, but through parody and exaggeration they hoped to go beyond mere imitation of mass fiction to accomplish a more serious literary task. All three authors belonged to the loose grouping of writers known as the Serapion Brothers, who were dedicated to exploring the potential of plot-driven prose as a way to push forwards the development of Russian literature.[35] The

Serapions' chief ideologue, Lev Lunts, complained that "Russian prose has ceased to move [*perestala dvigat'sia*], it just lies there. Nothing takes place, nothing happens."[36] The solution, he declared in a 1922 speech entitled "Go West!" (*Na zapad!*), was to "learn the techniques of story" (*uchit'sia fabul'noi tekhnike*) from Western mass literature in order to create prose that would match the success but improve upon the quality of Western imports.[37] Lunts saw "low" forms of story-driven culture as the most vital and worthy of imitation, not only for their popularity, but more importantly for their ability to "fertilize the soil ... for a new Russian literature" that would be driven by story (*fabula*).[38]

Both *Mess-Mend* and *Mustard Gas* can be seen as efforts to experiment with the devices of popular literature in order to bring them into the Russian literary tradition, and to renew that tradition from within.[39] Both novels not only borrow devices from mass literature, they also parody those devices – using them both to drive the story and to ironize story construction as such. For Shklovskii's contemporary and Formalist colleague Iurii Tynianov, such "dialectical play with the device" is the "essence of parody," and one of the major drivers behind literary evolution.[40] Put another way, when successful, the kind of play with devices of low literary genres that Shaginian, Shklovskii, and Ivanov perform can bring new forms and paradigms into the greater literary tradition.

The Serapions' efforts, however, were stymied by political developments. Shaginian's *Mess-Mend* fell out of favour in 1925, while Shklovskii and Ivanov's *Mustard Gas* never achieved popular success.[41] When the institutional processes that would mandate Socialist Realism were set in motion over the coming decade, they prevented further experimentation and removed the need for it. Strengthened censorship restricted access to undesirable mass literature, while Socialist Realism provided a broadly common culture that stabilized the rift between mass audiences and cultural authorities. Though émigré, dissident, unofficial, and even some official culture would provide various alternatives to the Socialist Realist paradigm over the ensuing decades, the Russian literary field would not experience the type of volatility that characterized the 1920s again until some seventy years later, when the Soviet Union's dissolution would once again throw institutional structures into turmoil. In the late 1990s, in the midst of the new post-Soviet institutional uncertainty, a renewed attempt to bring elements of mass literature together with the Russian literary tradition would find an extraordinarily successful incarnation in Grigorii Chkhartishvili's creation of B. Akunin and his series of Erast Fandorin detective novels.

Fandorin and *Azazel*: Sleuthing Between High and Low

Throughout the 1990s, Chkhartishvili showed an abiding interest in the forms of mass literature, even as he worked in the realm of serious literary fiction. Not only did he playfully propose founding a second *Foreign Literature*, an FL-2, as we have seen, completely devoted to "intellectual murder mysteries, provocative memoirs, literary games, and further amusements," he also took very real steps to promote the quality of entertainment reading. In 1996, along with colleagues from the *Inostranka* publishing house, Chkhartishvili launched a book series called *Worldwide Mystery* (*Mirovoi detektiv*) that translated internationally renowned mysteries by classic authors of the genre from G.K. Chesterton and Arthur Conan Doyle to Agatha Christie and Georges Simenon.[42] Chkhartishvili's decision to translate specifically detective fiction was no coincidence: detective fiction was by far the most popular genre among the general reading public at the time.[43] Like the proposed FL-2, the *Worldwide Mystery* series was intended in part to raise the culture of entertainment by bringing classic authors of higher literary quality into a market saturated with the latest genre pulp. In a similar fashion, when B. Akunin and the Erast Fandorin mystery series appeared in 1998, they bridged an analogous divide between popular detective fiction and intelligentsia values (and along the way, they attracted many more readers than either FL-2 or *Worldwide Mystery* could have ever imagined).

Whatever the specific aim of Chkhartishvili's many projects, their cumulative effect was much more than simply to "raise the culture of entertainment." The Fandorin series specifically had a twofold effect on Russian literature of the 1990s: first, it brought the plots and forms of popular fiction into contact with the Russian literary tradition, and, second, it imported a particular ideology of success, one that was already current among the general populace, into the realm of serious literary fiction. It is this ideology of success that makes Chkhartishvili's Fandorin series legible as "Socialist Realism inside-out." That is, if Socialist Realism was meant to bring great literature to the masses, then the Fandorin series can be seen as mass literature for the elites. It combines the structures and genre paradigms of popular fiction with literary allusions and a prose style designed to appeal to readers of serious literary fiction. But more than that, by doing so, the series smuggled a popular ideology of success into the field of respectable Russian literature.

The first book in the Fandorin series, *Azazel*, which appeared in 1998, introduced both Erast Petrovich and B. Akunin to the world. Set in 1876, *Azazel* takes its name from the vast underground conspiracy at the centre of the novel's mystery plot. That conspiracy involves an international network of orphanages and is bent on nothing less than world domination. The novel's hero, Erast Petrovich Fandorin, a lowly collegiate registrar in the Moscow police, peels away layers of the conspiracy through hard work, investigative brilliance, daring, and charm. As he does so, he climbs in the official ranks and blossoms into a full-fledged detective-protagonist, leading the reader's epistemological journey through the clues, intrigues, and false leads of the mystery plot. Along the way, the novel compiles genre clichés nearly as gleefully as Shaginian's *Mess-Mend* or Shklovskii and Ivanov's *Mustard Gas*. No fewer than five chapters end under the assumption that Fandorin has been killed. He is stabbed in a dark Moscow alleyway (chapter 5), drowned off the docks in London (chapter 11), shot at by his former mentor (chapter 13), and tortured by a mad scientist (chapter 14), among several other forms of certain death. Every time, however, he finds miraculous salvation in modes characteristic of genre fiction, "ex machina" and otherwise: a gun fails to fire, a knife is blocked by an undergarment, hand-to-hand combat overcomes firepower, and so on. The trope overload suggests parody, and indeed, the playful, overwrought language used around these scenes marks them out as ironically intended.

For instance, at the end of chapter 13 Fandorin, along with his boss, police captain Brilling, confronts suspected members of the criminal conspiracy, when without warning Brilling turns his gun on a suspect named Cunningham and kills him in cold blood. Shocked, Fandorin asks, "Oh Lord, boss, why [did you kill Cunningham]?!"[44] But instead of answering, Brilling turns the barrel of his gun to Fandorin: "'It was you who destroyed him,' Brilling pronounced in some kind of unnatural voice. 'You are too good a detective. And for that reason, my young friend, I have to kill you, which I sincerely regret.'"[45] The chapter closes, once again, with Fandorin destined to die. But in the opening of the next chapter, a genre cliché saves the protagonist once again. Instead of shooting "the poor, uncomprehending Erast Petrovich,"[46] Brilling explains the full extent of his iniquity in tones of arch irony: "I shall place [this revolver] in the hands of the unfortunate Cunningham, and it will look as if you killed each other in a shoot-out. You'll receive an honorable burial. A deeply felt eulogy is all but guaranteed. I know such things are important to you."[47] The drawn-out explanation – a familiar foible of evil masterminds from genre fiction such as Ian Fleming's James Bond series – provides Fandorin the time to regroup: "With a blood-curdling shriek, eyes tightly shut, Erast Petrovich threw himself forward, aiming his head at the boss's [Brilling's] chin. They were separated by no more than five paces. Fandorin never heard the click of the safety, but the shot thundered into the ceiling, as both of them – Brilling and Erast Petrovich – flew over the low sill and through the window."[48] This description suggests the unconscious nature of Fandorin's action ("eyes tightly shut," "never heard the click of the safety"), as if he gives over his agency to the mechanisms of the trope. As Fandorin dissolves into the role set out for him by the plot, Brilling is impaled on a tree branch while Fandorin tumbles away unscathed, and the plot marches on to its next cluster of genre clichés.

If borrowings from mass literature predominate in the plot's construction, then allusions to the classic Russian tradition are not far behind, nor are they treated with any less ironic distance. The novel, helpfully titled *Azazel*, opens on an idyllic park bench scene marred by an unexpected visitor and a death (alluding to Bulgakov's *Master and Margarita*, 1967). Later, conspirators are suspected of Dostoevskian nihilism (see Dostoevsky's *Demons*, 1872), and *Erast* Fandorin courts a character named Liza, who will end the novel, alas, in no better shape than her Karamzinian predecessor ("Poor Liza," 1792). In the course of his investigations, Fandorin wagers his life on a game of cards in order to avoid duelling a famed marksman, mixing fate and gambling in a mode reminiscent of Mikhail Lermontov's Pechorin (from *A Hero of Our Time*, 1840). At another point, he finds himself in the shoes of a yet another nineteenth-century hero, Prince Myshkin from Dostoevsky's *The Idiot* (1860), who is struck by a portrait of the "amazingly beautiful" Nastasia Filippovna shortly after arriving in Petersburg:

> Before Fandorin's impatient hand could touch the creaking leather [dossier], his gaze fell on a photo-portrait in a silver frame, standing just here, on the table in the most visible place. The face in the portrait was so remarkable that Erast Petrovich forgot entirely about the dossier: at a half-turn, a Cleopatra with luxuriant hair looked out at him with enormous matte-black eyes, a proudly curved long neck and a subtly drawn cruelty in the willful line of her mouth. More than anything, the Collegiate Registrar was enchanted by the expression of calm and confident power.[49]

The woman whose portrait so resembles that of Nastasia Filippovna turns out to be Amalia Bezhetskaia, a femme fatale and murderous lieutenant in the Azazel conspiracy. (If the Dostoevskian connection were not enough, the character's surname derives from Bezhetsk, the location of Anna Akhmatova's family dacha, and the title of her 1921 poem, doubly inscribing this villain's provenance in the Russian literary canon.) Just as much as genre conventions, tropes from classic Russian literature form the building blocks of the plot and the fictional world of *Azazel* and of the entire Fandorin series.[50]

The thickly woven tapestry of borrowings suggests a case of equal opportunity parody: Akunin brings popular literature together with the classic tradition by treating both with equal irony. Indeed, many critics read the novel in this way.[51] Others see the references to the classic Russian tradition as little more than a patina of respectability used to mask a straightforward caper, however successfully. One early reviewer's delight became emblematic of such a reading: "Finally a mystery writer has appeared in our country whose books aren't embarrassing for an intelligent person [*intelligent*] to hold in his hands."[52] Certainly, the joining of high and low culture became the calling card of the series. But a closer look reveals a patterning more intricate than a mere marketing ploy or postmodern pastiche.

Throughout *Azazel*, references to classic Russian literature are most often associated with the novel's villains, with danger, and with investigative dead ends. The murderous Amalia Bezhetskaia, as noted above, incorporates elements of both Nastasia Filippovna and Anna Akhmatova; Fandorin nearly dies from a card game reminiscent of Lermontov's "Fatalist" (1840); and, even more explicitly, an investigator outlines the dangers of a potential nihilist conspiracy with a direct literary reference: "[The revolutionaries] won't let us grow old in peace, mark my words. Have you read *Demons* by Mr. Dostoevsky?"[53] Though the conspiracy at the centre of this novel turns out to be not from Dostoevsky, it is nevertheless associated with a different Russian classic, as the reader is reminded each time a villain breathes the word "*Azazel'*" before shooting, stabbing, or drowning Fandorin. Classic literature seems constantly to threaten Fandorin, while it is, conversely, the tropes of genre fiction that save him from certain death – he wakes from feigned unconsciousness, a gun fails to fire, a friend unexpectedly shoots his assailant from the shadows, and so on.

This network of clichés and borrowings seems to indicate something beyond the formless postmodernist play that many critics and scholars have suggested.[54] If taken seriously, the pattern of allusions and genre tropes reveals a subject – Fandorin – who is constantly led into danger by the classical literary tradition, only to be saved by the conventions of genre literature. This sets up a value system that is somewhat unexpected for an *intellektual'nyi detektiv* written by a co-editor of a prestigious literary journal. Beyond simply "raising the culture of entertainment" or even elevating genre literature to something closer to literary fiction, this novel's combination of high and low elements might have something much more substantive to say about the development of Russian literature. Rather than bringing classical literary references into genre fiction simply to attract sophisticated readers, as has often been assumed and as Akunin has said publicly,[55] this novel – and the subsequent Fandorin series – suggest a critical stance *against* the over-idealization of Russia's literary heritage, something closer to what Elena Baraban reads in Akunin's use of Russia's historical past.[56] Like the Serapions' project of genre-based literature, the Fandorin project puts genre fiction on a collision course with the classical literary tradition in order to question that tradition, to puncture its hermetic seal, and ultimately to renew it through the introduction of new forms.

As mentioned above, it was, in part, an over-veneration of Russia's literary heritage that led to the crisis in contemporary literature of the 1990s. *Azazel* not only elevates entertainment literature by infusing it with references to the classic tradition, it also points a way forward for that tradition. On both a rhetorical and thematic level, it argues for the incorporation of the tropes and devices of genre literature. Like Socialist Realism, Chkhartishvili's *Azazel* relies on the communication strategies of mass culture; like Shaginian's *Mess-Mend* and Shklovskii and Ivanov's *Mustard Gas*, the novel uses exaggeration, irony, and travesty to bare the device and to expose its genre borrowings; but unlike either of its early-twentieth-century analogues, *Azazel*'s message for the elite largely *is* its mass culture codes, its genre borrowings, and its entertainment value. As he turns the formula of Socialist Realism inside-out, Chkhartishvili creates a mass literature for the elite not merely to fill a market niche or to create respectable genre fiction. For Chkhartishvili, as he outlined in the essay "If I Were a Newspaper Magnate," mass genre literature and the popular audience it would attract were precisely what the literary elite needed in order to create the conditions under which "Russian literature would blossom."

"B. Akunin": Success as Literary Communication

Beyond bringing mass literature in contact with the classical tradition, Chkhartishvili's project accomplishes something else as well. It imports an entire ideology of success and meritocracy into the elite pole of the literary field. In the immediate post-Soviet era, individual success took on an unprecedented importance in the Russian popular imagination. According to statistics collected by the All-Russian Centre for the Study of Public Opinion (*VTsIOM*), in 1994, a majority of Russians (56 per cent of 2,947 surveyed) for the first time said they related "most closely to those who aspire to success in everything they do," while only 24 per cent preferred "those who aspire to live like everyone else and not to stand out," and 20 per cent had difficulty answering.[57] Another survey the same year found that a full 60 per cent of respondents counted themselves among those who "in all their activities are oriented towards success."[58] The sociologist Boris Dubin (of *VTsIOM*) analyses this development in the statistical data as a "noticeable break in the declared relationship to success at the beginning of the 1990s" that arose due to the fall of Soviet institutions and norms, which were replaced by a privatized market economy apparently designed primarily to reward individual success.[59]

The new economic regime, according to Dubin, also gave rise to an emergent "rhetoric of mass communication," which structured narratives around this new value of individual success. In an essay entitled "The New Russian Dream and Its Heroes" (*Novaia russkaia mechta i ee geroi*), Dubin argues that by 1995 a Russian version of the "American success story" had become one of the dominant structuring principles in Russian mass communication.[60] Pointing to popular fiction, films, and especially television commercials, Dubin argues that the basic plot of this new mass communication strategy was constructed around a "new positive hero" (the Russian phrase *novyi polozhitel'nyi geroi* is a direct allusion to the Socialist Realist formula) and presents scenes which "follow one after another according to a single model of 'action-reward,'" propagating a straightforward understanding of success.[61] The attractiveness of this transparent model of success, Dubin suggests, lies in the promise of what he calls a "utopia of social order," in which positive actions are always rewarded, and in which one can "in a very simple manner bring order into life, and control it with elementary and generally understood ... methods."[62] In other words, these mass media models of success, the "American success stories," not only suggest the possibility for individual advancement in the new capitalist environment, they also project a world equipped to bestow predictable rewards for positive actions – a system of meritocracy that would be fair to all participants. In short, they are built to project the very attractive fantasy that lies at the heart of the capitalist worldview.

The "new Russian dream" of Dubin's essay, he makes clear, is predominantly a phenomenon of mass culture. High culture, especially literary culture, as Dubin would write in another essay, "The Failure Plot" (*Siuzhet porazheniia*), often avoids understanding the world through the prism of success:

> Whenever an attempt is made to somehow discuss the problem of success [in literary history] it immediately turns to the theme of failure [*krakh*] ... One could say that the inability, unwillingness, refusal to explain success and the norms behind it – including the recognition of classics, where the analytical abilities of the traditional historian of literature are paralyzed by the supra-valuation of the object, and only the poorest explanatory models

are applied, if any at all – is compensated for by a moral evaluation (a disqualifying over-evaluation).[63]

In the literary analyses Dubin has in mind, the "classic" or otherwise "worthy" literary object is evaluated as superior to the very system of success. Dubin claims that such "evaluation makes historians (especially 'advanced' historians) concentrate on negative phenomena – deviations, aberrations from the system, marginal phenomena, creative un-success, and so forth."[64] The very lack of attention to the accepted metrics of success can be framed as a value in itself, allowing authors and literary historians to supersede the social systems around success while nevertheless formulating their own alternative version of literary accomplishment.[65]

For Dubin, the divergence in understandings of success in the mid-1990s was emblematic of a broader divide in the culture, namely the divide between the forms of mass culture on the one hand, and on the other the ways in which the intelligentsia and cultural elites understood the place of culture in society. For Dubin, each year of the 1990s saw the decline "of those forms, which for decades had served as the foundation for the self-understanding and the production of the social role of the *intelligent*, for the self-affirmation of the intelligentsia in society."[66] As these forms of high culture lost their potency, mass culture provided the communication strategies most capable of appealing to the broad populace. This was no less true of understandings of success. As much as anything else, the valuation of success could be said to have characterized the bifurcation of the literary field of the 1990s. The emergent book market, which centred around mass literature and bestseller lists, came to value success at the expense of content, while increasingly niche intelligentsia-controlled publications concentrated on literary heritage and largely ignored indicators of success.[67]

When B. Akunin's Fandorin series appeared in bookstores beginning in 1998, it worked not only to bring together the two poles of the literary field, but also to bridge these two divergent understandings of success. Specifically, the Fandorin series did this by making the mass understanding of success, what Dubin dubbed the "new Russian dream," palatable to intelligentsia readers, and, perhaps most important for the further development of Russian literature, to the literary elite and the literary field as a whole.

In this light, *Azazel* was more than just a mystery novel that would not be "embarrassing for an *intelligent* to hold in his hands"; it was also the beginning of a fictional world deeply informed by the values of meritocracy and success.[68] In the broadest sense, as a successful sleuth, the unfailing protagonist Erast Fandorin confirms the expectations of the mystery genre, namely, that dogged pursuit, sharp observation, and logical reasoning can overcome any structural disadvantages the detective-protagonist might face.[69] But beyond that, Akunin situates Fandorin in a well-known hierarchical system originally designed to instantiate a specific vision of success: the Russian imperial table of ranks.[70] The very first appearance of the protagonist's name in the entire series identifies him first as "civil servant of the fourteenth rank [*chinovnik 14 klassa*] Erast Petrovich Fandorin."[71] A hardworking clerk (*pis'movoditel'*), he has already rewritten a police report three times, but completes the task once more without complaint for his boss, who "sincerely wished the boy well, as a father would."[72] The next paragraph makes clear that this paternal model of civil service takes the place of Fandorin's biological family and – perhaps more topical for the Russian reader of 1998 – gives him much needed relief from the caprices of capitalism:

> At nineteen years old he was left an orphan. He never knew his mother, and his father, a hot head, put their wealth into empty projects ... In the railroad rush he struck it rich but went broke during the bank rush. Just like last year, when the commercial banks went under one after the other and several respectable people all over the world went the same way. The most trusted securities turned to rubbish, to nothing. Such was Mr. Fandorin, retired lieutenant, suddenly deceased from the shock of it, having left his son nothing but promissory notes. The boy should have finished preparatory school, then university, but instead it was out on the street to earn his bread ... The orphan decided to take the [civil service] exam to become a Collegiate Registrar.[73]

In this way, the very first characteristics the reader learns of Fandorin include his work ethic, difficult circumstances, and embrace of government service as a meritocratic surrogate for his lost family. As the novel unfolds, Fandorin is revealed to be possessed of extraordinary intrinsic qualities. He is handsome, intelligent, brave, dogged, and lucky. And the system to which he has entrusted his fate, the imperial civil service, recognizes these qualities and promotes him. By the end of the first novel, Fandorin leaps from collegiate registrar (the lowest, fourteenth, rank) to titular counsellor (the ninth rank). Five more books and fourteen years later in the fictional series, Fandorin would reach the fifth rank of state counsellor (in the eponymous novel *Statskii sovetnik*, 1999).

As much as any other signs of personal or professional growth, Fandorin's rise through the imperial ranks defines the series' trajectory. His steady promotion recognizes hard work, integrity, bravery, and patriotism – that is, it arises from a meritocracy working exactly as it should, untroubled by corruption, nepotism, or incompetence.[74] In this way, Fandorin's trajectory through the series projects a world structured around a reliable meritocracy, capable of recognizing and rewarding extraordinary personal merit with extraordinary success.

The general ideology of success that informs Fandorin's world – and that Chkhartishvili would extend beyond his fiction through the persona of B. Akunin – is itself fairly straightforward, but its consequences and its potential to connect with a large audience in late-1990s Russia proved grand in scope. Put simply, this ideology of success holds that an extremely gifted and talented person should be recognized as such by contemporaries and by social institutions, should gain accolades for his or her accomplishments, and should be able to achieve prominence in the world. Crucially, this fairly standard, if rather idealistic, understanding of success implicitly depends on a surrounding system of benevolent meritocracy, through which the gifted individual would be recognized as such. By creating this kind of individual in Fandorin and showing his successful advancement through the table of ranks, Chkhartishvili instantiates this vision of success and projects an idealized meritocracy that pervades Fandorin's fictional world.

With the creation of the alter ego B. Akunin, Chkhartishvili expands that vision of success beyond Fandorin's fictional world and into the field of literary production and authorial self-presentation. Constructed specifically as a successful writer, the "author" B. Akunin is "disciplined, loquacious, and elegant ... Even his surname, which is easy to pronounce, testifies to his suitability for high society," according to Chkhartishvili in a 2007 interview, by which time the persona of Akunin was already well established.[75] Everything Akunin approaches he accomplishes with elegance, grace, and outstanding success. For instance, when Chkhartishvili (along with designer Art Lebedev) launched a personal website for the pseudonymous author (http:// akunin.ru), the site explained Akunin's approach in the following terms: "B. Akunin is an extremely advanced Internet user. This comes through in how he describes the World Wide Web: without the excessive elation of a novice and without the blunders often committed by authors who know the Internet only by hearsay. Sooner or later the experienced Internet user arrives at the conclusion that he needs a home page ... This is not *trendy*, it is *contemporary*, [*eto ne* modno, *eto* sovremenno] and Akunin takes an interest in everything contemporary."[76]

The framing of an author as already successful finds its antecedents in the commercialized book market. By the mid-1990s, the transliterated word "bestseller," the very marker of commercial success, had already become an advertising slogan for authors both domestic and foreign.

A 1994 series by the Moscow publisher Vedo, for instance, translated Western genre writers such as James Hadley Chase and Sidney Sheldon under the banner "World Bestseller" (*Mirovoi bestseller*), framing previous success abroad as a selling point for readers in Russia.[77] Following suit, many aspiring Russian writers borrowed the names of successful foreign authors or created "bestselling" alter egos in order to market under the banner of proven success.[78]

Chkhartishvili's presentation of Akunin, however, differs in important ways. First, Akunin is not framed as a foreign author who has achieved success elsewhere, but rather as a Russian author of a past epoch (the copyright claim on http://akunin.ru reads "© 1856–2001 Boris Akunin"). Second, his success is not primarily expressed through extrinsic markers such as bestseller status or cultural prominence, but through his intrinsic qualities ("disciplined, loquacious, and elegant," "extremely advanced," "contemporary," etc.). Put differently, if the marketing behind *Mirovoi bestseller* asked the reader to believe that James Hadley Chase is good because he has been proven successful, Chkhartishvili leads one to understand that Akunin is successful because he is good. In addition to importing the rhetoric of success into his Akunin project, Chkhartishvili's particular understanding of the vector of success – from intrinsic to extrinsic, rather than the other way around – implies a literary system capable of recognizing an author's intrinsic qualities and translating them into the extrinsic markers of success. In this way, Chkhartishvili's particular framing of Akunin as a successful writer not only creates a successful alter ego, it also projects an entire literary system of benevolent meritocracy. Crucially, that imagined system is meant to exist not in a different country, but in an alternative past of Russia itself, suggesting the possibility of recovering such a system in the present day. Indeed, in "If I Were a Newspaper Magnate," Chkhartishvili seems to imply that importing an ideology of success into the contemporary literary landscape might help bridge the gap between popular culture and the literary elites. Beyond the plans for new periodical publications, the essay imagines a literary world structured around success, where literary publications would once again attract large popular audiences, and at least as important, where the literary system would be able to recognize merit and reward it with success.

Conclusion

Chkhartishvili's entire project involving both B. Akunin and Erast Fandorin is built, in large part, around an ideology of success and meritocracy, both of which become structuring values for the worlds these characters inhabit. For each, success is imagined as the natural consequence of extraordinary intrinsic qualities within a system equipped to recognize them. It is this vision of success that defines the ideology of the Akunin/Fandorin universe at least as much as the interplay between genre tropes and allusions to classic literature. And it is this ideology of success that finally completes the connection between the Fandorin project and what I am calling "Socialist Realism inside-out." As the series combines tropes from high and low culture, it projects an implicit and pervasive worldview of success and meritocracy, a worldview that, as shown above, gained currency among the broad populace in the 1990s, and animated the newly capitalist book market. By bringing a sincere belief in meritocracy and success into a cultural product capable of appealing to elite readers – including members of the intelligentsia – Chkhartishvili not only helped introduce new genre forms into literary art, he also helped bring (for better and for worse) the ideology of the book market into the elite pole of the literary field.

If Socialist Realism used popular communication strategies to create art that would transmit a socialist ideology to the masses, then Chkhartishvili's project uses literary allusions along with genre tropes to create literature that communicates a mass ideology (and, not incidentally, an ideology of capitalist liberalism) to the elites. Many of the literary elites, it seems, have been receptive to that message. In 2003, the *Times Literary Supplement* wrote about the "Akuninization" of Russian literature, quoting the author, who said that since the release of his first book the literary landscape in Russia has changed: "First, it is no longer considered shameful to write detective stories. Second, reading this literature is no longer seen as a bad thing."[79] In the article, "Akuninization" is framed as the process of making genre literature more acceptable to the elites. Certainly, this has been one of Chkhartishvili's major contributions; however, as I have argued in this chapter, the "Akuninization" of Russian literature has brought about another change that is at least as important. It has made success into a central value in the field of contemporary Russian literature.

NOTES

1 Grigorii Chkhartishvili, "Esli by ia byl gazetnym magnatom," *Neprikosnovennyi zapas* 2 (1999). All translations from the Russian are my own unless otherwise noted. Please see my translation of the full article, included in Appendix 1 of this volume.

2 Ibid.

3 Chkhartishvili's first novels appeared under the pseudonym B. Akunin, highlighting the connection to the nineteenth-century Russian anarchist Mikhail Bakunin. Chkhartishvili filled out his pseudonym's first name only in 2000. See "Biografiia g-na Akunina," *Fandorin.ru*, accessed through The Internet Archive, 15 Nov 2016, http://web.archive.org/web /20010224070036/http://www.fandorin.ru/akunin/biography.html.

4 Chkhartishvili, under both Akunin and other pseudonyms, has gone on to create many other heroes, including several generations of the Fandorin family and the intrepid detective-nun Sister Pelagia. In this article, I focus on his first two characters: B. Akunin and Erast Fandorin.

5 Vanora Bennett, "Akuninization: *The Winter Queen* by Boris Akunin," *The Times Literary Supplement* 5224 (16 May 2003): 32.

6 Chkhartishvili, "Esli by ia byl"; see Appendix 1.

7 Though Socialist Realism was adopted as official state cultural policy only in 1934, many classic Socialist Realist works were in fact produced in the preceding decades, including Maksim Gorky's *Mat'* (*Mother*, 1906), Fyodor Gladkov's *Tsement* (*Cement*, 1925), and Marietta Shaginian's *Gidrotsentral'* (*Hydrocentral*, 1930–1). Indeed, the development of Socialist Realism as a mode of literary fiction largely took place before its official proclamation as policy, and it is this development that I trace here.

8 Boris Akunin, *Azazel'* (Moscow: Zakharov, 1998). The novel has been translated into English as *The Winter Queen*, trans. Andrew Bromfield (London: Random House, 2003), but in order to foreground the reference to Mikhail Bulgakov's character Azazello, I refer to the novel as *Azazel* throughout this chapter. In this chapter, all translations from the novel are mine.

9 Birgit Menzel, *Grazhdanskaia voina slov. Literaturnaia kritika perestroechnogo vremeni* (Moscow: Vremia, 2006), 46.

10 Stephen Lovell, for instance, writes that even in the late Soviet period "Popular entertainment culture still existed under very serious constraints. This situation began to change fast in the late 1980s, when the policy of 'openness' (glasnost) led to the publication of many forgotten and forbidden works ... These ideologically controversial works were joined by modern classics that had been taboo for a range of less obviously political reasons: for their formal experimentation, their lewdness, or their foreignness. The sudden appearance of all these 'rediscovered' treasures brought a huge reading boom: a mass reading public with enormous curiosity and pent-up demand came into contact with an entire century of literary heritage over a period of two or three years." "Literature and Entertainment in Russia: A Brief History," in *Reading for Entertainment in Contemporary Russia: Post-Soviet Popular Literature in Historical Perspective*, ed. Stephen Lovell and Birgit Menzel (Munich: Verlag Otto Sangner, 2005), 27–8. For legislative details relating to press policy in perestroika and post-Soviet

Russia see Andrei M. Il'nitskii, *Knigoizdanie sovremennoi Rossii* (Moscow: Vremia, 2002).

11. The fall of the Soviet Union caused financial and administrative problems for the "thick" journals, which were state-financed throughout the Soviet era. George Soros's Open Society Institute quickly stepped in to fund the most prominent of these periodicals in the 1990s. Even as their financial situation stabilized, however, their circulation numbers continued to fall throughout the decade. See Menzel, *Grazhdanskaia voina slov*, 46. For an updated analysis, see Olga Breininger, "A Scholarly Look at 'Thick' Journals Today: The Crisis of The Institution," *Russian Journal of Communication* 6, no. 1 (2014): 20–31.

12 Lev Gudkov, "The Institutional Framework of Reading: Preserving Cultural Discontinuity," trans. Liv Bliss, *Russian Social Science Review* 45, no. 5 (2004): 44–65. Translation modified throughout to preserve the original *zhurnal* as "journal" rather than "magazine." For original Russian text, see L.D. Gudkov, "Institutsional'nye ramki chteniia: konservatsiia kul'turnykh razryvov," *Chitaiushchii mir i mir chteniia: sbornik statei* (Moscow: Rudomino, 2003), 20–38.

13 Gudkov, "The Institutional Framework," 48.

14 Ibid.

15 Ibid., 47.

16 Birgit Menzel, "Writing, Reading and Selling Literature in Russia, 1986–2004," in Lovell and Menzel, *Reading for Entertainment*, 41–2.

17 Ibid., 42.

18 Ibid.

19 Natal'ia Ivanova, *Gibel' bogov: sbornik statei* (Moscow: Ogonek, 1991); Mikhail Berg, *Literaturokratiia: Problema prisvoeniia i pereraspredeleniia vlasti v literature* (Moscow: Novoe literaturnoe obozrenie, 2000), especially 269–307.

20 It is worth noting that the Russian version of Evgeny Dobrenko's classic study on *The Making of the State Reader, Formovka sovetskogo chitatelia*, appeared in *Novyi mir* in 1992 and 1993, just as the contemporary literary field was undergoing many changes analogous to the 1920s transformations Dobrenko investigates. *The Making of the State Reader: Social and Aesthetic Contexts of the Reception of Soviet Literature*, trans. Jesse Savage (Palo Alto, CA: Stanford University Press, 1997).

21 See Peter Kenez, "Lenin and the Freedom of the Press," in *Bolshevik Culture: Experiment and Order in the Russian Revolution*, ed. Abbott Gleason, Peter Kenez, and Richard Stites (Bloomington: Indiana University Press, 1985), 131–50.

22 Peter Kenez, for instance, mentions that surprisingly few manuscripts were either submitted to or blocked by Bolshevik censors in the first post-revolutionary decade. *The Birth of the Propaganda State: Soviet Methods*

in Mass Mobilization (Cambridge: Cambridge University Press, 1985), 28–9. On Glavlit in the first Soviet decade more generally, see A.V. Blium, *Za kulisami "Ministerstva pravdy": tainaia istoriia sovetskoi tsenzury, 1917–1929* (St. Petersburg: Akademicheskii proekt, 1994).

23 For an analysis of the debates among the various literary factions of the NEP era, see Natalia Kornienko, "Literary Criticism and Cultural Policy During the New Economic Policy, 1921–1927," in *A History of Russian Literary Theory and Criticism: The Soviet Age and Beyond,* ed. Galin Tihanov and Evgeny Dobrenko (Pittsburgh: University of Pittsburgh Press, 2011), 17–42.

24 Dobrenko, *Making of the State Reader,* 88.

25 Ibid.

26 Ibid., 129–32.

27 As Katerina Clark has shown, the *literary* formation of Socialist Realism was largely accomplished by 1927, when standard-bearers like Dmitry Furmanov's *Chapaev* (1923) and Fedor Gladkov's *Cement,* had already achieved popularity. The institutional consolidation of power began only in 1932. See Katerina Clark, *The Soviet Novel: History as Ritual,* 3rd ed. (Bloomington: Indiana University Press, 2000), 27–45.

28 Ibid., 42.

29 Ibid., 36.

30 Ibid., 35.

31 Ibid., 44.

32 Nikolai Bukharin, "Kommunisticheskoe vospitanie molodezhi v usloviiakh Nep'a," *Pravda,* 14 Oct 1922, 2. Quoted in Boris Dralyuk, *Western Crime Fiction Goes East: The Russian Pinkerton Craze 1907–1934* (Boston: Brill, 2012), 26.

33 On "Red Pinkertons" see Mariia Malikova, "'Kommunisticheskii Pinkerton': sotsial'nyi zakaz NEPa," *Vestnik istorii, literatury, iskusstva* 2 (2006): 278–91. For a broader exploration of crime fiction in the decades before and after the Russian revolution, see Dralyuk, *Western Crime Fiction Goes East;* specifically chapter 5, "The Red Pinkerton's Rise: Bukharin and the Komsomol," 83–98. On imported popular fiction after the Revolution and its interaction with the development of Russian literature of the time, see Mariia Malikova, "Khalturovedenie: sovetskii psevdoperevodnoi roman perioda NEPa," *Novoe literaturnoe obozrenie* 103 (2010): 109–39.

34 Aleksandr Sekatskii, "Geografiia v kartinkakh," introduction to new edition of Vsevelod Ivanov and Viktor Shklovskii, *Iprit: roman,* first published 1929 (St. Petersburg: Red Fish, 2005), 6.

35 While Ivanov was a core Serapion, Shaginian and Shklovskii were more peripheral members. For a time, Shaginian lived with Serapions in Maksim Gorky's *"Dom iskusstva"* and was often referred to, affectionately, as the Serapions' "sister-croaker" (*sestra-kvakersha*). T.M. Vakhitova,

"Marietta Shaginian," in *Russkaia literatura XX veka. Prozaiki, poety, drama-turgi. Bibliograficheskii slovar'*, vol. 3 *P-Ia*, ed. N.N. Skatov (Moscow: Olma-Press, 2005), 672. Shklovskii, who was of the older generation, and more involved in theoretical exploration than the other members, was referred to by Konstantin Fedin as "either the eleventh, or the first" of the Serapion Brothers. See Konstantin Fedin, *Gor'kii sredi nas: Kartiny literaturnoi zhizni* (Moscow: Sovetskii pisatel', 1968), 86.

36 Fedin, *Gor'kii sredi nas*, 73.

37 Lev Lunts, "Na zapad! Rech' na sobranii Serapionovykh Brat'ev 2-go deka-bria 1922 g.," in *"Rodina" i drugie proizvedeniia* (Moscow: Pamiat', 1981).

38 Ibid.

39 This goal has much in common with the Formalists' interest in what Viktor Erlich calls "sub-literary forms," which through adaptation could be "admitted into the parlor, raised to the status of *bona fide* literary art." Viktor Erlich, *Russian Formalism. History – Doctrine*, 3rd ed. (New Haven: Yale UP, 1981), 260. On the connections between the Formalists and the Serapions, see Dralyuk, *Western Crime Fiction Goes East*, 109–19; D.G.B. Piper, "Formalism and the Serapion Brothers," *Slavonic and East European Review* 47, no. 108 (1969): 78–93.

40 Iurii Tynianov, "Dostoevskii i Gogol' (k teorii parodii)," in *Formal'nyi metod: Antologiia russkogo modernizma. Tom 1: Sistemy*, ed. Sergei Ushakin, first published 1921 (Ekaterinburg: Kabinetnyi uchenyi, 2016), 561.

41 See, for instance, Grigorii Lelevich, "Retsenziia na *Lori Len*," *Oktiabr'* 8 (1925): 157–8, quoted in Dralyuk, *Western Crime Fiction Goes East*, 116.

42 Personal interview with the co-editor of the series, Varvara Gornostaeva, 15 June 2016, Moscow. The series continued after Chkhartishvili's departure from Inostranka in 2001, and is now published by Eksmo. Its current incarnation includes mostly contemporary mystery novels from all over the world.

43 Boris Dubin, "Chto chitaiut rossiiane," *Knizhnoe obozrenie* 11, no. 1449 (15 March 1994): 26.

44 Akunin, *Azazel'*, 170. Page references are to the Russian original. Translations from *Azazel'* are mine. The corresponding passage in the published translation: *Winter Queen*, 187.

45 Ibid., 170; *Winter Queen*, 187.

46 Ibid., 171; *Winter Queen*, 189.

47 Ibid., 171; *Winter Queen*, 189.

48 Ibid., 172; *Winter Queen*, 190.

49 Ibid., 18–19; *Winter Queen*, 18–19. Myshkin sees the portrait just as he completes his first task in Petersburg – a calligraphic sample for General Epanchin. Distracted by the portrait of "a woman of extraordinary beauty," Myshkin forgets about the issue at hand and instead contemplates her

"dark deep eyes, pensive brow; passionate and somehow haughty facial expression." F.M. Dostoevskii, *Polnoe sobranie sochinenii v 30-i tomakh, tom 8: Idiot* (Leningrad: Nauka, 1973), 27.

50 As the series advanced, Akunin would become even bolder in his borrowings. The tenth book in the series, *The Diamond Chariot* (*Almaznaia kolesnitsa*), for instance, opens with an entire passage borrowed unaltered from Aleksandr Kuprin's 1905 story "Staff-Captain Rybnikov" ("Shtab-skapitan Rybnikov").

51 See for instance Natalia Ivanova, "Zhizn' i smert' simuliakra v Rossii," *Druzhba narodov* 8 (2000); Alena Solntseva, "Mirovaia literatura mozhet byt' vozvyshennoi," *Vremia novostei* 121 (6 December 2000). In contrast to these critics, I see Chkhartishvili's project motivated by more than a desire to fill a market niche. Rather, I believe that the particular way he combines high and low sources suggests a much more serious attempt to bring genre forms into the realm of serious literary fiction.

52 Konstantin Bocharov, "Orkestr v kustakh," *Knizhnoe obozrenie*, no. 13 (3 April 2000): 16.

53 Akunin, *Azazel'*, 71; *Winter Queen*, 79.

54 See, for instance, Konstantin Bocharov, "Sekretnaia missiia postmodern-ista," *Knizhnoe obozrenie*, no. 14 (12 April 2000): 16–17; Aleksandr Ageev, "Golod 31: Prakticheskaia gastroenterologiia chteniia," *Russkii zhurnal*, 17 May 2001; and Ivanova, "Zhizn' i smert' simuliakra v Rossii."

55 Anna Verbieva, "Boris Akunin: Tak veselee mne i interesnee vzyskatel'nomu chitateliu ..." *Exlibris. Nezavisimaia gazeta*, 23 December 1999.

56 Baraban argues that Chkhartishvili's use of historical elements in his Fandorin novels pushes back against the characteristically post-Soviet idealization of pre-Revolutionary Russia by first representing that idealized past, and then emphasizing several of its negative aspects – such as his depiction of the Khodynka tragedy at the end of the seventh book in the series, *The Coronation* (*Koronatsiia, ili poslednii iz Romanov*, 2000). See Elena V. Baraban, "A Country Resembling Russia: The Use of History in Boris Akunin's Detective Novels," *Slavic and East European Journal (SEEJ)* 48, no. 3 (2004): 397 and passim.

57 Boris Dubin, "Uspekh po-russki," *Monitoring obshchestvennogo mneniia* 37, no. 5 (1998): 18.

58 Ibid.

59 Ibid.

60 Boris Dubin, "Novaia russkaia mechta i ee geroi," in *Slovo–pis'mo–literature* (Moscow: Novoe literaturnoe obozrenie, 2001), 200–11. First published in *Russkie utopii* (St. Petersburg: 1995), 281–304.

61 Ibid., 205–6.

62 Ibid., 201.

63 Boris Dubin, "Siuzhet porazheniia," in *Slovo–pis'mo–literature*, 262–72. First published as "Siuzhet porazheniia (Neskol'ko obshchesotsiologicheskikh primechanii k teme literaturnogo uspekha," *Novoe literaturnoe obozrenie* 25 (1997): 120–30.

64 Ibid.

65 For example, see Boris Eikhenbaum's analyses of both Pushkin and Tolstoy as writers who avoided the norms of success that developed in their times in his 1927 "Literatura i pisatel'," in *Formal'nyi metod: Antologiia russkogo modernizma. Tom 2: Tekhnologiia*, ed. Sergei Ushakin (Ekaterinburg: Kabinetnyi uchenyi, 2016), 630–42.

66 Boris Dubin, "Rossiiskaia intelligentsia mezhdu klassikoi i massovoi kul'turoi," in *Slovo–pis'mo–literatura*, 333.

67 For an analysis of the development of bestseller lists in 1990s Russia, see Bradley A. Gorski, "Authors of Success: Cultural Capitalism and Literary Evolution in Contemporary Russia" (PhD diss., Columbia University, 2018). For an analysis of the content of those lists, see Jeremy Dwyer, "The 'Knizhnoe obozrenie' Bestseller Lists, Russian Reading Habits, and the Development of Russian Literary Culture, 1994–98," *Russian Review* 66, no. 2 (2007): 295–315.

68 Bocharov, "Orkestr v kustakh," 16.

69 For a classic overview of the genre's social and psychological implications, see John G. Cawelti, *Adventure, Mystery, and Romance: Formula Stories as Art and Popular Culture* (Chicago: University of Chicago Press, 1976). For historical context on the mystery novel in Russia and Russian literature, see Abram Reitblat, "Detektivnaia literatura i russkii chitatel' (vtoraia polovina XIX–nachalo XX vv.)," in *Knizhnoe delo v Rossii vo vtoroi polovine XIX–nachale XX veka*, vol. 7, ed. V.E. Kel'ner (St. Petersburg: Rossiiskaia natsional'naia biblioteka, 1994), 126–40 [reprinted in Reitblat, *Ot Bovy k Bal'montu, i drugie raboty po istoricheskoi sotsiologii russkoi literatury* (Moscow: Novoe literaturnoe obozrenie, 2009), 294–306], and Louise McReynolds, "'Who Cares Who Killed Ivan Ivanovich?': The Literary Detective in Tsarist Russia," *Russian History* 36, no. 3 (2009): 391–406.

70 Chkhartishvili's emphasis on the table of ranks also situates the Fandorin novels within the Russian literary canon, whose nineteenth-century exemplars were particularly fascinated with the imperial system of meritocracy. On the table of ranks in Russian literature, see Irina Reyfman, *Rank and Style: Russians in State Service, Life, and Literature* (Brighton, MA: Academic Studies Press, 2012).

71 Akunin, *Azazel'*, 8. The corresponding page in *Winter Queen*: 7.

72 Ibid.

73 Ibid., 8–9. The corresponding pages in *Winter Queen*: 7–8.

74 It should be noted that several times throughout the series, Fandorin meets with precisely these vices, often in government service. (The corrupt police captain Brilling from *Azazel*, mentioned above, is one such example.) But they are treated as aberrations, frustrating Fandorin's uncompromising work, rather than intrinsic characteristics of the system itself.

75 Anna Zhebrovskaia, "Prilozhenie k Fandorinu," interview with Grigorii Chkhartishvili, Tema, 20 Jan 2007, http://www.tema.in.ua/article/1598 .html.

76 Grigorii Chkhartishvili, "Akunet," Fandorin.ru, accessed through The Internet Archive, 15 Nov 2016, http://web.archive.org/web/20010407194829/ http://www.fandorin.ru/akunet.html. Emphasis in the original.

77 Birgitte Beck Pristed, "Glasnost Noire: The Soviet and Post-Soviet Publication and Reception of James Hadley Chase," *Book History* 16 (2013): 351.

78 See, for instance, the popular series of (unauthorized) sequels to Margaret Mitchell's bestselling (in Russia and the United States) *Gone with the Wind*, including *Rhett Butler* (*Rett Batler*) and *Scarlett's Last Love* (*Posledniaia liubov' Skarlett*), by the pseudonymous D. Khilpatrik (Minsk: Belorusskaia assotsiatsiia detektivnogo politicheskogo i prikliuchencheskogo romana, 1992–4). By the end of the 1990s, the trend became so pervasive that it was parodied by a group of Russian writers, led by Viacheslav Rybakov and Igor' Alimov, who created the patently ridiculous pseudonym Khol'm van Zaichik, meant to be a bestselling Chinese author of mystery novels set in an alternate reality. See, for instance, the first in the series *Eurasian Symphony*: Khol'm van Zaichik, *Delo zhadnogo varvara* (St. Petersburg: Azbuka, 2000).

79 Bennett, "Akuninization," 32.

14 Boris Akunin and Cross-Media Marketing

NATALIA ERLENKAMP

Cross-Media and Boris Akunin's Creative Agenda

In 2000, poet and columnist Lev Rubinstein pointed out Boris Akunin's business-like quality, atypical in a Russian man of letters.[1] Indeed, since 1998, when his first novel appeared, "Boris Akunin" has become a peculiar brand, a versatile interactive profit-oriented project that intertwines literature, history, and media. With editions reaching up to half a million copies, Akunin's books regularly become bestsellers. The writer actively participates in various promotion campaigns while discussing sales of his books, plans for the future, and his literary credo with readers, scholars, and journalists. In 2001, Grigorii Chkhartishvili admitted that Boris Akunin was both a literary and business project.[2]

To be sure, contemporary cross-media campaigns like Akunin's require a well-coordinated collaboration of professionals in marketing and sales management, advertising, public relations, product and digital media design, and consulting, as well as publishing and information technology. This essay examines the phenomenon of Boris Akunin as a business project. An analysis of the market strategies that ensure its commercial success demonstrates that, in Akunin's case, the economic concept of "push marketing" is successfully applied to a literary project. Central to this study is the notion of cross-media, defined, following Niklas Mahrdt, as the implementation of at least three means of communication unified by a leading idea. While different media types are applied to each specific target group, they are integrated in terms of their content, form, and timing. Together, many channels of appeal, including interactive and multi-sensory ones, create an impression of the product's value for the consumer. A cross-media campaign typically relies on a combination of traditional and new media.[3] With the tremendous growth in the number of the means of communication and the proliferation of affordable (digital) media devices in the new millennium, bringing together various instruments of cross-media marketing into an effectively operating system has become increasingly important. A cross-media campaign influences the consumer non-stop in different life situations such as work, leisure, and transit (for example, work commute).[4]

Every cross-media campaign conveys a comprehensive *leading idea* that serves as a key content signal for the whole project. It can be a slogan or claim that captures essential features of the brand.[5] I propose that the leading idea of the Boris Akunin project is his self-positioning as an author of high-level entertainment literature. He has reiterated this idea in numerous claims that he is not a writer but is, instead, "a writer of *popular* fiction."[6] One can trace the origins of this idea to Chkhartishvili's literary criticism of the 1990s, when, while still working as deputy editor of *Inostrannaia literatura*, he discussed the challenges that faced Russia's literary market under capitalism. In his 1997 article "Shincho Magazine: Survival Experience of a High-brow Magazine in a Market Economy," Chkhartishvili questioned the future of Russian literary magazines. He explained the decline of Russia's literary journals ("thick journals")[7] by their disengagement from mass culture and lack of competitive attributes under the conditions of the market economy. During their 200-year history, Russian "thick journals" survived the pressures of autocracy, dictatorship, and "the complete idiocy of the Soviet empire"; yet in the 1990s, "under the weight of the market economy and its inevitable consequence – the dictate of mass culture" they were "fading away." In order to stop this decline, Chkhartishvili argued, these journals needed to reorganize and adjust their literary priorities in accordance with the changing cultural and publishing situation in the country. In his view, these journals should publish innovative literary works that would appeal to young generations of Russians.[8]

Additionally, in his somewhat humorous 1999 article "If I Were a Newspaper Magnate," Chkhartishvili emphasized the need to increase the quality of popular fiction. He argued that in order to give a different meaning to the concept of mass culture (which was then mostly in contempt), one could publish high-quality entertaining fiction such as intellectual detective novels, literary games, or piquant memoirs.[9] He reiterated this idea in 2000 at a round table titled Culture and Market (*Kul'tura i rynok*). He said, in particular, that under a market economy the writer was to produce marketable "merchandise" (*tovar*) in the genres of fantasy, detective, or adventure stories.[10] Instead of treating his prospective readers condescendingly, the writer should treat them as equals. Akunin has demonstrated such an attitude towards readers in his own work by probing his readers' ability to recognize allusions to literary classics and to historical events. At the above-mentioned round table, Akunin also suggested that each work of fiction should meet the expectations of the target group that could potentially buy the "product" (*produkt*). In other words, right from the start of his career as a writer of popular fiction, Akunin has thought of his writing in terms of a commercial project and applied specific writing and marketing strategies in order to achieve financial success.

Furthermore, in addition of thinking of how to make his literary project popular with his readers, Akunin also promoted its sales. Explicitly disagreeing with the opinion that a writer should create works with a view towards satisfying his own artistic demands, Chkhartishvili has repeatedly said that he writes in order to satisfy *his readers'* needs.[11] This, he believes, distinguishes him from a writer of serious fiction because "a writer writes for himself, whereas a belletrist writes for his reader."[12]

Lamenting the fact that poorly written popular fiction strengthened the negative view of mass literature, Chkhartishvili said that nothing in Russia spoke against the emergence of a high-level entertainment literature of the kind that already existed in the West: "We have either *Crime and Punishment* or *Gang's Lookout*.[13] There is no middle ground. There has never been normal entertainment literature for a discerning reader in Russia, something like *The Three Musketeers* or works by Agatha Christie and G. K. Chesterton in Europe."[14] Consequently, when working on his first three novels – *The Winter Queen* (*Azazel'*), *The Turkish Gambit* (*Turetskii gambit*), and *Murder on the Leviathan* (*Leviafan*), all published by Zakharov (Moscow) in 1998 – Chkhartishvili developed his idea of a *literary project* that was to introduce new standards for popular literature in Russia.[15]

Indeed, both Akunin's detective fiction and his *History of the Russian State* (*Istoriia Rossiiskogo gosudarstva*) are meant to promote the development of high-quality mainstream literature in Russia.[16] Directed at a mass readership and meant to reawaken the interest of Russians to the history of their country, Akunin's *History of the Russian State* is "entertaining" and "informative" while also offering "depth."[17] In contrast to professional historians, Akunin writes historical works that are "not boring."[18] The target group of this project is broad, including mostly "ordinary readers" who have no in-depth knowledge of history and read history books for pleasure and out of curiosity.[19] According to Akunin, historical works that offer a wealth of facts and dates while lacking entertainment overwhelm "ordinary readers," making them lose interest. As a writer of popular fiction, Akunin above all wants to win over his target group by meeting his readers' perceived needs: "My reader is free like a bird, he will fly away from me and I will remain quite unnecessary with all of my *Riurikovichi* uninteresting to anyone. Therefore, I keep it in mind all the time."[20] As his creative writing and interviews demonstrate, Akunin has for many years adhered to the leading idea of his project: writing high-level entertainment literature and popular history for mainstream readers. Keeping in mind this creative program as central for his cross-media campaign, let us now consider specific cross-media marketing strategies employed by Akunin's literary project.

Project Strategy 1: Engaging the Target Group and Market Research

In a cross-media campaign, the project's leading idea is communicated to the target group via several communication channels that usually rely on new and traditional media. The choice of a medium depends on a particular target group and its wishes.[21] In Akunin's case various media and at least three communication channels are used. One of them is the internet.[22]

In 2000, together with web designer Artemii Lebedev, Akunin created his official homepage, http://akunin.ru. Its nostalgic design supported Akunin's playful self-presentation as a writer from the second half of the nineteenth century.[23] The sepia-coloured page features headings in the pre-Revolutionary script. The use of an old-fashioned way to describe the author's photo as a "photographic portrait" (*fotograficheskii portret*) also renders the idea of the project's "historicity." In addition, the author's costume and the accessories such as a top hat and a pince-nez further recreate the atmosphere of the nineteenth century.

Akunin.ru is composed of sections dedicated to the Erast Fandorin mystery series (*Novyi detektiv*), the Sister Pelagia trilogy (*Provintsial'nyi detektiv*), and the Adventures of Nicholas Fandorin (*Priklucheniia magistra*). Interactive applications such as *Useful Historical Information, Facts, and Documents* as well as *Combined History of Moscow* are to compliment the novels by entertaining the reader. Both the novels and the interactive applications featured on this website capture the leading idea of the Boris Akunin project, namely writing high-level entertainment literature. Although this homepage was not fully developed and has not been updated since 2003, it is still accessible today, and thus still contributes to the success of the Akunin project.

The importance of digital media for Akunin's project is also evident when one considers his blog "Love of History" (*Liubov' k istorii*), published and frequently updated from 2010 until spring 2017 on *LiveJournal*.[24] Unlike the old homepage akunin.ru, the blog opened an opportunity for communication between the author and his readers and helped to form Akunin's fan base. As Christian Jakubetz notes of the possibilities opened by cross-media promotions, "what had only been possible as a monologue before ... turned into an accessible dialogue for

Self-portrait of the *Noble Assembly* (Screenshot), 9.

Source: Boris Akunin, "Avtoportret blagorodnogo sobraniia," *LiveJournal* (blog),
14 November 2010, http://borisakunin.livejournal.com/11499.html. Reprinted with
permission of Grigorii Chkhartishvili.

both sides."[25] Importantly, like Akunin's homepage akunin.ru, the design of the blog, its structure and the headlines of its sections refer to the pre-Revolutionary era in Russia, matching the blog's main subject: history. For example, to immerse his fans in the atmosphere the nineteenth-century Russia, followers of the blog joined Akunin's so-called Noble Assembly (*Blagorodnoe sobranie*) and completed the "Self-Portrait of the Noble Assembly" (*Avtoportret blagorodnogo sobraniia*). The latter served as a "common reader's profile" and provided relevant statistics for market research on Akunin's target group: of almost three thousand participants, around 56 per cent of the blog readers are women, and about 67 per cent live in Russia and are between twenty and forty years old.[26]

ВНИМАНИЕ!

Теперь вам предстоит выбрать, в каком направлении двинется наша реконструкция дальше. Всё будет зависеть от следующей фразы.

Опрос #1849668 *Выбираем алгоритм*
Открыт: **Всем**, подробные результаты видны: **Всем**. Участников: 6065

И не торопимся!

Показать ответы

«Ша, зелень! – крикнул Зайцев. - Слушай сюда!»
━━━━━━━━━━━━━━━━━ **1075** (17.9%)
В темноте раздался дрожащий Зинин голос: «Я... умерла?»
━━━━━━━━━━━━━━━━━━━━━ **1648** (27.4%)
«Спокойно, товарищи!», - бодрясь сказал Долотов.
━━━━━━━━━━━━━━━━━━━━━━━━━━━━━━ **3287** (54.7%)

Po sledam gruppy Diatlova: opinion poll (Screenshot), 9.
Source: Boris Akunin, "Po sledam gruppy Diatlova. Chast' pervaia," *LiveJournal* (blog), 26 June 2012, https://borisakunin.livejournal.com/67157.html. Reprinted with permission of Grigorii Chkhartishvili

Comments on Akunin's posts made it possible to monitor readers' response to his works as well as their expectations regarding the project. Usually, Akunin's followers expressed their desires for the release of audiobooks and paperback versions, discussed the prices of the new releases, or suggested alternative ways of payment such as using PayPal.[27] Furthermore, readers participated in questionnaires and polls, the results of which Akunin used afterwards in his books based on the blog entries. When in June 2012 Akunin began writing his own version of the widely discussed tragedy of Igor Diatlov's ski trekking group,[28] his followers were asked to choose one of the three endings suggested by the author or propose their own version of the ending. Akunin thus turned his readers into co-creators by way of completing the story following the most popular choice.[29]

When the short story based on this blog was published as a hard copy, Akunin's praised the blogger "telegammochka" for suggesting a highly original ending to the story.[30]

In addition to communicating the Boris Akunin project's leading idea, the blog on *LiveJournal* also opened other possibilities, including studying Akunin's target group, merchandising new publications, and keeping the audience involved.

On 5 April 2017, however, Akunin announced that he was abandoning his blog on the *LiveJournal* platform. Allegedly, the reason for this was Akunin's disagreement with the administration of *LiveJournal* regarding user policies.[31] Today Akunin continues posting, merchandising, and communicating with his followers via his Facebook page "Akunin Chkhartishvili," which has over 250,000 followers.[32]

Digital communication channels, including social media such as blogs and Facebook, mostly target a younger audience composed of more confident Internet users who frequently check updates regarding Akunin's creative works and his social and political statements. Overall, the progression in Akunin's use of media platforms is notable. In step with time, Akunin, starting from the personal homepage, which was a "must have" of the 2000s, to his Facebook account, without which today's marketing is unimaginable, has well used the growing influence of online-media with their potential of updates.

Akunin has also used traditional communication channels such as radio, print media, and TV. He frequently relies on radio and TV as complementary media that, thanks to their multi-sensory appeal, reach out to many potential new consumers while they engage in their everyday activities (office work, driving, or household chores). Additionally, Akunin's interviews about his work and personal life target his regular readership as well as random listeners, readers, and viewers from different generations. In this way the author potentially acquires a new audience while increasing the loyalty of the existing one.[33]

Similar goals are pursued through direct communication that normally takes place at special events, such as meetings with readers, book presentations, and book fairs. While this is standard practice in the West, in Russia it is still developing. As a project that is unusual for Russian literature, Akunin has actively relied on such direct interaction with his target group. In order to promote public participation in such events, the latter are usually announced in advance in press or in social media,[34] including Akunin's Facebook page, the Facebook page of an event organizer, or the website of the publishing house. For best cross-media marketing results, an announcement would simultaneously appear on all such platforms.

Besides having a strong emotional influence on the target group, such public events are openly used for marketing.[35] In 2013, for example, Akunin presented the first volume of *The History of the Russian State* at the major bookstores in Moscow (Biblio-Globus, Dom Knigi, Knizhnyi magazin Moskva, and Molodaia gvardiia). Akunin introduced his multi-volume project by conveying its "big idea" of "writing history that is not boring to read."[36] Among other things, Akunin emphasized the utility value, to use another marketing term, of his books. When meeting with his readers at the bookstore Biblio-Globus, for example, Akunin insisted that it would not make sense to read only the non-fiction parts of his *History of the Russian State* without also reading fictional narratives that accompany each historiographic volume, and vice versa. Both streams, he maintained, complement each other and provide the most worthwhile reading experience when read one after another. While in fictional narratives Akunin freely uses his fantasy to immerse the reader into the atmosphere of a particular historical period, in his non-fiction he is factual and analytical.[37] Providing a utility value for a new product in this way is one of the significant characteristics of cross-media.[38]

Various communication channels help to gather information on target groups of the Boris Akunin project. Depending on what product and product format they choose, Akunin's readers may be divided into those who buy: (1) expensive, high-quality bound editions intended for collectors and the most devoted fans; (2) pocket books intended for the mobile readership (who often read in the subway or on a bus); (3) e-books intended for readers who prefer to use modern devices; (4) a special, electronic *Akunin Book*[39] intended for Akunin's fans; (5) book-videogames envisioned for the "Quest Quizzers" who are looking for additional entertainment and challenge;[40] (6) audiobooks meant for mobile readers (driving a car or public transit commuters); and (7) screen adaptations and theatre performances that target both Akunin's regular audience and random visitors. The latter, influenced by the multi-sensory appeal of a movie or a theatre performance, might be motivated to buy the original text.[41] The Boris Akunin project thus applies different channels to communicate with its target groups while using media that are most appropriate for a particular group. Besides, based on market research, the project offers an array of suitable devices and products to cover different audience preferences.

Project Strategy 2: Advertising *Boris Akunin*

Part of Akunin's well-organized cross-media campaign is advertising, most of which takes place on the Internet, the widest channel of communication. Until April 2017, Akunin's blog *Love of History* had served as the writer's main online advertising site. It includes advertisement banners with Akunin's latest releases and books that appear on the right-hand side of the blog page. A mouse click on these banners transfers a visitor to the partner site where one can purchase a book. Additionally, the blog offers a subscription to Boris Akunin's newsletter. Furthermore, several visits to the blog web page trigger search engine marketing. Suggestions to purchase Akunin's work automatically appear on Yandex and Google. Finally, the blog is cross-linked with the Akunin project's partner sites, as hyperlinks that are embedded in Akunin's posts take the reader to partner sites (websites of publishers and bookstores) where one can buy the writer's work.[42]

In the case of Akunin, there are many examples of such cross-linking between different media platforms. In his blog post of 16 March 2016, for example, Akunin announced the release of his new book *The Widow's Shawl* (*Vdovii plat*).[43] The hyperlinks take a blog visitor from this book's description to online stores[44] that sell the book in various formats: e-version, print, or as an audiobook. Moreover, Akunin's blog post about *The Widow's Shawl* was also reposted on the "Akunin Chkhartishvili" Facebook page, further spreading the word about the new release. Like the readers of the blog, Akunin's Facebook followers were also transferred to the partner websites where they could purchase the novel.

Akunin's web project *Octopus* (*Os'minog*, 2016) is a good example of how free advertising is integrated into the writer's blog and Facebook page. *Octopus* and its first part, the novel *Sulazhin* (2016), have characteristics of a literary game. Several times the readers are invited to choose between different plot options in order to continue reading (playing). The development of the plot (including the narrative's ending) depends on the readers' decisions. Having introduced *Octopus* in his post "Literary Games" ("Literaturnye igry"), Akunin linked the announcement to the project's own homepage, where one can either read *Octopus* online or download it on iTunes (for iPhone/iPad) or Google Play (for Android).[45] However, only one chapter is free, and the reader then has to purchase the narrative in full or quit reading the novel. This free offer helped Akunin collect statistics on his readership. The writer then made these data public in his follow-up posts. Eventually he decided that it was also important to run a paid advertising campaign for this particular project.[46]

The online book *Sulazhin* is both a quest game and a psychological test. Similar to what he did with his earlier novel *Quest* and his blog on Diatlov's group, in *Sulazhin* Akunin also invites his readers to choose between various versions of the story, which influence its ending. As a bonus for participating in this process and for buying the book, the reader receives his or her psychological portrait. Thus, in addition to providing the joys of reading and playing, *Sulazhin* also provides a new utility value to the readers, as they want to learn the results of this psychological analysis.

The colourful and interactive design of the project *Octopus*, along with the nostalgic design of the blog, appeals to the reader through text, sound, and images. This multi-sensory appeal additionally stimulates a website visitor to purchase a book.[47] Eye-catching and elegant book designs influence the buyer's decision on the multi-sensory level. The followers of Akunin's blog admit that they prefer the expensive, attractive, hardcover editions of *The History of the Russian State* with their pleasant haptics over pocket books or cheaper electronic versions that do not have pictures and maps.[48]

Akunin's publishers also conduct online advertising campaigns. The writer's two main publishing houses, Zakharov and AST, advertise new and older releases on their corporate websites. In order to attract consumers' attention to a particular book, they make it appear under different rubrics such as "Bestsellers," "New publications," "Recommended," or "Best of...".[49] On Zakharov's website, once a reader becomes interested in a book by Akunin, he or she is automatically suggested to read a similar book by this author. Moreover, a variety of purchasing options are suggested, as the website provides addresses of physical bookstores and links to online stores.[50] In addition to featuring Akunin's *History of the Russian State* on its corporate website, the publishing house AST also released several video trailers for the book series. These trailers appear on the publisher's homepage and YouTube channel, and are also reposted on the social media platforms Vkontakte and Facebook.[51] The trailers rely on visual appeal (through pictures, colours, shapes, texts, and actions) and auditory appeal (through music, words, sounds, and noises). One can purchase a book by Akunin in electronic and hard-copy versions by clicking on the hyperlink below the trailer, which transfers a visitor to online stores.

The Boris Akunin project also relies on outdoor advertising. Out-of-home media offer various options for visualization, especially those that are close to points of sale and stimulate buying on impulse. For example, an advertising poster or banner that is located in close proximity to a metro station or a busy street can reach out to large masses of potential customers. Furthermore, if this advertising poster has a striking creative design, it has excellent chances of eliciting positive public response.[52] In 2007, Chkhartishvili used this method of advertising his work when he developed his *Authors* (*Avtory*) project, which allowed him to work outside of the topics, genres, and style of his Boris Akunin project. Chkhartishvili then used new pen names, Anatolii

Brusnikin (an author of historical adventure novels) and Anna Borisova (a writer of psychological prose). At first Chkhartishvili did not reveal his authorship, and the project started without being specifically connected to him or to Boris Akunin. Extensive advertising campaigns for both previously unknown authors caused much speculation about their identities.[53] More specifically, a striking advertising poster for *The Ninth Saviour* (*Deviatnyi Spas*, 2007), the first book that Chkhartishvili published under the pen name Brusnikin, provoked wide public response. The posters were placed in many frequently visited places in the centre of Moscow, including one of the most prominent Russian bookstores, Moskva, where one could purchase Brusnikin's book. The provocative text on these posters attracted buyers to a book by a completely unknown author: "Akunin is disheartened ... Dashkova is enchanted ... Luk'ianenko is impressed ... Minaev is stunned ..." The names of popular Russian authors, including Akunin himself, who gave kudos to Brusnikin, served as an excellent teaser that triggered excitement ahead of the revelation of Chkhartishvili's new pen name. Intrigued critics and journalists inadvertently supported the advertising campaign while coming up with various speculations about the true identity of the mysterious Brusnikin.[54]

This marketing technique of developing a new literary identity and organizing a strong advertising campaign that precedes the start of the sales was successful and economically effective. As a result of this advertising campaign, Brusnikin's first two novels, *The Ninth Saviour* and *A Hero of a Different Time* (*Geroi inogo vremeni*, 2010) became bestsellers, while the movie rights for his third novel *Bellona* (2012) were sold when the novel was only a manuscript.[55] Later Chkhartishvili acknowledged that he was both Brusnikin and Borisova. In further editions, besides the pseudonyms Anna Borisova and Anatolii Brusnikin, the name Boris Akunin also appeared, thus clarifying the authorship. In this way the *Authors* project was presented as "a new mask" of Boris Akunin.[56] In other words, the *Authors* project was explicitly subordinated to the Chkhartishvili's main project, Boris Akunin.

Apart from online and outdoor advertising, dialogue marketing plays an equally important role in the promotion of the Akunin project. It helps to create lasting relationships between the author and his readers, personalize the readers' experience, retain existing customers, and recruit new ones.[57] With its direct communication as, for example during question and answer periods, dialogue marketing takes place at book presentations, book fairs, and meetings with the readership. For instance, a presentation of the deluxe edition of Akunin's first mystery novel, *The Winter Queen*, was organized at the Moskva bookstore by Meshcheriakov Publishers (Izdatel'skii dom Meshcheriakova), who specialize in high-quality reprints of popular literature. During his presentation the author emphasized the advantages of reading the new illustrated hardcover edition of *The Winter Queen* over reading the original black-and-white edition that did not have any extras. With its nostalgic design, integrated maps and pictures, and pages that are made to look aged and are pleasant to the touch, the deluxe edition conveys to the readers "the sense and scent of an epoch." Akunin said that he sees the future of the literary market either in electronic books or in high-end printed editions.[58]

It is noteworthy that Akunin has consistently followed through with his own pronouncements. Since 2013 his books have been acquiring ever more exclusive and expensive designs. While his *History of the Russian State* is printed on high-quality glossy paper in Italy and is expensive, cheaper electronic versions of this book series have been created for readers of average income who cannot afford deluxe editions.

Dialogue marketing is an effective way to channel the ideas of the Boris Akunin project to readers, as well as to guide their buying behaviour. By the end of book presentations, readers are often convinced that they *must* have a high-quality edition of the book. Furthermore, meeting the author in person and getting a chance to ask him a question strengthens the bond between the author and his readers. As if to confirm that the emotional power and sustainable impact of such events are usually enormous,[59] one of the visitors of the presentation for *The Winter Queen* at the Moskva bookstore in 2013, for example, mentioned: "I am going to leave this evening with a charge of positive energy!"[60]

Project Strategy 3: Point of Purchase Marketing

Besides cross-media strategies that create a certain image of the Boris Akunin project, conceptualize its leading idea, communicate it to the target group, and help advertise Akunin's books, another important marketing tool that impacts the consumer is so-called Point of Purchase Marketing (POP-Marketing), used typically in bookstores. POP-Marketing sets buying impulses in motion at the time and place of the purchase decision. At the point of sale and purchase, the customer is influenced through multi-sensory means and is especially susceptible to advertising. Consequently, POP-Marketing is chiefly responsible for an increase in sales rather than in building a product's image, as compared with other elements of cross-media. The store space is divided into function zones including some that are ideal for presenting the product.[61] Initially, books by various authors can be found on regular shelves, where they are either arranged alphabetically by authors' names or sorted by genre. Checking these shelf placements is typical of both casual customers and those who are looking for a specific author or book.

The second placement, however, plays a strategic role in successful POP-selling. In this case a particular title, apart from its initial placement, is also placed on floor stands or on additional tables or displays. Such displays raise the visibility of books at the point of purchase. The more noticeable and attractive such placement is, the stronger the customer's impulse to buy. These second placements are hard to obtain and the publishing agencies and literary agents who represent an author have to negotiate their terms with the stores.

As observed in several metropolitan and regional bookstores in Russia,[62] Akunin's publications regularly obtain distinguished second placements. His books are frequently found on counter placements as well as on mixed second placements, where books are categorized by a certain topic. In one store the third volume of Akunin's *History of the Russian State* as well as his fiction book *The Widow's Shawl* were found on a mixed display of bestsellers. Unlike other authors, Akunin was additionally given an advertising poster above the mixed display.

At the bookstore Chitai-gorod in the city of Ivanovo, the books from the historical part of *The History of the Russian State* occupied a placement on a supporting beam under the rubric "The Best about History" (*Luchshee ob istorii*). Furthermore, Akunin's *Planet Water* (*Planeta voda*, 2015), the fifteenth book about Erast Fandorin, was placed in the category "The Best of Detective Writing" (*Luchshee iz detektivov*) in the same store. In the best-case scenario, the second placement is a clearly visible and highly frequented area such as the centre of the bookstore, a place directly past the store entrance, or at the counter. Every customer walks through these points.[63] Akunin's single-author display of *The Widow's Shawl*, for example, was on the aisle side of a smaller board at the Moskva bookstore, and customers could not pass by without noticing it. Additionally, a large-scale replica of the novel was exhibited in the bookstore window, which provided additional advertising and had an inviting effect on customers.

Even more striking was a thematic placement located right in the centre of the Moskva bookstore. Dedicated to Grigorii Chkhartishvili's sixtieth birthday, this display had the caption "To Boris Akunin's Anniversary" (*K iubileiu Borisa Akunina*). The display featured a selection of Akunin's works published over the previous twenty years. In agreement with the birthday theme, the display was decorated with gift boxes, the cardboard headline "Boris Akunin's Anniversary," and a curriculum vitae titled *"Istoriia pisatelia rossiiskogo!"* ([Hi]story of [the]

Russian Writer), which summarized the most important dates in his literary career. The colours and style of the cardboards matched those of Akunin's historical project *History of the Russian State*, while the title of the curriculum vitae also rhymed with the wording of its title to produce a pun.

It is noteworthy that Chkhartishvili eagerly shares his marketing and sales plans with his readership. At the presentation of *Bosch and Schelm* (*Bokh i Shel'ma*, 2014) at the Sixteenth International Fair for High-Quality Fiction and Non-Fiction, the writer mentioned organizing a permanent separate bookcase for his *History of the Russian State* project in most big bookstores.[64] Subsequently, he posted a picture of such a thematic display on his blog *Love of History* and commented, "The publishing house promises to arrange special racks for the project *History of the Russian State* in big bookstores. The main place will be occupied not by the books that I authored, but by the books from *History of the Russian State* collection comprised of the best works by historians and writers of each era."[65]

Besides the strategically planned book placements at the point of purchase, the Boris Akunin project also uses other methods of sales promotions, including discounts or special offers, banners, audiovisual presentations, and promotional items such as a special package deals and a bag with the project's logo. Promotional items are three-dimensional, touchable, and comprehensible so that they can elicit emotional response.[66]

While quite a few stores promote Akunin's work through the POP-Marketing, they differ in their use of such marketing depending on their size (small private bookstore or a big chain) and the location of the store (Moscow or a regional store; suburb or city centre). As my field research demonstrates, the Boris Akunin project has a strong position at the points of purchase. It has many times received the most important strategic placements in retail space. In addition, it offers a whole array of books (including audio books) in different sections of the stores. A high demand for the products of the Akunin project is thus matched by these products' active marketing and sales politic.

Conclusion

Chkhartishvili's ideas regarding marketing have been implemented in Akunin's creative program. The *big idea* of the Akunin project consists in filling the niche in the Russian book market for high-level popular literature while achieving commercial success. Over the years this big idea has evolved in accordance with the market demands;

its realization has required the use of various marketing instruments and strategies. The Boris Akunin project has employed state-of-the-art cross-media strategies in the areas of image-building, communication, market research, and sales promotion. His promotional campaign responds to the demands of a contemporary, mobile lifestyle. Building his readership in a cross-media fashion corresponds to the idea of being the author of modern-day high-end popular literature. Since, in contrast to Western practices, in today's Russia there are few writers and hardly any historians who make such an extensive use of cross-media marketing, advertising, and sales strategies, an examination of all these commercial characteristics of the Akunin project is crucial for understanding the phenomenon of Boris Akunin.

NOTES

1 Lev Rubinstein is one the founders of Russian conceptualism and a friend of Grigorii Chkhartishvili. See Lev Rubinshtein, "Chelovek proekta Grigorii Chkhartishvili," interview with Grigorii Chkhartishvili, *Itogi*, 22 January 2000, http://www.guelman.ru/culture/reviews/2000-01-22 /rubinstein/.
2 In an interview with *Argumenty i fakty*, Chkhartishvili said: "My project 'Boris Akunin' is not only a literary, but also a business project." "Boris Akunin: Ia ne pisatel', ia belletrist," *Argumenty i fakty* 37 (11 September 2001), http://www.aif.ru/archive/1724205. All translations in this chapter are my own unless otherwise noted.
3 Niklas Mahrdt, *Crossmedia. Werbekampagnen erfolgreich planen und umsetzen* (Wiesbaden: Gabler Verlag, 2009), 29, 36.
4 Many people mundanely listen to the radio at work or in the car, listen to audiobooks while on the way to work, watch TV while doing housework, or check social networks. Mahrdt, *Crossmedia*, 5, 13–15.
5 Ibid., 30.
6 "Boris Akunin: Ia ne pisatel', ia belletrist."
7 The "thick journals" *Oktiabr'*, *Novyi mir*, and *Znamia* claimed themselves as independent editions during the time of perestroika. This was one of the reasons for their decline in the 1990s.
8 Grigorii Chkhartishvili, "Zhurnal Sintë: opyt vyzhivaniia vysokolobogo literaturnogo zhurnala v usloviiakh rynochnoi ėkonomiki," *Inostrannaia literatura* 8 (1997), http://magazines.russ.ru/inostran/1997/8/sin.html.
9 Grigorii Chkhartishvili, "Esli by ia byl gazetnym magnatom," *Neprikosnovennyi zapas* 2, no. 4 (1999), http://magazines.russ.ru/nz/1999/2/chart.html. For Bradley Gorski's translation of the article, see Appendix 1 in this volume.

10 Dmitrii Astrakhan et al., "Kul'tura i rynok," *Znamia* 6 (2000), http://znamlit
    .ru/publication.php?id=1155.
11 Ibid.
12 "Boris Akunin: Ia ne pisatel', ia belletrist," *Argumenty i fakty* 37 (11 September
    11, 2001), http://www.aif.ru/archive/1724205. Similar statements have ap-
    peared in Chkhartishvili's interviews. See, for example, Anna Verbieva, "Boris
    Akunin: Tak veselee mne i interesnee vzyskatel'nomu chitateliu," interview
    with Boris Akunin, *Nezavisimaia gazeta*, 23 December 1999, http://www
    .ng.ru/person/1999-12-23/1_akunin.html; Vadim Boreiko, "Grigorii Chkhar-
    tishvili: ia ne balzamirovshchik trupov, a prodavets v roznitsy," interview
    with Grigorii Chkhartishvili, Arba.ru, 17 November 2006, http://www.arba
    .ru/art/849. See also Boris Akunin, "Ia stal pisatelem," *LiveJournal* (blog),
    23 May 2012, http://borisakunin.livejournal.com/63290.html.
13 *Gang's Lookout* is a reference to depictions of the life of criminals and
    gangs, which were popular in the 1990s.
14 Verbieva, "Boris Akunin: Tak veselee mne."
15 Astrakhan et al., "Kul'tura i rynok."
16 Rubinshtein, "Chelovek proekta."
17 Sergei Buntman, "Ne tak. Istoriia Rossiiskogo gosudarstva. V gostiakh
    Boris Akunin," interview with Boris Akunin, *Ekho Moskvy*, 18 January
    2014, https://echo.msk.ru/programs/netak/1238026-echo/.
18 See Boris Akunin, "Novyi Karamzin iavilsia," *LiveJournal* (blog), 20 March
    2013, http://borisakunin.livejournal.com/94544.html.
19 Buntman, "Ne tak. Istoriia Rossiiskogo gosudarstva."
20 Ibid.
21 Mahrdt, *Crossmedia*, 20, 31–2, 36.
22 On the role of the internet, see Christian Jakubetz, *Crossmedia* (Konstanz,
    Germany: UVK Verlagsgesellschaft, 2011), 14, 19.
23 Maria Brauckhoff, "Der Fall Akunin gegen Čchartišvili. Ein Krimiautor
    will nicht sterben," *JFSL* (2004): 7, http://www.jfsl.de/publikationen/2004
    /Druckversionen/brauckhoff.pdf, accessed 11 January 2016.
24 *LiveJournal* (in Russian *Zhivoi Zhurnal*) is a popular social networking
    platform in Russia. In the past four years, however, due to controversies
    resulting from some legal cases and censorship, *LiveJournal* has started
    losing its popularity.
25 Jakubetz, *Crossmedia*, 21.
26 Boris Akunin, "Avtoportret blagorodnogo sobraniia," *LiveJournal* (blog),
    14 November 2010, http://borisakunin.livejournal.com/11499.html.
27 See the comments on Boris Akunin, "Zima! Krest'ianin torzhestvuia," *LiveJour-
    nal* (blog), 1 December 2015, http://borisakunin.livejournal.com/149183.html.
28 Igor' Diatlov was the leader of a nine-person ski trekking group that perished
    under mysterious circumstances in the Ural Mountains on 2 February 1959.

29 See all the three posts on the story "Po sledam gruppy Diatlova" ("Tracking the Diatlov group"): Boris Akunin, "Po sledam gruppy Diatlova. Chast' pervaia," *LiveJournal* (blog), 26 June 2012, https://borisakunin.livejournal .com/67157.html; "Po sledam gruppy Diatlova. Chast' vtoraia," *LiveJournal* (blog), 28 June 2012, https://borisakunin.livejournal.com/67386.html; and "Po sledam gruppy Diatlova. Chast'tret'ia," *LiveJournal* (blog), 20 June 2012, https://borisakunin.livejournal.com/67794.html.

30 Boris Akunin, *Samaia tainstvennaia taina i drugie siuzhety* (Moscow: AST, 2014), 38.

31 Boris Akunin, "Pamiati Zhzh," *LiveJournal* (blog), 5 April 2017, https:// borisakunin.livejournal.com/150279.html.

32 Akunin Chkhartishvili, "Official Facebook page of Boris Akunin," Facebook, n.d, https://www.facebook.com/borisakunin, accessed 4 February 2020.

33 Mahrdt, *Crossmedia*, 36, 54, 65.

34 Ibid., 76.

35 Ibid., 65.

36 Boris Akunin, "Novyi Karamzin iavilsia," *LiveJournal* (blog), March 20, 2013, http://borisakunin.livejournal.com/94544.html.

37 "Boris Akunin v Biblio-Globuse," video, 32:36, filmed 30 November 2013 at Biblio-Globus, Moscow, posted 4 December 2013, https://www.youtube .com/watch?v=WH6zXZ3seF8.

38 Mahrdt, *Crossmedia*, 40.

39 Boris Akunin i kompaniia eBook Applications LLC, *Universal'nyi reader ot Borisa Akunina Akunin Book*, accessed 19 October 2017, http://akuninbook .ru/. The *Akunin Book* contains all of Akunin's creative works, as well as his reading recommendations of books by other authors.

40 For example, the online novel *Quest* (*Kvest*, 2008) and the online literary game *Project Octopus* (*Os'minog*, 2016) and its first novel, *Sulazhin* (2016), have their own homepages and are available on the App Store and Google Play. See Boris Akunin, *Kvest. Elektronnaia versiia romana Kvest* (Moscow: AST, 2009), https://www.elkniga.ru/akunin/descr .html; Boris Akunin i kompaniia eBook Applications LLC, *Os'minog. Proekt Borisa Akunina*, accessed 15 October 2017, http://osminogproject .com/.

41 Films based on Akunin's novels include *Azazel'* (*Azazel*, TV film, directed by Aleksandr Adabash'ian, 2002), *Turetskii gambit* (*The Turkish Gambit*, film, directed by Dzhanik Faiziev, 2005), and *Statskii sovetnik* (*The State Counsellor*, film, directed by Filipp Iankovskii, 2005). The theatre productions based on Akunin's works include *Erast Fandorin* (*Erast Fandorin*, directed by Aleksei Borodin, RAMT Theater, Moscow), *In' i Jan': chërnaia versiia* (*Yin and Yang: Black Version*, directed by Aleksei Borodin, RAMT

Theater, Moscow), *In' i Ian: belaia versiia* (*Yin and Yang: White Version*, directed by Aleksei Borodin, RAMT Theater, Moscow).

42 See Mahrdt, *Crossmedia*, 35, 56 about the features of product sites.

43 Boris Akunin, "Pro novuiu knizhku," *LiveJournal* (blog), 16 March 2016, http://borisakunin.livejournal.com/149582.

44 These include the site http://litres.ru as well as the App Store and Google Play.

45 Boris Akunin, "Literaturnye igry," *LiveJournal* (blog), 20 May 2016, http://borisakunin.livejournal.com/149760.html.

46 Boris Akunin, "Iz zhizni Os'minoga," *LiveJournal* (blog), 6 June 2016, https://borisakunin.livejournal.com/150082.html.

47 On multi-sensory influence on buying decisions, see Adcock Dennis, Al Halborg, and Caroline Ross, *Marketing: Principles and Practice*, 4th ed. (Harlow, UK: Financial Times / Prentice Hall, 2001), 76–8.

48 For example, see the comments by the blog readers "pure salt" and "roman mozgovoy" to Boris Akunin, "Zima! Krest'ianin torzhestvuia."

49 For example, "Best of Detective Novels."

50 See publisher's website, http://www.zakharov.ru.

51 For example, watch the trailer for *Vdovii plat*: AST Izdatel'stvo, "Boris Akunin. Vdovii plat," video, 1:00, 13 March 2016, https://www.youtube.com/watch?v=CwYkTyE8SJo; and the trailer for the fifth volume of *Historia Rossiskogo gosudarstva*: AST Izdatel'stvo, "Boris Akunin. Aziatskaia evropeizatsiia. Istoriia Rossiiskogo gosudarstva. Tsar' Pëtr Alekseevich," video, 0:18, 14 November, 2017, https://www.youtube.com/watch?v=y5hVMS_GtaQ.

52 Mahrdt, *Crossmedia*, 50.

53 Alla Latynina, "Tak smeëtsia maska maske. Boris Akunin i proekt Avtory," *Novyi mir* 6 (2012): 171–2.

54 Ibid., 173.

55 The novel *Deviatnyi Spas* has been reedited twelve times, with a total circulation of more than 500,000 copies. See annotation to Anatolii Brusnikin, *Deviatnyi Spas* (Moscow: AST, 2015).

56 See annotation to Brusnikin, *Deviatnyi Spas*.

57 Jakubetz, *Crossmedia*, 21.

58 Moscowbooks, "Boris Akunin v knizhnom magazine Moskva: novaia Azazel'," video, 7:03, filmed 22 March 2013 at Moskva, Moscow, uploaded 1 April 2013, https://www.youtube.com/watch?v=EW-RYj3Rzwo.

59 Mahrdt, *Crossmedia*, 16.

60 Moscowbooks, "Akunin v knizhnom magazine Moskva."

61 Mahrdt, *Crossmedia*, 70–2.

62 The store check was conducted by the author, mostly in May 2016 and June 2017. Bookstores visited in Moscow: Biblio-Globus, Knizhnyi

Magazin Moskva, and Moskovskii Dom Knigi; in Ivanovo: Chitai-gorod and Renessans; and in Nizhnii Novgorod: Chitaina, and Dom Knigi.

63 Mahrdt, *Crossmedia*, 70–2.

64 Redaktsiia Zhanry, "Boris Akunin Bokh i Shel'ma," video, 58:05, filmed 29 November 2014 at the Sixteenth International Fair for High-Quality Fiction and Non-Fiction, Moscow, uploaded 3 December 2014, https://www.youtube.com/watch?v=wIioj0oA4bY.

65 Akunin, "Zima! Krest'ianin torzhestvuia."

66 Mahrdt, *Crossmedia*, 85.

15 Conclusion: A Dozen Questions for Boris Akunin

1

Elena Baraban: By now you have published more than sixty books and have essentially created a blueprint of a commercially and aesthetically successful literary career in contemporary Russia. In your opinion, which of your projects are the most successful? Which of your books do you like the most? Following twenty years of an impressive literary career, how do you define *success*? Is this the same kind of success that you strove for at the end of the 1990s? If not, then how have your views on success changed? What could you tell beginning writers and also your readers about the main components of your success?

Boris Akunin: The success of my projects can be assessed according to three very different criteria: (1) successful sales, that is to say from the point of view of the readers' demand; (2) success as critical acclaim, awards, prizes, and so on; and (3) success from the author's own point of view. By the first criterion, the leader is of course the Erast Fandorin book series. The second factor has been inversely proportional to commercial success: the better the books sold, the less the critics and literary juries liked them (which is psychologically very understandable). My personal assessment of my various projects has nothing to do with the first two criteria of success. For example, I was satisfied with the not-so-popular book series *Brotherhood of Death* (*Smert' na brudershaft*) because I was interested in mastering a plain, minimalist style that was new for me. And I am also satisfied with the series *The Family Album* (*Semeinyi al'bom*), because in this case I am for the first time completely free from the desire to please my readers and I write for myself, in the manner that I deem necessary. Therefore, success can be very different. It all depends upon you and your aspirations. My evolution in this sense is from an initial orientation on quantity and working for "the public" to introversion.

The components of success, regardless of the task set by the author, are always the same: a clear understanding of the task and the means to achieve it, perseverance, and, most importantly, luck, without which the most flawless book, if it appears untimely, may remain unnoticed or barely noticed.

2

Baraban: What has changed in your views on Russian literature during the past twenty to twenty-five years? When you started writing popular fiction (belles-lettres), Russian literature was in a deplorable state: the literary canon of the previous decades had collapsed, "thick" literary journals were surviving thanks to subsidies from George Soros and other sources, and the book market was filled with pulp fiction. How do you assess the state of Russian literature today?

Akunin: I cannot comment on this. All these years I do not read fiction. In my profession, reading books by other authors is harmful, it confuses me.

3

Baraban: Back in 2001, in an interview with the newspaper *Agrumenty i fakty*, you explained that your Boris Akunin project is not only a literary but also "a business project," and that you wanted to "create a situation in which a writer living in Russia could earn enough money as well as create some kind of a cultural model, in the centre of which would be a writer instead of a publishing house, a literary agent, or a producer." Has your understanding of your activity and your mission in Russian literature changed over the past two decades?

Akunin: Yes, that is exactly how it happened. For a long time, I enjoyed conducting an orchestra comprised of publishing houses, film studios, theatres, and literary agents, while not starting an exclusive relationship with any of them. But now it no longer seems interesting to me; I "have left the big sport." I feel like Diocletian growing cabbage, and I enjoy it.

4

Baraban: On 23 May 2012, in a preface to *Aristonomy* (*Aristonomia*), the first novel in the *Family Album* series, you wrote that you had begun a narrative about the fate of a family in twentieth-century Russia in the hope of finding answers to questions about the meaning of life. Have you succeeded in finding an answer to this question? What is important for you in your work on the *Family Album* book series? Would you stop working on it if it sold poorly? In other words, is self-knowledge a luxury or a vital necessity?

Akunin: The *Family Album* is the most important project for me. I see it as a kind of homework: an answer to complex questions that life has set before me. As a writer, I respond with novels. In turn, question by question. What is the meaning of life and is there one anyway? – The novel *Aristonomy*. What is love and is it possible to combine private happiness with participation in some big, unsafe activity (this is an eternally acute problem for Russia)? – The novel *Another Way* (*Drugoi put'*). Can Russia become a prosperous country and under what conditions? – The novel *Happy Russia* (*Schastlivaia Rossiia*). How should children be raised? – The novel *Treasury* (*Trezorium*). Here you need to understand that I do not preach or even persuade, I do not "graze the nations," I do not pretend to be Leo Tolstoy. I give answers to myself. It is sufficient for me if I convince myself. Why then write a book, one could ask? It is for the reason that I can figure out a difficult problem only when I place it in some kind of imagined world. I need to see how my characters will behave.

These novels are quite difficult to read; not everything is thoroughly explained. These novels do not have too many readers. But those who read them are the best readers in the world.

5

Baraban: In 2012, you warned fans of your adventure novels that the *Family Album* books are "rather tedious reading." In your view, can such serious literature exist only on subsidies from commercial projects? In other words, could the *Family Album* feed you if there were no *History of the Russian State* and adventure novels?

Akunin: If *The Family Album* had been my first project, it would have been impossible to exist on such royalties. Now, thanks to my fame, many people buy these books too, so the count still goes by tens of thousands. However, if Fandorin had not worked for me, this would certainly not have happened.

6

Baraban: In the fall of 2019, *Treasury*, the fourth novel in the *Family Album* series, came out. Its action takes place in 1945. The publication time of this book seems ideal, since in Russia preparations for the

celebration of the seventy-fifth anniversary of the victory over Nazism
are already in full swing and public interest in the war topic is high.
What contribution does your book make to the war discourse in Russia? Do you think the war of the Soviet Union against Nazi Germany
should continue to be called the Great Patriotic War, or is it time to
consider that war as part of the Second World War?

Akunin: I don't know about my contribution to war prose, I have not
thought about it, and I do not care. For me, this novel is not about the
war; it is about happiness. The war in this case is nothing more than a
contrasting background.

It seems to me that it does not matter much what the 1941–5 war may
be called. The name "The Great Patriotic War" contains after all a reference to the other Patriotic War (1812–4), against Napoleon. This said,
the fact that the Great Patriotic War is part of the Second World War, of
course, should be written more clearly in Russian textbooks. Likewise,
in the textbooks of Western countries, one needs to say clearly that the
Second World War began not in 1939, but in 1937, in China. It began in
Asia and it ended in Asia.

7

Baraban: Do you work with experts who track the sales statistics of
your books, study readers' comments on your posts in social media,
suggest modern ways of keeping in touch with your audience, organ-
ize advertising campaigns, and generally help to develop a marketing
strategy for the Boris Akunin project? If in the late 1990s you said that
the author should write for the reader, in the last few years you have
been talking often (with regard to both the *History of the Russian State*
and the *Family Album*) about writing for yourself. How well do you
know your readers and take into account their wishes?

Akunin: I have no experts and have never had any. When I was
actively interested in the situation of the book market, I collected the
data myself from open-access and professional (for example, publishers') sources. Even now I sometimes conduct polls through social
media in order to better understand the evolution of the audience.
This activity may be considered phantom pains. But in general – yes,
for several years now I mainly play the glass bead game. I will complete my large-scale mass-culture project *History of the Russian State*
and then I will probably begin to write on a grain of rice. Although ...
we will see.

8

Baraban: Have you ever experienced the pangs of creativity? Say, it was difficult for Gogol to come up with a good plot, it was difficult for Pasternak to write a novel, while Nabokov, on the contrary, did not succeed in poetry. What difficulties do you experience in your writing? You used to say that since you were a belletrist and not a writer, you had no difficulties; you did not have to wait for inspiration and instead just followed the work plan for a day, for a week, and so on. What is your relationship with creativity now? What interests you in your literary work now?

Akunin: No, I do not like to suffer. In my case, writing resides in the centre of pleasure in my brain. In literary work, the most interesting thing for me is that for me it is not work, but leisure.

My main problem is language fatigue, which is natural after so many written texts. I get tired of using the same words, while there are no other ones to use. Of course, it is not always easy for me to write, but I never force myself. If a novel has slowed down, I put it aside and take up non-fiction or write the *History of the Russian State*, which requires no mysticism.

9

Baraban: At the beginning of your career as a belletrist, you noted that your education in oriental studies and knowledge of Japanese culture made it possible for you to look at Russia in a different way. How has your present life in Western Europe enriched your view of Russia? Does this closer acquaintance with a pragmatic and logical Western civilization affect your work?

Akunin: Living in the West does not affect my work, in my opinion. Maybe I'm too old. I really love Europe. It seems to me that this is the most advanced zone of human civilization. But life here – or rather, my long absence from Russia – is rather useful to me in another way. It allows me to get less annoyed at the absurdities and abominations of Russian politics and view Russia in a longer historical perspective. This is very important for writing the history of the country.

10

Baraban: On 20 March 2013, in your "Love of History" blog, you wrote that you started "your literary life" with adventure novels, but that already then you "secretly" hatched a "megalomaniac plan" to write a history of the Russian state. Now, when this mega-project is close to completion, what new large or small projects are you planning?

Akunin: Basically, these plans relate to territories that have been newly conquered by literature – the paperless. I see there, in the digital New World, great opportunities for a writer. I also want to start writing books that will please me. Not about difficult problems that need to be solved, but about what I love. You know, about pensioner's joys. For example, I want to write a novel about my love of Japan, a kind of Japonaiserie.

11

Baraban: A number of critics note that many images of women in your novels, including novels written under the pseudonym Anna Borisova, were created from patriarchal positions. How do you feel about such an assessment? How important are gender categories for your narratives?

Akunin: Gender categories are very important to me. As for all of us, I suppose. I have novels written from patriarchal positions, from matriarchal positions, from teenagers' positions, from gerontocratic positions, and so on. I would only warn critics and readers from confusing the author's position with the position of my characters. This, alas, often happens.

12

Baraban: Over the past twenty years, you have given many interviews and answered a variety of questions. What questions inspire you? Is there a question you would like to hear? How would you answer it?

Akunin: It is more interesting for me when I am asked about something I have never been asked about; this makes me move my brains. The best question a writer can be asked is: "Tell me, how do you manage to be so unbearably talented?" Here, however, the writer begins to suspect that he is being mocked and feels offended.

NOTES

In November 2019, Boris Akunin answered Elena V. Baraban's questions about his views on literature, his literary career, and his past and current projects. Translated from Russian by Elena V. Baraban.

Appendices: Excerpts from Boris Akunin's Untranslated Works

Appendix 1
Grigorii Chkhartishvili, "If I Were a Newspaper Magnate: Notes of a Restless Cow"(1999)[1]

Translated by BRADLEY A. GORSKI with Permission from GRIGORII CHKHARTISHVILI

If I were not I, but the most handsome, most intelligent, and best person in the world (and, naturally, the richest) – in a word, Gusinskii-Berezovskii[2] – I would immediately found a news and magazine empire. Television I would leave alone. To hell with it! It's for the broad masses, and the broad masses bore me. No, I would rather undertake publishing those periodicals that I find wanting in today's Russia – I'd give myself such a gift.

First Thing: A Daily Newspaper

First of all, I would open a decent daily newspaper because I don't understand why and for whom all the current daily papers exist. Okay, *Kommersant*, fine – if, of course, anyone cares about leasing, franchising, and the Dow Jones Industrial Average. The *Forest Gazette* (*Lesnaia gazeta*) and *At the Military Post* (*Na boevom postu*), I suppose, are also necessary. But it would be wonderful to have just one good paper of a standard variety – to read over breakfast or in the limousine on the way to my skyscraper. That kind of really necessary paper is something we lack. I don't know anyone who would subscribe to or regularly buy any of the existing newspapers, even though all my acquaintances seem interested in politics and economics and watch the TV news every day, sometimes even twice a day. My acquaintances used to subscribe to the newspaper *Today* (*Segodnia*). They would leaf through the first pages and, shaking their heads in disapproval, read the latest confessional by Boris Kuzminskii.[3] Then this mess came to an end; there was no longer anything to read in *Today* and by the tenth anniversary of glasnost most of us subscribed only to *Seven Days* (*Sem' dnei*). You read the photo credits there and you begin to doubt your values – maybe I'll vote for Zyuganov,[4] after all?

There's no point in today's daily papers. They tell you the same thing as the TV news does, only a day later, and the only difference among them is that some are for Luzhkov[5] and others are against him.

Oh! My newspaper would be different! My newspaper would become the missing link between the heat-of-the-moment radio and TV news and the critical analyses in the monthly magazines. Upon opening my paper in the morning, I would count on finding not news but explication and a first qualified interpretation. The previous evening, my colleagues would have managed to survey many intelligent experts and, in that morning edition, they would already explain to the reader how to interpret the mysterious mumblings of the prime minister and why the president still seems like a zombie,[6] and whether one should sell off one's dollars after the chairman of the Central Bank told that joke yesterday. With time it would become clear which of the experts is really perceptive and I would pay those clairvoyants enormous fees, and those who were not perceptive enough, I wouldn't print them at all.

I would also keep an entire pack of wolf-reporters, desperate cut-throats, who would without fail, a couple of times a month at the very least, dig up a sensational scoop and would be ready to provide proof of its veracity if necessary. By sensational scoop I mean not the piquant details of a pop star's personal life (such things are not meant for my respectable newspaper), but something like a law enforcement minister's visit to a sauna owned by the mafia.

My newspaper would be thick. Not four pages and not six, but at least thirty-two. I would decide ahead of time to publish it for, say, three demographic groups, and would address a few pages to each. A reader by the name of, say, Lopakhin would get the latest issue, look at the first two pages with news analysis and – if we had one that day – a sensational scoop, and then right away would turn to the economics section on page 7, then to finance on page 8, then to information about selling one's cherry orchard on page 9. A reader called Ranevskaia, after glancing at the front pages (of course), might turn her eyes to page 17 for cultural news, page 18 (society column), page 28 for an interview with Anton Chekhov, and page 19 for fashion. Petia Trofimov, another reader, would flip past all this nonsense. He's interested in sports, a survey of internet innovations, the science page, and the "Lonely Hearts Club." I wouldn't worry about readers like Epikhodov and Firs. The first would continue reading *Moscow Komsomolets* and the second would read *Tomorrow* (*Zavtra*).

I forgot the main thing. The writers and journalists in my newspaper would be the very best because I would pay them a pile of money. (I am, after all, the richest man in the world.) And my informants would penetrate all of society from the bottom up (especially to the very top), because I would also stimulate them somehow (precisely how would be a secret), and my wolves would never, even under torture, give up their sources.

Incidentally, the daily newspaper would not be led by me personally. It's a difficult job, a lot of stress, I understand little of it. I would invite Sergei Parkhomenko[7] as the editor-in-chief and he would set up everything as needed. But I would foster and cultivate the other publications of my expansive empire myself.

A Weekly Newspaper

Here, everything is straightforward. I would buy the long-suffering *Literary Newspaper* (*Literaturnaia gazeta*) and make it entirely literary, on all sixteen pages – and politics, economics, and the plagues of society would not be allowed anywhere near my property. After all, my *weekly* should be different from *The General Newspaper* (*Obshchaia gazeta*) and *The Moscow News* (*Moskovskie novosti*).

I would keep the division into four sections that was introduced into the *Literary Newspaper* at some point. I like it. I'd call the first "Literary News" (which of the big names has written what, who received what prize, where have writers been meeting, what have they been talking about, all manner of presentations, manifestoes, and declarations, para-literary gossip and so on). The second section would be "The Literary Conversation" (articles and essays, and also interviews, discussions, surveys, opinion pieces, and writers' squabbles). The third one, "Reviews," would comprise book reviews and evaluations of the latest issues of literary journals. The fourth one, "The Book Market," would consist of analytical reviews of the publishing industry and of mass literature, rankings, copyrights, and authors' royalties.

On second thought, four sections are not enough. We'd need one more: "Focus." And it would have a collection of materials on some unbelievably topical, or alternatively, perfectly timeless subject: "The Writer and the Bestseller," "The Writer and Death," "The Writer and Immortality," "The Writer and His Companion," "The Writer and His Partner," "The Writer and Her Companion," "The Writer and Her Partner," "The Writer and Gambling," or "How Should We Reorganize the PEN Club?" In short, there would be plenty of good topics.

Seriously, it'd be the best literary newspaper in the whole world, not *A Literary Newspaper*, but **The** *Literary Newspaper*, inimitable, the one and only. Without it, those who find themselves interested in the literary arts (and at least 100,000 such people could be found in our country) would simply be at a loss.

A Weekly Magazine

And those who count themselves part of respectable society would be at a loss if they didn't subscribe to my weekly illustrated magazine, fully devoted to culture.

It would be a relatively conservative publication, very restrained in its expressions and completely non-nepotistic. Sure, scandal and outrage would be a part of it, only not in form but in essence; not in diction but in argumentation.

The journal would be dressed accordingly, not in a blazer with gold buttons, but not with a navel ring either. Instead, it would appear in that kind of deceptively bourgeois tweed jacket and tie (or, fine, without a tie, but the jacket is required).

The sections would be simple, unpretentious: again "Literature" (for those who, unlike the bibliophiles who subscribe to the *Literary Newspaper*, simply want to keep up), "Theatre," "Cinema," "Television," "Art," and of course, "Latest Events," profiles, interviews. No lobbying or sectionalism, no disrespectful reviews, no dirty laundry, no portraits of stars against a freshly remodelled interior. Paging through the magazine, you'd feel like you lived in a civilized country, you'd respect yourself. You'd know where (not) to go, what (not) to watch, what (not) to read, and what (not) to listen to.

We need such a magazine terribly. I'd subscribe right away at any price.

Literary Journals

This has become the most painful part, and so I would take the most decisive action.

I would erect a memorial to George Soros (in place of Peter the Great or Marshal Zhukov) for saving Russian journals in their most difficult times, and I would say: "Thanks, I'll take it from here."

Immediately and irrevocably, I would deprive journals of their financial independence. No need to torture these pink flamingos any more. They should be taken to a nature reserve under a magnate's attentive care. Look how much weight they have lost, how their marvellously coloured feathers have fallen out, how their heavenly voices have grown hoarse from hunger. Let the editors and literary workers sit in their offices swamped with manuscripts, drink tea with authors, coffee and cocktails, tell jokes, gossip about mutual acquaintances, and among all those pleasant pursuits work out issues for an article, and think up a topic for discussion or a special issue. I was in the editorial offices of a Japanese literary journal and I shuddered: there, all the editors sit at one long table, silently rustling pages, and, when necessary, (brr) read proofs till dawn. That's not how my literary journals would work. A literary journal is no conveyer-belt factory, but a magical kingdom of luxuriance. That's why they are so thick and why they've been so fertile, not just anywhere but specifically in Russia.

I would immediately give my favourite journal, *Foreign Literature* (*Inostrannaia literatura*),[8] incalculable currency – buy, my dear, buy any novel you could want. A Barcelonan vampire, the holder of all Spanish-language copyrights, wants $30,000 for Marquez's most recent novel? Not a problem. Need to send translators to take questions to Milorad Pavić and Julian Barnes? As it happens, my private plane is waiting. And another thing. One *Foreign Literature* is too few, I want two. The second (let it be called simply *FL-2*) would be for entertainment: intellectual murder mysteries, provocative memoirs, literary games, and further amusements (in wonderful translations) for those who want to give their brains a break. This is the best contribution I can make to improving the quality of cultural life. I imagine *FL-2* would have ten times the readers of *FL-1*, and that is as it should be.

With the other thick journals, I would act severely. "Stop printing the same journal under five different covers," I would tell their editors-in-chief, shaking my chequebook. "We've had enough of all the same authors. Time to decide amongst yourselves which profile each of you has, which literary trends you represent, and to which generation of readers you cater. If it is too hard to come to an agreement, draw lots."

Friendship of the Peoples (*Druzhba narodov*) publishes writers of the older generation. The latter shouldn't worry about it and try to look younger; instead they should write in the way preferred by their readers, those who are ageing along with them. Why alarm respectable people with profanity and oral-anal sex?

The youth's Sturm und Drang will have grouped itself around *October* (*Oktiabr'*). Of course, we would have to redesign the cover, style, and layout, and maybe even change the name to *Torrid October* (*Znoinyi oktiabr'*).

As my empire's tentacles would stretch all the way to Petersburg, I would recommend *The Star* (*Zvezda*) print only true Petersburg writers. No Paramonovs or Bitovs.[9] Moved away from the city on the Neva River? Goodbye for good. Promised to return to Vasilievsky Island but actually ended up living on the Island of San Michele? Then maybe *Neva* will print you. (I would reserve *Neva* for publications about Petersburg in general).

Banner (*Znamia*) would become the official organ of forty-year-olds, the literary mainstream, and it would stop being shy about it, too.

For *New World* (*Novyi mir*), I would reserve the role of a catch-all journal: for the omnivorous reader who is not fixated on a certain age group, trend, or habit of mind and who reads a bit of everything. Those who really love literature could subscribe to all the literary journals of my empire, but those who do not have the time, money, or interest for *Friendship of the Peoples*, *Banner*, *Star*, and *October* – read *New World*.

And that's how a glorious news-and-periodical life would begin under the trustworthy wing of my many-headed oligarchic eagle. That's how Russian literature would blossom...

And here one can inevitably hear some critical realist asking: "And where would you, Grigorii Shalvovich, get the money to feed this entire, quite obviously unprofitable, encampment?"

"I don't know," I would answer, annoyed. "It's not important. That would ruin everything. I'm dreaming, after all. I'm 'an elm,' 'a refuge.'"

"Do you know, Pavel Ivanovich," said Manilov, who very much liked such thoughts, "how good it would actually be to have that kind of life together, under one roof, or in the shade of an elm, to philosophize about something, to plumb the depths."

"Oh! That would be a heavenly life!" Chichikov said, sighing.

Appendix 2

Boris Akunin, "A New Karamzin Has Appeared" (2013) and "General Introduction" to *The History of the Russian State* (*Istoriia Rossiiskogo gosudarstva*, 2013)

Translated by STEPHEN M. NORRIS with the permission of GRIGORII CHKHARTISHVILI

Introduction

These two translations outline Akunin's plans for his multi-volume history series. The first, an announcement on the author's popular blog, speaks to the way Akunin envisioned his *History of the Russian State* as a commercial project as well as a popular one. As Akunin writes, he began his project with a novel – the first in the Fandorin series – that deliberately invoked characters from Nikolai Karamzin's famous short story, "Poor Liza" ("Bednaia Liza"). Karamzin (1766–1826) became famous first for his travelogue, *Letters of a Russian Traveller* (*Pis'ma russkogo puteshestvennika*, 1791–92), then as a writer of sentimental prose, including "Poor Liza." He would go on to found an influential literary journal, *The Messenger of Europe* (*Vestnik Evropy*), before writing the first multi-volume history of Russia, one that stressed the role the state had played in shaping Russian history.

In a sense, Akunin is playing with his reader yet again in this blog post, "A New Karamzin Has Appeared," suggesting that he too has followed the path Karamzin once trod. In another sense, Akunin's announcement that he is writing a new history of the Russian state has a subtle political message to it: Karamzin famously wrote his volumes as a court historian for Alexander I (r. 1801–25) and trumpeted the autocratic system as a necessary part of Russia. Akunin claims that he is writing his new history as a corrective to the Putin state's plans to write its own state-approved history textbook. The second translation, a follow-up from the blog announcement, appears in all the

Boris Akunin as Nikolai Karamzin. Reprinted with the permission of Grigorii Chkhartishvili.

subsequent volumes of his *History* and lays out the three rules that govern it.

Boris Akunin's Original Blog Post:
https://borisakunin.livejournal.com/94544.html
"A New Karamzin Has Appeared"
20 March 2013

This post for me is historical (in both senses of the word). I have been preparing it for a long time and now I am somewhat worried.

I'll start from the beginning.

Some writers dream of becoming new Tolstoys, others of new Chekhovs. I (it is past time to admit it) have always dreamt of becoming the new Karamzin.

I began my literary life with the novel *Azazel'*, a transparent reference to the story about poor Liza and happy Erast. Even then, I secretly harboured a megalomaniacal plan: to repeat Karamzin's trajectory and, starting with fiction, then arrive at writing the history of the Russian state.

Now, a decade and a half later, this plan (well, and the attached inverse) has begun to be realized.

Dear readers, I want to make an announcement, which will upset some of you, but others, perhaps not.

I have stopped being a detective writer.

The series about Fandorin, of course, I will finish, but my main interest and the main direction of my work will be a multi-volume project, *The History of the Russian State*. In fact, I have worked on this great matter for a long time, and now the first volume is, uh, written.

"My God, why do we need to surrender to a new Karamzin? – you ask. – After Solov'ev, Kliuchevskii and many other historians?[10] Why replay events that are already so well known to everyone?"

I will answer.

A new Karamzin, in my opinion, is needed now because for two hundred years the "history of Russia" has been written by professional historians, and there are few who read it except for students and people deeply interested in the past. When the history of the country is told not by a professional, but by a dilettante belletrist, he, by virtue of his profession, cares about making the book *readable* – as did Nikolai Mikhailovich Karamzin. This is how Isaac Asimov wrote historical books.[11] Now a similar project is being carried out by the remarkable British novelist Peter Ackroyd – he is releasing volume after volume of the monumental "History of England," which is serious and entertaining all at once.[12]

About the fact that historical events are well known to everyone without me needing to write about them, I object: not all, and even, I would say, very few people know them. The overwhelming majority of people have only a very vague idea of the history of their own country – they only possess fragmentary information, and even then mostly obtained from novels and movies.

I myself, despite a historical education, have no solid idea of our history. And this is the main reason why I took up this task: *I want to understand how our state was formed, how it developed, and why it became what it is today.*

My *History* is not intended for historians – they will not learn anything new. I write for those who know the biography of their country poorly and would like to know it better.

My method is simple. I read the available sources, trying not to miss anything, and see how the information contained there is interpreted by various authors. From all of this mass of facts, names, figures, dates, and judgments, I try to choose all those that are undoubted, or at least the most believable. I cut out those that are minor and unreliable.

The peculiarity of my *History* is that it is not *ideologized*. I do not have any preconceived concept for which it would be necessary to find evidence. The current official attempts to create a new "truthful" history are a confirmation that a neutral and objective *History of the Russian State* can prove useful. We know what kind of textbooks state functionaries will write for us. Why such historiography is necessary was frankly explained by the court historian General Nechvolodov more than a hundred years ago: "It shows us from what kind of brave, wise, and noble people we developed." End of story.

Well, I have another problem. *I want to know how it really was.* The truest, or version closest to the truth – this is what I need.

I write using quite unscientific language, and sometimes (infrequently, do not be afraid) even allow myself to joke, but at the same time I do not permit factual liberties and do not get carried away by authorial digressions. I advise any reader not to learn history from my belletrist novels, but from this multi-volume series – please do so. Here everything will be weighed, measured, and checked by specialists.

But the belletrist is still a belletrist, and reading the historical works will inevitably fuel the reader's imagination. I solved this problem this way.

At the same time that I am publishing a "serious" volume I will publish an "unserious" one with historical stories, the action of which takes place in the same epoch. For example, the first volume of my *History of the Russian State* covers the period before the Mongol invasion. The events of the first fictional book will take place in the same century. And there I will really give full play to the worst-case scenarios.

Over time, the fictional stories will form a massive mega-story about the life of one Russian family across 1,000 years. (Yes, the main characters of the stories will be genealogically related to each other.) That is, the history of the state and *human* history will go side by side, testing each other for strength.

The design for both series will be similar (they are in fact part of one project), but they will be sold separately. I really hope that those who read the adventure volume will want to know how it happened in reality at that same time. Similarly, lovers of "dry" history, perhaps, will want to go deeper into the epoch – for this, they can try out the story.

That's what kind of work I intend to take up and God knows how many years it will take.

There was no publishing analogue for such a two-pronged long-term project. The entire strategy will be developed and calculated. In addition, both the historical and fictional volumes will be well illustrated, because it is one thing to read about the past; it also needs to be seen. So before the end of the year the first book tandem (how, dammit, this word has been compromised!) is unlikely to come out. While I am certain about the publishing house (although it is still not yet finalized), it will take many months before we develop the algorithm and prepare the design together.

I have announced my plans for two reasons.

First, I have been drawn to writing about the Middle Ages in this blog for a while now. I am now completely addicted to this era, and I have a lot of interesting stories in my files that I want to share. This obsession with the events of a thousand years ago, if not explained, would seem strange to you.

And second, from time to time I will need your help.

This is my question right now.

You have probably heard that today in the universities of the United States and Great Britain (perhaps elsewhere too) there exists DNA analysis for people interested in conducting interesting genetic and genealogical research, which easily reconstructs their paternal and maternal ancestry across many centuries.

Here's how this service is advertised:

▶ Trace both lines (paternal and maternal)

○ **Combo Package (Y-DNA 20 Marker + mtDNA HVR-1 Test)**, $238.00 US
Trace your own ancestry on your paternal and maternal lines. You may upgrade to Advanced Package at a later date.

I'm sure that out of curiosity someone has already done this test and obtained their results. They are very interesting to me. If you do not mind sharing, send them in a personal note. For example, Leonid Parfenov already passed his genealogy to me. (Yes, there is one essential condition: it is necessary that both parents are 100% Russian, and not some newly arrived riff-raff like yours truly).

In general, wait for posts about how our ancestors, in the words of Karamzin, *went to the theatre of history.*

Boris Akunin, General Introduction to *History of the Russian State*

From the author

Before you decide whether it makes sense for you to read this work, I must warn you about its peculiarities.

There are three.

I write for people who do not know Russian history well and who want to understand it. I myself am like this. All my life I have been interested in history, I received a historical education, I wrote several dozen historical novels, and yet one day I realized that my knowledge consists of separate fragments that do not fit well into a general picture. I did not have a clear idea of how and why Russia turned out like it did. And I understood: in order to answer such a concise question, first I must read tens of thousands of pages, and then write several thousand pages.

I do not formulate a concept. I do not have one. Any historian who creates his own theory cannot cope with the temptation to leave out facts inconvenient for him and to silence or question everything that does not fit into his logic. I have no such temptation.

In addition, I am a determined opponent of ideological history. Both self-praising and self-deprecating lines, presented abundantly in the writings of Russian historians, are equally uninteresting to me. I want to know (or calculate) how it really was. I do not have a preconceived opinion. There are questions and there is a desire to find answers to them.

This is not a history of the country [*strana*], but of the state [*gosudarstvo*], that is, a political history: state building, the mechanisms of governance, the relationship between the people [*narod*] and power [*vlast'*], the evolution of society. I only touch on culture, religion, and the economy to the extent that they are connected with politics.

Russia is primarily a state. It is not identical to the country, and in some moments of history it was even hostile to it, but it was the state of that invariably determined the vector of evolution (or degradation) of all spheres of Russian life. The state is the cause of both Russian ills and Russian victories.

Trying to understand our thousand-year state and what is and what is not so (and why): this is what this work eventually aims to do.

Appendix 3

Boris Akunin, *Spy Novel* (*Shpionskii roman*; Moscow: AST, 2005), 5–20

Translation by STEPHEN M. NORRIS with the permission of GRIGORII CHKHARTISHVILI

In 2006, Akunin initiated his "genre series," a group of novels written in different genres where the title conveys the genre. His first three books in this project came out that year: *Children's Book* (*Detskaia kniga*), *Spy Novel* (*Shpionskii roman*), and *Science Fiction* (*Fantastika*).

Spy Novel fictionalizes the events leading up to the German invasion of the USSR in June 1941 and explains the surprise attack as one involving spies from both countries. Stalin received numerous intelligence reports that the Wehrmacht planned to invade, including one from Pavel Fitin on June 17 that stated that an invasion was imminent, but chose to ignore them. Akunin's novel provides a reason for this lack of action.

Prologue

A Genius Pig

Three men sat in a marble office with red walls and a rosewood desk.

Two were silent, one spoke – slowly at first, as if by force, now and then wearily rubbing his swollen eyelids with his fingers, then louder, more energetic. Finally he jumped up, paced around the table, rapidly turned on his heels, and made nervous gestures with his hands. His blue eyes filled with radiance, his voice rang and vibrated his cheek, which twitched in an angry tick, but his mouth remained calm and its corners concealed a shadowy, dreamy smile.

The listeners (one of whom was wearing the black uniform of an admiral, the other the grey of a general) knew perfectly well that the alternation of lethargy and pressure, whispering and shouting, the language of numbers and inspired campaigns was no more than the method of a professional orator, and yet they inevitably felt the magic of this half-smile known in this country and around the world.

The speaker was the dictator of the most powerful state in Europe, the most loved and the most hated man on earth.

The listeners were the head of military intelligence and his deputy; the secret meeting took place in the Reich Chancellery, the outcome of which involved the life and death of tens of millions of people.

But the man with fierce eyes and a smiling mouth was not talking about death, but about happiness.

"... The happiness of the German people and its future is at stake. Two weeks ago, it seemed that our position was firm, and the prospects were tremendous. But the Yugoslav gamble of our enemies made me delay the training for 'Barbarossa.' I quickly had to put out the fire that arose in the rear. The sceptics whispered that time was lost, that the plan would have to wait for next spring. And what happened?"

His fingers quickly seized on the tip of his sharp nose, and with a powerful pull tugged at his little, prickly mustache. "I gave the world a lesson, I crushed the Yugoslav army in one week! The military operation began on 6 April, and today, the 12th, it can be considered a complete triumph."

A short pause, chin grimly dropped, his forehead fell, and the long, oblique strand of his voice wilted. "... But the transfer of thirty divisions from east to west and from west to east wastes precious time. A strike on 15 May, as contemplated in the plan, will not succeed. The General Staff reported that we now cannot start until the second or even the third week of June. The main question is whether we can meet our aims with such a tight deadline, before the onset of winter: to destroy the main forces of the Red Army and to create a line from Arkhangelsk to the Volga. We counted on five months, and now only have four. I am told that this stolen month will mean there is not enough time for final victory. Might it actually be better to wait until next year?"

His twitching hand made an uncertain gesture and rubbed his temple. His shoulders bent as if under a heavy burden of responsibility, his mournful eyes closed.

Now a long pause – perhaps half a minute.

The intelligence chief, a man not yet old but already grey, carefully looked at his assistant. He winced a little, which meant that a decision had already been taken anyway, so why these theatrical effects?

The Reich Chancellor raised his head, his wide-open eyes shone with an unflinching will. "My God, these clever people do not understand a simple thing!" He made a slashing motion with his clenched fist. "An avalanche that starts at the top cannot stop. Anyone who tries to stand in its way will die. Movement is victory, any stop means collapse. Yes, we spent a month on Yugoslavia. Now 'Barbarossa' is even riskier. But

I know how we will compensate for the loss of time. Until now we have relied on military superiority: human, technical, strategic. Preparing for a defence by the Bolsheviks does not scare us. On the contrary, we wanted them to be focused on the border forces as much as possible – then we would have destroyed the Red Army in the first onslaught. But now to prepare well for the battle with our adversary may be too risky: we cannot get caught up in border battles, and then in a long pursuit of a battered but not broken enemy. The impact must not only be devastating, but also" – here a pregnant pause – "unexpected."

The Admiral and his deputy, not saying a word, leaned forward slightly. His face remained impenetrable, but the hand of the General involuntarily cupped his right ear – after a bad concussion he did not hear very well.

Standing up, the dictator looked down on them. "Yes, yes, gentlemen, you heard correctly. The strike must catch the enemy off guard. In this situation, the factor of surprise takes priority, is even crucial."

Coughing, the intelligence chief said quietly: "But it is completely impossible, my Führer. We have been preparing for the eastern campaign for several months already. On the Russian border, from the Baltic to the Black Seas, are five and a half million soldiers, thousands of planes and tanks. Troop movements of this scale have never happened before. We did not ourselves set the task to cover up our preparations from the NKVD. In any case, it would be unrealistic. How can there be a surprise?"

"I do not know!" The Reich Chancellor's face was stony, his crossed arms no longer trembled. "On this question I want an answer from you. And no later than twenty-four hours from now. The Abwehr was created to solve impossible tasks!"

"And if the task does not have a solution?"

The louder and stronger the Führer spoke, the softer and more muffled sounded the Admiral's voice. "Then I refuse to enact 'Barbarossa' ..." A spasm ran across the dictator's face. "I will not place the fate of the Reich on too weak of a card."

The Führer impulsively leaned over, put his hand on the Admiral's twisted shoulder straps. "But you will solve this problem for me, I know you will. I will choose the exact date of the strike only after you guarantee me a surprise. For a combat deployment the troops will need ten days. Hence, Z-Day is the day of your report plus ten days ... That's all, gentlemen. Go on, think."

The intelligence heads rose slowly. Glancing at their gloomy faces, the Reich Chancellor shrugged and condescendingly remarked: "I'll give you a clue. Target the Asians, everyone else is immaterial. And another thing. Without Prussian purity. I authorize any action, any. Only the result matters. So, in twenty-four hours you will give me a solution. Or others will find one." And the great dictator bent over his papers, making it clear that the meeting was over.

The Admiral and the General walked silently through a suite of pompous halls lined with granite, by blond Liebstandarte guards under the outspread wings of imperial eagles, crowned with giant bronze doors.

At the western entrance to the Reich Chancellery, on Vossstrasse, a black Opel waited – it was not very new and, unlike the neighbouring limousines, did not have a dazzling shine. The admiral did not like showy external effects.

The setting sun coloured the granite steps an even carmine. The leaders of the Abwehr descended on them in a strictly hierarchical order: the chief in front, followed at a respectful half-step by the Deputy, also grey-haired, lean, and restrained in his movements – a sort of shadow of his boss, except that much taller, but the shadows in the late afternoon made him longer than the original. However, dropping into his seat, separated from the driver's soundproof glass partition, the General ceased to follow the chain of command.

"How do you like that, Willy?" he said evilly, and tapped his fingers on his knee.

"Hmmm ..." the Admiral replied vaguely.

They were silent, one looking to the left – at the darkened windows of the British embassy, the second to the right – where immediately after the gloomy building of the Prussian Ministry of Culture the embassy of the USSR was located.

The limousine turned on Unter den Linden, where marble columns with eagles and flags stood instead of the famous, recently felled lime trees.

"And what do you say, Sepp? The machine is clean, I checked this morning, so you need not be cautious."

It did not take long to beg the General. He muttered: "A pig. A vulgar, narcissistic pig. Thank God, I have had to admire him less frequently than you."

"He is a pig, of course, a pig," the Admiral agreed, "but a genius. And, most importantly, damn lucky. In the last war we were busy with Serbia for four years, and he dealt with them in one week. Let's be realistic. After the revolution Germany turned into a pile of dung, and without such a hog we would not have gotten ourselves out of the muck."

The Deputy seemed to have agreed with this. In any case, his tone went from evil to peevish: "It would be better if we would have been stuck in Yugoslavia for a month or two. Then the question would no longer matter, and so it turns out neither one thing nor the other. From this new victory, the pig has only become more inflamed, believes in his star even more."

"And maybe it was indeed a lucky star?" the Admiral said philosophically.

"Maybe. But I am not an astrologer. I am a specialist in information and disinformation strategies. As well as a surgeon with a highly specialized profile."

The chief smiled, appreciating the metaphor. "Well, so, go about your business, Sepp, and trust the movement of the stars and in the Lord God."

The Opel had already left the Tirpitz Embankment, where the building of the High Command and the study of the chief of intelligence is located. A quarter of an hour later, the old comrades were sitting in comfortable chairs facing each other and drinking thick oriental coffee brewed by the Admiral's Algerian servant. On the lap of the Abwehr chief luxuriated his favourite dachshund, Sabina, in tightly knitted raspberry-coloured panties. She had started to be in heat, and Sabina's master took her home so as not to worry Sepp's dog.

The Admiral's study was the complete opposite of the marble hall, where the intelligence scouts took them to the Reich Chancellor. The tidy, modestly furnished room created a sense of tranquillity and domesticity. The photographs hanging on the walls (the former intelligence chief, and also a personal friend and host of General Franco) were similar to the portraits of relatives. Even the maps on the walls were not suggestive of geopolitics, but awakened the imagination, making one think about exotic seas and distant journeys – furthering the maritime form of the study, complete with a model of a cruiser on the desk.

There was one more unusual item on the desk, well-known throughout the central office – three bronze monkeys: one covered its mouth with its legs, the other its ears, the third its eyes. The Admiral stretched out, absently stroked the three of them on the head – he had developed this habit in moments that required particular concentration.

"In the Abwehr we believe that it is a symbol of intelligence: to know how to look, to know how to listen, and to know when we should keep quiet," said the General. "But, in my opinion, a good intelligence scout should always keep his eyes and ears open, and use his mouth to fool the enemy's brain."

"Of course." The Admiral scratched Sabine's long, velvet ear – the dachshund squinted like a cat. "My monkey is not a symbol of intelligence. It is a reminder to myself about the commandments of Buddhism, without which it is impossible to achieve enlightenment: do no evil, hear no evil, speak no evil."

The Deputy chuckled: "Sorry, Willy, but being righteous is unlike you. Not that this is the same with your occupation."

The chief smiled. "I am not so presumptuous as to consider myself a warrior for Good. I've been living in the world for a long time, but have never seen how Good enters into combat against Evil. Every time one Evil fights another Evil. Therefore, my friend, I have never had a particular choice. But I am proud that I have always been on the side of the Lesser Evil. Anyway, I sincerely believe it, and continue to believe it now ..."

The host spoke slowly, measuredly, and the General lazily nodded, but both thought about something else, and that finally became clear when the Admiral, without any transition and without changing the tone, suddenly said:

"What, eh? 'I will give up on Operation Barbarossa.' He will not give up on a damn thing, he will just appoint other performers for you and me twenty-four hours later. And perhaps we should let him appoint them?" The General listened attentively, but for now said nothing.

"No, it is not necessary," the Admiral himself said. "And the point is not that such a turn of events is fraught with serious personal troubles for you and me. The trouble lies elsewhere: nobody except us can solve the riddle. Others would make up some nonsense and the pig would swallow it because he cannot and does not want to retreat. Them instead of a short war, we get a long one, which is 100 times worse. It is as the sage says: 'Trouble is better than misfortune and misfortune is better than catastrophe.' Again, I find myself on the side of the Lesser Evil, as opposed to the Greater Evil."

The Deputy grunted. "Willy, you're too fond of philosophizing. It is time to formulate the conditions of the problem."

"Well, then, let's." The Admiral gently spread out his little hands. "We need to ensure that the Russians, as they say in their own proverb, see the trees, but do not realize that it is a dark forest where toothy wolves hide."

"The proverb does not sound quite right, but it does not matter."

"And if it does not matter, do not interrupt me," the chief snapped.

The skirmish, however, was not serious. The Admiral continued: "So, the Russians see 200 divisions ready to attack, but they must be firmly convinced that Germany would not attack them." He shrugged eloquently.

The Deputy continued: "Add to that the fact that Soviet intelligence probably already got wind of the existence of the plan 'Barbarossa,' about which they daily receive alarming information from a hundred different sources. As you know, the NKVD has actively restored its German operations and in doing so, my old friend, the enemy has become very, very dangerous."

"The more difficult the obstacle, the less stigma on failure," the Admiral quoted another piece of eastern wisdom. "Let's start with the obvious. Point one: diplomacy. Ribbentrop should intensify the secret talks with Molotov about a strategic alliance between Germany, the Soviet Union and Japan. As a first step the Japanese should sign a neutrality pact with the Bolsheviks. The department 'Ausland' will supervise the diplomats. Point two: the paper tiger ..."

"As for me, I'm tired of your oriental flowery," the General complained. "What's a tiger?"

"England. In public speeches and especially in closed meetings the Führer must simulate a paranoid fear of unconquered Albion. This two-hoofed role will work out great. The General Staff will plan an urgent thrust through Turkey to Iran and the Middle East, the Suez Canal, to cut the umbilical cord connecting London with its major colonies. Work will take place in secrecy, but there will be carefully planned leaks. The operation division of the Abwehr-1 will oversee it. Furthermore. We will send English and Arabic translators to each military unit in Army Groups 'North,' 'Centre,' and 'South.' This will take the Abwehrstelle border districts. Next. We will make a mass transfer of agents to Iran through Soviet territory. They will provide cover for the group 'Ost.' With point two everything seems to be, go to step three, 'Wolf! Wolf!'

"Sorry, Sepp," the Admiral raised his hand. "I forgot, you do not like allegories. I mean the parable about the prankster who cried 'Wolf! Wolf!' and eventually everyone stopped believing him. There will be several false alarms: at first the Russians will receive information that we, despite the Yugoslav bother, will still strike on 15 May; then that the war will start on the 20th; then that it will start on 1 June. We will carry out this intelligence injection through Soviet agents known to us in order to discredit them in Moscow's eyes. I will personally lead this intelligence operation. Well, what do you think?"

"As a side dish it's not bad," admitted the General, looking away and blinking quickly. "But what is mashed potatoes and sauerkraut without a good piece of meat?"

"I agree. For success it needs a final touch, the exact flourish deposited in a properly designed moment. And only then, if successful, this action can be assigned the exact number and time of occurrence. And in case of failure – everything must be cancelled ..." The Admiral squinted, looking into the face of his deputy, who seemed to him to be not really listening. "Aha. By the strong flicker I see that your brain has already caught on. Come on, come on."

"You know, Willy, the pig, is indeed brilliant." The General rubbed his chin intently. "He actually uttered the keyword himself. Listen."

The two inclined towards each other, and the General spoke very quickly, barely keeping up with his thoughts. Because of the rush, he swallowed words and entire chunks of sentences, but the Admiral grasped on the fly, nodding vigorously. The dachshund restlessly whirled her head, barked, and jumped down to the floor.

The Chief and the Deputy constantly interrupted and re-interrupted each other, but this did not interfere with the course of the discussion. Now they were in their element and above all, perhaps, reminiscent of two jazz musicians in the midst of a jam session.

If some stranger overheard this chaotic conversation, it is unlikely that they would have understood it.

"The role of personality in history – " one threw a cue.

"Dry theory, my friend – " a knowing nod to the second.

"How do I make the trees not see the forest? It's very simple!" exclaimed the General.

"And there is nothing to be sprayed," echoed the Admiral to him. "And this intelligence, counter-intelligence, the NKVD, NKGB, 'communications service' – damn leg break ... A waste of time!"

After a quarter of an hour talking in an obscure way like this, the two sat back contentedly and puffed cigars.

"Well, there is the concept." The Admiral puffed bluish smoke. "And not bad."

The General was more categorical: "The only one possible."

"The likelihood of success?"

Thinking, the Deputy said: "Fifty per cent."

"Well, not so little. Our lucky pig has gotten used to acting on less. I hope you know, Sepp, that in case of loss we will have to pay with our own skin?"

"Is there a time in our profession when anything was different?" The General casually shrugged. "Only in the old days, before you put one bullet in a gun for yourself, and now you are just hung on a meat hook. In fact, there is little difference."

Both burst out laughing, for the mood of the old friends was excellent. The Admiral extinguished his cigar. "Well good. And who? It all depends on the performer. He must be a first-class agent, or fifty per cent may not be possible. What's your opinion?"

"'Wasser,'" the General said with certainty. It was evident that he had already thought about the issue.

The intelligence chief's face changed. He coughed once, then twice. He hesitated, choosing the right words. "Sepp, buddy, you know ...

When caught on live bait, the chances of the latter, to put it mildly, are small. Especially if the bait is swallowed safely. Right, that's too much. You're not a fanatic."

The creases on the Deputy's dry face sharpened. "I'm not a fanatic, but I respect his craft. And I am always ready to pay the bill with all that I have. Including with my life. I assure you, 'Wasser' is cut from the same cloth. So much for the emotions. And now for the case. I have been preparing agent 'Wasser' to do something like this for many years. 'Wasser' is ideal for the task in all respects – his personal qualities, his training, and according to legend. I say this objectively. Let's put the question: Who, if not 'Wasser'"?

They had a long look at each other. The General's face looked quite impassive, as the Admiral was clearly excited. "You're right, Sepp," he said in the end, and cleared his throat again. "You're the best of the best. And 'Wasser' is the best choice. Perhaps, we can count not on fifty per cent, but even sixty."

Appendix 4
Anatolii Brusnikin, *The Ninth Saviour* (*Deviatnyi Spas*; Moscow: Astrel', 2011), 5–37

Translated by YEKATERINA SEVERTS, with the permission of GRIGORII CHKHARTISHVILI[13]

Chapter 1

Of the Numerical Mysteries

On the flute I'll start my wistful verses,
As I gaze at Russia across faraway lands.
For this day it pleases me much
To meditate upon all her goodness.

Vasilii Trediakovskii

At the end of the seventeenth century, the country named Moscovia possessed a territory almost as large as present-day Russia but twenty times less populated. Its people clustered along the river banks and scanty highways, while the dense forests and desolate steppes occupied the rest of the space.

The subjects of this vast state ate poorly, lived in ignorance, and died early. At the same time, they were satisfied with what little they had and, without a second thought, believed in the Eternal Life. Although their faith did not turn their earthly life into a paragon of morality, at least it kept them from sinking into a beastly state, eased their suffering, and offered them Hope.

The edifice of their state, not all too harmonious but timbered soundly from ancient logs, lacked in comfort and terrified the foreigners with the austerity of its unpainted walls and indifference towards the outward prettiness; yet the skill and common sense showed through its squat outbuildings, rugged buttresses, and warily narrow windows. The corners and beams were held together by braces without a single nail; the roof darkened but did not cave in, and the golden dome shone above, and on the cross perched Alkonost, the white bird of joy.

As ordained by nature, the measure of the evil and the good in Rus was about the same. Following its simplistic instincts, the former ravaged and destroyed, spurred the history forwards; and the latter suffered, healed, and loved. But the people were still one, still undivided into two unequal halves that would be dissimilar in thought, clothing, and even manner of speaking. The rich were rich, and the poor were poor, yet they were the same Russian people, able to understand each other without unnecessary words, for they were united through the common religious and national sentiment.

The living proof of their natural unity could be observed on the last summer evening of *anno mundi* 7197, in the estate of the landowner Larion Nikitin, in Moscow vicinity, where three grubby boys were rolling in the dust – the master's offspring Mit'ka, the priest's son Aleshka, and Il'ia the peasant.

In those days, the New Year in Rus was reckoned starting with 1 September. Thus today the summer was nearing its end in more than one sense, except that our ancestors placed more value in the approach of autumn than in the year's change: wheat was harvested in autumn, which affected everyone, while few cared about the time which had passed since the world's creation.

As for the young friends, they couldn't care less about the New Year. Perhaps, Mitia and Alesha, after scratching their heads, would be able to recall what year was coming, but Il'ia, who had never studied bookish wisdom, kept his head free from such trifles. Needless to say, none of this trio had any notion that in the foreign reckoning, *anno domini*, today was 31 August 1689.

The brats, in the meantime, were engaged in a no-nonsense rough and tumble. Arms, legs, and teeth were put to good use; hair was ripped; and sniffling was loud. They didn't fight in malice but for the utmost or, as we would say now, principal cause. An argument arose as to which beast was the strongest of them all.

The fair-skinned and dark-haired, always earnest Mit'ka Larionov declared with an air of superiority that the king of all beasts was the unicorn. Recently, in a book, he had seen the marvellous creature, a long horn for its nose, and was charmed by the proud stature of this foreign habitant.

A freckled, red-head Aleshka did not see the picture and waived the unicorn aside as a tall tale, touting his own winner, a serpent. To this he added an insult: "An adder will sting your horned fool in his leg just once, and that would be it for him, he'll tumble hooves up."

The disputants sulked but hesitated to grapple. They wanted to see whose side the meticulous Il'ia would take. The peasant's son was thick-set, unhurried, and didn't use his words lightly.

"Whoa there, the thing is, why hurry? Let's put our heads together," he drawled his catchphrase, lowered his large head, and knitted his pale brows.

He thought and thought, then said with conviction – a bear. Never in his life had Il'ia seen a unicorn, and as for hearsay, he put no faith in it. Neither did he respect the adders who grovelled on their bellies, trying to sting on the sly. Now a bear is a different creature entirely. Last year Il'ia saw for himself how a bruin broke a birch tree. He scratched his mighty back on it, and it went crunch – and in half!

And so it began. Each of the three firmly held his own because, despite their differences, the boys had one thing in common – their stubbornness.

When in a passion, Mitia blanched. Alesha would mock and taunt his opponents. Il'ia kept a resolute silence.

At first the gentry son offered to fetch the book and show the unicorn, so that the fools would see just how magnificent and noble this animal was.

"I've seen the picture," Alesha lied. "Looked like a one-horned goat to me."

All the more reason for the peasant boy who mistrusted books. You never know what those clerks and other learned folks draw and scribble. If all their paperwork were simply burned, how much easier would it be for the people. There'd be no taxes, no levies, and no misery of serfdom.

He was a fortunate one, this Il'ia. As opposed to the other two, he had never been taught anything, never tortured with psalms and arithmetic. Mitia and Alesha envied him quite a bit. First of all, the peasant son led a carefree life. He could do whatever he wanted. Secondly, his Pa wound up dead, so there was no one to give him a whipping. He had a Ma, though, but she would always caress him and slip him a tasty morsel.

The lord's son and the priest's son, on the other hand, grew up with a father but motherless.

Not only had the disputants been friends from the cradle, they were also milk brothers. Mitia's mother died in labour, and Alesha's was sickly, tight in the teats, and unable to suckle her starveling. The three babes were born almost within one week, and the peasant wife had plenty of milk for all. It was so thick and nurturing that even the feeble priest's son, whom the father hastened to baptize on the first day, lest he die a heathen, surprised everyone by staying alive.

While Mitia and Alesha were quarrelling so much they started grabbing the other's shirtfront, Il'ia kept thinking.

"Whoa there, the thing is," he said finally, and at once the priest's son released the nobleman's embroidered collar, while Mit'ka stopped crumbling his adversary's canvas tunic. "What does your unicorn use for fighting?"

"His horn. It's a lance and a sword, all at once!"

"Here you go, then."

Ilya picked up a gnarly stick from the ground and put it to Mit'ka's nose.

"As for you, Alesha the Flea, the thing is, you must fall on your belly and grovel," the wise judge ordered the priest's son. "You can bite, you can fling your tail, but keep your hands down. If you manage to sting me or him, you win."

He himself spread his arms apart, like a bear, and slumped.

And so began the free-for-all. Il'ia was the strongest, with firm fists, yet unwieldy. Aleshka twisted and writhed – no catching this one – but the gentry's son fought in boots, and the peasant – in bast shoes. Try biting through that without getting up. Mitia with his stupid stick had it the hardest but refused to give in.

The friends raised the dust cloud almost to the sky and fought for victory with abandon, each after his own manner. Such brawls and squabbles were to them a daily occasion. But little did they know this game was destined to be their last.

Meanwhile in the estate's main house, which, in accordance with an ancient custom, was called *terem*, Larion Mikhailovich Nikitin was receiving his guest, Father Vikentii, an old friend and rector of the village church who happened to be a parent to the freckled Alesha and a god-father to Mit'ka; he also schooled both boys in book learning and spiritual wisdom.

The table was not set for a holiday because, as we have mentioned, the New Year was not deemed an important event; neither was it set in a mundane style, but rather for receiving. Apart from the regular country victuals, such as pies, cold chicken and goose, pears, apples, and berry decoctions, the linen tablecloth (used for moderate formality, unlike the damask) featured outlandish treats: raisins and candied fruit in a rather small *kovsh*, and *romanea*, and finally, red French wine, in a pot-bellied bottle of thick glass.

Although the priest greatly favoured the German jams, and the sweet wine as well, the refreshments remained untouched. The conversation at the table was far too uneasy.

The host, a stalwart man with large eyes and a well-groomed dark-blond beard, spoke little and mostly gave ear, while stroking a downward crease on his youthful forehead. The priest, gaunt and choking on a dry cough, was the narrator. Becoming agitated in the particularly dramatic spots, which were frequent, he would make the sign of the cross.

The subject was the pilgrimage, from which Father Vikentii had just returned.

He would pay a visit to the Trinity Lavra of St. Sergius no less than twice a year, to venerate the holy relics and order a memorial service for his own deceased wife and the spouse of Larion Mikhailovich. He would light two large candles: a pound in weight for the priest's wife, and half a *pood*, kindling through the night – for the noble lady. Nikitin covered all expenses for the candles and the journey himself.

This time, the pilgrim wanted to pay out of pocket for another large candle, before the icon Assuage My Sorrows, so that the Mother of God would not neglect the youth Alesha. Why this didn't work out, we will reveal later; but for now it suffices to say that for two months in a row the priest had been spitting blood. This signified his earthly days were numbered, and all Father Vikentii could care about was finding a situation for his son, who would be left an orphan. He hadn't told anyone of his misfortune, never shared his fears for his son. Even now he was telling his friend and benefactor not of his own miserable fate but about the great, pivotal events he chanced to witness on his way back from the pilgrimage.

Father Vikentii was a man of great scholarship, worthy to be a bishop, not a lowly parish priest. While in his younger years, he mastered to perfection not only Latin and Greek but the whole of the logic and rhetorical science, which held the following principle: the more important the discourse, the slower and more graceful it ought to be crafted. Therefore the speaker strung his words gradually, with a far-reaching goal in mind, which was to sink into the listener's mind all on its own, free of any discernible compulsion.

He did not wish to plead for his son directly. Not because of pride, a sin for a servant of God, but as to endow the giver with the pleasure of showing magnanimity. For if a man gives something on his own accord, without anyone begging him for a service, his contribution becomes more precious and more salutary for his soul.

Larion Mikhailovich was kind and merciful, the priest knew very well. After all, they had been friends for almost twenty years.

Once upon a time, in the reign of the young, dearly departed Tsar Fyodor Alekseevich, they both resided in Moscow. First Nikitin had been waiting for a position at the royal court, then received it and served as the tsar's *stol'nik*. Father Vikentii was a reader at the Patriarchal Metochion.

The nobleman was the first to leave the capital: he grieved for his departed spouse and languished among the throngs of courtiers.

The priest's wife, after delivering Alesha, ailed for a year before abandoning her husband and son for the sake of the Life Eternal.

Anyone who knew Vikentii perceived in this event the finger of God: fate itself was commanding the widower to take monastic vows. He would have gone far and risen high, no doubt about it. But the young priest did not want to retire from the world in name alone, not with all his soul. As for retiring with all his soul, he could not do so, what with feeling responsible for his little son.

At that time, Larion Mikhailovich rendered him the first inestimable service: he invited Vikentii to his village, Anikeevo, to take charge of a parish. Now, according to the Canons, a widowed priest, unless he took the vows, was banned from priesthood. But then, if here in Rus things were done in accordance to the canonical and not the human laws, what sort of life would it be? For every law there is a concession, for every rule an exception. The living soul holds more value than a letter, and man's destiny will not fit into every ordinance. So a special case was made for Father Vikentii, because the landowner was his friend, the bishop – a schoolfellow from Lavra – and the churchwarden a cousin-in-law. And this exception was much to everyone's benefit.

Nikitin built for the priest not only a fine log house, but also a new church of Martha and Mary, titled in memory of their most beloved wives, for one of the dear departed was Mary and the other one was Martha. Vikentii was provided with board and lodging, and even received a stipend which he spent entirely on books. Once he had started to cough blood, however, he repented of his profligacy: he should have been saving for a rainy day. But, of course, all is in God's hands. He did not fear the imminent death. Deep in his soul, he was even rejoicing, sinful as it was. For all these years he had pined for his wife, and now, it seemed, their meeting was nigh at hand. But he did worry about his son.

The full arc of his narration, the priest had thought through while travelling back. As the skilful rhetoricians of the past instructed, it was more effective to start with a deed instead of words, which would astound the listeners and make them harken to the speaker with twice the attention.

Therefore, as a start, the guest silently placed before Nikitin the candle money, unspent. After waiting through the surprised exclamations and unavoidable inquiries, he replied concisely, meaningfully, that he was never admitted into the Lavra. It was surrounded with pickets and tents, *strel'tsy* and soldiers in great numbers, and cannons loomed on the monastery walls, between the merlons. No, the pilgrims were not allowed anywhere near. The youngest Tsar Peter Alekseevich had encamped in the stronghold, together with his closest boyars who backed the Naryshkins, his mother's kinfolk.

The supporters of the regent Princess Sofia Alekseevna and the eldest Tsar Ivan Alekseevich, along with their relations the Miloslavskiis, had remained in Moscow. Before you know it, a strife may break out, even worse than in the year hundred and nine, seven years prior, when for months the country was being ripped into parts.

The companions, both the landlord and the priest, were provincials but not exactly country bumpkins. They knew a thing or two about state affairs, they had seen the Naryshkins and Miloslavskiis from up close, and as for Sofia, they remembered her while still a maiden, although each judged her differently.

Larion Mikhailovich, a man of old-fashioned views, disapproved that Rus was ruled over by a wench, albeit of royal blood. Such disgrace had never been seen in our land!

The priest, on the contrary, praised Sofia's rule, in reference to historical precedents – the wise and pious Princess Olga or Anna Yaroslavna, the Queen of France. Obviously, Father Vikentii condemned her for not heeding her maidenhood, for playing Jezebel with Vasilii Golitsyn, but he was willing to cut her some slack, because Eve's nature was well-known. May God be Sofia's sole judge. But for signing the eternal peace treaty with Poland, for bringing back Kiev, for showing what's what to the Crimean Tatars, for dispatching an embassy to the far-away Cathay – for all these she deserved honour and praise. A tenacious woman, strong, astute. She made the former Romanovs look like plucked chickens, judged the sagacious priest, who divined that the tsars, her younger brothers, could kiss goodbye to the crown. As long as Sofia lived, she would hold on to the helm of the state.

But today, still shaken by what he had seen, the priest changed his tune. Preparing a transition from *introductio* to *narratio*, being the principal part of the oration, Father Vikentii sighed, crossed himself, and spoke gravely:

"Verily, as thou knowest, churls are much afeared of this assault. They are gast of the dire wroth that wilt befall them. In my stead, I do lift up my hope unto thee, O Lord, and thy tender mercies!"

We will not trouble the reader with the word-for-word reproduction of the learned clergyman's speech. Our ancestors did not speak as we do now, but to them their language didn't seem either impenetrable or heavy-handed. Let's sacrifice, then, the historical verisimilitude for the sake of clarity. And thus, Father Vikentii said:

"Alas, the people have much to fear from this assault. They dread a terrible calamity may befall them. As for me, all I can do is place my faith in Lord's mercy! ... But if the brother and sister do not come to terms, the country may split into pieces, like in the Time of Troubles."

"Haven't you always said Sofia will get the best of the Naryshkins?" reminded Larion Mikhailovich.

"I did, but it seems I was mistaken..."

"How so? Tell me all!"

And the priest began to tell what he had seen with his own eyes, or heard from others, or deduced after the fact.

As he didn't gain entrance into the Lavra, on the way back he stopped in the royal village Vozdvizhenskoe, where his old acquaintance, Father Ambrose, served at the tsar's travelling palace. It so happened that precisely at the same time, from the Moscow via Troitsky Highway, Sofia's procession rode into the village, pompously, with many carriages, with retainers and mounted guards from the Stemyanny regiment. The regent decided to come to the Lavra in person and expostulate her obstinate brother. She took with her, in a special golden carriage, under an armed guard, the sacred royal icon the Ninth Saviour, which had hitherto remained solely in the household church at the palace. As the quick-witted priest surmised, bringing the icon was her chief design. Peter will be obliged to bend his knee before the Ninth Saviour. If the Saviour is in your hands, God is behind your back – everyone knows it.

Sofia was only ten *versts* away from the Lavra, when it came upon a court lady to go into labour. Prematurely, one must think, or else who'd let the fool travel so far into her pregnancy? This way or the other, Sofia ordered the travelling palace to be cleared of all people. Incense was burnt in the biggest chamber, water boiled, sheets and towels brought in. Until the baby arrived, said the princess, she wasn't going anywhere. A bad omen.

It was then that Father Vikentii, staying at his friend's house where the news and gossip reached with the shortest lag, had his first moment of doubt. Knowing Sofia, she would not slow down the whole business over some omen. She lacked in confidence, that's what it was all about.

"She let the time slip away, so the Naryshkins had a chance to come around," he said apprehensively. "In the evening, the boyar Troekurov came riding from the Lavra, by Peter's command. They didn't let the rider into the palace, so he stood there on the porch, hollering, yelling for the princess as though she was a common wench. This is Sofia we are talking about! Her single glance is enough to give generals a fainting spell!"

Nikitin shook his head at such an impudence. He wouldn't raise his voice at any woman, least of all at the royalty. In doing so, a man of honour disgraces himself.

"...Well, after a while, she walked out to him. She looked imposing and stout, and was leaning on a *stol'nik*. You know, Larion, how many times I have seen Sofia Alekseevna? Recall how she roared at that rabid dissenter, Nikita Pustosviat, in front of all boyars and bishops. She sounded like the Tsar Cannon itself, not merely a maiden. But this time, I barely recognized her. Her eyes looked dull, her face bloated, and oh, how pale she was! Troekurov read to her Peter's decree: I refuse to talk to you, go back whence you came, or else we'll treat you discourteously. She wanted to say something, but couldn't. She slumped in the *stol'nik*'s arms, and they carried her in unconscious."

"She must be ill," realized the landlord.

"Barely alive," Father Vikentii crossed himself. "When I saw her in such a state, it dawned on me why she didn't stir in Kremlin for so many days, while the Naryshkins dug in their heels. She must be suffering from a malady. Deadly, perhaps. So that's how things stand. And without Sofia's backing, what would become of the Miloslavskiis? Fie!"

"That's right," Nikitin agreed. He looked concerned, as was expected of a man who cared about his country's fate. Still, he had not arrived at the conclusion which the priest was steering towards. A clearer explanation was required.

But Father Vikentii made no haste, relying heavily on logic and rhetoric.

"It all happened yesterday, and I spent the night at the Ambrose's. What if Sofia came around by morning? As they said, the lady gave birth successfully, and for the princess, this was an auspicious omen. But nothing of the kind!" the priest waved his hand. "In the morning, her retinue was on their toes. They harnessed the horses and turned back to Moscow, like whipped dogs. It was all over for Sofia. Meanwhile, the delegates from *strel'tsy* regiments flocked in crowds to the Lavra, to swear fealty to Peter ..."

The perplexed Larion Mikhailovich shrugged.

"But why did Sofia turn back? It's not like her. Ailing or not, what difference does it make? She was only ten *versts* away!"

The priest had an answer ready. All the way home he was racking his brain and apparently solved the mystery.

"I believe, the Ninth Saviour was the cause," he said quietly and, with reverence, stroked the cross hanging from his neck. "It was a vicious deed, to disturb the holy icon in pursuit of worldly ambition. The miraculous icon was granted to the Romanovs for the protection of the motherland, not for their family squabbles. And so the Saviour punished the wicked regent, sent down a malady, sapped all her strength. I can think of no other reason ..."

Father Vikentii was bringing the conversation to a proper *conclusio*, and to do so he broke off for a short but pregnant pause.

But Larion, unfamiliar with rhetorical finesse, jumped in with a question:

"Tell me, Father, why do they call the icon the Ninth Saviour? I've also heard it named Filaret's Saviour. You've been to the tsar's house church many a time. Surely you must have seen this most glorious icon?"

"Never. Common mortals are not allowed to gaze upon it, only the royals and the patriarch, and only on solemn occasions. For the rest of the time, the Saviour remains hidden from view."

"How so?"

"Allow me to explain."

The priest wasn't upset their talk took a sharp turn aside. On the contrary, he felt relief. He was worried about how this conversation might end and delighted in the respite.

"As you well know, His Grace Filaret, the Patriarch of Moscow and noble father to the first Romanov, anguished long in Polish captivity. He was the head of the boyar embassy that came to the Poles to sign a peace treaty. But they received him ignobly and placed him in prison, where he was tormented and humiliated. Worse still, they took away his Orthodox icons and put a despicable papist Madonna on the wall – here, pray to that! As the old books tell us, Filaret was the first among the clergy, yet he was unsteady in spirit and a sinner in his former life. While still in the world, he was the tsar's closest boyar and kinsman but also a first-rate Moscow fop and ladies' man. Even later, when he was disgraced and took the vows, he sinned greatly against the truth. False Dmitrii himself bestowed on him the patriarchal cowl, and he wanted to pass the crown to the Polish Prince Sigismund, and many other shameful things. But when he advanced in years, he gave up wantonness, or maybe the Lord had chosen him for the great cause. In any case, in Polish prison, Filaret showed an uncrushable will and amazed his gaolers. Only at night, alone in his cell, would the patriarch weep bitterly and pray feebly to the empty wall. Without an icon, where was he to seek spiritual strength? In the meantime, his captors contrived to remove him from Lithuania to Poland, further away from the Russian border. Until one night was marked by a significant occurrence. It was on 9 May 7119, or 1611 by Polish reckoning ... Commit these dates to your memory, Larion," the narrator paused to lift a finger significantly. "That night, a stranger was admitted into the house where Filaret was kept in custody. The patriarch thought the guards had let him in, but the Polish guards swore they never opened the doors, nor did they lay eyes on a stranger."

The landlord leaned forwards. His eyes were open wide, and a joyous, child-like smile graced his face; he knew a story of a divine miracle was coming next, and his heart was ready to melt.

"So what did the elder say to the patriarch?"

"Why, nothing. He glanced at Filaret lying in his bed, blessed him with a cross, and departed in silence. The patriarch took it for a dream, but in the morning he saw on the table a flat wooden box with doors like shutters. He opened them and froze in place, dazzled with miraculous light."

"What lay hidden in the box?"

"The image of our Saviour. They say, the icon's eyes radiate light, that's why it is also named 'The Saviour with Bright Eyes.' Or sometimes 'The Window Icon.' The shutters that conceal the icon have nothing to do with it – rather, it is the window through which a Russian sovereign may see the Almighty and receive divine succour. When the tsar prays to the Saviour on a regular day, which is called a Minor or Everyday Prayer, the shutters remain closed. But when a disaster is approaching – be it a war, or pestilence, or famine – his Royal Majesty opens the shutters with reverence and starts the Great Prayer, mightier than anything else in the world. That's how powerful the icon is!" Father Vikentii exclaimed, tears in his eyes. "Were it to be lost, the Russian tsar would no longer be the God's chosen one. He'll be just another potentate, like those abroad, whom the rabble may depose and execute – that's what they did to King Carolus in England. And the piety, humility, and wisdom would vanish from Rus – only the fiendish unease and irreverence will remain! As long as the Romanovs keep the icon, neither themselves, nor our land have a cause for fear. But the shameless Sofia took it into her head to remove the icon and use it against her brother! What do you think she was hoping for, that sinful woman? Why, any Romanov would bow down before the royal who holds the icon!"

"And what if the patriarch possesses the icon?"

"His power is not of the same kind. A patriarch, you know, may reach his station through cunning schemes and intrigues. But only those with royal blood in their veins, although they may be men or women, are endowed with special grace. If this weren't true, what use would be the tsars, anyway? And who are the Romanovs without the icon? Do you think Filaret would put his weak son on the throne, if the Ninth Saviour wasn't helping? And how would Mikhail, and Aleksei, and Fedor keep the Monomakh's Cap on their frail heads, but for the Saviour with Bright Eyes?"

The landlord pondered this and could raise no objection.

"All right, I see why it is called the Saviour with Bright Eyes or Filaret's Saviour. The Window Icon also makes sense. But why the Ninth?"

The priest lowered his voice in a mysterious manner. This part of the legend, which for him was an undeniable truth, he approached with the greatest trepidation.

"I will relate to you now what is known to very few. Father Varsonifii, the confessor of the late Tsar Aleksei Mikhailovich, told me this tale. Aleksei Mikhailovich heard it from his father, who in turn heard it from Patriarch Filaret himself ... That same night, when Filaret saw the elder, in waking life or in a vision, the elder appeared before him again, this time definitely in a dream. Instead of tatters, he was dressed in a shining garment and spake thusly: 'Hark unto me, the father of the tsars, and remember. That which was given four times nine will disappear twice nine, but fear thrice eight and twice eight.'

"When he awakened, the patriarch recalled clearly those wondrous words but took them for a fanciful dream. The words made no sense to him, and as for being the father of the tsars, the thought hadn't even crossed his mind. But beholding the icon, which appeared out of nowhere, he also recorded the vague prophecy, word by word. Later, when, through the divine providence, he became the father of the new monarch and the founder of a dynasty, he would puzzle over the terrible mystery contained in the prophecy. Clearly, 'that which was given' referred to the Saviour. But why 'four times nine?' Be it as it may, the icon received its new name: at first it was called 'The Four Times Ninth Saviour,' then simply 'The Ninth Saviour.'"

"And the mystery remained unsolved?" asked the distressed Nikitin, who was listening with bated breath.

"It's no accident Father Varsonifii told me about Filaret's dream. He knew I was keen, of scholarly disposition and ambition. What if I applied my mind to the secret? And in truth, I kept thinking about those nines and eights night and day. I dreamt of solving the parable and distinguishing myself before the tsar and patriarch," Father Vikentii smiled dolefully. "But to a cow that butts, God gives short horns. And when my horns grew long, on the account of my great sorrow, I was too tired to butt ... Here, in this village, with peace of mind and plentiful leisure, I finally deciphered the prophecy. Not all of it, as I ran out of time, but at least a portion."

"Indeed?!"

"Or so it seems to me. You be the judge, as you are the first to hear it."

From the cassock's wide sleeve, serving him as a pocket, the priest produced a tiny slate pencil and a scroll of grey paper on which he habitually took down the thoughts that crossed his mind. Like any learned man, he nurtured a lifelong dream, now unattainable, of writing in his wise, venerable years an account of his life and ideas. Larion

Mikhailovich knew of his plan and stared at the scroll inquisitively. But instead of reading, the priest intended to write.

He wrote down the numbers: first 7119, then 1611, not in the old-fashioned Cyrillic figures but in Arabic numerals which Moscow scribes had long used for simplicity's sake.

"This is the year when the Romanovs received the icon, in Russian and Western reckoning. Go ahead, add up the numbers. See here? Seven and one, and one, and nine – twice nine. And one, six, one, and one – the same. The icon was revealed on 9 May, that is, on the ninth day of the ninth month, Russian style. This is why the Savior is 'four times ninth' however you look at it – *anno domini, anno mundi*, from the beginning of the year, and from the beginning of the month."

"Yes, that's exactly how it looks! What's the special meaning behind these nines?"

"Nine is the greatest of numbers, the highest of them all. Not to mention it is thrice blessed because it contains three times the Trinity."

Larion was delighted.

"How sage and far-seeing you are, Father! Truly, you are without an equal. Tsars themselves scratched their heads and got nowhere, but you figured it out! Let's write a letter to the palace, or perhaps to the patriarch. You are sure to receive great honour and reward!"

"If only I solved the future prophecy. But I lack foresight," the priest sighed. "Even if I guessed correctly, 'that which was given four times nine' refers to the past, so what use would it be to the tsars? Had I known what 'twice nine' stands for or why they should fear 'thrice eight and twice eight,' that's when Filaret's descendants would have rewarded me handsomely ... But I am short on time," he concluded, too softly for the landlord to hear.

Nikitin gave an inquiring look to the papers, on which Father Vikentii scribbled with a slate two more numbers: 7197 and 1689.

"There is, perhaps, a possibility," the priest shook his head with uncertainty. "Presently *anno mundi* 7197 is coming to an end, and, in summation, it would be twenty-four, or thrice eight. If we count from the birth of Christ, we'll end up with one, six, eight, and nine, or thrice eight."

The host counted for himself and gasped.

"Right you are! So what do you think it signifies?"

"God alone knows. But my lowly mind dares to think that this year will be dangerous for the Romanovs, and somehow the danger is linked to the Ninth Saviour. Sofia shouldn't have moved it from its rightful place ... That's as far as I can divine."

"Great and mysterious are the ways of the Lord," drawled out the host. "Far beyond our mortal comprehension."

The priest was seized with a bout of coughing. Covering his lips with a sleeve, he wiped them and looked stern.

The rough fabric was showing dark spots, and upon inspecting them, Father Vikentii decided to stop beating about the bush and get down to business. But, as it happens with the consumptives, he suddenly felt an extreme fatigue.

"Here's what I'm getting at, Larion," said the priest, clearing his throat. "The power is about to change. Before long, Sofia will be done for, and the young tsars will take the reign. As you know, Ivan, the elder one, is feeble-minded. What this means is that Peter and the Naryshkins will run things, so you should make haste and ingratiate your son with the new ruler. Peter eagerly accepts young men of breeding into his Toy Army. Up till now, few noble families wanted to send their sons to his village, Preobrazhenskoe. But come tomorrow, they will bolt for it. So make arrangements, Larion Mikhailovich, and take Dmitrii to Moscow today. Later you will thank me for this piece of advice."

Nikitin was startled.

"What are you talking about? My Mitia is far too young. He is not even twelve!"

"But he looks older. You can report him as fifteen years of age. Think about your son, Larion. He needs to live his life and serve his tsar. Loiter today, and you will clip his wings. But if you hurry and surrender him there on time, a wide road will open up before him."

The master of Anikeevo was not particularly sharp, but neither was he foolish, so after some deliberation he saw the true value of the priest's counsel. The change of power ushers in new opportunities for some, while others it may lead into trouble. The country will be shaken from top to bottom. As they say, a new broom sweeps clean, and when it starts sweeping, dust will fly. The closer to the court, the safer you will be. Otherwise, you have only yourself to blame.

At once Larion Mikhailovich lost interest in the cryptic numerology. As a man slow in conversation, he was quick to act once he made up his mind.

"If that's how the future may be, we must hurry," he said, getting up. "I'll order the horses and prepare a sweetener for the royal scribes, and then we'll be ready to go. We should reach the palace by morning. What about you, Father? How may I thank you for your precious guidance?"

Here's the result of rhetoric for you, rejoiced the priest in his thought. It takes you wherever you need to go, as promised. No need to plead.

"I know you will want nothing for yourself," the host insisted. "But how about your son? Tell me, don't be shy."

The landlord was not as simple-minded, after all. He must have guessed the priest's secret desire or felt it deep within his heart.

"My Alesha needs an education," spoke Father Vikentii in a trembling voice. "There is a fine school in Moscow, known as the Greek Latin Academy ... Except the tuition is high. Forty rubles per year, and this without the cost of clothing, of paper and quills. I could never afford it on my priestly income ..."

"Especially when I'm gone," he added to himself.

"I was hoping you'd allow your Alesha to stay by my Mit'ka's side," replied Nikitin nonchalantly, noticing how the priest, unaccustomed to supplication, blushed crimson. "In good company, they will have more fun in Moscow. I thought you might apprentice your son with a court official or a scribe. But the Latin school sounds even better. Perhaps, he'll teach my little recluse a thing or two. Don't worry about the tuition, I'll take care of it. And no need to thank me," he stopped the priest before he made a bow. "It's to our mutual benefit. Mit'ka will serve the tsar as a man at arms, and your Alesha will grow up to be a scholar. They will help each other, scratch each other's back. Go home now and prepare your son for travel. We'll take them both at once."

"Oh, but he's ready to go. I left his bundle in the entry," confessed the embarrassed priest and wiped off the tears – free from rhetorical ploys, straight from the heart.

But fate deemed otherwise, and that evening the fathers did not take their sons to Moscow. When they called for the boys, there was no response. They searched in the backyard, in the rooms, behind the fence, but to no avail. The boys had disappeared.

NOTES TO APPENDICES

1 Originally published as Grigorii Chkhartishvili, "Esli by ia byl gazetnym magnatom: Zapiski bodlivoi korovy," *Neprikosnovennyi zapas* 2, no. 4 (1999), http://magazines.russ.ru/nz/1999/2/chart-pr.html, accessed 25 October 2018.

2 Vladimir Gusinskii and Boris Berezovskii were Russian media magnates in the 1990s.

3 The literary critic and columnist Boris Kuzminskii wrote for *Today* from 1993 to 1996.

4 Gennadii Ziuganov was the Communist Party presidential candidate in 1996, 2000, 2008, and 2012.

5 Yury Luzhkov was Moscow mayor from 1992 to 2010.

6 Boris Yeltsin was Russia's President from 1991 to 1999.

7 Sergei Parkhomenko is a publisher, political observer, journalist, radio host, and columnist. In 1996 he founded the journal *Itogi* and was its first editor-in-chief from 1996 to 2001.

8 From 1986 to 2000, Chkhartishvili was an editor and later a deputy editor-in-chief of *Inostrannaia literatura*.

9 The Leningrad-born writers Boris Paramonov and Andrei Bitov both left the city by the 1990s. Paramonov emigrated to New York where he worked for Radio Liberty; Bitov moved to Moscow where he taught at the Gorky Literary Institute. Both continued publishing in *The Star*.

10 Sergei Solov'ev (1820–79) wrote twenty-nine volumes in his *Istoriia Rossii s drevneishikh vremen* (*History of Russia from the Earliest Times*) project before his death; he was also the founder of what has often been termed "the state school" of interpreting Russian history. Solov'ev's student, Vasilii Kliuchevskii (1841–1911) focused more on economic, geographical, and colonial forces in his highly influential history books.

11 Isaac Asimov (1920–92) is most famous for his science fiction works, but also wrote fourteen works of popular history.

12 Peter Ackroyd (b. 1949) has written well-regarded works of historical fiction, poetry, and biography. In 2000, he published *London: A Biography*, which he followed with *Albion: The Origins of the English Imagination* (2002) and *Thames: Sacred River* (2007), all published by Chatto and Windus (London), among other popular histories.

13 I thank Annika Severts for her inestimable help in editing my translation. Without her constant encouraging and stellar editing skills, this project would have hardly taken wing.

List of Works by Grigorii Chkhartishvili

As Boris Akunin

Adventures of Erast Fandorin **series /** *Prikliucheniia Erasta Fandorina* **(1998–2018):**

1 *The Winter Queen / Azazel'* (1998).
2 *The Turkish Gambit / Turetskii gambit* (1998).
3 *Murder on the Leviathan / Leviafan* (1998).
4 *The Death of Achilles / Smert' Akhillesa* (1998).
5 *Special Assignments / Osobye porucheniia* (1999), in two parts:
   A) *The Jack of Spades / Pikovyi valet.*
   B) *The Decorator / Dekorator.*
6 *The State Counsellor / Statskii sovetnik* (1999).
7 *The Coronation / Koronatsiia, ili Poslednii iz Romanov* (2000).
8 *She Lover of Death / Liubovnitsa smerti* (2001).
9 *He Lover of Death / Liubovnik smerti* (2001).
10 *The Diamond Chariot / Almaznaia kolesnitsa* (2003).
11 *Yin and Yang / In' i Ian* (2006). A play about Fandorin.
12 *The Jade Rosary / Nefritovye chetki* (2006). Seven short stories and three novellas.
13 *All the World's a Stage / Ves' mir teatr* (2009).
14 *Black City / Chernyi gorod* (2012).
15 *Planet Water / Planeta voda* (2015). Three novellas.
16 *Not Saying Goodbye / Ne proshchaius'* (2018).

Provincial Mystery, or Adventures of Sister Pelagia **series /** *Provintsial'nyi detektiv, ili Prikliucheniia sestry Pelagii* **(2000–3):**

1 *Pelagia and the White Bulldog / Pelagiia i belyi bul'dog* (2000).
2 *Pelagia and the Black Monk / Pelagiia i chernyi monakh* (2001).
3 *Pelagia and the Red Rooster / Pelagiia i krasnyi petukh* (2003).

Adventures of Nicholas Fandorin series / Prikliucheniia magistra (2000–9):

1 *Altyn Tolobas / Altyn-tolobas* (2000).
2 *Recommended Reading / Vneklassnoe chtenie* (2002).
3 *F.M. / F. M.* (2006).
4 *The Falcon and the Swallow / Sokol i lastochka* (2009).

Genres series/ Zhanry (2005–12):

1 *Children's Book / Detskaia kniga* (2005).
2 *Spy Novel / Shpionskii roman* (2006).
3 *Science Fiction / Fantastika* (2006).
4 *Quest / Kvest* (2008).
5 *Children's Book for Girls / Detskaia kniga dlia devochkek* (2012). Co-authored with Gloria Mu.

Brotherhood of Death cinema-novels / Smert' na brudershaft (2007–11):

1 *The Infant and the Devil / Mladenets i chert* (2007).
2 *The Torment of a Broken Heart / Muka razbitogo serdtsa* (2007).
3 *The Flying Elephant / Letaiushchii slon* (2008).
4 *Children of the Moon / Deti luny* (2008).
5 *The Wandering Man / Strannyi chelovek* (2009).
6 *Let the Thunder of Victory Rumble! / Grom pobedy, razdavaisia!* (2009).
7 *"Maria," Maria... / "Mariia," Mariia...* (2010).
8 *Nothing Sacred / Nichego sviatogo* (2010).
9 *Operation Transit / Operatsiia "Tranzit"* (2011).
10 *The Angels Battalion / Batal'on angelov* (2011).

History of the Russian State series / Istoriia Rossiiskogo gosudarstva (2013–):

1 *A Part of Europe – From the Beginnings to the Mongol Conquest / Chast' Evropy – Ot istokov do mongol'skogo nashestviia* (2013).
2 *The Fiery Finger / Ognennyi perst* (2013). Three novellas.
3 *A Part of Asia – The Horde Period / Chast' Azii – Ordynskii period* (2014).
4 *Bosch and Schelm / Bokh i Shel'ma* (2014). Two historical novels.
5 *Between Asia and Europe – From Ivan III to Boris Godunov / Mezhdu Aziei i Evropoi: Ot Ivana III do Borisa Godunova –* (2015).

 6 *Widow's Kerchief / Vdovii plat* (2016). Two historical novels.
 7 *Between Europe and Asia – The Seventeenth Century / Mezhdu Evropoi i Aziei – Semnadtsatyi vek* (2016).
 8 *Sennight of the Three-Eyed / Sedmitsa Trekhglazogo* (2017).
 9 *Asiatic Europeization – Tsar Peter Alexeyevich / Aziatskaia evropeizatsiia – Tsar' Petr Alekseevich* (2017).
10 *Nutshell Buddha / Orekhovyi Budda* (2018).
11 *Eurasian Empire – The Era of Tsarinas / Evraziiskaia imperiia – Epokha tsarits* (2018).
12 *The First Superpower – Alexander the Blessed and Nicholas Unforgettable / Pervaia sverkhderzhava – Aleksndr Blagoslovennyi i Nikolai Nezabvennyi* (2019).

Other works (not serialized):

 1 *The Seagull / Chaika* (2000).
 2 *Comedy/Tragedy / Komediia/Tragediia* (2000). Two plays, *Hamlet. A Version / Gamlet. Versiia* and *The Mirror of Saint Germain / Zerkalo Sen-Zhermena.*
 3 *Fairy Tales for Idiots / Skazki dlia idiotov* (2000).
 4 *Screenplays / Stsenarii* (2006).
 5 *Photos as Haiku / Foto kak khokku* (2011).
 6 *The Most Frightening Villain and Other Stories / Samyi strashnyi zlodei i drugie siuzhety* (2012).
 7 *A Real Princess and Other Stories / Nastoiashchaia printsessa i drugie siuzhety* (2013).
 8 *The Most Mysterious Secret and Other Stories / Samaia tainstvennaia taina i drugie siuzhety* (2014).
 9 *The Northern Sentry and Other Stories / Severnyi chasovoi i drugie siuzhety* (2015).

As Anatolii Brusnikin:

 1 *The Ninth Saviour / Deviatnyi Spas* (2007).
 2 *A Hero of a Different Time / Geroi inogo vremeni* (2010).
 3 *Bellona / Bellona* (2012).

As Anna Borisova:

 1 *Over There ... / Tam ...* (2008).
 2 *The Creator / Kreativshchik* (2008).
 3 *The Four Seasons / Vremena goda* (2011).

As Akunin-Chkhartishvili:

Family Album series / *Semeinyi al'bom* (2012–):

1 *Aristonomy* / *Aristonomiia* (2012).
2 *Another Way* / *Drugoi put'* (2015).
3 *Happy Russia* / *Schastlivaia Rossiia* (2017).
4 *Treasury* / *Trezorium* (2019).

As Grigorii Chkhartishvili:

1 *The Writer and Suicide* / *Pisatel' i samoubiistvo* (1999).
2 *Cemetery Tales* / *Kladbishchenskie istorii* (2004).

List of Contributors

Elena V. Baraban is an associate professor of Russian at the University of Manitoba. Her research focuses on Russian detective fiction as well as Soviet and post-Soviet films about the Second World War. Her publications include a co-edited volume, *Fighting Words and Images: Representing War across the Disciplines* (2012), and a number of articles on Russian literature, cinema, and culture.

Natalia Erlenkamp graduated from Ivanovo State University with a diploma in Russian. She received her MA in Russian and East Central European Studies from the University of Passau. Erlenkamp has taught Russian language at the University of Passau, Karl Eberhard University of Tübingen, and the Europa-Institut in Reutlingen. She is currently working for the non-profit organization GIZ LLC in Berlin.

Ilya Gerasimov is Executive Editor of *Ab Imperio* Quarterly. A historian of Imperial Russia, he is the author of two books in English: *Modernism and Public Reform in Late Imperial Russia: Rural Professionals and Self Organization, 1905–1930* (2009) and *Plebeian Modernity: Social Practices, Illegality, and the Urban Poor in Russia, 1906–1916* (2018).

Bradley A. Gorski received his PhD from the Department of Slavic Languages at Columbia University in 2017, completing his dissertation on "Authors of Success: Cultural Capitalism and Literary Evolution in Contemporary Russia." He is currently an assistant professor of Russian and East European Studies at Vanderbilt University. He is the author of several articles on contemporary Russian fiction and the guest editor of "A Culture of Institutions/Institutions of Culture," a special issue of *Ulbandus: The Slavic, East European, and Eurasian Review of Columbia University*, vol. 17 (2016).

Judith Kalb is an associate professor of Languages, Literatures, and Cultures at the University of South Carolina. Her research focuses on the interactions between Russian culture and the Greco-Roman classical tradition. Her book *Russia's Rome: Imperial Visions, Messianic Dreams, 1890–1930* (2008), examines the image of ancient Rome in the writings of Russian modernists. Her new project focuses on Russia's reception of Homer.

Stephen M. Norris is Walter E. Havighurst Professor of Russian History and Director of the Havighurst Center for Russian and Post-Soviet Studies at Miami University (OH). He is the author of *Blockbuster History in the New Russia: Movies, Memory, Patriotism* (2012) and *A War of Images: Russian Popular Prints, Wartime Culture, and National Identity, 1812–1945* (2006); co-editor of the edited volumes *Russia's People of Empire: Life Stories from Eurasia, 1500–Present* (2012); *Insiders and Outsiders in Russian Cinema* (2008); and *Preserving Petersburg: History, Memory, Nostalgia* (2008); and author of numerous articles on Russian nineteenth- and twentieth-century history and culture.

Elizabeth Richmond-Garza is University Distinguished Teaching Associate Professor of English at the University of Texas. The author of the monograph *Forgotten Cites/Sights: Interpretation and the Power of Classical Citation in Renaissance English Drama* (1994), she has also published many articles on Orientalism, the Gothic, Cleopatra, Oscar Wilde, and European drama. She is currently finishing a study of decadent culture at the end of the nineteenth century.

Yekaterina Severts holds a PhD in comparative literature from the University of Texas. A former lecturer at the University of Texas at Austin, she is a translator, freelance journalist, and the author of eleven books in Russian (fiction and non-fiction) on various topics from the history of Victorian England, including the Russian biography of Queen Victoria, *Koroleva Viktoria* (2015), published under the name Yekaterina Cotey. Severts's research interests include literature, folklore, and everyday culture of nineteenth-century England and Russia, Russian literature of the digital age, RuNet, Russian language pedagogy, and creative writing.

Zara M. Torlone is a professor of Classics and Faculty Associate of the Havighurst Center for Russian and Post-Soviet Studies at Miami University (OH). Her research primarily focuses on classical reception and the classical tradition in Russia. She is the author of four books, including *Russia and the Classics: Poetry's Foreign Muse* (2009) and *Vergil in Russia: National Identity and Classical Reception* (2015).

Claire Whitehead is a senior lecturer in the School of Modern Languages at the University of St. Andrews. Her research focuses on prose fiction in Russia (and France) from the nineteenth century onwards. She is the author of *The Fantastic in France and Russia in the Nineteenth Century: In Pursuit of Hesitation* (2006) and *The Poetics of Early Russian Crime Fiction, 1860–1917: Deciphering Tales of Detection* (2018).

Index